This book is dedicated to Sherree Anne
for all her help with the birds.

THE BLACKBIRD MAN
AUTOBIOGRAPHY OF AN AVICULTURIST

THE BLACKBIRD MAN
AUTOBIOGRAPHY OF AN AVICULTURIST

ISBN 978-0-955931-11-6

A catalogue record for this book is available from the
British Library.

Compiled and produced by: SPC Printers Ltd. Thetford, Norfolk, UK.

Proof reader Brenda Cooper.

Other titles by the author:

Seasons- 2008. ISBN 978-0-9559311-0-9. A book of poems

Photographic credits:

Dennis Avon, MIOP, ARPS.
Tony Tilford FRPS.
Tommy Milner
Frank Stark
Andrew Calvesbert
Ron Summers
Bozena Kalejta – Summers
Bernard Williams
Dave Cottrell
Alan Hoary
Rudy Driesman
Alois Van Mngeroet
Dave Henderson
Sergey Yeliseev
Luke Harvey
Brenda Cooper
Robb Brown

Many thanks are extended to all photographers.
A special thanks to Mrs. Avon for the use of her late husband's photographs.

Special thanks to Steve Dix for his assistance in the rearing of many of my birds.

Cage & Aviary Birds (www.cageandaviarybirds.co.uk) has kindly allowed me to
use my articles which were originally published in their newspaper, including
those printed as the British Bird File; these articles now form part of
Chapters 2 and 3 of this book. The photographs accompanying the text are
different to those originally used.

Photographers responsible for a few images posted in this book are unknown.
The author wishes to apologise to any photographer not accredited.

CHAPTER FOUR:
My Mules and Hybrids

CHAPTER FIVE:
Thrush Breeding Programme

CHAPTER SIX: Howlett vs Caton

CHAPTER SEVEN:
The evolution of bird fancy law

CHAPTER EIGHT:
Howlett vs Baldry

CHAPTER NINE:
Exhibition and Records

My little piece of England

Royal Army Veterinary Corps.

Policeman-Poet.

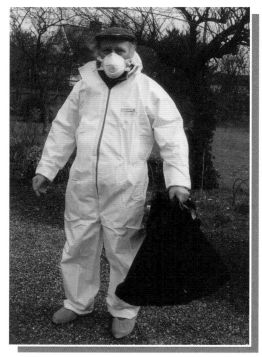

Government Consultant Wildlife Inspector
collecting dead waterfowl during bird flu outbreak.

Best Softbill 1984 National

This hen blackbird was a big winner in her day. The photo was taken when she was quite old. She is wearing a well worn British Bird Breeders Association closed ring, and a Government split metal ring, this was fitted to enable the bird to be shown after the 1981 Act became law - a transitional period.

Photograph by Dennis Avon

THE WILD BLACKBIRD

The blackbird (*Turdus merula*) is one of six common British thrushes belonging to the family Turdidae, which is a group of medium-sized perching birds with slender bills, long wings and tails.

Juveniles and females are spotted, but in its normal, non-mutant form the cock blackbird is unspotted. Most thrushes migrate at night and many occur in loose flocks outside the breeding season. They are mainly ground feeders.

The blackbird is one of the most commonest land birds living in Britain with a resident population of about 5 million breeding pairs, and is found almost everywhere. It is familiar to town dwellers and country folk alike. It is a successful species due to its adaptability, surviving anywhere where its varied food is found.

Once it was more adapted to a woodland environment, but as human populations grew and spread it too began to take up residence in hitherto alien locations, such as parks and gardens, to become one of Britain's best loved birds. These days it can be found even in the heart of cities.

LOCAL MIGRATION

The blackbird is a resident species within Britain, although some local migration takes place in the autumn from north to south and even across the English Channel.

The autumn also brings an influx of Continental birds to these shores where they forage for food in the fields and hedgerows with other thrushes, such as fieldfares and redwings. They appear in the meadows overnight to swell the local population.

Outside Britain, the blackbird inhabits most of Europe and North Africa, its range extending eastwards across South East Asia to eastern China. It has also been introduced to America, Australia, New Zealand and elsewhere.

The male blackbird is jet black in colour, with a bright orange-yellow bill and eye ring. The female is of a dark brown hue, lighter below, slightly mottled with a brownish bill; the young cocks resemble the female until their first moult, the mature, adult plumage occurs in their second year.

Mutations appear in the wild, notably albino. Some of these individuals have only a few white feathers, commonly around the head, while others have more and others still are totally albinos. My colour variant strains of cultivated blackbirds are derived from mutant wild stock.

The song of the blackbird is one of the loveliest bird songs heard in Britain. Its liquid beauty is a delight to the ear, albeit amidst the dawn chorus of a spring morning, or in the quietness of a balmy evening, when I feel it is at its best.

It also has a soft call, made by both sexes, which is only audible from a short distance. This soft call is often emitted by my birds, not only from within their flights, but also from their show cages, when they are being transported to and from exhibitions. A loud alarm call is usually uttered when the bird is disturbed, when frightened off its nest for instance. A harsh call is repeated at dusk, just before roosting, or when there is a predator in the vicinity, such as a cat or an owl. This din can continue for several minutes. Most evenings, as the sun is setting, my garden resounds to the avian orchestra of music, with the wild population of blackbirds chipping in with my home-bred stock.

The blackbird also has the capacity to mimic tunes. I remember one such cock bird in my collection mimicking the ditty emanating from an ice cream van, which always used to stop at the same place, nearby.

The breeding season of the wild blackbird can begin early in the year. It always surprises me to see young blackbirds, sometimes as early as around Christmas time, when bred in sheltered locations, and well before leaves appear on deciduous trees. Their season continues into July.

The blackbird will build its nest in a variety of places, in a tree or bush, or even in a building. As a child I often found blackbirds nesting in a hedge bank or even on the ground.

The nest is a large, stoutly built cup, comprising of plant stems, grasses, dead leaves, thin twigs and roots. The female builds it and lines it with a solid layer of mud, this is lined with finer, dry grasses. Two or three rounds, occasionally more, are reared during this period. The eggs, which number three to five in a clutch, are blue-green with brown spots. Incubation is 13 to 14 days, and is carried out by the female. Sometimes the male will cover the eggs for short periods while the female is away feeding.

During the first few days after hatching, the male will collect the food required for the brood. He will often break it up into small pieces to soften it, before returning to the nest, where he will present it to the sitting female, which, in turn, feeds it to the chicks.

Later on, both parents will sustain the brood with worms and insects, and any other invertebrate they can find within their territory. The young leave the nest after two weeks and continue to be fed by both parents for at least two further weeks. During this time the adult pair may well be incubating another clutch of eggs. Even then, well-grown young will badger their parents for top-ups whenever the opportunity arises.

GOLDEN VOICE

Most people share my love of the blackbird; the bird with the golden voice. In home-grown surroundings, blackbirds are easy to maintain. They become tame and long-lived. I have exhibited some of my birds up to their eighth year and have had fertile males living for eleven years.

I started keeping the blackbird during the early 1960s and began showing examples then at local shows. I first exhibited a specimen at the National Exhibition, when it was held at Alexandra Palace in 1969. It was at that time that I decided to breed a strain of these beautiful birds.

BREEDING MY FIRST BLACKBIRD

My unrelated pair of blackbirds was obtained under Home Office licence in 1969. They were hand-reared and very confiding from the outset. In 1970 they built a nest but no eggs were laid. In 1971 their enclosure was prepared in early March.

It measured 1.8m x 90cm x 2m high (6ft x 3ft x 7ft). Two perches were provided, one under the shelter at the rear, the other high at the front. The front perch was designed to provide a song position for the male.

On March 27th the birds were introduced to their quarters and they settled down immediately. The male came on song and used the high perch to deliver his beautiful liquid notes, his melody ringing out as if to proclaim that spring had arrived.

I placed nesting material, in the form of grasses and moss, in the aviary on April 10th. A few earthworms were added to the bird's normal poultry pellet diet. After 10 days I noticed the female with grasses in her bill.

No nest site had yet been considered, I rectified this by fixing a soap powder 'gift tray' onto a ledge at the front of the aviary, 90cm (3ft) from the ground.

I had bent the tray into an 'L' shape, the bottom of which formed the nest platform; the back gave privacy from one side. A plywood strip was nailed in front of the site to give added seclusion. I also placed a tin containing mud in the enclosure for the bird's use.

The female, unconcerned with the bright colours of the tray, built a solid nest on it neatly lined with mud and then with fine grasses. On April 29th she was sitting on the nest. In the subsequent days she incubated very tightly. Fly maggots and a few mealworms were added to their diet at this time.

During the morning of May 11th, I was near the aviary when I heard a very soft call. I saw the male standing on the rim of the nest, he was feeding the hen. I inspected the nest later in the day and found two young had hatched and two fertile eggs

remained, these hatched by the 14th. Live food was increased and the chicks grew at normal pace. The male did most of the feeding.

GROWING YOUNG

I entered the aviary on May 16th at an opportune moment, inspected the young and close-ringed them. The parents had no objection to these proceedings and the female returned to the nest after a short while. The young continued to grow. They were fed mainly on earthworms and maggots, although a few mealworms were taken morning and evening. I thought it remarkable that the parent birds did not consume the mealworms, passing them instead to the chicks.

On May 23rd two young fledged. They were joined by the remaining two the next day.

The female made repairs to the nest and laid the first egg of the second clutch on May 27th. The next morning I could not find one of the youngsters. After a search I found it trapped behind a plywood strip, at the rear of the aviary. On release it recovered with no ill effects.

The second clutch consisted of five eggs and the hen started incubation after the second had been laid.

By the end of the month the first round chicks had grown well and proved to be two males and two females.

The cock continued to feed them, emitting a low whistle when he did so. Mealworms were withheld and fewer earthworms given. On one occasion I noticed pellets being fed.

On June 5th, I found an egg from the second clutch on the aviary floor; whether it had been discarded I don't know. I put it in the nest.

On June 11th the first chick of the second round hatched out. At this time the old male was still feeding the first round young. However he found time to feed the new arrival. By the 13th three young had hatched; the remaining two eggs failed to hatch.

I noticed that the young from the first round were taking their own food so I separated them by placing them in another aviary in sight and sound of the parent birds.

The second round young grew at normal rate, being fed almost entirely by the male parent. The live food was increased during the first 10 days of their existence. They were close-ringed early on and by June 26th they had left the nest, all three in good condition.

At the other end of the aviary, linnets were incubating a clutch of four eggs, their nest being situated in a bunch of thorn provided for that purpose. On June 27th the female blackbird had destroyed the linnet's nest and I was unable to save any of the eggs.

By the 29th she had built a strong nest on the site, 1.2m (4ft) from the ground. The first egg of the third round was laid the next day and by July 4th the clutch of four eggs was complete and being incubated.

GOOD TEMPER

The chicks of the second round continued to thrive, they often sat on the nest or on top of their mother as she was incubating and I was amazed at her good temper. By July 11th the second round young were self-sufficient and were transferred to another enclosure.

On inspecting the first round young I noticed one was singing softly from the floor of its flight. This bird was of good type and I later trained it for the shows.

Two young of the third round hatched on July 14th and a third the next day. This bird died a few days later, not having developed in the normal way. The remaining two were close-ringed on the 21st.
Live food had become scarce as I had a pair of song thrushes with young at this time. The blackbirds grew steadily and were fed blowflies instead of mealworms. They flew on the 28th and were of the same size at that stage as were the young from the previous rounds.
All my blackbirds were of normal colour at that time, and I was on the lookout for colour variant forms. My first breeding of the blackbird gave me valuable data that could be put to good use.

ADULT COCK BLACKBIRD

Photograph by Dennis Avon

ADULT HEN BLACKBIRD

Photograph by Dennis Avon

COLOUR VARIANT BLACKBIRDS

At the 1971 National Exhibition held at Alexandra Palace, I met Richard Baglow and Ron McCluskey, both ardent blackbird enthusiasts. Richard had two albinos on show and Ron was exhibiting a fine cinnamon hen, a bird bred by Mr J. Thompson. In 1956, Mr Thompson acquired a visual cinnamon hen blackbird and when the bird was 12 years old he managed to breed a carrier cock from it, the cinnamon mutation being sex-linked. In 1969 he paired the carrier cock to a normal hen, the first eggs were discarded by the birds, but all five of the second clutch hatched into three visual hens and two normal coloured cocks.

Mr Thompson passed the old cinnamon hen to Ron, who was living in Bedford, and subsequently he also passed to Ron one of the young cinnamon hens. Ron exhibited these birds to perfection,

1991 CINNAMON BLACKBIRD HEN - MAJOR WINNER

Photograph by Dennis Avon

winning well with them; unfortunately no on-going strain was developed.

In 1976 I was granted a licence to take blackbirds and other species from the wild and the same year I acquired a visual cinnamon hen blackbird. It was a wonderful specimen of good size and colour and proved very prolific. I was able to create the strain I have today, from this lovely bird.

At first several carrier cocks were bred, five in one year and later visual cinnamon hens. I had never seen a visual cinnamon cock blackbird prior to breeding one and, so far as I could ascertain, none of my avicultural friends had seen one either; so it was with mounting excitement I waited for the first breeding of such a bird in the UK. I was not disappointed, it is a beautiful mutation, and is bred in numbers every year now. I believe most cinnamon blackbirds seen in Britain today can be traced back through the generations to my strain and the bird I acquired in the early 1970s.

The first albino blackbirds I saw were those shown by Richard Baglow in 1971. He managed to breed two carrier cocks before losing the visual hen in a freak accident when a large piece of wood fell on it. He later sold the visual cock and as far as I

know no further breeding was made, so no strain was created. The albino mutation is recessive and little was known about it in those days. This may have been one reason as to why no further examples were raised at the time.

TRAGIC EVENT

My first albino, a visual hen, came into my possession in 1974. Later, I bred a visual cock and from these beginnings bred an on-going strain of these beautiful birds. They were excellent show birds and did well at the National events. A difficulty arose, however, when they were photographed in their show cage. They were so white that they almost became invisible and did not appear clearly when the pictures were developed. (Page 279).

All went well with the albino strain until I moved to my present address in 1983. Within two years I was almost certain that I had lost all the birds which had constituted the strain, all the visual and known splits were lost, the possibility that the albino gene had survived in the remaining blackbird stock was hope, nothing more.

I built new aviaries when I moved, and made the mistake of placing two visual albino blackbirds together in one flight and not ensuring that their accommodation was vermin-proof. Whilst I was at work one day, a weasel managed to gain entry to their aviary and killed both birds.

I had already lost one or two members of the strain as a consequence of moving and this further tragedy left me with only two birds, both carriers, a normal cock and a normal hen. No problem you may think?

Try as I might I was unable to get a fertile egg from the hen. The carrier cock lost his top mandible when a sparrow hawk attacked it in its aviary. The bird could not be saved, so this particular strain was lost. It was the most tragic event that I have ever suffered so far in my avicultural career.

Late in 1988 I acquired a three-year old hen from another keeper. This bird was as white as snow. It had an orange-yellow bill, pink legs and white toe nails, its eyes were very dark, but in bright sunshine appeared plum-coloured, it was a lovely large specimen, in all aspects an albino, or was it? I paired the bird in 1988 to the best normal cock within my stud, and two young were reared; a cock and a hen, which I hoped, would carry the albino gene. In 1990 the old pair produced six young, all hens and all carriers, or so I thought, but the lack of additional cocks held up the programme somewhat.

GREAT EXPECTATIONS

In 1991 I paired the 1988 cock to its mother, the old visual hen, but they fought all summer and no young were raised. In 1992, I again paired them together and a further cock and hen, both normals, were reared. If the visual hen was indeed albino, I would have expected from such pairing to obtain 50 per cent visual albino and 50 per cent albino carriers. My faith in the visual bird was steadfast, because I thought that one day the visual albino gene would manifest itself. I also paired the 1988 bred cock to one of the 1990 hens, but they were unsuccessful. Some of the other hens bred from the visual hen, were paired to unrelated cocks; these produced two cocks, which if from a recessive strain had a 50 per cent chance of being carriers.

In 1993 I paired the old visual 'white' hen with a carrier cinnamon cock and bred a beautiful cinnamon pied hen, a very large bird. Somehow white had merged with cinnamon!

During the following years I tried every possible mating with the descendants of the lovely white hen, but have yet to breed a white or albino specimen.

Some of the normal offspring continued to display a few white feathers.

My original albino blackbirds were wonderful, very large with silky feathers and did extremely well on the show bench, as did the cinnamon pied hen.

Visitors to the National Exhibition, who visited the British Bird Council stand, will have seen two lovely colour photographs taken by Dennis Avon and produced there, of the 'white' hen and her daughter, the cinnamon pied.

Pair of albino blackbirds

Satinette blackbirds at their nests 1987

My first cinnamon blackbird 1970's

My first satinette blackbird 1982

SATINETTE BLACKBIRDS

I am also the first keeper in Britain to breed an on-going strain of satinette blackbirds. These birds, which are sex-linked, are also called creams, inos and sometimes cinnamon inos. It all started in 1982 when I acquired a visual hen. I was able to breed carriers, visual cocks and hens.

I exhibited a satinette at the National Exhibition for the first time in 1989 and it created a bit of a stir. Like my cinnamon strain I have passed examples on to numerous keepers around Britain and most of these birds held now can be traced back through their ancestry to my first hen.

Each spring a number of white blackbirds emerge countrywide, most of them are sex-linked satinettes, but on occasions two birds each with the recessive gene for albino, will pair up by chance and an albino will be produced.

A LIKELY STORY

On May 21st 1994, the Daily Mail ran an article about albino birds spotted by the public. Several photographs of white blackbirds were featured and the centrepiece was one of my best hens, a bird that was suitably close-ringed.

The image of the bird had been taken inside my garage by Dennis Avon and had been supplied to the newspaper by another interested party, Roger Caton. The caption read that the bird had been spotted near Wolverhampton – a likely story! Soon after the story appeared, Roger wrote to me, saying he had been misquoted. The money paid to him for the feature was equally shared by Dennis, Roger and myself, which I thought was a very nice gesture.

At the 1995 National Exhibition I took best softbill with an adult cream (satinette) blackbird, my fourth variety of blackbird to win such an award, the others being normal, albino and cinnamon.

NORMAL BLACKBIRD

During the 1980s I bred a normal blackbird hen from a visual albino cock. I exhibited this specimen as a normal-coloured bird at the National Exhibition.

It was a large bird, nicely marked, with wonderful feather quality. When I explained its parentage to 'experts', they all considered that the bird should have been a visual albino like its father, the fact that albinos are recessive never occurred to them, so rife was ignorance of genetics among keepers at that time.

Continued on page 20

**ADULT COCK
CINNAMON BLACKBIRD**

Photograph by Dennis Avon

ALBINO OR NOT ALBINO ?
(some dominant genes perhaps)

Photograph by Dennis Avon

Photograph by Dennis Avon

CINNAMON PIED HEN
BLACKBIRD - DAUGHTER OF ABOVE

PERFECT SHAPE

Photograph by Dennis Avon

Mail Blackbird not 'snapped' in wild

SOME readers may have spotted the excellent double page spread in *The Daily Mail* recently featuring Albino Blackbirds in the wild. But it gave little credit to birdkeepers, and, worse, suggested that the main photograph by Dennis Avon of an Albino Blackbird bred by Bernard Howlett was of a bird "spotted in the wild by professional aviculturalist Roger Caton".

The fact that the bird is closed ringed obviously meant little to the journalists responsible for the feature.

Mutation British Birds are, of course, nothing new. My pictures include one of a White Magpie taken by former British BBA secretary, Peter Howe, and a very old picture – possibly taken before the Second World War – of the late Fred Jefferson with a Light Fawn Rook.

■ Pre-war picture of Fred Jefferson with a Light Fawn Rook.

■ White Magpie in the London Zoo.

■ Colour variant Blackbird bred by Bernard Howlett.

BLUE VARIANT

A dominant colour variant blackbird, known as blue, but also often referred to as silver, is making its presence known in both shades: the light coloured birds are double factor and the dark ones single factor. Many of these are being bred and shown nowadays.

These birds originated on the Continent, where they first appeared in the 1960s. They arrived in this country in the early 1980s and I have been keeping them for a few years.

Normals bred from visuals are not carriers, but nevertheless they are unlike all other normal-coloured blackbirds in that their ancestral colours come through to some extent, giving the cocks a blue black sheen and the hens a streakier pattern. This makes it difficult for judges who have to decide whether such a bird is of sound normal colour.

I believe strongly that colour variant British birds should be excluded from the ringing process. To advertise this point I obtained a licence to show an aviary bred, unringed, single factor blue blackbird cock. This specimen was successfully exhibited at Lancashire British Bird & Hybrid Club and at the National Exhibition. (See photo below).

The last blackbird mutation to be mentioned, is the so-called grizzle whose feather patterns consist of blue, black/grey and white, an attractive type. This colour variant first appeared in Britain in the aviaries of Mr. Alan Dawson. In the 1980s he bred many wonderful specimens and achieved much with them on the show bench, they are still in existence in Britain today. I now have them in my collection and hope to breed a strain.

THE BLUE BLACKBIRD

The blue blackbird is a dominant variety and double factored. The single factor is blue-grey and the double factor is a silvery colour. As a standard term, "blue" has been adopted by the fancy, though some think of the single factor colour as agate, or even lavender.

COCK SINGLE FACTOR BLUE BLACKBIRD

Photograph by Dennis Avon

These blue birds originated in Europe and have been bred in Britain for many years. I know of no other dominant variety of softbill, though this mutation is apparent in some hardbills such as the greenfinch, siskin and house sparrow.

Single factor young leave the nest with the blue-grey wings and tail. At this stage the body and head are dark and speckled. Slowly, the colour spreads to the back and body and finally the head gets its new attire, the first moult is complete when birds are about three months old.

It wasn't until 2003 that I became interested in this variety. I paired a double-factor cock to one of my best normal hens. Two single factor cocks were produced, the best of which was not close-ringed. Nevertheless, I decided to exhibit it. I obtained the necessary licence and prepared it for the shows.

I believe that colour-variant British birds should not be subjected by law to the close-ringing regime. Though many Schedule 3 British birds are shown each year with Continental rings under licence, I was dumbfounded by the attitude of some keepers and some clubs. They were totally against a blackbird being shown without a ring. Schedule 3 birds wearing Continental rings are considered not ringed in law; that is why a licence must be in force if such a bird is to be shown. One influential expert phoned, however, to congratulate me on my stance. After the bird had been rejected at one major club, it was accepted by the Lancashire British Bird and Hybrid club that November.

The bird had already been entered in the National Exhibition of 2003 and I talked to the National show manager Bernard Williams at the Lancashire event and subsequently, he wasn't happy about the bird being shown. Finally, Donald Taylor, the then editor of Cage & Aviary Birds, sponsors of the event, gave me the go-ahead to exhibit the bird. So the point was made that, with a licence, an un-ringed British bird can (and should) be shown. During the 2005 breeding season, I paired the old silver cock with a good normal hen. From this pairing of my pure strain, I knew every chick would be a visual single-factor. Eleven were bred from three rounds, all very nice large birds.

The pair shared a sizeable aviary with other birds. Their first nest was ready on May 10th. Five eggs were laid, the nest being built within a small open flight inside the large aviary. Four chicks hatched on May 27th. Two days later, I shut the pair in the small aviary, with food and water, but the hen forsook the young. They were fostered out and all survived.

A second nest was built elsewhere in the large aviary, and by June 7th five eggs had been laid. On June 17th, these began to hatch, and all were successfully reared by their parents. By July 4th, the hen was sitting on a new nest that contained five more eggs, from which the old birds successfully reared two chicks.

That season three nests were built, all successful. Fifteen eggs were laid and 11 chicks reared – all single-factor blue, of course. The young consisted of six cocks and five hens and all moulted out wonderfully well. Some I passed on to other breeders and two (a cock and hen) were prepared for the shows. I called the hen - 'Two spot', I close-ringed all the birds. The young hen I retained was an outstanding bird and did well for me on the show bench.

Blue blackbirds would make interesting hybridisers, because of their dominant nature. For instance, if a visual blue hen was paired to a cinnamon song thrush cock split for satinette, the three colours red, white and blue would emerge, possibly in the same nest – with maybe a fourth if the colours merged in some way. (Note: ringing laws are under review).

THE SONG THRUSH

The song thrush *(Turdus philomelos)* is resident in most areas of Britain. There is movement during the winter. Also at this time there is usually an influx of birds from northern Europe which forage with blackbirds, fieldfares and redwings in the fields and meadows for worms and wild fruits.

The song thrush is smaller than the mistle thrush and is dressed in a warmer shade of brown. Its underparts are whitish brown with a slight orange tinge on the breast and flanks. The breast is covered with dark brown streaks and spots.

Its golden-brown underwing is very obvious in flight and its tail is completely brown, unlike that of the mistle thrush whose tail is edged with white. The bill is brown and the legs are pale yellow-horn.

The sexes are alike. In my experience cocks usually appear lighter on the breast than hens and their spots are slightly smaller and rounder. In contrast, the hens are much warmer looking. However, the sexes are very difficult to tell apart at a glance. Even with experience, mistakes can be made in the visual sexing of these birds.

The loud, clear song of the song thrush is unique through the repetition of its notes, which can be heard almost every month of the year, sometimes late in the evening when the moon is up. I have listened to it often at this time, competing as it does with the robin and the nightingale. The song of the song thrush, however, is somewhat less mellow than that of the blackbird. Hens utter a few quiet notes now and then.

COCK SONG THRUSH

Photograph by Dennis Avon

The song thrush has for centuries been ideally suited as an avian subject owing to its long association with man as a garden bird, its endearing ways and readiness to breed in home-conditions. In former days, cock birds were kept solely for their song.

However these days home-bred strains have been developed and many beautiful specimens are raised each year.

Usually young cocks within my stud begin singing at around Christmas time, but I have had some sing as early as November. By the end of January, though, they are singing in earnest, and it is at this time that they pair up in the wild.

An aviary measuring 2.7m x 1.2m x 2.1m high (9ft x 4ft x 7ft) is about the right size to house a pair of these delightful softbills.

As they come into breeding condition, the cock will often be the first of the pair to carry leaves and other items of nesting material. He will invariably drop these near the hen as an indication to her that it is time to build a nest. Although the cock bird has no elaborate spring display, the puffing up of his breast feathers is his chief method of attracting his mate.

Open nest-boxes or even canary nest pans form an alternative to natural sites within a planted aviary, and will be readily used. Care should be taken to protect them from the ravages of inclement weather, including the direct heat of the sun.

Some shelter is advisable for the birds. It need not be elaborate, merely sufficient for the stock to retreat into – a small wooden box suitably positioned would indeed suffice, providing it is draught-proof.

PROLIFIC LAYERS

In these conditions, the hen will soon construct a nest using any material available, including roots, grasses, small twigs and moss. She will line this with mud, which she will leave for a day or two to dry out, before laying.

Several clutches are laid in a season, making these birds very prolific. I have reared as many as 13 from one pair in a single season, the last chicks leaving the nest in October of that year.

Young from the first round were seen feeding their siblings as the hot summer went by, a phenomenon not seen, so far as I am aware, in the wild.

The eggs, usually numbering between three and five in a clutch, are a beautiful blue in colour and are usually marked and spotted with black. The hen also incubates them for a fortnight and the young are fed by both parents for a further two weeks whilst in the nest and for a similar time when they have fledged.

Young thrushes are more rufous in colour than their parents, having the feathers of the upper surface and wing coverts broadly edged with golden-buff. Their yellowish underparts are much deeper in colour and the spots smaller than those of the adult.

My song thrushes are fed all year round on poultry pellets, supplemented with fruit. During the breeding season, earthworms, snails and mealworms are offered, together with added vitamins and calcium.

Breeding a top class exhibition strain of song thrushes is difficult to accomplish and takes years to achieve. From the first sketchy plans, the project will near its goal little by little, year by year, until such a high degree of progress has been obtained that only slight improvements are possible or expected.

The need to continue improving a strain is endless, but once a strain has developed sufficiently to enable a noticeable number of its exhibits to make real progress amid strong opposition on the show bench, the first of many targets has been reached.

Size and shape are essential components in the make-up of a good song thrush. I would suggest that both are of equal merit, because unless both are present in an exhibit, its chances of making any headway on the show bench are minimal.

The shape of an exhibition bird should be conical, short and nicely rounded, with a good head, feather and wing carriage. If a bird of this quality is as large as possible and stands well, then it is near to the ideal.

Producing a bird with good breast markings is a must. Such markings should be universally scattered over the required areas in individual spots. The pairing of nicely spotted birds together is obviously important, but even so the outcome is by no means guaranteed.

Strain building is a fascinating hobby to pursue because there are so many facets to consider and options to contemplate. When top birds from top studs clash on the show bench, differences between them are apparent, but their important features are similar because, while each strain has evolved separately, the same goals and ideals are sought.

My stud of song thrushes contains normally coloured and colour variant birds.

COLOUR VARIANT SONG THRUSHES

Photograph by Dennis Avon

SATINETTE SONG THRUSH

I have two colour variants of the song thrush, in my collection – the cream, sometimes called satinette, and the cinnamon – both of which are sex-linked mutations. I will start here with the cream mutation. The cream song thrush has been with us in Britain as an aviary bird for a very long time. The first strain to evolve of cream song thrushes was developed by Wilfred Rolph of Lakenheath, Suffolk. He bred and exhibited both this mutation and the cinnamon at National Exhibitions and elsewhere, after the Second World War, and following his death, his son Robin carried on the tradition.

My first cream song thrushes came from the Rolph stud in the late 1960s. I had several examples and bred from them, the best of which was a very nice hen reared in 1984. This bird took the best in show award at Colchester that year, and went on to win second place in a class of 11 at the National. However, it was not until 1993 that my present strain began to significantly prosper.

That year I bought a carrier cock and, in 1994, bred a lovely cream hen. A bird that was both strong and healthy, it was of a creamy-white colour, with plum-coloured eyes, and with a hint of dark spots on its breast.

MAJOR WINNER

I had paired its parents up in the May of 1994. Their first round came to nothing. The second round produced two chicks, one of which was a cream, but a weasel penetrated their aviary and disrupted the pair. The chicks were lost, the parent birds survived. By June 14th 1994 the third nest to be built contained four eggs, two of which hatched and again one was cream. Both chicks were strong and healthy from the outset and grew quickly. After fledging, I noticed that the young cream was a nice, compact bird with a good head, and thought it would do well as an exhibition bird.

I mentioned the breeding to my late friend, Richard Baglow of Dunfermline, who expressed his desire to see it. That winter I took it up to the Dunfermline open show as part of my team, to his delight, where it was well received.

Over the next eight years the cream thrush won many major awards at the big events and locally. It was never beaten by another cream. During this time mutations of all descriptions were being imported and shown, but it was rare to see another cream song thrush on the benches until recently. Many more are beginning to appear nowadays. This cream, show-winning song thrush proved difficult to breed from and it was not until 1998, when it was four years old, that I managed to breed a carrier cock from it. I now breed several examples of this mutation every year and have won World Show medals with them.

CINNAMONS

My association with cinnamon song thrushes goes back to 1990 when I was loaned a 1988 visual cock by Roger Caton. This bird had taken the best British award at an all British show, and was much admired.

I was able to pair it with my best normal hen and bred two carrier cocks from it, which became the foundation of my cinnamon stud. I returned the bird to Roger, but later bought it from him and bred again from it.

In 1991 I exhibited a young cinnamon hen at the National where it won its class of nine, then went on to win best current year British bird or hybrid in show and second best British bird.

I soon built up a lovely strain of cinnamon song thrushes. These birds took the show arena by storm locally, winning best in show at many events. They also won many specials at the big events. The 1990s was a decade where cinnamon song thrushes really made their mark, and of course there were several breeders with good birds during this period. I had been winning with them at the beginning of the decade and yet my best win was at the end of it, at the 1999 National Exhibition. I won numerous specials with an unflighted cinnamon hen, the most important of which was the K & R Books trophy for the best current-year bird in the whole show (page 278).

This particular winner was bred in early May of 1999 from a visual cinnamon cock and a normal hen. As soon as the bird became independent of its parents I moved it to separate quarters. After a few weeks I felt it had potential as a show bird, due to its size, shape, and good spot formations on its breast and flanks. After training I entered it at three shows, including the Yorkshire British Bird & Hybrid Club annual open show, and at each it performed extremely well.

At the National, in becoming best young bird in show, it had beaten Albert Lawson's clear greenfinch mule, which went on to challenge for the supreme award. An understandable anomaly within the system at that time.

The win had elevated colour variant softbills to an unprecedented level.

In 1999, the National Exhibition was held at the Telford International Centre. I was unable to attend that year. My show team was conveyed to and from the event by my friends from North Walsham, who did a wonderful job. I was unaware of my big win until they unloaded the birds from their van, late on the Sunday evening. A great moment!

In 2009 one of my cinnamon hens won a gold medal in Italy, at the World Show.

CINNAMON HEN SONG THRUSH
MAJOR WINNER

Photograph by Dennis Avon

Photograph by Dennis Avon

CINNAMON SONG THRUSH

A SHADE OF BROWN

by BERNARD HOWLETT

THIS young Cinnamon Song Thrush hen is a product of the strain I have established since 1990 and was bred from a Cinnamon carrier cock and a Normal hen. The cock's sire was best Softbill at the All-British show at Winsford in 1990. I have bred other big winners from this strain, including a hen which was second best British Bird at the 1991 National Exhibition.

This young bird had a good first show, winning many awards, including best current year-bred British Bird at the East Anglian National and best current year Softbill at the London & Home Counties event. I am particularly pleased with the extension of throat and breast markings on this bird. These need to be even and as extensive as possible.

Written in 1994
and refers to that date

Written in 1995
and refers to that date

Quality Song Thrush

by BERNARD HOWLETT

I BRED this Cream Song Thrush hen last year, and it left the nest very late, on July 27. My present strain only goes back to 1992, and will take a few more seasons to consolidate.

I exhibited this bird four times during the show season and have been very pleased with its progress. It will mature into quite a nice bird.

I last exhibited a Cream Song Thrush at the National in 1989, and am looking forward to doing so again this year.

Clippings from
"CAGE & AVIARY BIRDS"

with original
photographs by
Dennis Avon.

MISTLE THRUSH

The mistle thrush (*Turdus viscivorus*) takes its name from its fondness of mistletoe berries. It is also the prime vehicle for transporting their seed from one tree to another. After feeding on the berries it flies off to wipe its bill elsewhere, and without being aware, deposits the sticky seeds which adhere to their new location and flourish, benefiting the parasitic plant and the bird.

The largest of the British thrushes, the mistle thrush is resident throughout the year but it is also a partial migrant. Some birds leave the UK in the autumn and winter on the Continent, while many arrive from northern Europe to winter in Britain. Before the introduction of the Wildlife and Countryside Act 1981, the mistle thrush was a popular aviary bird, and many were bred and exhibited. The Act prohibited fancies from freely showing the species and many were disposed of because of this. I had quite a nice strain at the time, but as I could no longer show examples, I lost interest in the species.

During the show season 1994 and 1995 display licences were introduced by the Government to allow the exhibition of the mistle thrush after a lapse of some years, and I was able to exhibit examples from the birds I had bred. The reappearance of the bird on the benches created further interest within the fancy.

Although they are not as popular as the song thrush, partly due to there being no strains of colour variants of the species available, there are plenty within collections.

The species presents the breeder with a real challenge because it is unpredictable, and often spiteful to its own kind when housed in a small, confined area.

It is important that any selected pair of mistle thrushes are compatible with each other. If not they should not be housed together, for they will undoubtedly attack each other, causing injury or even death.

Birds intended as a new pair should be gradually introduced to each other and a close watch maintained on their progress. Their aviary should be as large as possible and secluded, preferably well away from the quarters of other thrushes. This will give them security and the knowledge that their new territory is relatively safe from intruders.

In a planted enclosure, the birds will select their own nesting sites, and provided suitable nesting material is available, will build a perfectly sound nest. Open boxes can be provided if required. Every effort should be made to keep the nest site protected from inclement weather.

The bulky nest of the mistle thrush is similar to that of the blackbird, but a little larger. Supply the birds with fresh, dry grasses, mosses and mud. Put the mud in an old pan or similar container.

The nest is built in about three days. A little mud is used as its base and then the bulk of the nest is fashioned with dry materials. The shape of the cup is achieved by the hen sitting inside it and rotating. Mud is used to line the inner structure, and finally soft grasses are used to line the cup, ready for the eggs and young.

I have bred the species on a number of occasions, my description of one successful breeding occurred in 1995, when I tried during March and April to find a compatible pair. It was not an easy task, and it was not until late April that a particular pair had settled down. Within a few days the hen had built a strong nest on a ledge. I checked the nest only when both birds were away from it. On May 7th there were two eggs; four were laid altogether. They are slightly larger than those of the blackbird, smooth and glossy with greenish-blue spots and blotches of reddish-brown, reddish-purple or pale purple.

Juvenile mistle thrush bred by the author. (photograph: Dennis Avon)

During the evening of May 20th I noticed the hen standing up in the nest with her head bowed. This I considered to be a good sign that the eggs were beginning to hatch. Later, I gave the birds a liberal supply of mealworms. The next morning I looked into the nest at an opportune moment to discover one chick had hatched and its shell was still inside the nest. One more chick hatched the following day. The remaining eggs were clear.

On hatching, the chicks had down on their heads and backs. They had yellow mouths and pale yellow gape flanges. When ringing the young, I noticed that one chick was smaller than the other, the first ring came off this little bird's leg and was lost in the nest, it had to be replaced with a new one.

The young were fed by both parents on earthworms, snails, mealworms and softfood, with some food being regurgitated by the parent birds in the early stages.

Snails were consumed but, unlike song thrushes, no anvil was used to smash open the shells. The mistle thrushes scraped the fleshy parts of the snail from within the shell, discarding the whole empty shell on the aviary floor, an activity I have not observed in the wild. The two young birds had left the nest by June 7th.

In their juvenile state the young birds' back and wing feathers were covered with white marks on their tips, creating a patterned effect. They were transferred to their own quarters on June 25th that year. The old birds re-built the nest and a further four eggs were laid, but at this time the local pair of sparrow hawks had their young to feed and frequently disrupted the mistle thrushes from their breeding activities, so no more chicks were bred that year.

A General Licence is now in force, enabling keepers to exhibit their mistle thrushes and today the species is widespread among fanciers, and some nice examples are once again on show.

THE REDWING

The redwing, (*Turdus iliacus*) is the smallest of the six common thrushes to inhabit Britain. There are two distinict races of the species, which occur here each winter, one from Scandinavia, the other from Iceland. The Icelandic birds are darker and larger and have longer wings. If specimens of this race were available to a keeper, and quality offspring bred, I have no doubt they would fare better on the show bench than birds from elsewhere.

About 50-100 pairs of redwing are thought to nest in Scotland each year, confined to the northernmost areas, where the first wild breeding in the UK was recorded in 1925. I have personal knowledge of the species in the Torridon region in the early 1990s, at that time the birds were breeding there in May.

FACT FROM FICTION

One hears of tales from time to time where the siblings of a rare bird have fallen from their nest or undergone some other unusual misfortune, and someone has hand-reared them and later bred from them in their first year, in a tiny flight. I take these stories with an extra large pinch of salt. When however, the late Richard Baglow of Dunfermline told me he had bred the redwing. I believed him, for Richard was no Walter Mitty character!

Richard went to the aid of redwings which had succumbed to the ravages of the 1969 northern winter. He was, indeed, able to help quite a few of these birds back to health. However, four were retained due to their poor state, and were placed in a planted aviary. The birds turned out to be a cock and three hens. They built their nests at heights of 80cm -1.5m (3-5ft) in his aviary and produced chicks. The youngsters were parent reared.

At the National British Bird & Mule Club all-British show held in Telford in 1973, Richard exhibited several generations of aviary-bred redwings - the first keeper to breed such a strain. In 1972 he was awarded the British Bird Breeders' Association Medal for his achievements. Richard emphasised that like the waxwing, redwings will not breed in the first year of confinement if they have been taken from the wild. Just before he died in 1994, Richard Baglow gave me his medal, which I still have; a photograph of it is reproduced in this chapter.

I have kept redwings off and on since the 1960s, and in 1970 had taken a few on licence. When the 1981 Wildlife and Countryside Act became law, the species was placed on Schedule 4 of the Act, birds had to be ringed and registered, keepers lost interest in the species and by 1989 they had died out within British aviculture. In 1988, I applied for a licence, but it was turned down.

In 1990 the British Bird Council set up a thrush breeding programme and I became its co-ordinator, and during my watch about six wild disabled redwings were collected, which I registered at my own expense; no breeding pairs emerged.

I made another application to take wild redwings, this time under the auspices of the British Bird Council, but again it was turned down.

At their 1995 meeting, the BBC closed down the programme. I set up a new, independent one with a few associates, and in the following years real progress was made. Redwings were imported in. I had my first consignment delivered in April 1997. Imported birds were split-ringed, so it was necessary to obtain a licence in order to show them, this I did, and exhibited the redwing once more.

Norman Woodhouse, who had imported them in

1997, bred them the following year, and he was mainly responsible for the re-introduction of this lovely little thrush into British aviculture.

A new redwing breeding programme was set up by the British Bird Council, and at its September meeting members announced that they had been granted a licence to take up to sixty redwings from the wild during the following November, December and January.

On October 4th 1998 I was contacted by a top official of the BBC and asked to take part in the programme, but when he pointed out the strings attached – for example, no bird to be used in hybridisation, and no bird to be used in colour variant breeding, I declined. My independently run programme was going well at the time, and I had this species already in my collection. I certainly didn't want to be restrained by further government diktat. I understand about ten members did however join the new programme and four useful birds, all cocks, were snaffled during the licencing period. A vital opportunity to make real progress had been largely missed.

LIKE A BLACKBIRD

I recall one breeding of the redwing when I only managed to breed two youngsters. This was after the pair had failed in their first two attempts.

I watched the old pair during their courtship. The male would puff up his chest and chase the female around the aviary floor. He sang for long periods, a scratchy tune, which I found most irritating.

The successful nest was built in a wooden box 1m (3ft 3in) above the ground of their planted aviary. Grasses were used to complete the frame, which was lined with mud and grasses. A redwing's nest is similar to that of a blackbird, but smaller.

Three eggs were laid, very similar to those of the blackbird, but smaller. Two chicks hatched on June 23rd, and were fed mainly on earthworms and mealworms. They were very dark when they fledged, and the eye stripe was most noticeable. A General Licence is now in force enabling the species to be shown without registration.

REDWING

Photograph by Dennis Avon

Photograph by Dennis Avon

Medal won by Richard Baglow
For breeding the Redwing

THE FIELDFARE

The fieldfare (*Turdus pilaris*) is primarily a winter visitor to British shores, arriving here in flocks in the autumn and departing again in early spring. It is often found, during the winter months, foraging in fields, orchards, parks and gardens with other members of the thrush tribe.

Their food consists of worms, snails and insects, but berries and fruit are often taken. The fieldfare is also a passage migrant.

It is now an established breeding bird here in Britain, where breeding was first recorded in the Orkneys in 1967. Since then their population has grown in north-east Scotland, where possibly 50 pairs are breeding at the present time.

The fieldfare is one of the most colourful members of the thrush family with its contrasting plumage patterns. It has a smooth blue-grey head and rump, large spots and crescents on its breast and belly, and a yellow base to its bill. It is slightly larger than the blackbird. Sexes are very similar, but cock birds appear to be a little brighter in colour than hens.

I have kept several fieldfares over the years, and in 1970 was granted a licence to take specimens from the wild, and during the years that followed I maintained them within my aviary complex.

When the 1981 Wildlife and Countryside Act became law, many keepers, including myself, disposed of stock as the species could no longer be shown. It was placed on Schedule 4 of the Act and birds kept had to be ringed and registered. No breeding pairs were being kept at that time and in retrospect, most of the wildlife legislation has undergone changes and U-turns by the Government since 1981.

A General Licence is now in force to enable their exhibition. The species with all other passerine kinds have now been removed from Schedule 4, and any bird can be imported without much difficulty these days.

UNDER LICENCE

Post-1981, there were four legal ways of obtaining fieldfares: captive bred, import, wild disabled and under licence. I had acted too hastily in disposing of my fieldfares due to the legislation, but I was determined to acquire new stock.

There were no aviary-bred fieldfares registered as captive-bred at that time. The other three options, however, were available to me. I applied to take a few specimens on licence, but this was turned down. I wrote an article on the subject in Cage & Aviary Birds, and following this I received a small number of wild disabled stock, one of which came to me all the way from the Isle of Man, but I was unable to find a compatible breeding pair. In 1990 the British Bird Council set up a thrush-breeding programme, with myself as its co-ordinator. Its intention was to re-establish breeding pairs of mistle thrush, fieldfare, redwing and ring ouzel. Headway was made with the mistle thrush and ring ouzel, but not with the other two.

DELICATE DISH

I was aware of aviary-bred fieldfares in Europe and made enquiries about them, but I was not able at that time to import any. On one visit on my behalf, a friend called on a fieldfare breeder to obtain stock, but was informed that the birds were a delicacy and had been eaten!

Norman Woodhouse imported fieldfares from Europe and in 1998 he bred them. From then on they became readily available.

On a cold, damp, autumn evening in 1998 I collected two young fieldfares from a friend who had kindly ferried them from Norman's premises. When I placed them in my birdroom I was taken aback by their beauty.

As spring approached, the fieldfares became vocal and restless within their aviary. The hen frequently visited a nesting platform, and by April 7th, grasses were being deposited by the birds onto the platform and the nest gradually took shape.

FIELDFARE

Photograph by Dennis Avon

The song of the fieldfare is a repeated sequence of some eight notes, and during nest building this song was often heard.

It was not until June 13th that the first egg hatched. This chick was on the wing 11 days later - my first ever breeding of the species.

In 2003 I bred five fieldfares. The most successful pair consisted of a young cock bred by me in 2002, and an old hen. They were housed in a large, planted aviary, and had been together since February 24th 2003. By April 30th the hen had built a stout nest within a small wooden box, situated about 1.2m (4ft) from the ground. Five eggs were laid, but these were all clear.

By May 22nd the old hen had built a second nest in a privet bush. Again five eggs were laid, three of which hatched and were reared to maturity, mainly on earthworms, and on any invertebrates found within their large aviary. All these young turned out to be nice birds – probably the best I have bred so far. At that time my strain consisted of several generations, and line breeding in the future will enhance the stock.

The chicks were ringed as required, with DEFRA close rings. One bird was also close-ringed with an International Ornithological Association closed band, and this bird was entered in the 2004 World Show in Lausanne.

Since then I have exhibited the fieldfare on many occasions, and was the first exhibitor to win a special at a major event after the species had again become an aviary bird.

THE RING OUZEL

The ring ouzel (*Turdus torquatus*) is slightly smaller than the blackbird. It is a summer resident in Britain and is also a bird of passage here in spring and summer. It is similar to the blackbird in colour, but can always be distinguished from it by its white gorget which is more apparent in the male than in the female.

The ring ouzel's habitat is wild moorland amid rocks, heather and stunted alders around the 300m (1,000ft) contour line. Here they forage for earthworms, which are their staple diet.

It is an early arrival, the first birds reaching the south in early March. Swiftly, they move on to occupy their nesting grounds in the wild, open country of the hills.

At the beginning of the breeding season the cocks map out well defined territories and begin to sing, their liquid notes resembling the more familiar mistle thrush. The alarm note of the ring ouzel is a loud and persistent 'chac chac', similar to that of the blackbird but much harsher.

RARE IN CAPTIVITY

Before the introduction of the Wildlife and Countryside Act 1981, birds were kept for exhibition with little attempt made to breed strains from them. In fact, I can only recall one breeding of the species; this was by Percy Carr, whose birds built nests high up in his aviary.

The ring ouzel was not placed on Schedule 3 of the Act, so could not be shown in the early days of the new system. Keepers lost interest, and numbers fell dramatically within aviculture. However, in recent years, and with a General Licence in force enabling enthusiasts to exhibit them once more, numbers of ring ouzels are beginning to climb, and there are some very nice examples around.

About a dozen dedicated breeders are involved in its recovery as an aviary bird. Many fine examples have been displayed in recent years. The ring ouzel is, I believe, the most difficult to keep and breed of all the large British thrushes, being very susceptible to disease. There is always a demand for pairs, and yet they are still comparatively rare in captivity.

If they were as easy to propagate as other thrushes, there would be more than enough to go round. When birds are available, they are sold at a premium. However, I take my hat off to those keepers who have mastered their stockmanship of this lovely species.

An aviary which measures 2.7m (9ft) square is suitable to house a breeding pair of ring ouzels. It should be furnished with a rocky area with built-in ledges, and if possible a small hut or imitation ruin. In the wild, ouzels often use old buildings such as shepherds' bothies. Ivy should be encouraged to climb over the structure, and other plants such as heathers, encouraged to grow within the enclosure – all to stimulate the type of habitat favoured by the birds.

I had partial success in 1995, when my pair of ring ouzels were placed in a nicely prepared aviary measuring 7.3m (24ft) square x 2.7m (9ft) high. By March 22nd the cock bird was singing, and by early April the hen was building a nest in an elder bush. Both birds were unhappy with me intruding into their territory and would signal this with alarm calls. Subsequently this nest came to nothing, as did the second attempt.

On May 27th the hen was sitting on her original nest, and by June 5th the first egg was laid. I stayed completely clear of the nest and on June 10th, I noticed the cock bird with a mealworm in his bill, but it was a false alarm.

By June 16th the hen was seen re-building the nest and three or four eggs were laid so I

Photograph by Dennis Avon

RING OUZEL

increased the volume of livefood. On June 30th I heard 'clicking' coming from the nest and realised I had at last bred the species.

UNEXPLAINED DEATHS

As the parent birds began to moult, something dreadful happened. They both became lethargic and listless, remaining on the aviary floor. Their feathers were neither fluffed up, nor was there any discharge from their bill or vent.

I did what I could for them, but having never experienced anything like it, I had no way of helping them. They deteriorated rapidly and died, their condition lasting only a few hours; no other birds in my collection became ill.

In 1997 I again acquired a pair of ring ouzels, however they failed to breed. The female developed an eye problem, and I gave the male to a friend to make up a pair.

On July 28th 2003 I once again took home a lovely pair of ring ouzels: an adult male and a young female. I released the birds into separately prepared outside quarters straight from their respective carrying boxes without handling them. They appeared fit and well and began to settle. On August 7th when I went to feed them, the cock was standing in a corner of his flight. Thoughts of my 1995 experience came flooding back to me. I took it to my local vet straight away. He administered medicine to it orally and gave it an injection, but to no avail. It died that evening.

The hen seemed well enough, as it was in a separate aviary. I decided to watch it closely and gave it some medicine in its water. On August 16th, however, the hen had the same symptoms as the cock and died before I could get it to the vet. A post-mortem examination was carried out on both birds. All internal organs appeared normal, and the cause of their deaths was unknown at that stage. Body tissue was sent away and this confirmed that the birds died of septicaemia (blood poisoning), caused by bacteria.

The vet, who had experience with zoo birds, told me I had done nothing wrong, which was a relief. She said the disease develops so rapidly that little can be done.

I had not handled the birds at the outset, but when I caught them up I noticed that each had at least one flat fly on it. I have had such flies on birds from time to time, but have always considered them non toxic, as I have had no deaths of similar nature, except with the ring ouzels.

MEDICAL RESEARCH

I decided to carry out some research on flat flies and discovered that these particular ones were of the species hippoboscid and a common external parasite. They suck blood, and can cause anaemia in their hosts, but they cannot cause septicaemia by themselves. They can, however, carry certain blood parasites themselves, such as Haemoproteus and Leaucocytozoon, which can be passed on into the bloodstream of birds they infest. When this occurs the incubation period is between four and ten days.

My birds, according to my vet, died of septicaemia caused through bacteria, with no blood protozoa being found, so the flies appear not to be involved. Another veterinary surgeon told me. "It is common for birds to become stricken with an infectious illness soon after arriving in a new environment, since the stress of the move lowers their resistance to infection, and allows pre-existing dominant infections to take hold; or else contact with new germs to which they have no immunity will affect them."

I have to learn the lesson that ring ouzels, however well bred are very susceptible to stress, which lowers their immunity and allows bugs to gain an upper hold.

I understand that even during the breeding season, birds will become stressed and unless steps are taken to alleviate stress, problems are likely to occur later on, especially during the moult, which is stressful in itself.

COMMON SENSE

I have learnt the hard way, but now understand why so few ring ouzels are home-bred. They will become far more common when the stress factor has been overcome.

When a potential buyer makes contact with the seller, the stress factor must be emphasised. Birds must be healthy; ideally they should be checked over by a veterinary surgeon before they leave the seller, and again when the buyer gets them home. Medicines will be prescribed if required to help boost immune systems. Birds should never be moved just before, during, or just after the moult. If these common sense steps are taken I am sure many more ring ouzels, which after all are becoming rare in the wild, will live healthy lives within home-bred stocks.

Photograph by Dennis Avon

HEN RING OUZEL

STRAIN AND STUD BUILDING – BLACKBIRDS

For me the hobby of keeping blackbirds is an all year round affair; and not one where January means very much. This is because at this time of the year the British bird show season is already in full swing. It begins in October and is destined to go on until early March. As soon as the moult is over, the birds go back on the exhibition trail. January can, however, be a starter for the breeding season, as this is the time when wild, resident blackbirds are seen in pairs on garden lawns and in our parks. Most of my birds are also paired at this time. A few birds needed for exhibition remain isolated, and are placed into their breeding flights later on, when the shows are over. My home-bred stud of blackbirds has been built up over many years and contains birds whose silhouettes all share a common shape, consistent with the uniqueness of the strain.

CAREFUL PAIRING

This standardisation process has been achieved through line breeding of the best inter-related birds at my disposal, and a careful and controlled integration of any outside new blood.
I try to avoid in-breeding my blackbirds too closely,

CINNAMON BLACKBIRD'S EXCELLENT PEDIGREE

by BERNARD HOWLETT

THIS Cinnamon Blackbird hen comes from my line-bred strain of pedigree Blackbirds, which I have had since 1973. It was bred in May 1991 from a visual Cinnamon cock and Normal hen. The cock won numerous major awards including three red tickets at consecutive National Exhibitions between 1989-90; these awards included best British Softbill and best colour variant, the latter twice.

The Cinnamon hen has already achieved much, including a first at the National Exhibition. Among the awards it achieved in the 1994-5 season were best Softbill and best colour variant at the Eastern Federation of British Bird Fanciers' show, as well as the best Softbill at the Dunfermline show.

brother to sister is always avoided for instance. Close in-breeding will weaken the strain and if pursued will bring about its demise. I keep the members of each pair as distant as possible from each other so far as the family tree is concerned; in this way only healthy stock capable of producing strong young in their turn, are propagated, thus sustaining the stud.

My stud, as previously mentioned, consists of normals, cinnamons, satinettes, possible albinos, blues and grizzles. With the exception of the blues and grizzles, all the other strains within the stud are of my own creation over many years. Albino and grizzle are recessive, cinnamon and satinette sex-linked and the blue dominant.

On rare occasions I have brought in a bird and a supply of new blood. I once attended a National Exhibition where I met a man who said his blackbirds were "as big as jackdaws" – twice the size of mine. He sent me a pair, and the cock bird was indeed slightly larger than any I had. I integrated it into my stud and managed to breed several good birds from it.

I regard each individual bird as part of a jigsaw, which I strive to complete each year. The complete puzzle should comprise quality cocks and hens in visual form, with all the mutant colours in the stud also represented, together with normals and carriers. Invariably each spring only brings partial success, leaving pieces of the jigsaw missing. The emphasis of any plan is often concentrated on one or two aspects, or 'missing pieces.'

Each year brings with it new challenges, highlights and disappointments. Even with meticulous planning and a disciplined regime there are sometimes problems. There is no guarantee that success will be automatic. A positive approach is necessary, however, and the addition of only one or two new pieces to the jigsaw is success enough in any one season.

So, in January, the plans for the forthcoming breeding season, fashioned from my dreams, have already been made and goals set – a first rate normal hen here, a high class cinnamon cock there, and so on. Looking through my stock books, calling on experience and considering what my needs might be, the pairings are made and each is allotted a breeding flight.

By the end of March the pairs have become accustomed to their surroundings and are settled down in readiness for the weeks ahead. A careful watch is maintained to make sure peace reigns with each pair, and any specimen hostile to its spouse is given extra attention.

If hostilities persist, I usually place a piece of plywood up against the inside wire of the flight, behind which a bird being bullied can hide. Two

food and water stations are also provided at this time. In rare cases I remove the offending bird for a couple of days. This usually has the desired effect.

DAWN CHORUS

I am satisfied if the pairs settle down to breed in the middle of April. The dawn chorus begins around 4am and is magical, each bird trying to outdo its neighbour. The nest-boxes and ledges secured during the winter months are screened with brushwood. Dry grasses and dishes of mud are made available for the birds so that the nest building can get underway. It gives me great pleasure to walk round my aviaries during the breeding season and observe a bird on a nest or young being fed.

I tend to leave first-round youngsters with their parents for quite some time. This usually has an advantage in providing fledglings with an insight into the breeding process. The cock singing and the sight of the hen reconstructing the old nest, for instance, helps them to be firmly imprinted on their own kind.

The most I've ever reared from a single brood is five. One such breeding consisted of a cock split for cinnamon and satinette; the hen was visual cinnamon. From this clutch I bred two cinnamon cocks, two normal hens and a splendid satinette hen. A seasons work pretty well achieved in the one nest! Following the moult, a programme is put into place to train the best stock, young and old, for the shows.

THE SIX SPECIES OF BRITISH THRUSH

Thrushes have a charm and beauty rarely equalled in the bird world. Their songs are golden, mellow and varied, and as an aviculturist they are a joy to keep. The six species of large thrushes that commonly inhabit Great Britain are comparatively easy to breed and cater for in captive surroundings, and are among the most favoured of softbill show birds. Some are propagated in a variety of colours, both here and on the Continent. They are in order of size, mistle thrush, fieldfare, blackbird, ring ouzel, song thrush and redwing. Although there is migratory movement in all, and all six species breed in Britain, three - the mistle thrush, blackbird and song thrush are regarded mainly as residents. The fieldfare and redwing are predominately winter visitors to our shores and the ring ouzel visits our upland and mountainous regions to breed in spring.

These six species of thrush fell into three categories so far as the law was concerned. The blackbird and song thrush are listed on

Schedule 3 of the Wildlife & Countryside Act 1981, and can be sold or shown, provided they are close-ringed when young, with an approved ring. There are only two approved suppliers, these being the British Bird Council and the International Ornithological Association. The birds must have been bred in captivity from legally held stock.

The mistle thrush and ring ouzel are not listed on any Schedule, but may be sold or shown under General Licence if bred in captivity and ringed with a legible individually numbered metal closed-ring.This ring or band is a continuous circle, without any break, join, or any sign of tampering since it was manufactured, and which cannot be removed from the bird when its leg is fully grown. In the case of non-scheduled, the rings fitted need not be BBC or IOA, but I strongly advise that they are, because uniformity is good for the hobby.

The last of these intricacies of law concerned the fieldfare and redwing. These thrushes initially had to be registered within Great Britain. They can now be sold or shown under the terms of General Licence.

Documentary evidence of captive breeding must accompany a non-scheduled specimen. I keep my written evidence as brief as possible and usually write it out on the certificate of entry form, confirming that the exhibit in question was aviary-bred from legally held stock. Or hand a copy to a buyer; in the latter situation, I add details of the parent birds and hatch dates.

Schedule 3 birds, such as the blackbird and song thrush, wearing foreign rings here, or no ring at all, can be shown if an individual licence for such a bird is obtained specifically for that purpose, from the authorities. A bird listed on Schedule 3, which is fitted with a foreign ring, is not ringed within the meaning of the Act or its regulations. I always send a copy of any individual licence with any such exhibit that I show. (changes in ring laws pending)

SPACIOUS FLIGHTS

Thrushes are best kept in spacious flights, with sheltered roosting and nesting sites. Outside the breeding season they can be fed on a diet of poultry pellets and fruit, but livefood is essential if chicks are to be reared. Ring ouzels need a more varied diet, which includes livefood, and in particular, earthworms, all year.

All six species require moss, dry grasses and mud with which to build a nest. In my experience, all six species can be kept in pairs all year round, with the exception of the mistle thrush – where pairs should be parted outside the breeding season. All pairs must be watched at all times, as sometimes one partner can become a danger to the other.

THE MAVIS AND THE STORM COCK

What's the difference between the song thrush (Turdus philomelos) and the mistle thrush (T.viscivorus)? These are two birds which are superficially similar and often confused, but in fact are quite different when you get to know them. The mistle thrush's bullish character is well suggested by its old country name of 'storm-cock', whereas the gentler song thrush is known by the quainter name 'Mavis.'

The mistle thrush is the larger at 27cm (11in) in length, and weighs 110-140g (4-5oz), while the song thrush is 23cm (8.5in) long and only 70-90g (2.5-3oz) in weight. The two birds are closely related members of the genus Turdus. There are about 60 Turdus thrush species around the world. In Britain, apart from our featured two, we have the blackbird, redwing, fieldfare and ring ouzel.

The mistle thrush is paler than the song thrush, and more bulky. Its spots are larger, more rounded and darker. Its tail has white tips to its outer feathers, whereas the song thrush's tail is uniform in colour. The gait of the mistle thrush is more bouncing and exaggerated; its head is held high, whereas the song thrush's is level.

The song thrush holds its body horizontally while running on the grass. Its feathers are of a much warmer brown colour than the pale shades of its near relative. The underwing of the mistle thrush is white and is seen as an obvious flash when the bird is in its characteristic deeply, undulating flight. In the song thrush, the flight is steadier and the underwing is creamy buff, and hence less contrasting. Both species are early nesters. The mistle thrush in late February, the song thrush in early March. The mistle thrush's breeding period is much shorter.

Although equally fluent and beautiful, the songs of these birds are quite different. A mistle thrush can be told by its short, emphatic song phrases, and also by the fact that its main singing period begins in early January and tapers off in mid May. The song thrush, on the other hand, begins to sing with full vigour in early December and continues until the middle of July.

The key to recognising a song thrush's song is its repetition. It will utter a phrase, reproduce it once or several times, then move on to a completely different phrase, usually repeated too, then on and on, each phrase is a new invention. It often sings from dawn until and even beyond dusk. Both species often sing from the topmost branches of the tallest trees, but the mistle thrush is much more robust, and will skirl away in the teeth of a gale (hence 'storm-cock').

The mistle thrush is bold in appearance and behaviour, a pugnacious bird that will fiercely drive off any intruder near its nest. It is often able to see off a sparrow hawk or even a cat, which comes too close. The song thrush has none of these traits.

A song thrush's nest is a well-shaped cup of grass, thin twigs, roots, moss and dry leaves and lichens, with a neat inner cup of rotten wood pulp or solidified mud, built by the female. But the male is often the first of the pair to carry material to a chosen site, egging the female on to build and usually puffing out its breast feathers. Mistle thrush's nests are bulkier affairs, built by the hen, again with an inner layer of mud lined with soft grasses.

Many early song thrush nests are built in bare branches before the leaves appear. A mistle thrush's nest is usually less obvious, perhaps lodged in the fork of an ivy-clad tree.

Song thrush eggs usually number four to six in a clutch. Mistle thrush eggs number three to six in a clutch. The song thrush often undertakes four broods in a season, whereas the mistle thrush is double-brooded. Incubation in both takes 13-14 days, and in each case is carried out by the female.

The offspring of both kinds are similar, with down on the head and back. This is fairly long, yellowish buff in the song thrush and buffish white in the mistle thrush. Chicks of both species have yellow mouths and gape-flanges. They are tendered by both parents in the nest for about a fortnight and for about the same period after fledging.

A juvenile song thrush differs from the adult in the profusely speckled appearance of the upperparts. The back feathers have pale buff streaks and dark tips, and the wing feathers have distinct yellowish tips. In a juvenile mistle thrush, the back and wings are covered with white marks on the feather tips, creating a patterned effect.

The diet of both species is similar: worms, snails, fruits, berries and insects. The song thrush uses a stone or other hard object as an anvil on which to smash open snails, whereas the mistle thrush prises the meat from the shell without breaking it.

FEATURED IN THE FANCY

Both thrush species are well represented in British aviculture. The song thrush is the more popular, being easy to breed and exhibit. Cinnamon and cream mutations are common, making the species an attractive proposition for experienced and novice fanciers alike. But the mistle thrush is not easy to breed, owing to its aggressive nature, and few are shown.

Photograph by Dennis Avon

CHAPTER TWO

Other Softbills
- Including Thrushes

Satinette Blackbird

THE DUNNOCK-AVIARY HISTORY

The name 'dunnock' is the old English country word for the hedge sparrow (Prunella modularis), meaning 'the little grey-brown bird' or 'dun-coloured bird'. The name 'hedge sparrow' is widely used by ornithologists, but the bird is not related to the sparrow family (Passeridea) which includes the house and tree sparrows.

In the Middle Ages it was common practice to give the name 'sparrow' to any small bird, and in this case, the name has stuck.

Known also as the hedge accentor, the name that is perhaps the most suitable, as the bird is a member of the accentor family and frequents every part of the British Isles, except some remote islands in the north of Scotland. A separate race of the species inhabits the Hebrides.

DETAILED PLUMAGE DESCRIPTION

The dunnock is dressed in shades of glowing browns and greys. The wings, tail and back are brown; the head, neck and breast grey with brownish streaks, and the underparts merge into a paler grey. The thin, sharp bill is dark brown, with the lower mandible slightly paler than the upper, and the feet and legs are light brown. The iris is brown. The body length is 14.5cm (5 ¾in) and the weight 20-22g (about ¾oz).

The sexes are quite similar in colour, but generally, the male is brighter than the female, often showing a blue-grey hue.

INSISTENT SINGER

The short, musical, high-pitched song is beautiful and is constantly repeated. It is not commanding but insistent. It is at its height in spring, although it can be heard almost all year round, by night as well as by day.

The dunnock's song is at its best from January to July and is audible from a good distance.

Autumn sees some movement of birds from the continent to eastern Britain. British birds tend to be sedentary. In mid-winter, the population of dunnocks may rise to about 12 million.

In summer the dunnock is probably the cuckoo's most common victim in the south of England – some cuckoos specialise in the dunnock as a host species, producing eggs which resemble its victim's own.

SEXUAL GOINGS-ON

In the wild, studies have revealed bizarre sexual activities in the dunnock, where furtive matings are favoured in a deliberate reproductive strategy. Many dunnocks are polyandrous, which means the females mate with more than one male.

CAPTIVE HUSBANDRY

In home breeding, birds are usually housed in pairs, in small flights, where such activity cannot arise, although wild males will flit about around such an enclosure in order to attract the resident female.

Many more females die in cold weather than males. Females compete amongst themselves for territory. Often, territories are defended by two males and one female.

In order to mimic nature, dunnocks should be bred in trios, two males and one female. The female should be placed into the breeding compartment a few days before the males are introduced. Such experiments are worth considering, especially if a large aviary is available.

A vermin-proof planted aviary, measuring 1.8m x 0.9m x 1.8m high (6ft x 3ft x 6ft), is about the size universally used for these insectivorous birds. The stock should consist of good-sized, well-coloured birds. Breeding usually begins in March.

On no account should they be housed with any other small birds, because, when in breeding condition, they do become territorial and will attack any rival to their food supply, especially fledglings of other species, with their sharp bills.

Twigs, grass, roots, moss, hair and feathers will be required by the birds to build their somewhat bulky, cup-shaped, open nest. They will choose their own site amid the vegetation of the enclosure if left to their own devices, but will readily occupy a wicker basket, plastic nest-pan or even an old tea pot in which to build their nest.

Twigs about 10cm (4in) long will be used as a base if a natural site is chosen. The nest itself is composed almost entirely of moss and dry grass, lined with hair and feathers. It is built by the female, and it takes her about three days to construct it.

There are usually four or five smooth, glossy, bright blue eggs, which are incubated by the female for 12-13 days. The young, covered with fairly long, black feathers on the head and back, have bright orange mouths with gape-flanges of whitish-pink. They are fed in the nest by their parents for about 12 days.

It is wise to offer a selection of different insect foods when the chicks hatch, as some birds tend to be fussy early on and may decline items such as mealworms, so alternatives should be on hand. Armfuls of material infested with aphids will encourage feeding. After a few days, any insect food available will be fed to the young, which should then be reared successfully.

The chicks grow very quickly.

Three or more broods can be expected in a season. Young birds should be separated from their parents when they are seen feeding independently.

For many years, during the 1980s and early 1990s, the dunnock was the only small British softbill available for exhibition, due to restrictions in law, and during this time, a great opportunity to breed viable strains, which included colour variants, was lost by the fancy.

Nowadays specimens of any small softbill species can be shown, and the dunnock remains in the background, with no viable mutation strains in its armoury. Why is this? The species is easy to maintain and propagate.

Numerous species are bred in a host of colours, including the greenfinch, bullfinch, siskin, song thrush, blackbird and starling, to mention a few, but not the dunnock. I find this quite frustrating, I have tried myself and have failed. It is not that mutant material in the species is unavailable. It is quite frequently at hand.

The bird has occurred in opal, white, cinnamon, albino and in other colours, and any one of these could have become the foundation of a perceived strain, but for reasons I am less than sure about, all attempts have failed or fizzled out. Maybe its bizarre sexual inclinations have something to do with it. Perhaps normal coloured birds are put off by variants, by their unusual colours! Or maybe no aviculturist has made producing a variant dunnock strain his/her dedicated aim.

Only two colour variant dunnocks have been exhibited at the English National to the best of my knowledge, the first in 1984 by Tom Bailey and in 1985. On the first occasion, it came second of five variant birds (I managed to beat it with a blackbird). A year later, however, Tom turned the tables on me and won the class comfortably, taking the best softbill in show award.

This bird was a good size and was described as a cinnamon. It was however, paler in some areas of its body than in others. Its head and wings were of a light cinnamon colour, the rest of its body and its tail were much darker.

Soon after the 1985 event, Tom Bailey transferred the bird to me, it was then of some age, and during the spring and summer of 1986, I tried to breed from it, but was unsuccessful; the bird laid two chalky eggs which were infertile. During this time, Tom phoned me to say that the cock birds previously bred from it by himself and by the late Derek Oldknow had not produced any coloured hens. The bird was thought to be a sex-linked cinnamon.

Coloured females are bred from split cocks of the sex-linked mode of inheritance on a ratio of one from any four eggs. Tom went on to say that many birds bred from the cinnamon hen had not been kept. He advised me to keep all young bred, as he now considered the bird to be recessive. I heard later that Derek Oldknow did breed a visual from his normal – coloured stock, but it never reached maturity. It was years later before I processed another one.

The second mutation dunnock of this period was an adult dilute shown at the 1994 event by J.J. Tite. I judged the National that year, and found this particular bird very interesting indeed.

During the Spring of 1988, an East Anglian fancier, Robin Rolph, produced a black-eyed, pure white dunnock and a pied sibling from a normal-looking pair.

Photograph by Alois Van Mngeroet

ALBINO DUNNOCK

A dilute dunnock.

PHAEO DUNNOCK

DUNNOCK

Photograph by Tommy Milner

SHOW SPECIMEN

Robin Rolph transferred the white specimen to a local fancier, Roy Easter who exhibited it around the area, where it won well on the show bench. I first saw this specimen at the 1989 Eastern Federation show: it looked marvellous and in sparkling health, singing heartily in its nicely decorated cage. This bird became a great favourite with fanciers, but, alas, no useful strain was bred from it.

During the late 1990s, Peter Bailey, sadly now deceased, son of Tom, made great strides with light coloured variant dunnocks, which I considered to be opals or silvers. He showed these birds at the Yorkshire British Bird & Hybrid show at Scawsby, and I had the privilege of seeing them there, after that Peter told me he had little luck in breeding more of them, and the line eventually faded.

In 2006, I became the owner of a visual cock albino dunnock, quite a nice bird, which had bred a daughter, a split albino, which had been killed by the cock, its father. I tried in vain in 2007 and 2008, to breed from it but unfortunately failed to do so. I never exhibited it or the cinnamon hen, and regret this very much.

Variants are being bred on the continent from time to time, two fanciers, working as a partnership, have several satinettes between them. I am still hopeful of owning variant dunnocks.

The best normal coloured dunnock I have seen, was owned by Peter Jermy, an excellently shaped bird, it did well for him at the shows. Rob Windle successfully exhibits the species in pairs, quite an achievement considering the spiteful behaviour for which these little songsters are renowned.

BREEDING THE REDSTART

The common redstart (*Phoenicurus phoenicurus*) is a most beautiful little songster, and one I've had the pleasure of breeding in my aviaries. In 2007 I bred five from five eggs, and watched them develop with great interest.

The redstart is about 11.5cm long, (4½in) slightly smaller than our goldfinch. In avicultural terms, it is a "softbill", living mainly on insects, It is well suited to aviary life and is bred in quite good numbers by specialist enthusiasts each year. The biggest problem, early on, is to establish a compatible pair – but when this has been achieved a successful breeding is attainable.

OUT OF AFRICA

The wild redstart is a summer visitor to these islands from its wintering quarters of the Savannah and scrub belt of northern, tropical Africa, and it nests throughout Britain. It has a particular liking to oak woodlands and favours our western regions most. It nests in tree holes, but will readily take to nest-boxes.

The cock is particularly beautiful, with its chestnut tail, white forehead, black throat and grey mantle. It's one of the most handsome of our smaller birds. The hen lacks this bright plumage of the upper body and head, but retains the tail coloration.

My mature pair was housed separately during the winter of 2006/7; indeed, I had shown the cock bird on a number of occasions. The large, boisterous hen had been residing in one of my larger aviaries with a few other birds for almost a year, and had come through the winter strong and well. The enclosure was fully planted out with bushes, including box and elder. Also growing were plenty of honeysuckle and nettles. I affixed a variety of nesting receptacles at different heights, including one that was nailed to an upright, some 1.8m (6ft) from the ground. It had a round entrance hole cut into the front, and the pair raised their brood in this box.

On April 14th, I introduced the cock, a ferocious character that had nearly killed its mate in 2006. This time, after a few minor skirmishes, they settled down and by May 2nd they were observed perching together. At times, the cock pursued the hen, in a natural courting procedure. He bowed, showing off his white (frosted) forehead, and at the same time stretched out his neck and dropped his wings. He also spread his tail feathers to show off his flame-red colour. The hen would fly off with him in pursuit and on landing both would quiver their tails.

Nesting was under way in the little green box by May 23rd. I estimated that the nest had been completed by the 30th. The eggs take about 13 days to hatch, so they would do so around June 13th. On June 4th, I observed the cock enter the box followed by the hen. I decided to check the nest at the first opportune moment.

Three days later, using a small ladder, I opened the box lid and peered inside. There were five beautiful blue eggs in a well-constructed nest.

I now had a problem. All the aviary birds, which included pairs of blackbirds and song thrushes, were being fed mealworms each day as well as poultry pellets. Now I had to provide food more suited to the redstarts if I had any chance of them rearing a family.

I approached the problem in two ways. First, I placed a shelf under an aviary cross-member, and hooked utensils containing the required foods beneath it. This gave access to the redstarts but not the larger inmates. I did this in stages.

Second, I placed food for the birds in a half-open nest box, which I had placed nearby. The food was contained inside it, in a dish. I tied single stranded garden wire around the box so only the redstarts could enter and gain the contents. The hinged top of the box acted as a lid.

The young were fed on mini-mealworms, buffalo worms and waxmoth larvae.

My estimate of hatching proved to be spot-on, as I witnessed food being carried into the nest-box for the first time on June 13th. The heavens opened in Norfolk around this time, and poured torrents. All seemed well, though, and the chicks thrived.

On June 18th I decided to attempt to ring the chicks. I used code C closed rings, colour black for 2007 with my own code number, issued by the International Ornithological Association. As I exhibit birds at the World Show, I wondered if a British-bred redstart had ever been exhibited there.

I hoped I would be able to train a young redstart for the 2008 event. I was able to ring four of the five chicks: the smallest sibling was closed-ringed the following day. I estimated that they had hatched on June 12th and were at the five-or six-day stage.

I added small crickets to the diet. Aphids were flourishing in the aviary, on the elders and nettles, and the birds took them to the box. By June 27th, the first chick had left the nest, a strong bird. By June 29th three were on the wing. All eventually fledged. It was fascinating to watch the young redstarts change from being robin-like, with their speckled plumage, into their juvenile coats.

Redstarts show their full colours in their second year. My dilemma was whether to bring them into the birdroom to moult out or to leave them alone. I decided on the latter, although it would make it harder for me to train them for the shows. Most exhibition redstarts are hand-reared and very tame from the outset, mine being parent-reared, were less so. I didn't want to stress them so I allowed them to moult out naturally with their parents.

By the end of August, the old cock bird had regained his winter splendour and he began to intimidate the young cock pretenders, which were also beginning to "look the part". They, in turn, were bickering with each other. It was time to bring them in to train them for the shows.

THE STARLING AND ITS MUTATIONS

The song of the starling can be heard at almost any time of the year; only during July's moult is the species relatively quiet.

The song comprises a series of musical whistles, chatters and clicks, which is especially pleasant in the early spring. When alarmed, the starling utters a harsh scream.

The bird is a very good mimic of sounds, including the songs of other birds such as the blackbird, which it has almost perfected, as well as those of mechanical nature, such as farmyard machinery or passing trains.

Its plumage is amongst the most beautiful of all our native birds, and varies in intensity according to the density of the sun's gamma rays, which brings out the otherwise hidden iridescent purples, greens and blues, spangled with white, which are projected at their brilliant best. The plumage of the female has a less metallic sheen.

Aviary accommodation for a pair of starlings should not be less than 1.8m x 0.9m x 1.8m high (6ft x 3ft x 6ft) and should be made as vermin proof as possible to keep out rats and weasels.

Starlings are intelligent and inquisitive birds, so I would recommend that their flight be furbished in such a way as to induce interest and movement. Perches and platforms should be well spaced, and there should be an abundance of leaf mould on the floor.

A varied diet that includes fruit should be provided, together with a bowl of clean water, which may need to be replenished frequently, perhaps more than once a day, as they are avid bathers. This type of habit will stimulate the birds, ensuring they remain active and healthy.

Nest sites are best suited in sheltered positions. I use wooden boxes, which I have designed. Each has a hinged roof or top, one that can be lifted to allow easy access to the interior. I like to provide each pair with a choice of boxes. The birds readily take to these. The male starling selects the nest site and starts to build the foundations for the nest, which is completed by both parents. It's usually a rather untidy affair. Straw, grasses and other items of material found in the aviary, are used, the cup is lined with softer material such as feather, so all the various nesting materials must be provided for the birds. Nest building can begin as early as February, but I endeavour to get my birds started in early April, as this is the time when they come into breeding condition.

Four to six eggs are laid in April. They are pale blue in colour – sometimes white – and smooth and glossy. They are incubated by both sexes in the wild, for about two weeks. The male incubates the eggs during the day and the female at night. Some breeders choose to isolate the cock bird nearby, in sight and sound of the hen when the clutch is complete, to allow the hen to incubate the eggs and rear the young to about the fifth day, when the cock is reintroduced. This will prevent him interfering with the nest or removing the eggs, which often happens in confined conditions.

Concise records should be kept so one can estimate the day of hatching. When the chicks hatch, the eggshells usually appear on the aviary floor.

The chicks should be close-ringed on the fourth day if they have progressed well, and if it is intended to sell or exhibit the young. It is important to visit the nest-box as little as possible because I have known birds to forsake a nest when inspections are too frequent.

Given the opportunity, both parents will feed the young for about three weeks. However, food is brought to the nest only for the first 13 days; after that the chicks are at the nest-box hole. After fledging, they continue to be fed for a few more days. Juvenile plumage is replaced as autumn approaches.

Breeding starlings is difficult. In the wild these birds will breed in huge colonies and feed their young on almost anything edible. In confinement it's entirely different. The live food offered and the quality of it has to be to their liking. Earthworms, white mealworms, crickets and invertebrates found locally should be supplied. But in an aviary they rarely feed their young on pet foods or kitchen scraps.

Hand rearing is an easy option, one which must avoid mal-imprinting at all costs, to ensure the stock raised will behave in a normal, natural way. Although starlings have been represented in specialists' collections for many years, and shown from time to time at the National Exhibition and elsewhere, it's only during the past 20 years or so that the species has been bred, here and on the Continent, in numbers, both in normal and colour variant forms.

Roger Caton is, without doubt, this country's most prolific breeder of the starling. His birds have graced many an aviary, including my own. In the autumn of 1989 I met Roger at his home in the West Midlands, where he showed me his starlings and the mobile aviary built for them.

During the 1991 breeding season, Roger incubated 60 starling eggs, and from the resulting chicks 14 were outstanding quality – they were mainly pastels and browns which he retained for breeding.

By the end of the 1992 breeding season, Roger had established in British aviculture for the first time the phaeo-melanin recessive mutation, formally referred to as 'whites'. At that time he had a stock of 12, these included four visuals and eight carriers.

Before scaling down his project in 1998, Roger had bred over 40 phaeoes. At one time he had a collection of over 70 starlings of nine different mutations, these being opal, phaeo, dark-eyed clear white, greywing and pied, all recessive mutations, and four sex-linked varieties, namely cinnamon, Isabel, brown-pastel and agate pastel – a wonderful achievement.

I exhibited my first colour-variant starling, a cinnamon, at the 1975 National Exhibition. In 1977, I became the owner of a silver coloured starling. I entered this at the National Exhibition that year, the year of the Queen's Silver Jubilee. I described it as a Silver Jubilee Starling, and that's how it appeared in the catalogue. It won its class and best large softbill overall. I showed the bird again the following January at the Scottish National, where it also won its class. It was much admired. In retrospect the mutation was probably opal.

I purchased a hen phaeo-melanin starling from a London friend in the 1990's. The bird had been bred by Roger Caton and gave me enormous pleasure over many years. I bred several young from this beautiful bird; and it won a host of awards over many years for me. (See page 48).

The starling presents a challenge for the serious breeder. They are enchanting and entertaining birds, full of personality. Due to Roger's efforts, their place in aviculture seems secured, but the fancy cannot be complacent and efforts must be made to increase the population, in aviculture, so that these beautiful birds with their multitude of variant colours can be enjoyed by the generations to come.

At the present time I have a pair of cinnamon starlings. In 2012 they nested, but the eggs although fertile, failed to hatch.

They are young birds and it is hoped I will have better results in 2013.

OPAL STARLING

Photograph by Dennis Avon

Photograph by Dennis Avon

PHAEO STARLING

NIGHTINGALE PICTURE

Photograph by Dennis Avon

**PAIR OF NIGHTINGALES
OWNED BY THE AUTHOR**

THE CUCKOO

The cuckoo (*Cuculus canorus*) is the only completely parasitic bird that lives in Britain, and is as well known as our national bird, the robin. Its popularity, however, depends almost entirely on its call and the fact that it is associated with the arrival of spring.

The cuckoo's extraordinary habit of laying its eggs in the nest of other unrelated species, has interested nature lovers everywhere from early times.

One question which has long puzzled observers was how the cuckoo inserted its eggs into other birds' nests, some of which are of the cup-shaped variety like that of the reed warbler, others like the chiff-chaff are domed in shape, or built within a cavity such as those of the common redstart. Many cuckoos have been seen carrying an egg; it was thought that these were their own, but it has long been established that eggs carried by a cuckoo are those of their victim. These eggs are usually eaten by the cuckoo, thus gaining their nutritional value. The appearance of the cuckoo resembles that of a small falcon with its narrow wings and long tail. It has a low, direct flight with fast, shallow wing beats, which never rise above its back, followed by a glide when alighting.

It is often mobbed by small birds because of its shape, and probably because their instincts tells them that it is a bird which is not conducive to their family values.

The male cuckoo has a blue-grey head, throat and upperparts. The underparts are whitish barred with black. The tail is graduated, dark blue and spotted with white. The upperparts are whitish, barred with black. Its eyes and feet are yellow. The female, which is slightly smaller, has a rufous tinge on the upper breast. The young, after fledging have the upper surface and tail a rufous brown, barred with dusky blue. They have a white spot on head and nape. A redder phase also occurs in the adult female. The length of the adult male is 33cm (13in).

The structure of the feet also distinguishes it from all other British birds. It has zygodactyl feet, which means that of its four slender toes, the second and third (which are the largest) point forwards, and the first and fourth backwards.

Every cuckoo's call that I have heard has varied somewhat in pitch and tone, and this is most evident during the breeding season. When excited, the birds' voice becomes hoarse and low. Sometimes I have heard an audible stammering note, especially if a male rival is nearby. The female does not 'cuckoo' but produces a bubbling trill. The young birds cheep persistently, resembling a fledging, small songbird, which attracts other birds as well as its foster parents to feed it. The cuckoo's song is at its best from April to June.

By the middle of May, the cuckoo has taken up its territory, usually the one left the previous year, to lay its eggs primarily in the nests of the species of its birth.

After mating, the female cuckoo will perch in a tree or bush, where she will remain quietly, maybe for hours, watching a pair of birds going about their nest-building activities. At an opportune moment, she will fly down, usually uttering her bubbling cry, and neatly lay an egg directly into the host's nest, at the same time removing one, sometimes two, to make room for her own. When she next alights she often swallows her victim's egg.

The procedure of watching, waiting and laying is continued, on average, around a dozen times during May and early June. The record for the number of eggs laid in the same season by one female is around 25. Eggs are generally laid during the afternoon or early evening.

The eggs are usually laid on alternative days. Generally when two or three cuckoo's eggs are found in one nest they are from different females. Why the second bird, for instance, fails to remove a rival's egg, which would make the survival of her own chick hopeful, is unknown.

Occasionally, at the end of season, a female may lay two eggs in the one nest. The first, if fertile, being the older and stronger, would probably oust the other sibling - along, of course, with the foster's own chicks. Young cuckoos have a shorter incubation period, because eggs and young grow faster than those of the host species.

The cuckoo's eggs resemble the shape, colour and size of those already in the chosen nest; the size is slightly larger but small for the bulk of the bird. The commonest host species in Britain are probably the meadow pipit, hedge sparrow, reed and sedge warblers.

British cuckoo eggs show comparatively little variation except in ground colour, but on the Continent and in Asia, extraordinarily close mimicry of the eggs of the host bird is not uncommon. British eggs are sometimes reddish, spotted, marbled and freckled with various shades of grey and brown, and with fine blackish spots. Abroad pure blue eggs occur and there is a greater diversity of colour.

In the British Museum clutches of common redstart eggs are displayed, which are blue, together with pure blue eggs laid by the cuckoo. The museum also has a display of pure blue eggs placed by the cuckoo in the nest of the pied flycatcher, a species that also lays blue eggs.

The fact that the cuckoo produces blue eggs was for some time doubted in this country, although known in Germany. The question was set to rest by two English ornithologists in the 19th century - Mr Henry Seebohm and Mr H.J Elwes - who, when collecting together in Holland, received a nest of common redstart's eggs, one of which was larger than the others, and was said to be that of a cuckoo.

The eggs proved to contain well-formed chicks, and when investigated further, the chick found in the larger egg was a cuckoo, identified by its zygodactyl feet. These eggs were light blue in colour. Among the various types of eggs stored in the museum, many are exact copies of the eggs of host species.

Host species frequented by cuckoos include hedge sparrow, sedge warbler, wren, pied wagtail, reed warbler, tree pipit, meadow pipit, greenfinch, redstart, blackbird, nightingale, robin, chiffchaff, grasshopper warbler, linnet, chaffinch, Orphean warbler, reed bunting, yellowhammer, spotted flycatcher, whinchat and yellow wagtail.

As soon as the young cuckoo hatches, it ensures its wellbeing by deftly pushing out other chicks or eggs from the nest until it remains the only occupant. Evolution has equipped the young cuckoo with a very sensitive and somewhat concaved back, so that for a day or so after hatching it will instinctively throw out of the nest any egg or chick that comes into contact with its back.

The food of the adult cuckoo consists almost entirely of insects and their larvae. The larvae of crane flies, sawflies, ermine, magpie, fox and winter moths are consumed in large numbers. Also slugs, woodlice and spiders are taken. They feed on hairy caterpillars that are poisonous to other birds. Their stomachs are protected from the irritation of the caterpillars by a lining, which can be shed or renewed.

Young cuckoos move to their wintering quarters in Africa, not having ever seen their parents, in August and September, long after the adults have gone. Mr R. Bowler-Sharpe, in the late 19th century, shot three young cuckoos at around the same time and place. This indicates they may fly south in small groups. They, too, will consume large quantities of hairy caterpillars on their journey, especially those of garden tiger moth, which, are called 'woolly bears'. Over the centuries, the cuckoo, with its wandering voice and exotic colours, has captured the hearts of many country folk. Evolution has given it a niche in the natural world, which is complicated, bizarre and wondrous, yet there is so much more to learn about its habits.

WHERE DO THEY COME FROM?

The ornithologist John Parslow, an expert on bird distribution, believes the cuckoo is possibly of Palearctic origin, the area of northern Europe and Asia. It breeds through virtually the whole of continental Africa south of the Sahara, and in Himalayan India, Assam, Burma and northern Indochina, throughout the palearctic region east to Japan. Also, throughout North Africa and the Mediterranean islands.

In Britain it breeds in every county where its numbers at the present time are about 30,000 pairs. Its numbers have been in decline in the British Isles for a number of years, although they are healthy in Europe; I have particularly noticed this in the area I know best, East Anglia, with fewer birds calling in the spring than 20 or so years ago.

CUCKOO TAKES FLIGHT

Photograph by Tony Tilford

PASTEL SKYLARKS

In 2007 I obtained a pair of skylarks from Belgium, these consisted of a normal cock split for pastel, bred in 2005 and a pastel hen raised in 2006, quite large birds. In 2007 no chicks were bred. In 2008, I had a misfortune with the male, so no chicks were bred. I obtained an ordinary new cock bird for the 2009 season. I paired this to the visual hen and two large, healthy young cocks, split for pastel were bred, pastel being a recessive mode of inheritance. I believe this is the first occasion in the UK that young skylarks with mutant blood have been reared. The programme is on-going, I have yet to breed a visual, but one day I hope to do so.

**PASTEL HEN SKYLARK
MOTHER OF MY TWO SPLIT COCKS**

Photographs by Rudy Driesman

**PAIR OF SKYLARKS
PASTEL IN FOREGROUND**

BLACK REDSTARTS ARE FULL OF CHARACTER

The black redstart (*Phoenicurus ochruros*) is a member of the thrush family, but is very robin-like in habit. The male is mainly black in summer and dark grey in winter, and has white wing patches. The female is grey-brown. Both birds have a chestnut rump and a rufous tail. Juveniles resemble the adult female.

It is a summer visitor to the UK, taking up residence in old buildings, stable complexes and local authority work areas, such as sewage works, a similar habitat to that of the pied wagtail. A century ago, however, the species was very rare in Britain; it was not until after the Second World War that it appeared here as a regular nesting bird. It formerly took a liking to the bombed out buildings of London and the south-east, where it raised its families amid the debris.

Photograph by Dennis Avon

**PAIR OF BLACK REDSTARTS
OWNED BY THE AUTHOR**

The black redstart is listed on Schedule 1, Part 1, of the Wildlife and Countryside Act 1981 and has special protection. A goodly number of pairs are presently kept in the UK, and many are bred each year on the continent.

Sometimes the black redstart is referred to as the blackstart; this is misleading for there is a blackstart (Cercomela melanura), a closely related bird but which inhabits the Horn of Africa region.

I have kept a few black redstarts over the years, in one spring a pair nested in one of my old blackbirds nests, an unusual event, because the species prefers a nest box or cavity in which to nest. I kept the birds inside the birdroom during the winter months. Some breeders keep them outside during this time. I find a small-planted aviary with a shelter suits them very well when spring arrives. They are delightful birds to keep, endearing in their ways, and full of character. They are easy to cater for. An insect-based formula and added mealworms seem to suit them. Many insects and other invertebrates can be caught by them inside an aviary, or added when available by the keeper. This additional protein helps to maintain them in good feather and condition.

If the pairs are indeed maintained inside during the cold months, then they can be released into their breeding quarters at the end of March or in early April. They are less aggressive to each other than redstarts, but a close eye should be kept on them until they have settled down.

The cock will begin to sing in April, a pleasant warble. When I approached my breeding pairs, I was always greeted with a short "tsip" and a "tucc-tucc", reminding me that I was nearing their domain. In my experience breeding did not commence until July.

In 1994, I exhibited a cock bird, as a DOE licence was in force. It reminded me then of former times when these and many other species of small insectivorous birds were shown on a regular basis. Those times have returned as a General Licence is in existence enabling exhibitors to show their birds provided that they are legally bred and close ringed, from parents of which the keeper has full details.

THE HOOPOE

The Hoopoe (*Upupa epops*) is an annual passage-migrant to the UK, with a smaller number of pairs attempting to breed here every year.

It would be quite successful as a breeding species today if it had not been so persecuted by man in the past. Almost every bird sighted in the past was shot, and many nests were forsaken after being disturbed by egg-collectors. However with current conservation measures and a less hostile society, the Hoopoe might gain a better foothold here in the future.

It is a beautiful bird with a wonderful fan-like crest of pinkish-brown feathers, tipped with black. It has a pinkish-brown mantle and breast and its tail and wing feathers are barred in black and white. The bill is long and curved, while the legs are grey. Both male and female are alike, but the young are less brightly coloured and have shorter bills. The hoopoe is slightly smaller than a jay.

In the wild the hoopoe is quite confiding and unafraid of human company, which may have been a disadvantage in the past, making it an easy target for sportsmen. It walks in a similar way to the starling and the two birds can often be seen together. The hoopoe's flight is usually slow and undulating and appears feeble, but it is capable of fast flight and can use this ability to escape a hawk by climbing rapidly to an extreme height.

Its call is distinctive and carries far a "hoop-hoop-hoop-hoop", repeated 3-5 times. This made with a distended neck with the head lowered, and is carried out from a tree or the ground. This curious "hooping" sound is less musical than the cuckoo's.

In the UK, hoopoes are at the extreme northern limits of their range, thus are very rare breeders here, nesting mainly in the south-eastern coastal counties from May to June. Nesting sites are varied – any kind of hole in a tree, building, or quarry will suffice, although a nest box will also attract it. Little or no material is used in nest making.

Five to eight pale non-glossy eggs are laid, conspicuously marked with pores, and the hen begins incubation before the last egg is laid. Incubation takes about 18 days during which time the cock feeds the hen. Because the chicks hatch at intervals they differ in size, with the first being brooded by the hen and subsequently fed by the cock. However, after a few days both parents carry out this task.

The chicks have scanty white down and pink mouths with waxy white flanges. They remain in the nest for between 2-4 weeks and two broods in a season are not uncommon.

Most food is obtained on the ground, where the birds search diligently, probing widely turning over leaves and stones. Hoopoes feed on a wide variety of insects, including crickets, also grasshoppers and berries, but are partial to lizards and worms, which they probe the soil for with their long beaks. A lack of the right food may have reduced the number of successful breedings in the UK. The replacement of hedgerows and the implantation of set-aside schemes in agriculture, together with the high protection the law now gives to this species, may help redress this situation.

Many legends relate to the hoopoe - one involving King Solomon. It also appeared in ancient literature in Egypt and Crete, and portraits of the bird have been discovered in their ancient murals.

Several sub-species are found in Africa and Asia. The chief differences are overall size and the darkness of the body plumage, which varies from sandy-grey to dark rufous-brown.

The hoopoe has been bred in captivity in this country on a number of occasions, notably by Norfolk aviculturist Brian Fisher. I have had the privilege of seeing first-round young flying in their spacious aviary while second-round eggs were being incubated. Food for captive hoopoes includes mealworms, crickets, locusts and other foods offered by the trade.

Photograph by Tony Tilford

Photograph by Dennis Avon

**OPAL JAY
OWNED BY THE AUTHOR**

The pages which follow are what the author refers to as the British Bird File, and
sequence species in their genera, from wood pigeon to Lapland bunting.

WOOD PIGEON

Columba palumbus.

Related species: Stock dove and rock dove.

DESCRIPTION: Distinguished by the white patch on the wing, conspicuous in flight and by a white patch on the side of the neck. Head, neck, lower back, rump and tail blueish-grey, with purple and green reflections on the nape and neck; the mantle and wing-coverts are brown, tail dusky with dark bar. Underparts vinous purple on breast, blueish-grey on flanks and belly. Female slightly duller and smaller than male. Young birds lack the white patch on neck. Length 41cm (16in).

STATUS IN THE WILD: A steep increase in numbers in recent years. More than three million pairs breed in Britain. Bird of gardens, parks, woods and farm land. Flocks are swelled by continental birds in winter.

HARDBILL OR SOFTBILL? Noted as a softbill.

AVAILABILITY FOR BIRDKEEPERS: Sometimes available within aviculture. Rare mutant birds always wanted, and these would be expensive to purchase.

ADVANTAGES TO KEEPING: Subtle iridescence is a please.

DISADVANTAGES TO KEEPING: Persistent cooing, especially during the early hours of the morning!

DIET: Mainly vegetarian, especially seeds. Wood pigeons grind down hard foods into digestible fragments using their gizzard, a special digestive organ, deliberately consumes bits of gravel to store in the gizzard to assist grinding process.

HOUSING: Aviary about 9ft square, suitable for one pair. Sturdy perches should be available. Breeding pairs require plenty of twigs to construct their nest, and shelves or small wooden platforms to build on.

BREEDING: Nests built in trees or high hedges, in woods, often among ivy. Nest often flimsy, usually two eggs form a clutch, these are white, smooth and slightly glossy - often seen through the nest from the ground. Laying begins in March, often two or more broods taken. Incubation by both sexes, beginning with the first egg for 17 days. Nestlings are downy, absent about eyes and throat, skin underneath blueish-grey, bill flanges pale. Squabs fledge after 29-35 days. Fed on pigeon milk, which is a secretion from the lining of the crop. After fledging, they continue to be fed by both parents for several weeks. During courtship, the male glides in a gentle climb, then at the top of flight, gives several deliberate flaps, and then glides back down, to proclaim territory.

CALL: A five-note *coo*.

RING SIZE: Code P.

SHOWING REQUIREMENTS: Unlikely to be seen at the shows, although variants would attract attention. Show cage, wooden, painted black outside including wire front, and white inside, with two solid perches, floor covering optional. Cage must have plenty of space for bird to move around. Exhibit: As large as possible, with good wing and tail carriage and with bright eyes.

LEGAL REQUIREMENTS: May be killed or taken, under a General Licence. Can be shown if bred in captivity and ringed under present law.

SPECIAL NOTES: Wood pigeons often snap twigs from living trees and bushes for their nests, more so by male than female. Wing flapping among males in the tree canopy is common. When birds are ground feeding and are disturbed, loud wing flapping occurs as an alarm signal.

Photograph by Frank Stark

ROCK DOVE

Columba livia.

Related species: Stock dove and wood pigeon.

DESCRIPTION: The wild bird has a blue body, greyer back, black wing-bars white rump. Length 33cm (13in).

STATUS IN THE WILD: Resident, with 100,000 pairs, including feral types. True type birds inhabit west coast of Ireland, west Scotland, Scottish islands, the Yorkshire coast and elsewhere.

HARDBILL OR SOFTBILL? Regarded within British aviculture as a softbill.

AVAILABILITY FOR BIRDKEEPERS: Available in all guises. Racing birds can fetch huge sums.

ADVANTAGES TO KEEPING: Hugely desirable, with large following. Many clubs catering for all the specialised types.

DISADVANTAGES TO KEEPING: Racing and flying flocks likely to be predated by peregrine falcons. Possible conflict with house-holders in vicinity of lofts due to fouling, also with land owners if birds raid crops.

DIET: (wild bird) Mainly cereals, but also weed seeds, buds and small molluscs.

HOUSING: Lofts.

BREEDING: Slow flapping display flight, and elaborate strutting and breast puffing by male in courtship display. Usually nests in colonies, in caves and crevices of sea-cliffs, gorges or rock outcrops. The nest is a scanty layer of fine stems, roots and twigs. Both sexes build, but usually the male brings material to the female for construction. The breeding season is from March to August or September. Double or treble brooded. The eggs, two usually, rarely one, smooth and glossy, colour white. Incubation is by both sexes, beginning with the first eggs for 17-19 days. The squabs are downy, sparse and course, mainly yellowish with a slight reddish-pink; bill dull grey with pale, flesh-coloured tip, legs and feet greying pink. Young are brooded continually at first, and fed by both parents with pigeon milk regurgitated from the crop and later as regurgitated grain. After flying they are still fed by parents for some time. They become independent in 30-35 days. Feral birds build on ledges and nooks in buildings etc. Other kept varieties are maintained in purpose built facilities such as pens and dove coops, where they are fed propriety branded foods such as pigeon mixture and red band conditioner.

CALL: A moaning *oorh* or *oh-oo-oor*, longer crooning in display.

RING SIZE. Code R.

LEGAL REQUIREMENTS: Wild bird protected at all times, can be sold or shown. Feral birds may be killed or taken by authorised person within terms of a General Licence.

SHOWING/DISPLAYING: Royal Pigeon Racing Association feature classes for both racing and show racers. Racing pigeons return to their lofts from great distances. Fancy pigeons have numerous varieties, colour and types include kings, runts, Chinese owl, yellow tipplers, helmets, Hungarian feleg-laz, tumblers and many, many more; some used for flying competitions. Peace birds usually white and with homing instinct, and used at weddings and events. Carrier pigeons were used during the war, and no doubt are still used in some roles.

SPECIAL NOTES: First bird species to be domesticated. Now found in some form throughout the world.

Photograph by Frank Stark

STOCK DOVE
Columba oenas.
Related species: Rock dove and wood pigeon.

DESCRIPTION: Blue-grey dove, looks a darker, bluer bird than woodpigeon, with shorter tail and neater shape, two small black wingbars, has green and purple sheen on side of neck. Some feral pigeons do however resemble this species. Likely to be seen in pairs rather than in flocks. Flight is fast, has quicker action than woodpigeon. Bird of open spaces such as arable land. Length 33cm (13in).

STATUS IN THE WILD: Resident in British Isles, with small number of regular winter visitors from the Continent. About 270,000 pairs breed here.

HARDBILL OR SOFTBILL? Softbill.

AVAILABILITY FOR BIRDKEEPERS: Usually available. Cost inexpensive.

ADVANTAGES TO KEEPING: I have kept them and found them interesting, long lived and ready nesters.

DISADVANTAGES TO KEEPING: Bird for a large collection. Not usually considered as a show bird. Song could become an irritant, perhaps with neighbours.

DIET: Mainly vegetable, grain of all kinds, clover, turnip and swede leaves, peas and beans, and seeds of many plants. Some small snails also taken.

HOUSING: Sheltered aviary 1.8m (6ft) square, with strong perches and food and water dishes.

BREEDING: Generally breeds in tree holes, rabbit holes, in cliff hollows, ruins and old buildings, also within very thick ivy. Will use old crow and magpie nests; also nest boxes. Season begins in early March, when pair displays and postures like other pigeons and doves, including a slow wing-flapping. Double or treble brooded. Nest made of twigs, roots, straw and dead leaves. Usually two sometimes only one egg is laid, these are smaller than the woodpigeon, they are smooth and slightly glossy, white with a slight creamy tint. Incubation is by both sexes, beginning with the first egg, for 16-18 days. Nestlings are downy, warm yellowish-buff. They are fed by both parents on pigeon's milk and fledge after 27-28 days. They continue to be fed for a few days after leaving the nest. In home-bred conditions, nest boxes are essential. Food should include pigeon mix, wheat and plenty of fresh greens.

CALL: Alarm call a short *'hru'*. Song heard as early as March, is quite a quiet, rapidly repeated *goo-roo*, with the stress on the first syllable.

RING SIZE: Code R, which has an internal diameter of 7.1mm.

SHOWING REQUIREMENTS: Unlikely show bird; needs to be in good feather, tame, with bright eye and good wings and tail carriage. Cage: Painted black outside including wire front, white inside. Size no smaller than 24in long, 20in high and 16in deep, with two stout perches. Floor covering optional.

LEGAL REQUIREMENTS: Protected at all times. Can be shown within the terms of a General Licence, if ringed and bred in captivity.

SPECIAL NOTES: Local names; wood dove, blue rock and stock pigeon. Sits closely. Is readily distinguished from rock dove by lack of white rump.

Photograph by Tony Tilford

COLLARED DOVE
Streptopelia decaocto.
Related species: Turtle dove.

DESCRIPTION: This is a medium sized dove, which has a pale greyish-buff, pale pink and subtle blue-grey appearance. A black half collar, with which it got its name; and a long tail. The black wing tips and white outer tail feathers are more noticeable in flight. The short legs are red and the bill is black. The iris is reddish brown, but from a distance the eyes appear to be black, as the pupil is relatively large and only a narrow rim of reddish-brown eye colour can be seen around the black pupil. Juvenile birds are paler with no black collar at first. Length 31-33cm (12-13in).

STATUS IN THE WILD: The ancestral home of the species is Asia, in particular India. The collared dove is now one of the greatest colonisers of the avian world, arriving in Britain in the 1950's. It now breeds north of the Arctic circle in Scandinavia. Some introductions have enabled it to spread to North America and elsewhere. Resident in the UK with 230,000 pairs.

HARDBILL OR SOFTBILL? Softbill.

AVAILABILITY FOR BIRDKEEPERS: Taken up by dove fanciers to some degree, and available. Inexpensive.

ADVANTAGES TO KEEPING: Most interest rests with rarer doves, but for specialists, one to add to a collection.

DISADVANTAGES TO KEEPING: Lack of interest, and its monotonous call.

DIET: Food, chiefly seeds of various species of weed, also corn and leaves of seedlings. Common visitor to bird tables. Will consume prepared dove and pigeon mixtures in captivity, even poultry pellets.

HOUSING: An outside aviary with a shelter, fitted with strong perches. They can be kept with smaller birds such as finches and canaries.

BREEDING: In the wild the species breeds wherever there are trees for nesting, and is often found around human habitation. Two white eggs are laid in a nest made of sticks. They are incubated by the male during the day and by the female during the night. Incubation takes between 15-19 days. The male has an unusual mating display, consisting of a rapid, nearly vertical climb to height, followed by a long glide downwards in a spiral. The breeding season lasts from March to October.

CALL: The song is a *coocoo, coo*, repeated many times. Occasionally it also makes a harsh loud call lasting about two seconds, particularly when landing during the summer.

RING SIZE: Code R.

SHOWING REQUIREMENTS: Cage must be no smaller than 51cm long x 38cm high x 30cm wide (20in x 15in x 12in), with two sturdy perches. The exhibit should be in fine feather and condition with good markings and bright eye. Mutations exist. Very rarely exhibited within the British (native) bird fancy, due to lack of interest. Shown singly.

LEGAL REQUIREMENTS: Can be killed or taken due to General Licence. Can be sold or shown on separate General Licence for non Schedule 3 birds, if captive bred and close-ringed.

SPECIAL NOTES: Collareds can interbreed with the Barbary dove with many hybrids kept. Thought to be domesticated from the African ringed dove (Streptopelia risoria). Barbaries are sometimes released at weddings, etc. Unfortunately, they do not return like the homing pigeons.

Photograph by Frank Stark

TURTLE DOVE

Streptopelia turtur.

Related species: Collared dove.

DESCRIPTION: Very attractive dove, grey crown, sides of head, breast and belly pink, a black and white patch on side of neck, long rounded dark tail, white tips to outer tail feathers, showing a clear white band on the under tail in flight, the upperparts are black and brown. Female rather smaller in size, lack the black feathers tipped with white on the sides of the neck, and is of a duller hue. Length 27cm (11in).

STATUS IN THE WILD: Summer visitor, arriving April and May, departing in September or later, also a passage migrant wintering in Africa, south of the Sahara. About 75,000 pairs breed in U.K. but declining. Habitat; open ground, woods, high hedges, orchards and parks. One of the last summer migrants to arrive.

HARDBILL OR SOFTBILL? Softbill.

AVAILABILITY FOR BIRDKEEPERS: Numbers bred each year, some raised under other dove kinds. It is far better to allow chicks to be reared by their own kind, to help prevent behaviour problems.

ADVANTAGES TO KEEPING: Enchanting species with a wonderful purring song.

DISADVANTAGES TO KEEPING: CITES species, Government paperwork required for sale or movement.

DIET: Mainly seeds and cereals.

HOUSING: An aviary about 1.8m x 1.8m x 2.1m high (6ft x 6ft x 7ft) or larger, partly sheltered, is suitable to accommodate one pair of these lovely doves. Nesting sites in form of large wicker baskets, or platforms, secured and secreted in brush-wood would be suitable. Small twigs should be scattered around the floor for the bird's use.

BREEDING: Nest built of sticks and twigs, almost randomly, as often clutch can be seen through the nest from below. Two creamy white eggs are laid, these are glossy and oval shaped. Breeds May to August. Nest placed in tree or bush from 4ft-20ft high. The eggs are incubated by both parents for 13-14 days. The nestlings are downy, pale straw-buff, lighter than wood pigeon; skin blue-grey. They are fed on pigeon milk, which is a secretion from the lining of the crop, for 19-21 days.

CALL: A cat-like *purr*, *roor-r-r*, repeated.

RING SIZE: Code P.

SHOWING REQUIREMENTS: Wooden show cage, 24in long, 20in high and 16in wide, painted black outside, including the wire front, white inside, fitted with two strong perches, floor covering optional. Exhibit; as large as possible, of excellent condition, with good wing and tail carriage and bright eyes.

LEGAL REQUIREMENTS: Protected at all times. Listed on CITES. Specimens can be kept and bred without the need for an Article 10 certificate. An Article 10 Certificate from DEFRA is required for movement or sale; to obtain an Article 10 a bird must be close ringed or micro-chipped. Any keeper wishing to exhibit a turtle dove is advised to get in touch with the authorities first, so as to keep within the law.

SPECIAL NOTES: Local and other names; wreckin dove, ring-necked turtle and common turtle. Sits pretty tightly when incubation has advanced. If disturbed flies off without vocal sound.

Photograph by Tony Tilford

GREAT SPOTTED WOODPECKER

Dendrocopus major.

Related species: Lesser spotted woodpecker.

DESCRIPTION: The upperparts of the male are glossy black, with buff on the forehead, a crimson spot on the nape and white on the sides of the face and neck; on the shoulder is a large white patch, the flight feathers are barred with black and white. The three outer tail feathers are also barred; these show when the short, stiff tail is outspread. The underparts are buffish-white. The lower body and under tail coverts are crimson. The beak is slate-black, the legs greenish-grey, and the eyes crimson. The female is a slightly smaller bird, and has no crimson on the nape. In the young, this nape spot is absent, but the crown is crimson. Length 22cm (9in).

STATUS IN THE WILD: Resident with about 28,000 breeding pairs.

HARDBILL OR SOFTBILL? Known as a softbill.

AVAILABILITY FOR BIRDKEEPERS: Kept in some large collections, but of very little interest to the average keeper. Advertising may produce positive results. Price would be in excess of £200 a pair.

ADVANTAGES TO KEEPING: Would provide colour and interest.

DISADVANTAGES TO KEEPING: Their drumming in the spring could become irritating. The aviary would need to be specially constructed in order to keep them in.

DIET: Chiefly larvae of wood-boring insects, beetles and their larvae, moth larvae, spiders, woodlice, young chicks of several species including house martins, sparrows and blue tits also vegetable matter, such as hazel nuts, berries of rowan, beech mast, pips of crab apples and cherries.

HOUSING: A pair of these beautiful birds would require quite a large aviary. Any wood used in its construction would need to be covered, to prevent damage by the birds. A metal one would give better security. Dead branches affixed to the aviary netting in erect positions would provide plenty of interest for the birds, especially those with the bark still on. Strong perches are also desired.

BREEDING: If undisturbed a pair will use the same tree in the wild year after year, often making a new hole below the old one if space permits. No nesting material is used, the white eggs usually number five or six in a clutch. Laying begins in May, incubation is carried out by both birds for 16 days. The young are tendered by both sexes until they leave the nest at between 18-21 days. The species is single brooded. In captive conditions, the birds are likely to construct their own cavities. However those made by the keeper would be taken up; for instance a space cut out in an upright branch and a nest box inserted therein would suffice. Livefood suitable for these birds, and for raising their young includes; large mealworms, locusts, and crickets, which are readily available on the market.

CALL: No song, metallic 'kich', repeated as an alarm call, drumming carried out on hollow tree, dry branches, posts, or even on metal is regarded as their spring "song".

RING SIZE: Code K.

SHOWING REQUIREMENTS: Cage must be much higher than its length, so the exhibit can climb up any erect timber affixed at the back. The bird is usually shown singly, and should be in excellent condition.

LEGAL REQUIREMENTS: Not on any Schedule. Legislation enables the species to be sold or shown if ringed and bred in captivity. It is fully protected.

SPECIAL NOTES: Local and other names include, whitwall, woodnacker, wood-pie, French-pie and speckled-pied woodpecker. A very close sitter.

Photograph by Tommy Milner

LESSER SPOTTED WOODPECKER

Dendrocopus minor.

Related species: Great spotted woodpecker.

DESCRIPTION: Recognised by its black and white plumage. It is much smaller than the great spotted, sparrow size in fact. The back is white barred with black, there is no scarlet under the tail. Wings similar to great spotted, the male has a crimson crown, the female's is dull white, both sexes have white patches on their cheeks and side of neck. The central tail feathers are black, the rest barred with white. The underparts are whitish, streaked with black on the flanks. The young are similar to adults, but their markings are less defined, there is some crimson on the crown, their underparts are buff, with short brown streaks. Length 15cm (6in).

STATUS IN THE WILD: Resident in Britain, with about 5,000 breeding pairs, smallest European woodpecker. Species more likely to be found in England and Wales than elsewhere, majority in South-East.

HARDBILL OR SOFTBILL? Softbill.

AVAILABILITY FOR BIRDKEEPERS: Rarely available, would cost about £100 each.

ADVANTAGES TO KEEPING: If successful would bring much prestige to a genuine breeder, specimens make exquisite show birds.

DISADVANTAGES TO KEEPING: Limited aviary stock making it difficult to acquire a genuine, unrelated legal pair.

DIET: Chiefly larvae of bark-hunting and tree-boring insects, including beetles and moths, also ants, fly larvae, gall insects and spiders. Will also take soft fruit like blackberries.

HOUSING: Being tiny, not so destructive to aviary timber, as great spotted, but the fact that these wood bangers are likely to escape should be borne in mind. Flight should be no smaller than 2.75m x 1.2m x 2.1m high (9ft x 4ft x 7ft), furnished with old timber and strong perching. Sheltered nest boxes should be in place to encourage nesting. These filled to 3in below nesting hole with untreated wood chippings, shavings or other suitable material.

BREEDING: Drills nest hole in very soft and decaying timber, sometimes quite low down, or at a considerable height. The nest chamber is almost spherical, not much below the entrance, no material is used. The eggs number four to six in a clutch, white and glossy. Laying begins in April, but usually in first half of May. The incubation is carried out by both parents for a period of 11-14 days. Single brooded. Food for aviary stock must be provided in insect form all through the year, increased in volume at breeding time, items offered can include small mealworms, wax moth larvae, crickets, buffalo worms and clean fly maggots. During the winter months fruit such as mountain ash berries can be added, together with an insectivorous compound and nuts.

CALL: Call note, *tic tic*, or *kink, kink*.

RING SIZE: Code J.

SHOWING REQUIREMENTS: Show cage should be taller than its length and of good size, to allow the exhibit to climb any plant material, such as bark, fitted to the back, inside the cage. Two springy perches should also be affixed. An exhibit must be in fine feather and condition, with bright eyes and good tail and wing carriage, in order to catch the judge's eye. Species can be shown singly or in pairs.

LEGAL REQUIREMENTS: Protected at all times. Not listed on any schedule. May be sold or shown within terms of General Licences.

SPECIAL NOTES: Since the advent of Dutch elm disease, the species has fallen in numbers. Other names: Crank bird, pump bird, and hickwell.

Photograph by Tony Tilford

WRYNECK

Jynx torquilla.

Related species: No others in genus.

DESCRIPTION: Beak rather short, straight-pointed, and brown. The whole of the upperparts of the body consist of varying shades of brown mixed with grey, pencilled, mottled, barred and streaked with buff, greyish-white, brownish-black and black. The top of the head, nape, and neck, is barred with blackish-brown. The wings are dark brown, barred with buff. Tail greyish brown with irregular bars, underparts white, tinged with yellowish-buff. The breast and belly are marked with small triangular spots. Female is somewhat duller. Length 18cm (7in).

STATUS IN THE WILD: Summer visitor. Very rare breeding bird, perhaps only 5 pairs nest in England at the present time. I have only come across one nest in my lifetime, birds used to forage on my lawn. Habitat; open broad leafed woodland, copses, parks and orchards. Our birds return to Africa to winter. Some continental birds regularly occur, especially in autumn, mainly in east coast as passage migrants.

HARDBILL OR SOFTBILL? Known in aviculture as a softbill.

AVAILABILITY FOR BIRDKEEPERS: Just a few have been kept during the last 20 years, all obtained from continental breeders. Consideration was given to re-introduce species into the Waveney Valley in Norfolk, but no progress was made.

ADVANTAGES TO KEEPING: Very interesting species, especially for private enterprises. It makes a nice show bird.

DISADVANTAGES TO KEEPING: Obtaining true and legal pairs.

DIET: Mainly ants taken from the ground, also other insects including beetles.

HOUSING: Aviary no smaller than 1.8m square x 2.1m high (6ft sq x 7ft high) with plenty of old branches propped up all round the inside. Nest boxes fitted in sheltered locations for breeding and roosting purposes. Winter quarters must be warm and roomy.

BREEDING: Nest in holes in trees, at varying heights from the ground. The deserted hole of a woodpecker is a favourite site, in former days holes in old apple trees in Kent orchards, were frequently used. Six to ten white eggs are laid in May or June.

Incubation is by both sexes, but mainly by female for 12-14 days. The young are fed by both parents on ants and ant pupae. Young leave the nest at 19-21 days. The bird arrives in April and leaves for Africa in September.

CALL: A shrill repeated *kee-kee-kee-kee*, the song heard from April and ceases when the clutch is complete in May.

RING SIZE: Code G.

SHOWING REQUIREMENTS: Exhibit as large as possible, good wing and tail carriage and bright eye. Show cage desk or box type, size no smaller than 20in long, 24in high and 12in wide, painted black outside, including wire front and white inside. Decorated out with cork bark and perches, so bird can climb. Should have a grass floor.

LEGAL REQUIREMENTS: Listed on Schedule 1, birds protected by special penalties at all times. Can be sold or shown if ringed and legally bred.

SPECIAL NOTES: Local and other names: Snake bird, cuckoo's mate, tongue bird, emmet hunter, and long tongue. Sits closely and hisses if disturbed.

Photograph by Tony Tilford

SKYLARK

Alauda arvensis.

Related species: No others in genus in Britain.

DESCRIPTION: A dull brown bird, heavily streaked upperparts and a streaked breast. The crown has an erectile crest that rises at will to a point above the nape. The bird spends most of its time on the ground, rising when disturbed on fluttering wings. In the air it shows white outer tail feathers and hovers and circles at great height singing continuously. During migration and in hard winters often forms sizeable flocks in search of food. Bird of open landscapes. Length 18cm (7in).

STATUS: Resident and partial migrant. 2,500,000 pairs in Britain.

HARDBILL OR SOFTBILL? Softbill.

AVAILABILITY FOR BIRDKEEPERS: Usually available, due to surge in interest. Cost about £50 for single bird.

ADVANTAGES TO KEEPING: Willing breeder, lovely song. A very interesting species to keep.

DISADVANTAGES TO KEEPING: Banned by most clubs from the show bench in years gone by. Now being exhibited on a regular basis.

DIET: Vegetable and animal matter. Seeds of weeds as well as cereals, leaves of growing root crops and clover, worms, insects and their larvae, spiders and slugs.

HOUSING: An aviary 1.8m square x 2.1m high (6ft sq x 7ft high) is suitable for a pair. Grass floor ideal, if not wood chips will suffice. Old logs placed at back of flight will induce birds to build at their base. Also high perches at each end or "singing" posts to encourage male to sing. Song also often delivered from the ground.

BREEDING: Nest slight depression in the ground, sometimes sheltered, but often exposed. Shallow cup of grasses, with lining of finer grasses and at times hair. Built by the hen alone, in late April, double brooded. Eggs usually three to five, smooth, dull greyish white or tinted buff or greenish, heavily spotted overall with brown or olive. Incubation by female alone for 11 days. Chicks are downy at first. Fed by both parents. On leaving the nest, unable to fly, hide by crouching motionless, fly well at three weeks. In home-bred conditions, grasses, hair and coconut fibre should be provided for nesting,

and although birds will survive on seed and mealworms, additional livefood must be added if young birds are to prosper. Small mealworms, buffalo worms and wax moth larvae are ideal, the latter especially valuable.

CALL: Song consists of several strains, trilling, warbling notes with much variety, and interrupted by loud whistles. After aerial song, plummets to the ground.

RING SIZE: Code G.

SHOWING REQUIREMENTS: As large as possible, long body, with well filled, nicely rounded breast, gentle rise over shoulder to rump. Head well rounded with rise of crest, neat wing and tail carriage. Cage no smaller than 18in long, 15in high and 12in wide, black outside and white inside. Decorated out to replicate habitat.

LEGAL REQUIREMENTS: Not listed on any schedule. May be sold or shown under General Licence.

SPECIAL NOTES: In olden times were lured down from the sky, netted, plucked and eaten. Other names: Lavrock and field lark. Predated by the merlin.

Photograph by Dennis Avon

WOODLARK

Lullula arborea.

Related species: No others in genus in Britain.

DESCRIPTION: Smaller and slighter than skylark, plumage similar, but crest more pronounced. It has buff upperparts, which are heavily streaked blackish. Adult's face is boldly marked with long white supercilia (stripes above the eye) which meets at the nape, dark brown surround to warm buff cheeks. The closed wings show a black and white bar, tail short and dark. Upperparts buff-white with necklace of prominent black streaks. Hind claw is shorter than that of a skylark. On the ground, woodlarks both walk and run. Juvenile is similar to adults. Length 15cm (6in).

STATUS IN THE WILD: Resident and partial migrant. Distribution is patchy. About 350 pairs breed in Britain. Found only in southern England, particularly south-east and among the Brecks of East Anglia.

HARDBILL OR SOFTBILL? Softbill.

AVAILABILITY FOR BIRDKEEPERS: Until recently, only disabled wild birds were kept. Now however, aviary-bred birds are being reared. Price about £90 each.

ADVANTAGES TO KEEPING: Makes attractive show bird. Experience already gained by some fanciers with skylarks, woodlarks present no unfamiliar problems.

DISADVANTAGES TO KEEPING: Insufficient home-bred birds available to fulfil demand at present time.

DIET: Insects during breeding season, mainly seeds at other times.

HOUSING: An aviary about 1.8m square x 2.1m high (6ft sq x7ft high) would suffice for a pair of these interesting birds. Planted with heather and long grasses, and with song-posts.

BREEDING: The nest is placed on the ground; the neat cup is built by both sexes, among grass or heather. It is lined with grass and finer material, including hair. Three to four grey-white, finely spotted eggs are laid from March onwards. Incubation is by the female alone for 13-15 days. The nestlings are downy, mouth yellow with three black spots, one on tip of tongue and two smaller ones on either side of base of tongue. The gape flanges are yellowish-white, they are tendered by both parents and leave the nest at about 12 days. They cannot fly at this stage, and remain together nearby for some time. Two broods are raised in a season, sometimes three.

CALL: The call note is a double or triple, *tweedlie* or *to-lui-ie*. Richly varied repertoire; sings from February. Flight song is a beautiful descending series of rich, mellow, fluty whistles.

RING SIZE: Code E, which has an internal diameter of 2.4mm.

SHOWING REQUIREMENTS: Show cage, desk or box type, no smaller than 46cm x 38cm x 30cm (18in x 15in x 12in). Painted black outside including wire front, and with white interior. Food and water vessels white and placed inside the cage. Exhibit should be as large as possible, in good feather, bright eyes and with neat wing and tail carriage.

LEGAL REQUIREMENTS: Listed on Schedule 1 of the Wildlife and Countryside Act 1981 - birds are protected by special penalties at all times.

Photograph by Sergey Yeliseev

SHORE LARK

Eremophila alpestris.

Related species: No others in genus in Britain.

DESCRIPTION: A rather tame and confiding bird, which spends most of its time on the ground in small winter flocks. The upperparts are cinnamon-buff, heavily streaked on back and wings, whitish below, yellow and black head markings, less distinct in winter, especially in the female. During breeding season, male has small black "horns". The stubby bill and legs are black. Its natural breeding quarters are in the Arctic. Length 16.5cm (6½in).

STATUS IN THE WILD: Since 1970 has bred erratically in Central Highlands of Scotland. A scarce visitor to the east coast of Britain from late October onwards.

HARDBILL OR SOFTBILL? Certainly a softbill.

AVAILABILITY FOR BIRDKEEPERS: Very rarely seen in home-bred collections, although available through continental sources.

ADVANTAGES TO KEEPING: Would be ideal for an experienced fancier, and would make welcome addition to exhibition benches. It is hard to understand why it is not kept in numbers.

DISADVANTAGES TO KEEPING: General lack of interest and some difficulty in obtaining true, legal pairs.

HOUSING: Aviary 1.8m (6ft) square, furnished with rocks and boulders, and with sandy floor, small pond would be ideal for the birds.

DIET: Seeds of weeds, together with insects, and in winter, crustaceans and molluscs.

BREEDING: Breeds in large open grass areas of tundra or barren higher ground - usually bare, sandy and stony, but also in sparse ground in a hollow, usually in the shelter of a plant, turf or stone. The cup is of dry grasses and plant stems, loosely put together, with a finer inner lining of plant down and hair. Small pieces of peat and pebbles may be accumulated around the nest. Breeding begins in May, usually double brooded. Eggs - usually four - are smooth and glossy, pale greenish-white, heavily speckled with fine buffish-brown, they are laid at daily intervals. Incubation is by female alone for 10 -14 days. Young are tendered by both parents. They leave the nest at 9 -12 days, are tendered by both parents for some days after fledging.

CALL: A thin *tseep* or *tsee-ree*, nearer to a pipit than a lark. The song which is produced in a song flight similar to that of a skylark, is a high pitched tinkling.

RING SIZE: Code C.

SHOWING REQUIREMENTS: Show cage of the desk or box type, painted black outside including the wire front and white inside, door on right. No smaller than 18in high x 15in high x 12in wide. Decorated to imitate habitat, with grassy turfs, rocks and sand. Exhibit to be as large as possible, of good feather and bearing with good wing and tail carriage and bright eye.

LEGAL REQUIREMENTS: Listed on Schedule 1 Part 1, of the Wildlife and Countryside Act 1981 and specially protected. Can be sold or shown if legally bred in home conditions by virtue of General Licence.

SPECIAL NOTES: Shuffles close to the ground picking up small food items among the vegetation.

Other name; horned lark.

Photograph by Bozena Kalejta-Summers

65

TREE PIPIT

Anthus trivialis.

Related species: Olive-backed pipit, meadow pipit, rock pipit, water pipit, red-throated pipit, tawny pipit and Richard's pipit.

DESCRIPTION: The crown, nape, and back, dark brown, wings darkish-brown, secondary coverts edged with pale brown, primaries edged with pale brown. Rump, upper-tail coverts brown, outer tail feathers whitish, chin and throat pale brownish-white. A brown streak runs from the gape. Sides of neck and breast pale buff, with streaks of brown on the former and round spots on the latter, belly, vent and under tail-coverts whitish. Legs, toes and claws pale yellowish-brown. Hind claw shorter than that of the meadow pipit. Bill medium length, nearly straight. Eyes hazel. Length 15cm (6in).

STATUS IN THE WILD: Summer visitor to British Isles, with about 120,000 pairs arriving in April and departing in September or October. Habitat woods, plantations and tree-fringed streams, plus areas of scattered trees and heathland.

HARDBILL OR SOFTBILL? Softbill.

AVAILABILITY FOR BIRDKEEPERS: Occasionally available, with a price tag of about £80 each.

ADVANTAGES TO KEEPING: Easy to propagate, interesting species with nice song.

DISADVANTAGES TO KEEPING: Require good sheltered quarters during winter months.

HOUSING: Flight about 1.8m x 0.9m x 1.8m high (6ft x 3ft x 6ft), with perches either end or song posts, floor planted with heather or similar clumps. Potted shrubs ideal.

BREEDING: Breeding takes place in May and June, pairs often return to the same spot each year. Nest on the ground in cover, usually bordering open spaces, consists of large cup of dried grasses, with some moss, lined with plant fibre and hair. Eggs number four to six, smooth and glossy, very variable in colour, and variably speckled and blotched. They are incubated by the female for 12-14 days. Chicks have long and thick dark grey down. Mouth orange, gape flanges light yellow. The young are tendered by both parents. They leave the nest at the 12-13 day stage, and continue to be fed for some days after fledging.

CALL NOTES: A sweet, ringing *tsee, tsee, tsee*. Followed by pretty, canary-like phrases. Cocks use the same tree - often the same branch - to start from and return to after their short, parachuting display flight.

RING SIZE: Code D, which has an internal diameter of 2.7mm.

SHOWING REQUIREMENTS: Exhibits to be as large as possible, cone shaped, but of plumpish build, full, nicely rounded head, well filled breast, gentle rise of shoulder to rump. Neat wing and carriage. Show cage, desk or box type, 18in long, 15in high and 12in wide, painted black outside including the wire front, and white inside. Decorated out to familiarise the onlooker of the exhibit's habitat and with two springy perches.

LEGAL REQUIREMENTS: Protected at all times. Not listed on any Schedule. Can be shown under General Licence, if closed-ringed and bred in captivity from lawfully held stock.

SPECIAL NOTES: Other names; field lark, field titling, pipit lark, tree lark and grasshopper lark. Sits closely.

Photograph by Tony Tilford

ROCK PIPIT

Anthus petrosus.

Related species: Olive-backed pipit, meadow pipit, water pipit, tree pipit, red-throated pipit, Richard's pipit and tawny pipit.

DESCRIPTION: A darker and larger bird than the meadow pipit. Upperparts are olive-grey streaked with black, outer tail feathers are grey. The underparts are streaked with black. The legs are darker than those of the meadow pipit. The hind claw is curved. Length 16-17cm (6½in).

STATUS IN THE WILD: Population about 50,000 pairs. Birds of our coastline, prefers a rocky habitat. Resident, and as numbers leave here in the autumn and return in the spring it is also a summer visitor.

HARDBILL OR SOFTBILL? Softbill.

AVAILABILITY FOR BIRDKEEPERS: Rock pipits are being bred in numbers in British aviculture and are usually available.

ADVANTAGES TO KEEPING: Makes lovely addition to a collection. Interesting subject.

DISADVANTAGES TO KEEPING: None.

DIET: Almost entirely animal matter - insects, including beetles, larvae and aphids, also slugs and snails, remains of fish and sandhoppers, worms and some seeds.

HOUSING: An aviary, furnished with rocks and a small pool, grass clumps and shingle areas is suitable, two of these flights should be prepared side by side, a breeding pair in each. This system will encourage the birds to pair-bond and successfully breed.

BREEDING: The nest is usually above the reaches of the tideline. It is sometimes constructed on a bank, under a clump of thrift or other maritime plant, but more commonly in a hole or crack in a rock. It is built of grasses, sometimes seaweed; the lining is of fine grass or hair. The bird nests late and eggs are seldom laid until May. A second brood is often reared. The eggs number four or five, they are closely speckled with grey or reddish spots. They are incubated by the female for 14 days and the young are fed by both parents for 16 days before fledging. In home-breeding half-open boxes and holes either in the rocks or in a roughly built wall will be used for nesting. The chicks can be fed on white maggots, pinkie maggots, fruit flies and small mealworms.

CALL: A high-pitched *tsip*; song uttered in display flight similar to meadow pipit, but more melodic. Song period from March to August.

RING SIZE: Code D.

SHOWING REQUIREMENTS: An exhibition bird should be as large as possible, cone-shaped but full bodied with a nicely rounded head and well filled breast. There should be a gentle rise from shoulder to rump. Neat wing and tail carriage is important. Nice slate blue colour overall, legs and feet dark.

LEGAL REQUIREMENTS: Not listed on any schedule, may be sold or shown under General Licence.

SPECIAL NOTES: Closely related to the water pipit, many experts believe the rock and water pipits are one and the same. They differ in colouration and habits however.

Photograph by Frank Stark

MEADOW PIPIT

Anthus pratensis.

Related species: Tree pipit, rock pipit, olive-backed pipit, water pipit, red-throated pipit, tawny pipit and Richard's pipit.

DESCRIPTION: The crown, nape, back and upper tail coverts dark brown. Wings brownish-black, the feathers being edged with light brown; the tail is dark brown, the two outer tail feathers on each side are margined with white, the rest with light brown, the chin and throat are dull white; side of neck and breast pale-buffish white or yellowish brown, with numerous spots, the belly and under tail-coverts dull white, lined with brown. The hind toe is almost straight, the claw is longer than the toe, and longer than that of the tree pipit. The sexes are alike. Length 14.5cm (5½in).

STATUS IN THE WILD: Resident in British Isles with some local movement, about 2,000,000 pairs. Bird of moorlands, meadows, heaths and dunes.

HARDBILL OR SOFTBILL? Softbill.

AVAILABILITY FOR BIRDKEEPERS: Generally available and a popular aviary subject. Worth £60 each.

ADVANTAGES TO KEEPING: Hardy species, easy to maintain and breed. Makes nice exhibition bird.

DISADVANTAGES TO KEEPING: Best suited to experienced keeper.

DIET: Chiefly insects, including beetles and their larvae, moths, spiders, small earth worms and seeds.

HOUSING: Best kept outside all year in a planted and partly sheltered flight. Grassy floor covering would be ideal.

BREEDING: Nests on the ground in rough grass or at side of tussock. It is built of bents and lined with finer grasses and with some hair. The eggs usually number four to five, and are almost covered with mottling of browns and greys. They are laid about the middle of April. Incubation is about 13-14 days, by female alone. The nestlings are covered with long and thick brownish-grey down. They are tendered by both adults for about two weeks in the nest and for a few days on fledging. Usually double brooded. In aviary conditions, live food should be as varied as possible. First round young can be removed when fully independent, to allow old pair to raise second brood.

CALL: Usually rises to sing in the air from the ground or a bush, and continues as it floats down. The note on ascent is ze-ut repeated, and in descent several *wheet* notes followed by a final trill. The song may also be delivered from a post and is inferior to the tree pipit's.

RING SIZE: Code C.

SHOWING REQUIREMENTS: Size and type: As large as possible. Cone shaped with nicely rounded head, well filled breast and gentle rise of shoulder to rump. Neat wing and tail-carriage. Show cage can be desk or box type, painted black outside and white inside, 18in long, 15in high and 12in wide. Nicely decorated to imitate habitat. Two perches.

LEGAL REQUIREMENTS: Protected at all times. Not listed on any Schedule of the Wildlife and Countryside Act 1981. Can be shown or sold under current legislation.

SPECIAL NOTES: Irish legend has it that if a meadow pipit host climbs into a young cuckoo's mouth (as it often seems to be trying to do) the end of the world will come! Other names include titling, moor tite, titlark, ling bird, teetick, moss creeper wekeen, pipit lark, heath lintie, moor titling, moor tit, meadow lark. Sits closely and hovers around if disturbed.

Photograph by Dennis Avon

PIED WAGTAIL

Motacilla alba.
Other race white wagtail.
Related species: Yellow wagtail, grey wagtail and citrine wagtail.

DESCRIPTION: In the male pied wagtail the upperparts are pure black, marked with white wing bars and edges to the primaries. The tail is black with white outer feathers and is frequently bobbed. The belly and under tail coverts are white as is the face and forehead. The chin and breast have a large black bib that joins with a black back. Females are similar, but are dark grey on the back. The young are paler than their parents. Length 18cm (7in) weight 19-27g. White wagtails have a pale grey back and rump at all times, and are basically European mainland based but many pass through Britain in April and May.

STATUS IN THE WILD: Resident and partial migrant. In Britain about 430,000 pairs breed.

HARDBILL OR SOFTBILL? Regarded as a softbill.

AVAILABILITY FOR BIRDKEEPERS: Bred in numbers annually, so some always available. Cost about £60 each.

ADVANTAGES TO KEEPING: Hardy, easy species to breed.

DISADVANTAGES TO KEEPING: Best suited to an aviary with water feature.

DIET: Chiefly insects, especially gnats, mosquitoes, small beetles, seeds and tiny fry (fish) also taken.

HOUSING: An outside partly sheltered aviary, about 1.8m (6ft) square, would suit a pair of these delightful birds. It should be planted out with grasses and tiny bushes, and with a shallow pool frequently refreshed. This design is to give the birds opportunities to find insect food by wading in the water. Half-open nest boxes placed about 1.2m (4ft) up and in climbers would be used by the birds as nesting sites. This type of small aviary must be kept watered and green. An all year supply of insects must be provided, greatly increased during the breeding season.

BREEDING: In the wild, nest in bank sides, ivy, pollarded trees, sheds, holes in walls, cavities in bridges and utility complexes, built of moss, dead leaves, bents and grasses, lined with hair, feather or wool. The eggs usually number five or six, greyish white, freckled with grey, laid in April and incubation chiefly by the female for 13-14 days. Double brooded. The chicks are fed by both parents for 13-16 days

before fledging and for a similar period when on the wing.

CALL: Song consists of a series of short phrases. The call sounds like a sharp *tchissik*.

RING SIZE: Code C.

SHOWING REQUIREMENTS: Show cage no smaller than 18in long, 15in high and 12in wide, painted black outside and white inside, decorated out to mimic habitat in miniature with mosses and semblance of water (mirror). Two springy perches also desired. Exhibit must be as large as possible, cone shaped, well filled breast tapering to vent, gentle rise at shoulder to rump, good length of tail, wings and tail neat and well carried.

LEGAL REQUIREMENTS: Protected at all times. Not on any Schedule. Can be sold or shown within terms of General Licence if ringed and captive bred.

SPECIAL NOTES: In winter gather in roosts, often numbering hundreds. Other names; dishwasher, washtail, wagster and water wagtail. Often victim of the cuckoo.

Photograph by Dennis Avon

YELLOW WAGTAIL

Motacilla flava.

Related species: Grey wagtail, citrine wagtail and pied wagtail.

DESCRIPTION: The male in spring is greenish olive on the upper areas, yellowish on the tail, with brownish-black wings and tail, the former with buffish edges, forming bars, and the latter with two outer pairs of feathers mainly white. Below the eye and the whole of the underparts are canary yellow. The female is browner, and eye stripe and wing-bars are buff, chin and throat whitish, underparts paler. It is the smallest and most compact of our wagtails. Much variation occurs within the species. Length 16.5cm (6½in).

STATUS IN THE WILD: Summer visitor with about 23,000 pairs. Favours fresh water margins and damp pastures where cattle graze, such as water meadows.

HARDBILL OR SOFTBILL? Regarded as a softbill.

AVAILABILITY FOR BIRDKEEPERS: Numbers bred in captive conditions each year, also birds imported from Europe.

ADVANTAGES TO KEEPING: Beautiful, easy to breed and cater for and makes splendid show bird.

DISADVANTAGES TO KEEPING: Needs good-quality sheltered accommodation during the winter months.

DIET: Small invertebrates.

HOUSING: Aviary at least 1.6m (6ft) square, with small pool and plenty of grasses, at varying heights, suitable for nesting. Small wall, perhaps!

BREEDING: Nest on ground in a hollow or in thick herbage, the nest is built of grasses, plant stems and roots, lined with hair, wool or fur. The season begins in May. Single or double brooded. Eggs usually five to six, smooth and glossy, heavily speckled with yellowish-buff or buffish-brown. The incubation is chiefly by the female, beginning with the last egg for 12-14 days. The nestlings are tendered by both parents. Leave the nest at 10-13 days, fly at 17 days. In home-bred conditions, there are plenty of foods available nowadays to sustain these birds, young can be reared on small mealworms, buffalo worms and wax moth larvae.

CALL: A shrill *pseeep*. Song is a rhythmic series of twittering notes.

RING SIZE: Code C.

SHOWING REQUIREMENTS: Show cage box or desk type, no smaller than 18in long, 15in high and 12in wide, painted black outside including wire front and white inside, decorated out to imitate habitat of species. Exhibit: As large as possible. Long bodied of slender upstanding build. Nicely rounded head, gentle rise of shoulder, good length of tail. Wings and tail neat and carried well. Autumn/winter plumage, brown overlay more obvious in young birds. Shown singly or in pairs.

LEGAL REQUIREMENTS: Protected at all times. Not listed on any schedule, but may be shown or sold under current legislation.

SPECIAL NOTES: The yellow wagtail is slowly evolving into several species. At the present time there are a number of subspecies, these generally live in separate locations across Europe, Asia and north Africa, some of these visit Britain occasionally the blue-headed wagtail for example. Local and other names: Cowbird, Ray's wagtail, and yellow wagster. Sits lightly, and although by no means shy, is very wary.

Photograph by Dennis Avon

GREY WAGTAIL

Motacilla cinerea.

Related species: Yellow wagtail, citrine wagtail and pied wagtail.

DESCRIPTION: Uniform slate blue of upperparts and very long tail. In spring the male has a black throat, white stripes above and below the eye, sulphur yellow underparts, and white on outer tail feathers. Female has little or no black on throat. After autumn moult, both sexes have white throats and buff eye stripe. The chin in juveniles is also white. Length 18cm (7in).

STATUS IN THE WILD: Resident and partial migrant. About 56,000 pairs in Britain, bird of fast, flowing streams.

HARDBILL OR SOFTBILL? Softbill.

AVAILABILITY FOR BIRDKEEPERS: Some bred in home-conditions each year, and available from a small number of enthusiasts. Cost about £90 per bird.

ADVANTAGES TO KEEPING: Bring beauty and interest to any collection, will breed if conditions are right.

DISADVANTAGES TO KEEPING: Species require a semblance of natural conditions during the breeding season, the most important element is running water, which is not always achievable in a small area.

DIET: Chiefly insects, also other invertebrates that thrive within a watery territory, including small mollusc and crustacean.

HOUSING: It is a challenge for any keeper wishing to breed these delightful birds and essential that consideration be given to their requirements. They will enjoy a planted enclosure, within which should be a pond with a waterfall set-up. This should consist of a pump where the water can overflow off a shelf and back into the reservoir. These features need not be elaborate. Plants around the pond will bring in invertebrate life as will the water itself, and the addition of a few, well placed rocks, would provide nesting opportunities. Livefood must be increased if young are to be raised, and can include mealworms, buffalo worms, and wax moth larvae.

BREEDING: The species usually nests in a hole in a wall, steep bank, or in the roots of a tree close to running water; also under bridges and on lock gates. The nest is built of course stalks, moss, leaves and grasses, neatly lined with horsehair and feathers. The clutch number five or six eggs,

and have a buff or stone ground colour, faintly speckled. Laying begins in April, sometimes earlier, incubation is carried out by both sexes for 13-14 days. The species is usually double brooded.

At first the chicks have fairly long down, their mouth is orange and gape flanges pale yellow. They are tendered by both parents and leave the nest at 11-13 days: they can fly at 17 days.

CALL: Sharp *'tseet tseet'*. Song is made up of high pitched twittering phases.

RING SIZE: Code C.

SHOWING REQUIREMENTS: Softbill cage No. 5, can be of desk or box type; no smaller than 18in long, 15in high and 12in wide. Nicely decorated to mimic habitat in miniature, with perches in form of rock, wood or slate. (A small mirror could represent water.) Size and type: As large as possible, very long body, well-filled breast, nicely rounded head, gentle rise of shoulder, well tapered, cone shape, and with good length of tail.

LEGAL REQUIREMENTS: Fully protected. Not on any Schedule. May be sold or shown if ringed and bred in captivity under current legislation.

SPECIAL NOTES: Local and other names: Dun wagtail, nanny wagtail, grey wagster. Sits closely, and when disturbed hovers around with mate, uttering calls of alarm.

Photograph by Tommy Milner

WREN

Troglodytes troglodytes.

No related species.

DESCRIPTION: The wren is rufous brown above, greyer beneath, barred with darker brown and grey even on wings and tail. The bill is dark brown, the legs pale brown, the eyes hazel. It has a stumpy tail. Length 8.90cm (3½in). The young are less distinctly barred. There are three other insular forms on St. Kilda, the Shetlands and Outer Hebrides, these "subspecies" are slightly larger with stronger legs and beak than the nominate form.

STATUS IN THE WILD: Resident, with about 10,000,000 pairs.

HARDBILL OR SOFTBILL? Softbill.

AVAILABILITY FOR BIRDKEEPERS: Available from time to time, at about £70 each.

ADVANTAGES TO KEEPING: Interesting species, quite easy to breed by experienced keeper, if conditions are right in planted aviary and with varied diet.

DISADVANTAGES TO KEEPING: Very little interest to keepers. Aviary must be well-constructed or escapes may occur.

DIET: The young are fed almost exclusively on a diet of moth larvae; together with fly and other insect larvae and spiders.

HOUSING: A small, well constructed aviary, with small flowering bushes and twiggy perches, is suitable for one pair.

BREEDING: Breeds in a wide range of habitats which provide low cover. Any cavity seems suitable for the nest from ground level upwards, most often in side of tree, wall or bank. The male is often polygamous, building a number of nests within its territory for its several females. The nest itself is a stout, domed structure of leaves, moss, grass and other plant material, and lined with feathers. The male builds the outer nest layers and if selected by a female she will line it. Five to eight eggs are laid in April, they are smooth and glossy, sometimes white, but usually speckled. These are incubated by the female alone for 14-17 days. Nestlings are fed by both parents. Polygamous males usually have broods which hatch at intervals, the male helping the first, then another. The chicks are 15-20 days in the nest.

CALL: Alarm call, a loud *teck-teck-teck*. Song a loud, clear warble with trills.

RING SIZE: Code A.

SHOWING REQUIREMENTS: As large as possible. Short, plump well rounded body, well filled nicely rounded head, neat wing and tail carriage, latter short, full and nicely piped. Active but with confidence, tail to be well cocked, head feathers slightly raised. Cage no. 5 18in long, 15in high and 12in wide. Painted black outside including the wire front, white inside, decorated out in an appropriate setting.

LEGAL REQUIREMENTS: Fully protected at all times. Not listed on any Schedule of the Wildlife and Country Act 1981, can be exhibited if conforms with General Licence, and is bred in captivity from legally held stock, and closed ringed.

SPECIAL NOTES: Local and other names: Cutty wren, titty wren, stumpy, Jenny Wren, Kitty Wren. A close sitter. Collective noun - A Chime.

Photograph by Tommy Milner

WAXWING

Bombycilla garrulus.

No related species in Europe.

DESCRIPTION: A plump looking bird with rich dark brown back and pinkish-brown underparts. A curved pinkish-brown and erectile crest rises from the crown and the eye, is set in an area of black extending from base of bill. There is a white flash at the gape below which is a black bib. The tail is grey shading to black and boldly tipped with yellow; the under tail coverts are a rusty colour. The wings are tipped with yellow and white and with red, wax like appendages to the secondaries. Sexes are alike. Length 18cm (7in).

STATUS IN THE WILD: Winter visitor to Britain from northern climes. Numbers vary, some years large numbers arrive due to irruptions. This was so in 1996 when more than 10,000 arrived in Britain to feast on berries. Most are recorded along the east coast.

HARDBILL OR SOFTBILL? Softbill.

AVAILABILITY FOR BIRDKEEPERS: Continental breeders can supply birds at a price of about £200 a pair. A few are bred in the UK. each year.

ADVANTAGES TO KEEPING: Very attractive. Will breed in suitable surroundings. Makes nice show bird.

DISADVANTAGES TO KEEPING: Droppings are fluid, so floor covering of show cages must be absorbent.

DIET: Mainly insects, worms, spiders and berries in summer. Berries, fruits and plant bulbs in winter.

HOUSING: Colony breeder. Aviary should be about 3.5m square x 2m high (12ft x 12ft x 7ft), suitable for two pairs, plenty of perches of various thicknesses. Nest sites should be secluded with conifer sprays.

BREEDING: Breeds in coniferous and birch forests, nest usually in conifer, often on forest edge. The nest consists of a cup of conifer twigs, reindeer moss and grass, lined with hair and down. The breeding season begins in late May or early June. Single brooded. Eggs number four to six, smooth and glossy, pale blue or greenish blue in colour, marked with black or grey spots. The incubation is by female alone, fed by male for 13-14 days. The nestlings are naked at first. Mouth bright red with violet-blue on either side, tongue purplish. They are tendered by both parents as they mature, leaving the nest at the 15-17 day stage. Aviary birds can be fed on insectivorous compound, scrambled egg, grated cheese, peanuts and carrots, plenty of fresh fruit, especially berries. Adults will feed chicks on berries, wax worms, mealworms and earth worms.

CALL: A buzzing *snee*, song a mixture of humming and chattering notes.

RING SIZE: Code K.

SHOWING REQUIREMENTS: Size and type: As large as possible, of thick set full-bodied appearance. Head well-cushioned at front with good length of crest. Neat wing and tail carriage. Show cage: desk or box type, 18in long, 15in high and 12in wide. Painted black outside including wire front and white inside, with two strong perches. Floor covering optional.

LEGAL REQUIREMENTS: Not listed on any schedule, can be shown within terms of General Licence.

SPECIAL NOTES: Flocks may be mistaken for starlings.

Photograph by Tony Tilford

DUNNOCK

Prunella modularis. (Accentor or Hedge sparrow)
Related species: Alpine accentor.

DESCRIPTION: Head, neck and upper breast are slate grey, streaked with brown. Back brown. Wings and tail dusky brown with paler margins. There is a thin buff wing-bar. Beak slender. The female is duller. Juveniles are browner-looking, more spotted and streaked below. Length: 14cm (5½in).

STATUS IN THE WILD: Resident with roughly 2.8 million pairs. Generally distributed throughout the British Isles, but scarce in northern Scotland and Orkney. The Outer Hebrides have their own, slightly different, local subspecies.

HARDBILL OR SOFTBILL? In aviculture, described as a softbill.

AVAILABILITY FOR BIRDKEEPERS: Readily available, costing about £60. Mutation would cost more.

ADVANTAGES TO KEEPING: Comparatively easy to breed, easy to maintain, long-lived and interesting. Good exhibition birds.

DISADVANTAGES TO KEEPING: Highly territorial; in a shared aviary may be aggressive towards other small inmates. House separately.

DIET: Insects - beetles, caterpillars, etc - plus earthworms and spiders, and seeds of numerous weeds. In home-bred conditions, a staple diet when not breeding could consist of seed and insect-based softfood. When breeding, all types of livefood are required.

HOUSING: A small flight dedicated to a single pair is ideal, planted with plenty of shrubs to provide cover. Wicker baskets for nesting.

BREEDING: Early breeders, from late March or early April. The nest, only a few feet from the ground, is of moss with some twigs, and neatly lined with hair and feathers. Four or five clear blue eggs to a clutch. Incubation 11-13 days. Two or three broods are reared each spring. The young leave the nest after about a fortnight and are cared for by the parents for a further two weeks before becoming independent.

CALL: The hedge sparrow sounds more striking than it looks! In the spring it has a high-pitched, repeated call. Its main song is a sweet warble, not unlike the blackcap's. It is constantly repeated and can be heard from quite a distance. The bird sings from January to July.

RING SIZE: Closed rings are code E, with internal diameter of 2.9mm.

SHOWING REQUIREMENTS: A show specimen should be as large as possible, of chubby build, with a neat tail and wing-carriage. In autumn birds, the slate-blue colour is suffused with brown. Consideration should be given to yellow birds, which will be bluer, but show less work (markings). The show cage, of the desk or the box type, should be no smaller than 18in long, 15in high and 12in wide, painted black on the outside and white on the inside, door on the right. Decoration to suit the species' habitat - including two springy perches - is essential to take the judge's eye. Usually shown singly.

LEGAL REQUIREMENTS: The bird is referred to within the Wildlife and Countryside Act, 1981 as dunnock. It appears on Schedule 3 and can be sold or exhibited if ringed and bred in captivity.

SPECIAL NOTES: A favourite of the cuckoo. In the wild, the species is often polygamous. The accentor name is probably likened to "accenter", the leading singer of a choir.

Photograph by Tommy Milner

ROBIN

Erithacus rubecula.

No related species in Europe.

DESCRIPTION: Bill of medium length, nearly straight, and black. Crown, nape, back, wings and tail, olive brown. Round the base of the beak, eyes and upon the throat and upper breast, orange red, succeeding which is a narrow space of blueish-grey. The rest of the underparts white, tinged with brown on the sides, flanks and tail coverts. Legs, toes, and claws reddish-brown. Female smaller. Juveniles lack the red and are mainly mottled brown. Length 14.5cm (5¾in).

STATUS IN THE WILD: Resident and partial migrant, with about 6,000,000 pairs in Britain. Bird of the garden and broad leafed woodland here, inhabits coniferous woodland in Europe.

HARDBILL OR SOFTBILL? Known as a softbill.

AVAILABILITY FOR BIRDKEEPERS: Some bred in home conditions each year, readily available from continental sources.

ADVANTAGES TO KEEPING: Ready breeder in aviaries. Will also foster other small softbills.

DISADVANTAGES TO KEEPING: Showing is frowned upon, due to species being our national bird.

DIET: Invertebrates, especially beetles, some fruit and seed in autumn and winter. Will eat carrion (peck at road kills).

HOUSING: A flight or aviary approximately 1.8m (6ft) square with dry shelter would suit a pair of these endearing birds, bearing in mind compatibility must be assured. A few twiggy perches would enable the cock to find singing positions. The nest would most probably be built within the shelter on a ledge, or in a half-open sheltered box within the flight.

BREEDING: The nest of the robin has been located in holes in walls, inside and outside buildings, in flowerpots, old boots, teapots and nest-boxes. It is built of fibrous roots and moss lined with dead leaves and hair. Five or six eggs make up a clutch, they are white or very pale-grey, blotched and freckled with dull light-red. They are laid in March, April, May, June and July. The incubation is carried out by the female, fed by the male, for 12-15 days. The chicks are downy, mouth yellow and gape flanges pale yellow. They are tendered by both parents. At first the female broods while the male brings food, then both feed the young for 12-15 days, whilst they are in the nest and for a few days afterwards. Male takes care of the young if broods overlap. In home-grown conditions, plenty of live food is required, small mealworms, buffalo worms, fly larvae, (maggots), worms and wax moth larvae.

CALL: Sharp *tick*. Tuneful, sweet song, with liquid warbling phrases. Begins in the autumn.

RING SIZE: Code E.

SHOWING REQUIREMENTS: In olden days, the robin was banned by clubs from the show bench. Nowadays, although it is quite legal to exhibit the bird, it is still frowned on. They are kept for breeding and study. Sometimes shown. Any cage would be decorated to resemble the habitat. An exhibit would need to be in good health and feather.

LEGAL REQUIREMENTS: Not listed on any Schedule, but can be sold or shown under terms of General Licence.

SPECIAL NOTES: Local and other names; Redbreast, robin redbreast, robinet, bob robin and ruddock.

Photograph by Tommy Milner

RED-FLANKED BLUETAIL

Tarsiger cyanurus.

No related species in Europe.

DESCRIPTION: The adult male has dark blue upperparts including tail and pale underparts, pure white only on throat, flanks are washed with orange-red. Adult female has blue tail, but otherwise brown upperparts. Underparts pale, whitish on throat and with orange-red wash to flanks. Eye has white eye ring. Juveniles similar to adult female, but with pale spots on upperparts. First autumn male and female similar to adult female, legs and bill dark. Species tend to bob up and down while spreading or flicking the tail. Length 14cm (5½in).

STATUS IN THE WILD: Bird of northern Europe. Breeds in taiga forests and upland conifers and mixed woodlands. Maybe spreading west. It is an irregular visitor to the British Isles.

HARDBILL OR SOFTBILL? Softbill.

AVAILABILITY FOR BIRDKEEPERS: Sometimes available at a cost of about £300 per pair. Has been bred in British aviaries.

ADVANTAGES TO KEEPING: Of interest to fanciers due to its beauty.

DISADVANTAGES TO KEEPING: Pairs difficult to obtain.

DIET: Mainly insects and other invertebrates, but also some fruit in autumn and winter.

HOUSING: A partly sheltered, planted out, flight of about 6ft square, would house a pair of these delightful birds. Wicker baskets positioned low in a bush are necessary to encourage nesting.

BREEDING: The nest is a mossy cup-shaped affair, lined with soft grasses and pine needles, hair and wool, constructed on the ground or among tree roots, the eggs five to seven, colour white, unmarked or speckled, spotted or finely mottled with pale and often faint reddish-brown. Incubation by the female alone, the chicks remain in the nest for about 15 days. Breeding begins in late May. Usually single brooded. Captive stock will require a balanced diet consisting of an insectivorous softfood and a constant variety of insects, which could include mealworms, buffalo worms, clean fly maggots and wax moth larvae, greatly increased when young are being reared.

CALL: Call includes a soft *hueet*. Male has high pitched whistling song, similar to redstart.

RING SIZE: Rings optional, but recommended. Suggest code C. Internal diameter of 2.5mm.

SHOWING REQUIREMENTS: Show cage no smaller than 18in long, 15in high and 12in wide, painted black outside and white inside. Cage should be tastefully decorated out and to include two springy perches. Exhibit should be as large as possible, nice clear colours, especially the blue areas. Must be in good condition in health and feather. Shown singly, or in pairs.

LEGAL REQUIREMENTS: Fully protected. Can be shown or sold under terms of a General Licence which permits the competition of certain captive birds which have occurred as vagrants in Britain providing that they have been bred in captivity from parents lawfully held in captivity.

SPECIAL NOTES: Bird stands with an upright posture when on the ground. Often referred to as bush robin.

Photograph by Sergey Yeliseev

NIGHTINGALE

Luscinia megarhynchos.

Related species: Bluethroat, thrush nightingale (page 218) and Siberian rubythroat.

DESCRIPTION: The upperparts are russet brown, the tail coverts and tail pale chestnut, underparts white, breast and flanks greyish brown. Young have upperparts rufous with buff spots, underparts whitish with dark edgings forming bars, and chestnut tail. Length 16.5cm (6½in).

STATUS IN THE WILD: Summer visitor, wintering in tropical Africa. About 5,500 pairs in Britain. Arrive in April, depart in August.

HARDBILL OR SOFTBILL? A delightful softbill.

AVAILABILITY FOR BIRDKEEPERS: A few available each year, with an increasing number being bred in aviary conditions. Cost £100 each.

ADVANTAGES TO KEEPING: Quite easy to breed in appropriate aviaries, if stock maintained in good health.

DISADVANTAGES TO KEEPING: Might bring unwanted attention to genuine keeper by their song.

DIET: Chiefly insects, including beetles, flies, caterpillars, especially those of tree-infesting species, also ants, worms, spiders and fruit.

HOUSING: An outside, partly sheltered aviary of a size no smaller than 3m (10ft) square, and 2.1m (7ft) high, would suit one pair, if planted out with small bushes, including oak, brambles and nettles, and to include a few rotten logs strewn about, beside which birds will be tempted to breed. Aviary should include oak leaves, a favoured nesting material. Winter quarters should be snug, unless completely acclimatised.

BREEDING: Generally breeds in deciduous woodland, where oaks abound. Nest on or near the ground in thick vegetation, often in nettles or brambles, well concealed. Nest bulky, built of oak leaves, inner cup of grasses, lined with hair. Eggs four to five, generally greenish or brownish olive and uniform in colour. Laid in early May. Incubation period is 14 days, mainly by the hen. The chicks are fed by both parents for 11-12 days and for several days after leaving the nest. Single brooded. Home-bred birds must be supplied with a varied insect diet, wax moth larvae and small mealworms are readily taken.

CALL: The nightingale's song is heard both night and day.

It is divided by pauses with separate strains. The most characteristics are the *jug-jug-jug-jug* and the marvellous crescendo on a single note, which is unique among birds.

RING SIZE: Code E which has an internal diameter of 2.9mm, should be placed on a young bird at the six-day stage.

SHOWING REQUIREMENTS: As large as possible, with nice rounded head, and with neat wing and tail carriage, latter being broad. To be shown in a cage, desk or box type, 18in long, 15in high and 12in high, painted black outside including the wire front, white inside, with decorations to emphasise habitat with bark, moss etc, and two springy perches, with food and water vessels placed firmly inside.

LEGAL REQUIREMENTS: Fully protected. Not listed on any Schedule of the Wildlife and Countryside Act 1981. Can be sold or shown under terms of a General Licence.

SPECIAL NOTES: Other names include Philomel. Sits closely and slips away without fuss. Only rare visitor to Ireland.

Photograph by Dennis Avon

BLUETHROAT

Luscinia svecica.

Related species: Nightingale, thrush nightingale and Siberian rubythroat.

DESCRIPTION: The upperparts of the male are brown in the spring, and has a near white or buff superciliary stripe, the tail is chestnut. The throat and breast is blue with a broad band-like spot of chestnut, and below the blue area are bands of black, white and chestnut, above its whitish underparts. The bill is black, the legs brown and the eye dark brown. The female has tawny white underparts, except for a dark band across the breast. At first the young are spotted and streaked. (This describes the red-spotted type - shown). The central European race has a white spot on the blue throat. Length 14cm (5½in).

STATUS IN THE WILD: Breeds mainly in north and east Europe, also in France and Spain. Has bred in Scotland, but normally a scarce passage migrant to Britain, mainly along the east coast. Rare in winter.

HARDBILL OR SOFTBILL? Softbill.

AVAILABILITY FOR BIRDKEEPERS: Rarely kept, of interest only to the specialist. Can be purchased from home-bred stock from continental sources. Cost £200 or more a pair.

ADVANTAGES TO KEEPING: Relatively easy to breed and maintain, and in these respects should be treated similar to robin.

DISADVANTGES TO KEEPING: Stock not easy to come by.

DIET: Mainly insects, various aquatic animals, small earthworms, seeds and berries.

BREEDING: Nests near the ground, like robin, well concealed. Nest built of dry grasses and bents. Eggs number five to seven, they are greyish green or occasionally blue, freckled over with fine speckles of red-brown. Laying begins in April.

In captive conditions birds should be fed on a quality insectivorous diet, with added live food, such as mealworms, buffalo worms and wax moth larvae; with the volume dramatically increased when young are in the nest, until they are self-supporting.

CALL: Alarm note is a hard *tack*. Song is a hurried delivery of long phrases, made of varied notes. Often imitates other birds.

RING SIZE: Code D, which has an internal diameter of 2.7mm.

SHOWING REQUIREMENTS: Its show cage should be no smaller than 18in long, 15in high and 12in wide. Decoration to represent damp, wooded habitat to include two springy perches. Exhibit should be as large as possible, with good feather, with a bright eye. Now being exhibited occasionally.

LEGAL REQUIREMENTS: Listed on Schedule 1 of the Wildlife and Countryside Act 1981. Can be shown on General Licence if ringed and bred in captivity.

SPECIAL NOTES: Chicks usually unable to fly when they leave the nest.

Photograph by Sergey Yeliseev

SIBERIAN RUBYTHROAT

Luscinia calliope.

Related species: Bluethroat, thrush nightingale and nightingale.

DESCRIPTION: In size and shape similar to bluethroat; adult male grey-brown plumage, palest underneath. Head well marked with pale eye stripe, white sub-moustachial stripe and ruby-red throat. Juvenile plumage mostly brown with pale spots on upperparts and dark spots underneath. Bill dark, legs pinkish. Bird of the open taiga forest and damp woodland. First autumn birds look superficially similar to thrush nightingale, but facial markings of rubythroat are evident. Length 14cm (5½in).

STATUS IN THE WILD: Very rare vagrant to British Isles, mainly in autumn, mostly by young birds.

HARDBILL OR SOFTBILL? Softbill.

AVAILABILITY FOR BIRDKEEPERS: Sometimes available from European sources. Has been bred by British bird enthusiasts. The cost of a true pair would be high.

ADVANTAGES TO KEEPING: Makes wonderful addition to the small softbill benches at the shows.

DISADVANTAGES TO KEEPING: Difficulty in obtaining true, legal pairs and the expense.

DIET: Mainly insects.

HOUSING: Aviary should be no smaller than 1.8m long x 1.8m wide x 2.1m high (6ft x 6ft x 7ft), partly sheltered, and with a grassy bank, planted with flowers and small shrubs would provide a pair of these beautiful European birds with a homely habitat. Small branches for perching are essential, and a large, very shallow container for water, a must.

BREEDING: Breeds in forests with undergrowth and in scrub and woodland edges. Nests on the ground, built into a grassy tussock or vegetation at the base of a bush. Loosely built, the cup of thin stems, grass and fibre, hair and plant down. The breeding season begins in late May. Single brooded. The eggs number five, sometimes four to six, smooth and glossy, light blue, finely speckled and mottled with reddish-brown. They are incubated by the female alone for about a fortnight. They leave the nest at the 12th day stage. In captive conditions, nest baskets placed and secured would be accepted by the birds. Their diet could include an insectivorous mixture and soft fruit, together with cleaned fly maggots, wax moth larvae, buffalo worms and small mealworms.

CALL: Includes a loud whistle and a harsh *tshak*. Song rich and melodious, tuneful phrases often include elements of mimicry of local species.

RING SIZE: Code D.

SHOWING REQUIREMENTS: Size 5 cage for small softbills, 18in long, 15in high and 12in wide. The recommended colours are black on the outside - this includes the wire front and white on the inside. Vessels for food and water placed inside. Floor covering optional, but nicely decorated out to mimic habitat of the species and with two springy perches. Exhibit to be large, tightly feathered, with bright eye and good wing and tail carriage.

LEGAL REQUIREMENTS: Not listed on any Schedule of the Wildlife and Countryside Act 1981, but appears on an annex to a General Licence, made under the Act, due to the fact that the bird is on the British list. Can be sold or shown if bred in captivity from legally held stock. Rings optional.

SPECIAL NOTES: Generally shy and skulking bird. One known specialist breeder of this species in UK.

Photograph by Sergey Yeliseev

REDSTART

Phoenicurus phoenicurus.

Related species: Black redstart.

DESCRIPTION: Male in summer has forehead white, throat and sides of face black, rump and tail coverts chestnut, black slate-grey breast, belly white. Female has paler underside and is grey-brown above. Length 14cm (5½in).

STATUS IN THE WILD: Summer visitor to Britain with about 150,000 pairs arriving in April departing in September. Haunts old woodlands, and stone wall country where trees are scarce, also moorland edges.

HARDBILL OR SOFTBILL? Softbill.

AVAILABILITY FOR BIRDKEEPERS: Sufficient numbers are always available to satisfy fancy interests. Each bird costs about £70.

ADVANTAGES TO KEEPING: Most sought after of all our small softbills. Often a major winner at the main events. This is due to its beauty and its apparent adaptability to home-bred life.

DISADVANTAGES TO KEEPING: Care required to ensure breeding pairs are compatible, otherwise fighting will occur. Bird requires carefully balanced diet.

DIET: Chiefly insects, including small beetles, small butterflies and moths, caterpillars, flies, fly maggots, sawfly larvae, spiders and small earthworms; also takes elder and juniper berries.

HOUSING: An outside, partly sheltered aviary, no smaller than 1.8m square x 2.1m high (6ft square x 7ft high), planted out with small bushes and climbers would suit a compatible pair. Foliage needs to be watered frequently to keep it green. Tit type nest boxes with easy access for ringing chicks would eagerly be taken up by the birds.

BREEDING: Nests in hole of tree or stump at varying heights, sometimes in out-buildings, or in cavity of old wall. The nest itself is built by the female and is constructed of grass, moss, roots and strips of bark, lined with hair. Eggs five to seven, pale uniform blue, occasionally with fine red-brown speckles. The incubation period is 14 days, chiefly by female. Chicks are fed by both parents for 14-20 days, with the male taking sole responsibility when the female lays a second clutch. Juveniles resemble speckled female. In home-bred conditions

pairs must be compatible before being placed in their breeding aviary. Rearing food can include mealworms, buffalo worms, fly larvae and wax moth larvae, the latter seems to be very important.

CALL: Soft *hweet* and a louder *twick,* also a *hwee-tuc-tuc* of alarm. Song is a brief, varied warble.

RING SIZE: Code C, which has an internal diameter of 2.5mm.

SHOWING REQUIREMENTS: The cage should be no smaller than 18in long, 15in high and 12in wide. Painted black outside and white inside, nicely decorated out and with springy perches, to show bird off to its best advantage. Size and type: As large as possible. Full-bodied but of somewhat slender upright stance. Gentle rise of shoulder, reasonably straight back to rump, neat wing and tail carriage.

LEGAL REQUIREMENTS: Fully protected. Not listed on any Schedule. Can be sold or shown under terms of a General Licence.

SPECIAL NOTES: Other names include red-tail, firetail, brantail and fire flit. Sometimes mimics other birds.

Photograph by Tommy Milner

BLACK REDSTART

Phoenicurus ochruros.

Related species: Redstart.

DESCRIPTION: The male has cheeks, throat and breast black; the tail and rump are chestnut, the two central feathers of the tail are dark. There is white on the outer edges of the primary and secondary feathers, the lower belly is white. The female and young are sooty brown, their underside being lighter. First year males resemble females, they are able to sing, build territories and breed; obtaining their adult plumage in the second year. Length 14cm (5½in).

STATUS IN THE WILD: Resident and summer visitor, with about 100 breeding pairs.

HARDBILL OR SOFTBILL? Softbill.

AVAILABILITY FOR BIRDKEEPERS: It has a small following of specialist breeders in the UK. Surplus stock readily change hands. Aviary birds are also available from the continent. Individuals command a price of about £100.

ADVANTAGES TO KEEPING: They are beautiful birds, robin-like, and make an attractive aviary subject.

DISADVANTAGES TO KEEPING: Not suitable for the beginner.

DIET: Mainly insects of all kinds, also spiders, fruit and berries. The diet of aviary birds should be supplemented with mealworms, buffalo worms and wax moth larvae, together with an insectivorous mixture.

HOUSING: Sheltered flights and aviaries should be no smaller than 2m x 1m x 2m high (6ft 6in x 3ft 3in x 6ft 6in) - the larger, the better. Some fanciers build a wall with gaps within the brickwork to encourage nesting, or even a mini building.

BREEDING: The species tend to nest in holes and cavities, or perhaps in the rafters, like a swallow. Half-open wooden nest-boxes will be used. Nest quite bulky, built of dry grasses, and moss, lined with hair and feathers. Four to six pure white, but faintly tinged (blueish eggs have been recorded). Laying begins in late April. The incubation period is between 12-13 days, and carried out chiefly by the hen. Double brooded. In home-bred conditions insects of as many types as possible should be offered, together with spiders, small mealworms, buffalo worms, small, cleaned fly maggots and wax moth larvae.

CALL: Quick warbling song, ending with a trill. Its call is a *tuck* sound.

RING SIZE: Code C.

SHOWING REQUIREMENTS: Show cages should be no smaller than 18in long, 15in high 12in wide, box or desk type and decorated in a pleasing way to show off the exhibit. An exhibition black redstart should be as large as possible, full bodied, of nice rounded appearance. The head well rounded with good rise. Neat wing and tail-carriage.

LEGAL REQUIREMENTS: Listed on Schedule 1, of the Wildlife and Countryside Act 1981. Can be sold or shown if aviary-bred and closed-ringed within terms of General Licences.

SPECIAL NOTES: Species was extremely rare until the blitz in targeted cites. Pairs moved into bombed building sites and bred. Now they nest in ruins, power stations and even stable yards.

Juvenile Black Redstart

WHINCHAT

Saxicola rubetra.

Related species: Stonechat and Siberian stonechat.

DESCRIPTION: Slimmer and paler than stonechat, is squat and short-tailed. Male has white stripe above the eye, this is paler in the female. Males have streaked brown upperparts, reddish underparts. The white eye stripe and white sides at the base of the tail are also shared by the young. Length 12.5cm (5in).

STATUS IN THE WILD: Migratory, arriving in Britain in April and departing in September or October. Winters in Senegal, Nigeria and Uganda. (Sub-Saharan Africa.) About 20,000 pairs nest here. Like open bushy meadows, wasteland, dry heaths, and marshy areas. In coastal and upland areas.

HARDBILL OR SOFTBILL? Smart little softbill.

AVAILABILITY FOR BIRDKEEPERS: A few pairs breed in home-conditions each year. Would cost about £80 per specimen.

ADVANTAGES TO KEEPING: Sought after show bird, ideal for experienced softbill fancier.

DISADVANTAGES TO KEEPING: Pairs must be compatible if breeding is to take place. Require sheltered accommodation during winter months.

DIET: Mainly insects, spiders and worms, seeds and fruit in autumn and winter.

HOUSING: A flight no smaller than 1.8m x 1.8m x 1m high (6ft x 6ft x 3ft) would be large enough for a pair of these birds to settle. It should be planted with small shrubs and grasses and fitted out with twiggy perches.

BREEDING: The birds breed in May and June, the nest is built on or near the ground in grassy fields, rough pasture land, and on commons. It is of dead grass and moss, with an inner lining of horsehair. Four to six eggs form a clutch, they are of a beautiful greenish-blue, sparingly speckled round the larger end with spots of reddish-brown. They are incubated by the female alone for 12-14 days. The nestlings are downy, mouth pale orange to deep yellow. Gape flanges pale yellow to creamy white, they are tendered by both parents whilst in the nest for up to 17 days. In home conditions, it is essential to bring the birds into high breeding condition, and to provide a varied supply of invertebrates before and during the rearing process.

CALL: Hard, very short *tsek tsek*. Song is a mixture of short, hurried phrases made up of scratchy, warbling and fluty notes, these include mimicry of other birds' voices.

RING SIZE: Code D.

SHOWING REQUIREMENTS: Desk or box type cage, no smaller than 18in long, 15in wide and 12in high. Painted black outside, including wire front, and white interior, door on right, water and food vessels placed inside. Exhibit, as large as possible. Not so plump and more upright than stonechat. Head to be well filled with nice rise. Neat wing and tail carriage. Natural trait to drop wings below tail. Autumn/winter plumage, brown overlay more general, particularly in current year birds. Shown singly or in pairs.

LEGAL REQUIREMENTS: Protected at all times. Not listed on any Schedule of Wildlife and Countryside Act 1981. May be sold or shown under current legislation.

SPECIAL NOTES: Local and other names include furze chat, and grass chat. Sits lightly, extremely wary.

Photograph by Dennis Avon

STONECHAT

Saxicola torquata.

Related species: Whinchat and Siberian stonechat.

DESCRIPTION: Head, nape and back edged with tawny-brown, rump and upper tail coverts white, tipped with brown and black. Wing coverts black-edged and tipped with brown. Tail black, sides of neck white, breast rich rust colour, underparts much lighter. Female is dull brown on head, nape and back, the rump is brownish and the breast and belly duller. Juvenile speckled and robin-like. Length 12.5cm (5in). Smaller than robin.

STATUS IN THE WILD: Resident and partial migrant, with about 20,000 breeding pairs in Britain.

HARDBILL OR SOFTBILL? Most definitely a softbill.

AVAILABILITY FOR BIRDKEEPERS: A few individuals usually available towards the end of summer, at about £80 each.

ADVANTAGES TO KEEPING: Interesting subject. Sought-after show bird, with sheltered accommodation can thrive outside all year round.

DISADVANTAGES TO KEEPING: More suitable for advanced keeper, one with specific knowledge of its needs.

DIET: Mainly insects, spiders and worms, seeds and fruit in autumn and winter.

HOUSING: A sheltered aviary no smaller than 1.8m long, 0.9m wide and 1.8m high (6ft x 3ft x 6ft) suitable for a compatible pair; planted out with climbers and small gorse bushes, twiggy perches at either end.

BREEDING: Inhabits dry scrubby areas, particularly heaths and sandy downs, occasionally near wet areas, where male likes to take up prominent positions, on top of a gorse bush or other shrub. The nest consists of a loose cup of dry stems and leaves lined with hair, feathers and wool; hidden near the ground. The eggs which are laid in April or May number four to six, smooth, glossy pale blue or greenish blue, closely mottled with reddish-brown spots, some without any spots at all. Incubation by female alone (rarely the male may sit) for 14-15 days. The nestlings are downy, tendered by both parents for a fortnight in the nest and for several days after fledging, double or sometimes treble brooded.

CALL: A harsh *tchack*, or *it-tic* and *chuck, chuck* when chicks are hatching. Song shrill and monotonous series of short scratches and whistled phrases.

RING SIZE: Code D.

SHOWING REQUIREMENTS: As large as possible, rather robin like, plump with large rounded head. Cage no smaller than 18in long x 15in high x 12in wide. Decorated to emphasise exhibit's habitat, with heath-type features, perches for an exhibit to settle on, can be small rocks or gorse stems.

LEGAL REQUIREMENTS: Protected at all times. Not listed on any Schedule of the Wildlife and Countryside Act 1981, but can be sold or shown subject to demands of General Licence, provided it is close-ringed and bred in home-conditions from legally held stock.

SPECIAL NOTES: Local and other names: Stoneclink, stone chatter, stone smick, stone chack, stonesmith and clink stone. A fairly close sitter, but when at the foot of its nesting bush will run for some distance before taking flight.

Photograph by Frank Stark

Photograph by Frank Stark

WHEATEAR

Oenanthe oenanthe.

Related species: No close relatives in British Isles.
(Larger race, the Greenland wheatear is a passage migrant here.)

DESCRIPTION: Both sexes have conspicuous white rump. Male has upperparts mostly grey, and a white strip passing round forehead and over eyes, lores and ear-coverts black, wings dark brown, underparts buff, except belly which is white. Female has upperparts and ear-coverts brown, under surface buff. In autumn males resemble females. Young have back greying brown, throat and forehead barred brown. Length 15cm (6in).

STATUS IN THE WILD: Summer visitor to these islands, with about 70,000 breeding pairs. Visits open stony or rocky country, pastureland, moorland and heath.

HARDBILL OR SOFTBILL? Known within the fancy as a softbill.

AVAILABILITY FOR BIRDKEEPERS: Bred every year in numbers by specialist keepers.

ADVANTAGES TO KEEPING: Beautiful species. Makes splendid show bird. Need insectivorous diet.

DISADVANTAGES TO KEEPING: Requires extra care during the colder months. Kept singly in roomy flight within birdroom is, perhaps, the safest option.

HOUSING: Aviary for breeding pair should resemble natural habitat, and should be as large as possible, at least 1.8m (6ft) square and 2.1m (7ft) high. It should have a sandy floor with rocks real or imitation, some heather either planted or available in tubs. Nest sites in form of half open nest boxes, placed amid boulders, or underground cavities.

BREEDING: Breeding season begins in late March, can be single or double brooded. Nests in a hole in rocks, walls, quarries, and ground burrows. Made of grasses, moss, plant stems, roots and leaves, with a shallow cup lined with grass, hair, wool and feathers, built mainly by the female. The five to six eggs are smooth and non-glossy, very pale blue. Incubation by both sexes, but mainly by the female. The chicks are tendered by both parents for 15 days in the nest, and for some time after fledging. In aviary conditions young fed on live food.

CALL: Alarm call *chack*, song short, rapid warbling phrase made up of hard notes and soft whistles; heard from April to June, sometimes later.

RING SIZE: Code E, which has an internal diameter of 2.9mm.

SHOWING REQUIREMENTS: Show cage no smaller than 18in long, 15in high and 12in wide. Painted black outside including wire front, and white interior, door on right. Decorated to imitate a rocky, heathland habitat. Exhibit: as large as possible; full bodied with gentle rise over shoulders to rump. Full, nicely rounded head, neat wings and tail carriage. Male and female differ in colour. Shown singly or in pairs. In days of yore specimens of the Greenland race were much admired at the shows, due to their larger size.

LEGAL REQUIREMENTS: Protected at all times. Unscheduled. Can be sold or shown under current legislation, must be closed-ringed and aviary bred from lawfully held stock.

SPECIAL NOTES: Local and other names; white rump, fallow chat, fallow smick, chacher, chack-bird, clodhopper and fallow finch. A close sitter.

Photograph by Tommy Milner

BLACKBIRD

Turdus merula.

Related species: Song thrush, mistle thrush, fieldfare, redwing and ring ouzel.

DESCRIPTION: The male is recognised by its black plumage, orange bill, and yellow eye ring. The female is dark brown with brownish bill, and a lighter breast. Juvenile birds are dark and spotted, similar to the adult female. The colour of young males is dark until the second year. Length 25cm (10in).

STATUS IN THE WILD: Common resident, pretty well country wide and found in many habitats, including gardens, woods, towns, and open country. Large numbers migrate here from northern climes in the autumn. About 5,000,000 pairs breed in Britain.

HARDBILL OR SOFTBILL? For avicultural purposes, the species is referred to as a softbill.

AVAILABILITY FOR BIRDKEEPERS: Readily available, as many are home-bred each year. Cost depends on quality, an ordinary pair would fetch about £60.

ADVANTAGES TO KEEPING: Easy to keep and breed, long lived, their singing very pleasing. The best are sought-after show-birds, and the species is probably the most successful of all softbill exhibits.

DISADVANTAGES TO KEEPING: Dominant partner can be very hostile, so a constant eye must be kept until the birds settle down. A hiding place should be provided to enable a victim some respite.

DIET: In the wild the blackbird will consume all manner of fruit and berries, also seeds of many weeds. Earthworms, insects of numerous kinds and spiders are taken when breeding and fed to their young. Aviary stock will consume poultry pellets, an insectivorous mixture and fruit as a staple diet. Earthworms and mealworms are essential when chicks are in the nest.

BREEDING: In the wild the range of nest sites include trees, bushes, out-building and hedges. The large, open nest is constructed of grasses and moss, well built, and solidified with mud, and is lined with finer grasses. The eggs in a clutch number three to five as a rule, greenish colour and generally freckled with reddish brown which sometimes forms a cap at the larger end. An aviary should be no smaller than one of 2m long x 1m wide x 2m high, (6ft 6in x 3ft 3in x 6ft 6in). Although blackbirds will build in a bush or on a ledge, open nest boxes make an ideal site for a nest.

CALL: The blackbird's song is made up of short warbles, with varied notes, the best being flute like sounds, not surpassed in the song of any bird. It can be heard from February to the end of July.

RING SIZE: Code M, placed on the leg on the 4th day.

SHOWING REQUIREMENTS: The cage should be no smaller than 24in long, 20in high and 12in wide, desk or box type. An exhibition bird should be as large as possible, full bodied and of strong appearance. Eyes set centrally in head, wings carried well in straight line with tail. Mutations have separate standards. Shown singly.

LEGAL REQUIREMENTS: The bird is listed on Schedule 3 of the Wildlife and Countryside Act 1981 and can be sold or shown if close-ringed and bred in captivity from legally held stock.

SPECIAL NOTES: Mutations include cinnamon, albino, satinette, grizzle, opal and blue. Some northern male blackbirds have dark bills.

Photograph by Dennis Avon

RING OUZEL

Turdus torquatus.

Related species: Blackbird, song thrush, mistle thrush, redwing and fieldfare.

DESCRIPTION: The bird is recognised by its blackish brown plumage, black-tipped bill and white crescent. The female is browner, with narrower and duller crescent. Young have throat feathers tipped with white; the upper breast is mottled black and white. Length 24cm (9½in).

STATUS IN THE WILD: Early summer migrant from Mediterranean region to mountain areas, with about 10,000 pairs. Departs towards end of October.

HARDBILL OR SOFTBILL? Regarded as a softbill.

AVAILABILITY TO KEEPING: Numbers bred in home conditions vary from year to year, but usually a few available at a cost of more than £100 each.

ADVANTAGES TO KEEPING: Makes beautiful show bird, a challenge for any keeper.

DISADVANTAGES TO KEEPING: In captivity, it is difficult to build up populations, as a proportion of specimens die quickly of septicaemia (blood poisoning), caused by bacteria. This is virtually unknown to me, in other captive thrushes. Any keeper considering obtaining stock should discuss this aspect with the vendor to check that the birds are not carrying hippoboscid louse flies (also called flat flies). Before receiving them, an appointment should be made with a vet, so that the stock can be taken straightaway for examination. West Country keepers seemingly have less problems with these birds than others, elsewhere. Much more research is needed as to why this is.

DIET: Chiefly berries and seeds of moorland plants in summer, also earthworms, flies and their larvae (maggots), small molluscs and caterpillars.

HOUSING: A flight partly sheltered, no smaller than 2.7m long x 1.2m wide x 2.1m high (9ft x 4ft x 7ft), planted with heather, and with piles of rocks with cavities, together with half-open nest boxes for nesting purposes, would be ideal.

BREEDING: Will nest on the side of banks, beside tracks, in quarries, and occasionally in bushes, in mountainous or moorland terrain. Nest is similar to blackbird's, substantially made, with grasses, sometimes on a heather foundation, lined first with earth, then with dry grasses. Clutch usually four. Eggs are greenish or creamy yellow with bold blotches and spots of red brown and ashy. Laid in late April to early May. The incubation period is 14 days and is shared by both parents. Single brooded.

CALL: Usual alarm note, *tschk* or *tchuck*. Song consists of three short monosyllabic whistles followed by a double whistle, these are repeated. Quite monotonous.

RING SIZE: Code M, placed on the leg on the 4th day.

SHOWING REQUIREMENTS: Size and type: As large as possible, full-bodied of strong appearance with broad, nicely rounded head in proportion with well rounded body, neat wing and tail carriage. Female browner than male with less distinct crescent and heavily laced throughout. Current year birds less intensely coloured. Cage, desk or box type, 24in long, 20in high and 12in deep. Black outside, white inside, with two strong perches. Decoration optional.

LEGAL REQUIREMENTS: Not listed on any Schedule. Can be shown or sold under terms of a General Licence.

SPECIAL NOTES: Local and other names: rock thrush, ring thrush, rock ouzel, tor ouzel and ring blackbird. Sits pretty closely, and somewhat demonstrative when disturbed.

Photograph by Dennis Avon

MISTLE THRUSH

Turdus viscivorus.

Related species: Song thrush, blackbird, fieldfare, redwing and ring ouzel.

DESCRIPTION: Whitish underparts covered with large wedged shaped black spots, flanks and breast marked with buff, upperparts and wings greyish brown. Tail grey-brown with white tips to outer feathers noticeable when bird flies away. Juveniles similar to adults, but spotted white on head, mantle and wing coverts. Sexes similar. Length 27-28cm (10-11in).

STATUS IN THE WILD: Resident, with about 320,000 pairs. In open woodland, gardens and parks.

HARDBILL OR SOFTBILL? Known within the fancy as a softbill.

AVAILABILITY FOR BIRDKEEPERS: Usually available, cost about £70 each.

ADVANTAGES TO KEEPING: Easy to breed, if pair is compatible, long-lived. Make nice show birds.

DISADVANTAGES TO KEEPING: Require large flight, will often attack each other in confined space. Will also attack keeper, so beware!

DIET: Chiefly berries and fruits, including those of yew, holly, rowan, ivy, hawthorn, rose, juniper, honeysuckle, mistletoe, ash, as well as cherry, apple, plum, damson, and currant, also insects, snails, slugs, spiders and worms.

HOUSING: Outside, partly sheltered aviary, with strong perches, and places to hide if one spouse becomes too dominant.

BREEDING: Often places nest on bare fork of tree, sometimes at a height, occasionally lower down. Nest big and substantially built of grasses, mosses, lichens and roots, first lined with mud then with dry grasses. Eggs usually four, creamy, tawny or even blue, with blotches and spots of red-brown and lilac shell marks. They are laid in late February or March. The incubation period is 13-14 days, by female alone. Usually double brooded. In home-bred conditions, birds will build on a shelf or ledge, or in one of the larger wicker baskets. Earthworms and mealworms are important in their diet when young are being fed. Chicks are tendered by both parents for 12-14 days, young are able to fly at 15-20 days, they are fed by both adults after fledging, but male may take over if female begins new brood.

CALL: The song can be heard from January, similar to blackbirds, but more melancholy and penetrating, less variable and shorter. Often sings from highest perch in the teeth of a storm.

RING SIZE: Code M.

SHOWING REQUIREMENTS: As large as possible, full bodied, of strong appearance, well rounded, half-moon shaped spots from throat to vent, well rounded head, set on thick neck, nice, gentle rise from nape to rump, good wing and tail carriage. Show cage; 24in long, 20in high and 12in wide, painted black outside, including wire front. White inside with two strong perches. Floor covering optional. Shown singly.

LEGAL REQUIREMENTS: Protected at all times. Not on any schedule. Can be sold or shown within terms of General Licence if ringed and captive bred.

SPECIAL NOTES: Other names; holm thrush, holm screech, mistle throat, missel bird, bull thrush and storm cock. Sits closely, and makes a great deal of demonstration when disturbed.

Photograph by Tommy Milner

SONG THRUSH

Turdus philomelos.

Related species: Blackbird, ring ouzel, mistle thrush, fieldfare and redwing.

DESCRIPTION: Warm-brown upperparts, buffish underparts covered with black spots. Upright stance, but more horizontal when running. Juvenile, very speckled appearance, back feathers have pale buff streaks and dark tips, wing feathers have yellowish tips. Sexes similar. Length 23cm (9in).

STATUS IN THE WILD: Resident, however many move south for winter and are replaced by northern birds. Bird of hedgerow, garden and woodland. About 1,380,000 pairs breed in Britain.

HARDBILL OR SOFTBILL? Softbill.

AVAILABILITY FOR BIRDKEEPERS: Readily available, many bred each year. Worth about £30 each. Some variants may be more.

ADVANTAGES TO KEEPING: Easy to keep, breed and maintain. Excellent show bird.

DISADVANTAGES TO KEEPING: None known, however knowledge of keeping softbills required before obtaining stock.

DIET: Wide variety of invertebrates, snails, worms and fruit. Uses 'anvil', usually a large stone to open snails.

HOUSING: An aviary 1.8m (6ft) square is ideal for a pair of these confiding birds. Perches either end are essential, as is a secluded area where a subordinate bird of a pair can get respite. Sheltered nest sites should be secluded.

BREEDING: In evergreens, especially in early spring, hedgerows, bushes and trees, between 4ft-12ft up. Nest made of twigs, grasses and moss, with an inner lining of mud. Eggs number four or five, of a beautiful greenish-blue, spotted with black, occasionally unmarked. These are laid from February to July, sometimes later. Usually double or treble-brooded. Incubation usually begins with the last egg for 11-14 days, young are downy, mouth yellow, gape flanges pale yellow, they are tendered by both parents for 12-16 days. Aviary pairs will use large canary nest pans or baskets, or wide ledges and wooden boxes. Long dried grass, moss and even coconut fibre will be used, a container of mud is essential. Young can be reared on earthworms, mealworms and snails.

CALL: A sip flight note and a *tchook-tchook* alarm call. Song is a flute-like whistling in which each phrase is repeated 3 or 4 times followed by a brief pause before another phrase is similarly repeated.

RING SIZE: Code K.

SHOWING REQUIREMENTS: As large as possible, broad, nicely rounded head, full bodied of strong appearance with gentle rise over back, neat wing and tail carriage. Colour and markings: rich brown upperparts, sandy buff breast, profuse, large, even, well defined, very dark brown spots, carried well down breast and flanks receding towards vent. Show cage: 20in long, 12in wide and 15in high. Black outside, white inside, with two sturdy perches. Floor covering optional. Shown singly.

LEGAL REQUIREMENTS: Listed on Schedule 3 of the Wildlife and Countryside Act 1981. Can be sold or shown due to regulations made under the Act, if close ringed and captive bred from legally held stock.

SPECIAL NOTES: Other names: Mavis and throstle.

cinnamon hen

Photograph by Dennis Avon

FIELDFARE

Turdus pilaris.

Related species: Redwing, blackbird, song thrush, mistle thrush and ring ouzel.

DESCRIPTION: In winter, the slate-grey head is streaked with black, and the grey rump tinged with buff, the wings and tail are dark brown, the back and mantle warm chestnut. The rich brown throat and breast are streaked with black and with dark brown on the coverts. The bill is dark brown, yellowish on the lower mandible, the legs and eyes are dark brown. By the spring, the feathers are brighter, and the rump is clear, uniform grey, and the bill is completely yellow. Length 26cm (10¼in).

STATUS IN THE WILD: The fieldfare is a winter visitor to our shores from northern Europe, arriving in their tens of thousands in September and October, returning during April and May. About 25-30 pairs breed in Scotland.

HARDBILL OR SOFTBILL? Softbill.

AVAILABILITY FOR BIRDKEEPERS: A few pairs are kept within British aviculture. The species is also bred in numbers on the continent. Specimens cost about £80 each.

ADVANTAGES TO KEEPING: Easy to breed, hardy and long lived. Make a nice show bird.

DISADVANTAGES TO KEEPING: None obvious.

DIET: Snails, slugs, earthworms, insects, beetles, fly larvae, berries and seeds of yew, grain, and root crops, also fallen fruit.

HOUSING: A sheltered flight, about 2.75m long x 1.2m wide x 2.1m high (9ft x 4ft x 7ft) is ideal for a single pair, two strong perches, one affixed at each end, will suit the birds. Open wooden nest boxes placed in position under cover are usually taken up.

BREEDING: Breeds in colonies in woods of birch and conifer. Nest-site varies, occasionally built in out buildings, rocks or even on the ground. The nest is big and solidly built with grasses, and lined with mud. The inner layer is made up of dry grasses. The eggs number three to six as a rule; these are of a deep greenish ground colour, (varying to blue or yellowish), freckled and spotted reddish brown, and often much like the blackbird's. Laying begins in April and May, later in the far north. Incubation is chiefly by the female for 13-14 days. Young require parent care for a further, similar period. Home-bred birds require a staple diet, together with live food, just before the eggs hatch until the young are self-supporting.

CALL: Low warbling and twittering song, quite sweet. Also harsh note when disturbed.

RING SIZE: Code M. Young need to be ringed on the fourth day.

SHOWING REQUIREMENTS: Cage no smaller than 20in long, 15in high and 12in wide, painted black on the outside and white on the inside, with two strong perches. Floor cover optional. Size and type: As large as possible, of strong-bodied appearance, nicely rounded head. Gentle rise over shoulder to rump. Neat wing and tail carriage.

LEGAL REQUIREMENTS: Specially protected. Listed on Schedule 1, of the Wildlife and Countryside Act 1981. May be shown or sold if ringed and bred in captivity under terms of a General Licence.

SPECIAL NOTES: Anglo Saxon name felde fare. When in flocks birds are constantly chattering.

Photograph by Dennis Avon

REDWING

Turdus iliacus.

Related species: Fieldfare, blackbird, song thrush, mistle thrush and ring ouzel.

DESCRIPTION: Like a song thrush, earth brown above and with streaked breast and flanks on a warm creamy background that becomes white on the belly and under tail coverts. Bold, creamy supercilium and moustachial streak. Its name derives from the wash of rust-red along the flanks. Shows red under wing when in flight. Sexes similar. Length 21cm (8¼in)

STATUS IN THE WILD: Winter visitor, two races, T.i.iliacus from Scandinavia and T.i. coburni from Iceland. In British Isles about 50 pairs breed, mainly in Scotland. Icelandic birds spend winter in the west, around Irish Sea, Scandinavian birds in the east.

HARDBILL OR SOFTBILL? Softbill.

AVAILABILITY FOR BIRDKEEPERS: Tiny British avicultural population, birds, however available on the continent. Cost about £100 each.

ADVANTAGES TO KEEPING: Obvious alternative to the song thrush, breeds well in home conditions, and makes nice show bird.

DISADVANTAGES TO KEEPING: Difficult to come by due to insufficient interest.

DIET: Insects and their larvae, worms, snails, fruit and berries.

HOUSING: An outside, partly sheltered flight, at least 1.8m x 0.9m x 2.1m high (6ft x 3ft x 7ft) would suit a pair. This should be fitted out with strong perches and nest sites which could include open boxes and shelves protected by foliage.

BREEDING: Nest is a thick cup of grass, fine twigs, moss and lichen, usually lined with an inner cup of mud, this in turn is lined with fine grass, built by the female. Breeding begins in late April or early May in the south of its range to July in the north. Eggs number four or five, similar to those of the blackbird, light blue or greenish-blue, marked overall with fine speckling or mottling in reddish-brown. The incubation is carried out by the female alone, beginning with the last or next to last for 11-15 days. The nestlings are downy. They are tendered by both parents for 10-15 days in the nest and for a similar period afterwards. In home-bred conditions will eat staple diet of poultry pellets and fruit. When breeding will require supplies of earthworms, mealworms and any other invertebrates available.

CALL: A thin *seep*. Song is a repetition of a single phrase.

RING SIZE: K, internal diameter 3.9mm.

SHOWING REQUIREMENTS: Show birds should be as large as possible, with nicely rounded head and full body tapering through to vent. Gentle rise over shoulder to rump and with neat wing and tail carriage. In good feather and condition with bright eye. Cages, box or desk type, no smaller than 20in long, 15in high and 12in wide. Painted black outside and white inside, with door on right. Food and water vessels white, and inside the cage. Two strong perches, floor covering optional.

LEGAL REQUIREMENTS: Listed on Schedule 1 of the Wildlife and Countryside Act 1981, and specially protected. Can be sold or shown under terms of a General Licence.

SPECIAL NOTES: Both populations of the redwing are similar, the Icelandic birds are darker and larger, their greater size gives them longer wings, necessary for a lengthy sea journey. It is thought that both races breed in Britain. Old names include wind-throstle and windle.

Photograph by Frank Stark

CETTI'S WARBLER

Cettia cetti.

Related species: No close relatives in Britain.

DESCRIPTION: Chestnut back, rufous, rounded head, ten feathered tail, white underparts and conspicuous whitish superciliary stripe. The wings short and rounded, species flicks tail downwards. Male much heavier than female. Length 14cm (5½in).

STATUS IN THE WILD: Resident in south of England and Wales, with about 450 breeding pairs, which it colonised in the 1970s. Suffers badly in harsh weather, and is at the limit of its range.

HARDBILL OR SOFTBILL? Softbill.

AVAILABILITY FOR BIRDKEEPERS: Available from continental sources - not currently in UK.

ADVANTAGES TO KEEPING: They bring a pleasant song and their movements would be of interest.

DISADVANTAGES TO KEEPING: Best suited to experienced keeper.

DIET: Insects that are found within its habitat of hedges, ditches, streams and swamps. These include dragonflies, damselflies, gnats, mayflies and also spiders.

HOUSING: Would benefit from a fairly large aviary that is planted out with bushes (many of which should be evergreen) to give cover all year round, and with a shallow pool. Can be kept outside all year.

BREEDING: In the wild, it breeds in low bushes in moist places, or in reeds. It builds the nest about 0.9m (3ft) from the ground. The nest is made of dead leaves etc, and has a deep inner cup, which is lined with fine grasses, hair, feathers and reed flowers. The breeding season begins in April to early May and is single-brooded. There are usually four eggs produced, which are smooth and glossy. They are bright chestnut to deep brick-red and sometimes to paler and duller shades of purplish-pink.

The eggs are incubated by the female alone and the young are tendered by both parents. In captivity, habitat would have to be mirrored as above. Livefood obtained from the market place and elsewhere, should be as varied as possible.

CALL: Very distinctive, a loud - very explosive - burst of song from dense cover: *PLIT*! *Twik-a-twick-a-twick*! *Twick-a-twick*!

RING SIZE: Code D.

SHOWING REQUIREMENTS: As large as possible, full bodied, nicely filled breast and well-rounded head. Neat wing and tail carriage. Can be shown singly or in pairs. Show cages must be no smaller than 46cm long x 38cm high x 30cm wide (18in x 15in x 12in), decorated out in a natural way.

LEGAL REQUIREMENTS: Not on Schedule 3. General Licence in force for non-Schedule 3 birds enabling sale or exhibition of home-bred ringed specimens.

SPECIAL NOTES: This is one of the most skulking of British birds and when it is not singing it tends to go undetected. Can be mistaken for the nightingale (to look at, but not listen to).

Photograph by Sergey Yeliseev

SAVI'S WARBLER

Locustella luscinioides.

Related species: Grasshopper warbler, river warbler and lanceolated warbler.

DESCRIPTION: This rare warbler can be distinguished from others by its dark, unstreaked, reddish-brown head and underparts. It has a faint, buff eye-stripe, which fades behind the eye. The underparts are brownish white with rufous-brown on the breast and flanks to undertail coverts. Wings and tail are reddish-brown, similar to upperparts. The tail is broad and graduated towards the tip. The bill is dark grey-brown and the legs pale brown. Juvenile similar to adult. Length 12.7cm (5in).

STATUS IN THE WILD: Summer visitor to UK, with up to 15 pairs, mainly in the south-east. Bird of unbroken swamps and reed beds. Re-colonised England in 1960. Winters in Africa.

HARDBILL OR SOFTBILL? Soft-billed species.

AVAILABILITY FOR BIRDKEEPERS: Would need to be obtained from the Continent.

ADVANTAGES TO KEEPING: Well worth studying in captive conditions.

DISADVANTAGES TO KEEPING: Just one, availability.

DIET: Adult and larvae of flies, butterflies, moths, other insects and spiders.

HOUSING: Aviary, partly sheltered, some 1.8m (6ft) square, 2.1m (7ft) high, would suit single pair provided it is furnished with growing reeds (potted or otherwise) and a shallow pool. Housed inside from November to April. Mealworms, maggots, wax worms and buffalo worms should be offered all year, considerably increased at breeding time.

BREEDING: Breeds in reedy swamps and fens, overgrown lake edges with reeds and sedge beds. The nest is built into the bases of reeds, sedges or tall grasses in swampy places on or near the ground or above water. The nest cup's outer structure loosely built of dead leaves or waterside plants, inner section often woven more firmly from grass stems, and inner cup firm and smooth, lined with fine grasses, leaves and fibres; well concealed. Built by female.

The eggs number four to five, smooth and glossy, white and profusely speckled overall with brown, greyish-brown or purple-brown, and with a more densely speckled area at or around the larger end. The incubation is by female alone, fed by male, for 12 days. The nestlings are downy, mouth deep yellow. The nestling period lasts for 12-14 days, young fed by female alone at first, male often assists later on.

CALL: *Pit*, alarm sharp rattle, long, reeling song.

RING SIZE: Code D, 2.7mm.

SHOWING REQUIREMENTS: As large as possible, good feather and condition with bright eye and confident movement. Cage: 18in long,15in high and 12in wide, painted black outside, including wire front, white inside. White vessels for food and water inside. Door at right end. Decorated in a way to imitate habitat of exhibit, and with two springy perches.

LEGAL REQUIREMENTS: Listed on Schedule 1, Part 1, of the Wildlife and Countryside Act 1981, birds protected by special penalties at all times. Can be sold or shown under current legislation if bred in captivity from legally-held stock.

SPECIAL NOTES: Less shy than other warblers. Regularly sings from prominent position.

Often sings throughout the night.

Photograph by Tony Tilford

GRASSHOPPER WARBLER

Locustella naevia.

Related species: Savi's warbler, river warbler and lanceolated warbler.

DESCRIPTION: Upperparts olive-brown, black-brown markings, which appear to be in lines, there is a faint eye stripe. The underparts pale brownish, with a few darker streaks on the breast. Tail graduated, slightly barred. The bill brown, legs pale yellowish-brown, eyes are hazel. Length 13cm (5in).

STATUS IN THE WILD: Summer visitor to these shores, fairly local, with about 16,000 pairs. Usually haunts marshland and osier beds, but also found on heaths and commons.

HARDBILL OR SOFTBILL? Softbill.

AVAILABILITY FOR BIRDKEEPERS: Extremely rare in captivity. Specimens cost about £80 each.

ADVANTAGES TO KEEPING: Would suit a specialist breeder. The distinctive spring song would be a big plus to any collection.

DISADVANTAGES TO KEEPING: Difficulty in obtaining true pairs.

DIET: Chiefly insects, beetles, moths, caterpillars, flies, dragonflies, mayflies, woodlice and spiders.

HOUSING: Outside, sheltered aviary, about 2.75m long x 1.2m wide x 2.1m high (9ft x 4ft x 7ft) planted with small bushes, heather and grasses. This brings in insects and provides security for the birds, enabling the male to sing in confidence and for the pair to raise their brood.

BREEDING: Breeds in undergrowth. Nest of dead grasses and bents, well concealed on the ground or in rank grasses above it. Bird usually leaves the nest by a run (path) through the grass and tangle. Usually six, pinkish-white eggs, finely freckled all over with red specks. Breeding begins in mid May. Incubation period 13-14 days by both sexes, chiefly the female. Sometimes double-brooded especially in the south. Nestlings have long, dark grey down. Their mouths are yellow, with yellow-white gape flanges. Both parents tend them in the nest for nearly a fortnight and about the same period afterwards. Aviary birds, when breeding, must receive a varied, livefood diet, including small mealworms, buffalo worms, wax moth larvae and small maggots.

CALL: A "reeling" song, like the noise of a fisherman's reel. It often continues for several minutes. The singer's location is difficult to pinpoint. A ventriloquial effect increased by the bird moving its head from side to side. This serves to broadcast its territorial song and to make it less easy for a predator to locate. Alarm call 'tschek-tschek'.

RING SIZE: Code D.

SHOWING REQUIREMENTS: Exhibit must be in excellent health and condition, with good wing and tail carriage and bright eye. Show cage no smaller than 45cm long x 38cm high x 30cm wide (18in x 15in x 12in) painted black outside and white inside, with two springy perches and decorated out to mimic the natural habitat. Shown singly or in pairs.

LEGAL REQUIREMENTS: Fully protected. Not listed on any Schedule of the Wildlife and Countryside Act 1981. Can be sold or shown under General Licence.

SPECIAL NOTES: Local and other names: reeler, cricket bird, grasshopper lark. Leaves the nest quietly and quickly, and hides in the undergrowth.

Photograph by Sergey Yeliseev

SEDGE WARBLER

Acrocephalus schoenobaenus.

Related species: Marsh warbler, reed warbler, great reed warbler, aquatic warbler and moustached warbler.

DESCRIPTION: In summer the general colour is reddish-brown with dark centres to the feathers, forming streaks on the back, but not on the tawny rump. A conspicuous yellowish white eye stripe is bounded above by an almost black streak, and the centre of the crown is streaked with light and dark brown; the ear-coverts are brown. Light edges show on the wing feathers. The underparts are buff, whitish on the throat, and warmest on the flanks. The bill is dark brown, the legs pale brown, the eyes hazel. Length 13cm (5in).

STATUS IN THE WILD: Most widespread and numerous of Acrocephalus warblers. Summer visitor with about 360,000 pairs in British Isles.

HARDBILL OR SOFTBILL? Recognised as a softbill.

AVAILABILITY FOR BIRDKEEPERS: Thought to be only a few pairs kept in British aviculture, so surplus stock difficult to come by.

ADVANTAGES TO KEEPING: Interesting and busy bird with splendid song.

DISADVANTAGES TO KEEPING: Very little interest in the species, seems unlikely to be chosen as a show bird.

DIET: Chiefly insects from aphids to dragon flies, also spiders.

HOUSING: Aviary 1.8m x 1.8m x 2.1m high (6ft x 6ft x 7ft), partly sheltered and planted with reeds, or with stacked bunches of cut reeds, would be accepted by a pair of these striking warblers. A small pond would be of enormous interest to them. Frost free winter quarters.

BREEDING: Breeds by water in rank herbage and scrub. Also nests on the ground or a foot or two up in tall herbage or base of shrub, or bound to plant stems over water. Nest a rather bulky deep cup, cylindrical or rounded. Looser outer structure of dry grasses, plant stems, moss, sedges and spiders' webs; with thicker internal layer of fine grass stems and leaves, lined with grass, leaves, grass flower-heads, hair and plant down. Breeds in May and June. Single brooded. Eggs, five or six are smooth and glossy, tinged with pale green or pale olive-buff, finely speckled. Incubation by female for 12-14 days. The nestlings are naked, mouth orange-yellow. They are cared for by both parents for 10-12 days in the nest and for a further period after fledging. Juvenile, creamier than parents.

CALL: *tuc;* alarm *churr.* Song is a loud and varied mix of harsh and musical notes.

RING SIZE: Code D.

SHOWING REQUIREMENTS: As large as possible, of good feather and condition, with bright eye and showing creamy-white eye stripe. Cage no smaller than 18in long, 15in high and 12in wide. Painted black outside, including wire fronts, white inside. Decorated to imitate habitat of exhibit, with reeds and perhaps a mirror to indicate water, and with two twiggy perches to enable movement.

LEGAL REQUIREMENTS: Not listed on any Schedule of Wildlife and Countryside Act 1981. Can be shown under terms of a General Licence if ringed and bred in captivity.

SPECIAL NOTES: Song offered during night as well as by day, sometimes mistaken for nightingale. Young leave nest early to avoid predation.

Photograph by Tony Tilford

MARSH WARBLER
Acrocephalus palustris.
Related species: Reed warbler, great reed warbler, sedge warbler, moustached warbler and aquatic warbler.

DESCRIPTION: A medium sized warbler, very similar to reed warbler, but fuller bodied and heavier, with slightly shorter bill and rounded crown. Sexes are similar. Adults usually have more olive-brown upperparts than reed warbler, also lacks rufous rump. Juvenile similar to adults. Length 12.5cm (5in).

STATUS IN THE WILD: Summer visitor to British Isles with about 12 pairs. Numbers vary from year to year. Favour sites of dense vegetation in Severn and Avon valleys.

HARDBILL OR SOFTBILL? Cited as a softbill.

AVAILABILITY FOR BIRDKEEPERS: No data available.

ADVANTAGES TO KEEPING: Was on Schedule 4 until recently. Now paperwork is no longer required, specialist fanciers may consider taking the species up.

DISADVANTAGES TO KEEPING: Present lack of interest in the species.

DIET: Chiefly insects and spiders, some snails and berries.

BREEDING: Breeds in bushes near water or in damp thickets. Nest is built in tall herbage or in shrubs, consists of a cup, sometimes cylindrical like reed warblers, the rim of which is intertwined around stems. Outer part more loosely constructed of dry grass etc., the inner cup is more compact, of thinner material with some roots and hair. It is built by both sexes, but mainly by the female. The breeding season is from May to mid June. The species is single brooded. The eggs number four or five, very pale blueish, greenish or greyish with speckling. The incubation is by both parents for 12 days, the young are tendered for 10-14 days in the nest and for a further week on fledging. Aviary birds need natural nesting materials. Live food should be of the greatest variety possible. Small wicker baskets would be of interest to the birds.

CALL: Alarm note *tschak*. Song is loud, pleasant and very varied, mixed with squeaking and rattling notes, an unstructured medley, incorporating much mimicry.

RING SIZE: Code E.

SHOWING REQUIREMENTS: Show cage of desk or box type, no smaller than 18in long, 15in high and 12in wide. Painted black outside, white inside. Decorated to suit species with two thin perches. Shown singly or in pairs. Exhibit must be in excellent condition, with bright eyes, and well set wings and tail, must be fully trained for the show in order to catch the judges' eye.

LEGAL REQUIREMENTS: Listed on Schedule 1, Wildlife and Countryside Act 1981. Can be shown or sold if captive bred and ringed, from lawfully held stock.

SPECIAL NOTES: Songs may be 90 per cent mimicry, all learnt by the bird in its first year. At least 99 European and 113 African species' calls have been recorded. Spends 12-15 hours singing each day, by day and night, during breeding period.

Photograph by Tony Tilford

REED WARBLER

Acrocephalus scirpaceus.

Related species: Marsh warbler, great reed warbler, moustached warbler, aquatic warbler and sedge warbler.

DESCRIPTION: Adult upperparts are uniform olive-brown, with often noticeably more rufous rump and upper tail coverts, and dark-brown primaries. Underparts white with buff under tail coverts and sides of breast. Bill dark grey or greyish-brown with pale base. Legs sturdy, variable, but usually greyish. Juvenile brighter and rustier than adult, but face pattern less distinct. Medium-sized warbler. Sexes similar. Length 12.5cm (5in). Wingspan 18-21cm. Weight: 10-13g.

STATUS IN WILD: Summer visitor to British Isles with about 60,000 pairs, less than 50 in Ireland and only a few in Scotland.

HARDBILL OR SOFTBILL? Regarded in fancy circles as a softbill.

AVAILABILITY FOR BIRDKEEPERS: Species not bred in any numbers due to lack of interest.

ADVANTAGES TO KEEPING: Would make a nice addition to a collection.

DISADVANTAGES TO KEEPING: Interested parties may be obliged to search far and wide for a pair.

DIET: Chiefly insects especially flies, also spiders and small snails.

HOUSING: Outside, partly sheltered flight for use from April to October; should simulate reedy habitat, with water; so birds feel naturally at home. A small pond with reed and other vegetation would suit a pair of these interesting birds. Winter accommodation should be warm and draught free.

BREEDING: Breeds by or over water among reed-beds and marshes, built around stems of growing reeds, or in bushes. Nest deep, cylindrical-walled cup, the sides woven around several upright stems, of grass stems and flower heads, some plant down and spider's webs, lined with white material. Breeding begins in mid-April to mid-June. The species is single brooded. Usually four, rarely three to six eggs, smooth and glossy, greenish white, blotched and spotted. Incubation is carried out by both sexes for 11-12 days. The nestlings are naked at first, mouth orange-yellow, with a pair of long, oval black spots at the back of the tongue. Gape flanges are yellow. The young are tendered by both parents for 11-13 days in the nest and for a similar period afterwards. Reed stems would provide a base for any aviary nest. Invertebrates could include mealworms, fly larvae (maggots), and wax worms.

CALL: *churr-churr*, alarm harsher, song low, guttural churring with long phrases.

RING SIZE: Code D.

SHOWING REQUIREMENTS: Show cage, desk or box type, painted black outside, including wire front, and white inside, food and water vessels inside. Decorated out to mimic natural habitat with reeds and, perhaps a flat mirror situated on floor to illustrate water. Show specimen should be as large as possible, in good feather and condition and with bright eye.

LEGAL REQUIREMENTS: Protected at all times. Not listed on any Schedule, but can be sold or shown under terms of a General Licence, if close ringed and aviary bred from legally held parents.

SPECIAL NOTES: Species has broad feet, especially adapted to hold onto reed stems.

Photograph by Tony Tilford

ICTERINE WARBLER

Hippolais icterina.

Related species: Melodious warbler (page 301) and Olivaceous warbler.

DESCRIPTION: Medium sized warbler, with long bill, rather flat crown and long wings. Adults basically green and yellow below. Area between beak and below eye yellow, giving a pale-faced effect. The wings have a pale panel formed by yellow edge to dark olive secondaries. The legs are bright blue-grey. Juvenile usually flushed with yellow. Stance very reed warbler like. Length 12.5cm (5in).

STATUS IN THE WILD: Mainly central and eastern Europe. Scarce, but regular migrant to Britain. Turns up occasionally, mainly along coastal sites in autumn, also in spring, when males have been singing. Has bred in Britain, winters in southern tropical Africa. May occur more frequently in near future, due to climate warming.

HARDBILL OR SOFTBILL? Softbill.

AVAILABILITY FOR BIRDKEEPERS: Not readily available, if they were, would cost about £80 each.

ADVANTAGES TO KEEPING: No data available, but would do well if treated in a similar way as other warblers such as the blackcap.

DISADVANTAGES TO KEEPING: Difficulty in obtaining stock.

DIET: Insects, these include small beetles, moths, butterflies, caterpillars, flies and aphides, also spiders and berries.

BREEDING: The nest is deep, cup-shaped, positioned in the fork of a tree or bush, usually about 3 metres above the ground, and is made of plant fibre, lined with fur, hair and feathers. The eggs which number four to five are pale purple-pink, sparingly spotted with pink. The incubation is carried out by both parents for 13 days. The nestlings are naked, mouth pale orange-yellow, the gape flanges are yellow. Young are tendered by both parents for a fortnight before leaving the nest, and for about the same period when they have fledged. Aviary birds would accept varieties of live food such as small mealworms, buffalo worms and wax moth larvae. Breeds naturally in open woodland, parkland and orchards.

CALL: Common call *tec*. Song rather hoarse and sustained, but including musical whistles, and long drawn out notes with many imitations, these include blackbird, fieldfare, starling, swallow, blue tit, chaffinch, golden oriole, and great spotted woodpecker. Many phrases repeated one or more times. Usually sings hidden in tree tops. Song can last 40 seconds and can carry for about 500 metres on a still evening.

RING SIZE : Code E. Fitted on about the 6th day.

SHOWING REQUIREMENTS: Show cage should be no smaller than one of 18in long,15in high and 12in wide, either desk or box type, with the door fitted in the right hand end, made of wood, painted black on the outside, including the wire front, and white on the inside, with two white vessels placed inside for food and water, and two springy perches to allow movement. General decoration should mimic the bird's natural habitat. The exhibit must be in good health and condition, with a bright eye, and move with confidence, in order to catch the judges' eye.

LEGAL REQUIREMENTS: Not listed on any Schedule of the Wildlife and Countryside Act 1981. Bird on British list. General Licence in force, the terms of which allows species on British list to be sold or shown if ringed and bred in captivity.

SPECIAL NOTES: Bird could go unnoticed unless trapped by authorised persons, or its beautiful song is heard.

Photograph by Sergey Yeliseev

DARTFORD WARBLER

Sylvia undata.

Related species: Whitethroat, lesser whitethroat, blackcap and garden warbler.

DESCRIPTION: In summer the male has dark brown upper parts, shading to slate-grey on the head and the brown wings are shown up by paler edgings on the secondaries. The two outer tail feathers have white margins and tips, obvious when the tail is spread out. The underparts are rufous-chestnut. The bill is pale brown, the legs are light brown, the eyes are red, and the ring around the eye, reddish-orange. In autumn the underparts, especially on the throat, are streaked with white. The female is browner above, and paler beneath, and lacks the ruddy tints. Length 13cm (5in).

STATUS IN THE WILD: Resident bird of the furze-splattered southern heath-land. In Britain about 900 pairs.

HARDBILL OR SOFTBILL? Softbill.

AVAILABILITY FOR BIRDKEEPERS: Bred but pairs somewhat difficult to locate. When available, fetch about £200 a pair.

ADVANTAGES TO KEEPING: Gives specialist softbill keepers a challenge. Easy to maintain if given suitable conditions.

DISADVANTAGES TO KEEPING: Bird for the specialist - I have yet to see one on the show bench.

DIET: Mainly insects, including small beetles, butterflies and moths and their larvae, flies, spiders, some fruit such as berries.

HOUSING: Sheltered accommodation, about 6ft square would suffice for a pair, planted out with heather and gorse, where insects and spiders can abide. Large indoor cage during very harsh winters.

BREEDING: Breeds generally in gorse, or in long heather. The nest is built of stalks and bents, lined with finer grasses, sometimes hair and feathers. Eggs number three to four in a clutch. They have a ground colour white or faintly greenish, marbled and spotted with umber and ashy. Incubation is entirely by the female, the species is double brooded. In home-bred conditions, coconut fibre could be added to the nesting material offered. An open wicker basket situated near the bottom of aviary plants would, I believe, be taken up by the birds. Mealworms, buffalo worms and wax moth larvae should be added to the diet, especially when young are being raised.

CALL: The song is a subdued liquid warble, which lasts for some considerable time. Short bursts of song are also uttered on the wing. Its alarm call is a *pitcla-cla*, followed by repeated *tacks*. It sings in every month, chiefly March to May.

RING SIZE: Code B.

SHOWING REQUIREMENTS: Cage size 5, 18in long, 15in high and 12in wide, larger if possible. Painted black outside, white inside. Decorated to show off exhibit in a natural environment and with two springy perches. An exhibit should be as large as possible but of slender build, and with a nicely filled breast and head, neat wing and tail carriage, latter of good length and nicely graduated. Shown singly or in pairs.

LEGAL REQUIREMENTS: Specially protected at all times. Present law allows bird to be sold or shown if ringed and bred in captivity from legally held stock.

SPECIAL NOTES: Suffers in cold winters. Roosts in groups to conserve body heat.

Photograph by Tony Tilford

WHITETHROAT
Sylvia communis.
Related species: Lesser whitethroat, Dartford warbler, blackcap and garden warbler.

DESCRIPTION: Male in spring has an ash-grey head, upperparts are brown, underparts whitish, throat pure white; fore-breast rosy, wings and tail brown, wing coverts and secondaries edged with rusty brown. The outer tail feathers are white. The head of the female is of a duller brown. The young are like the female, but browner. Length 14cm (5½in).

STATUS IN THE WILD: Summer visitor with about 780,000 pairs in Britain, recovered from great population crash of 1969. Bird of the scrub, hedgerows, banks and woodland edges.

HARDBILL OR SOFTBILL? Softbill.

AVAILABILITY FOR BIRDKEEPERS: Generally available, at about £60 per bird.

ADVANTAGES TO KEEPING: To be recognised as one of the small group interested in the captive breeding of this species.

DISADVANTAGES TO KEEPING: Needs indoor quarters in winter.

DIET: Insects, including beetles, moths, caterpillars and flies, also spiders and their eggs and aphids and, in autumn, berries.

HOUSING: An outside, sheltered flight some 1.8m x 0.9m x 2m high (6ft x 3ft x 7ft) will house one pair. This should be planted out especially at the back, with honeysuckle, bramble and nettles to induce insects and provide cover and nesting sites. In winter, a cage in the birdroom fitted with two springy perches.

BREEDING: Generally two broods are reared in a season; nesting begins early May. Nests near the ground among nettles, brambles and hedges. The nest is a well-built open cup of dead grasses and bents lined with hair and down. The eggs are greenish-white or creamy spotted with brown, four or five to a clutch. Incubation lasts for 11-12 days, carried out by both parents though brooded continually by female for first few days. The chicks are naked, mouths pink with yellow edges and gape flanges pale yellow.

CALL: The alarm note is a scolding *churr*. Also a sharp and repeated *check* or *chuck*. The song is a vigorous warble, usually during its display flight. This is a loop in the air, just enough to sing its short song, landing with open wings down in the herbage.

RING SIZE: Closed ring, code C.

SHOWING REQUIREMENTS: Cage no smaller than 18in long 15in high and 12in wide, desk or box type painted black outside and white inside, with two springy perches and decorated in a manner that reflects the bird's habitat. An exhibit must be as large as possible of slender build, with well-filled breast, nice rise of forehead, gentle rise of shoulder to rump, neat wing and tail carriage, latter of good length and well tapered. Shown singly or in pairs.

LEGAL REQUIREMENTS: Fully protected. Not listed on any Schedule of the Wildlife and Countryside Act 1981. Can be sold or shown under terms of a General Licence.

SPECIAL NOTES: Often referred to in former times as nettle creeper. Sits closely.

Photograph by Tony Tilford

LESSER WHITETHROAT

Sylvia curruca.

Related species: Whitethroat, Dartford warbler, blackcap and garden warbler.

DESCRIPTION: The male in spring is slate-grey, with a brownish tinge on the back, brown wings and tail, the outer feathers of which are bordered with white. The chin and throat are also white, the breast and flanks are pale brown. The bill and legs are blueish-grey, the eyes yellowish-white, browner in young birds. The breast and flights are browner after the autumn moult. The female is very similar to the male. Length 12.7cm (5in). Smaller than the whitethroat.

STATUS IN THE WILD: Summer visitor. About 80,000 pairs in Great Britain. Inhabits scrub, hedgerows, woodland edges and larger gardens. More secretive than the whitethroat.

HARDBILL OR SOFTBILL? Softbill.

AVAILABILITY FOR BIRDKEEPERS: Regularly bred, and therefore available in small numbers, usually in the autumn, at about £70 each.

ADVANTAGES TO KEEPING: Well worthwhile, nice exhibition bird.

DISADVANTAGES TO KEEPING: For the experienced aviculturist, one who can supply the species' dietary needs and winter housing.

DIET: Chiefly insects and their larvae, including beetles, flies, ants and caterpillars; also spiders and aphides. Some fruit is taken.

HOUSING: Small, sheltered and planted outside aviary is ideal for one pair. Plants should include bramble, honeysuckle, hop and nettles. Several twiggy perches should be installed for movement and song. A roomy inside cage as winter quarters.

BREEDING: Breeds in hedgerows, thickets and shrubbery. Nest usually within a few feet of the ground. Home-bred birds will accept small wicker baskets fixed in foliage about 90cm (3ft) off the ground. Nest of grasses and dead plant stalks, lined with horsehair or fine roots. Four or five white eggs with bold markings and spots of dark brown and grey are laid in May. Incubation period 10-11 days, mainly by the female. The young are tendered by both parents, brooded by the female for the first few days. Young leave the nest when only able to flutter. This is to lessen predation in the wild. Livefood should be supplied in liberal quantities, especially when breeding is underway.

CALL: Alarm call is a sharp *tchek* which becomes a chatter when excited. Song is composed of a low prelude followed by an outburst of high notes, all at the same pitch.

RING SIZE: Code B, which should be fitted on the sixth day.

SHOWING REQUIREMENTS: Show cage is of box or desk type, no smaller than 18in long, 15in high and 12in deep. Painted black outside and white inside, suitably decorated to mimic bird's habitat, and with two springy perches. An exhibit should be as large as possible, of neat, sleek appearance, nicely filled body, well rounded head, with gentle rise of shoulder to rump, and neat wing and tail carriage. Shown singly or in pairs.

LEGAL REQUIREMENTS: Fully protected, not listed on any Schedule, but can be sold or exhibited under the terms of a General Licence.

SPECIAL NOTES: Leaves for northern Africa in late August and early September. Sits closely.

Photograph by Tony Tilford

GARDEN WARBLER
Sylvia borin.
Related species: Blackcap, whitethroat, lesser whitethroat and Dartford warbler.

DESCRIPTION: The species is plump and rather drab, with no obvious markings. During the summer months both sexes are olive brown above and white, shading into buff, beneath. The throat, breast and side of face are ashy grey. The tail is short and square shaped at the end. There are no white edges to the feathers. Moults in winter quarters. The bill is dark brown, paler at the base of both mandibles, the legs are lead-coloured and the eyes hazel. Hint of an eye-stripe and pale eye-ring. Length 12cm (5in).

STATUS IN THE WILD: Summer visitor April - October. About 200, 000 pairs breed in Britain.

HARDBILL OR SOFTBILL? Softbill.

AVAILABILITY FOR BIRDKEEPERS: Available to keepers, usually specialists. Species is being bred in British aviaries in small numbers.

ADVANTAGES TO KEEPING: Interesting species, both as a breeding subject, and as a show bird.

DISADVANTAGES TO KEEPING: None known.

DIET: Insects, including small beetles, flies, small caterpillars, also aphides, spiders and small worms, together with cherries, raspberries, currants, blackberries and berries of ivy, privet, elder and honeysuckle.

HOUSING: A small outside sheltered aviary will suffice for a pair of these delightful birds, within this should be planted a variety of plants, including small bushes, and climbers such as honeysuckle. These will be visited by insect life and provide suitable nesting sites for the birds.

BREEDING: The bird breeds in bushes, such as bramble, and thickets. The nest is built of grass stalks, and rather stouter than blackcap's and is lined with fine bents and some hair. The clutch comprises of four to five eggs, they have a ground colour which is yellowish or whitish, with yellowish brown spots and blotches. They are laid in mid-May, sometimes later. Incubation period is 11 or 12 days, the male shares the incubation. The species is single brooded. Home-bred pairs will use an open wicker basket, if it is sited low down in a bush or other vegetation. Live food comprises of its natural diet, together with mini mealworms, buffalo worms and wax moth larvae.

CALL: The song is wonderfully beautiful, a continuous mellow warble, more sustained than that of the blackcap. The alarm note teck resembles the sound of two pebbles being struck together.

RING SIZE: Code E, these should be fitted on the 6th day.

SHOWING REQUIREMENTS: Show cage must be 18in long, 15in high and 12in wide, or larger, painted black outside and white inside. Decorated to mimic species habitat in miniature, and with two springy perches. Exhibit must be as large as possible, of chubby appearance, stocky build, nicely rounded head, neat wing and tail carriage. Can be shown singly or in pairs.

LEGAL REQUIREMENTS: Fully protected. Not listed on any Schedule. General Licences in force allowing it to be sold or shown if ringed and bred in captivity.

SPECIAL NOTES: Local and other names: Pettychaps, fig bird.

Photograph by Tony Tilford

BLACKCAP

Sylvia atricapilla.

Related species: Garden warbler, whitethroat, lesser whitethroat and Dartford warbler.

DESCRIPTION: In the male bird the upperparts are blueish grey in spring, the back is tinged olive brown, and the darker primaries and tail have pale grey edges. The crown and nape are black. The underparts are paler grey, whitish on the chin and belly, brownest on the flanks. The bill is dark brown, the legs lead coloured and the eye hazel. The head colour of the female is rusty brown and is also more olive brown above and buffer below. After the moult there is a subdued change in feather colour. The young resemble the female at first, but by the autumn the young males have developed their black cap. Length 14cm (5½in).

STATUS IN THE WILD: The blackcap is a summer visitor to our shores, from Africa (some overwinter), widespread in most of England, Northern Ireland and in parts of Wales and Scotland. Around 800,000 pairs nest in the UK.

HARDBILL OR SOFTBILL? Softbill.

AVAILABILITY FOR BIRDKEEPERS: Favoured by a few keepers, usually a few available. A pair would cost £100.

ADVANTAGES TO KEEPING: Delightful species with a lovely song. Ready breeder in specialist care. Can be kept outside all year.

DISADVANTAGES TO KEEPING: Needs that little extra attention to maintain its health.

DIET: Insects of all kinds, including small beetles, caterpillars, flies, aphides and also spiders. Fruit and berries form a larger part of its diet during autumn and winter. These foods should be added to the diet of home-bred specimens when available, together with livefood and softfoods obtained from the market place.

HOUSING: A small, well-planted aviary, lots of shrubs should be planted within it including bramble, nettles, snowberry and honeysuckle. There should be a sheltered area and twiggy perches.

BREEDING: Nest rather flimsy, built with dead grasses, stems and bents, lined with finer bents and horse hair. Aviary pairs will occupy open wicker nest baskets, where coconut fibre and dog hair can be utilised. The clutch of eggs number four to five, these have light buff ground colour and are blotched with

brown of varying shades. Laying begins in late April or May. Incubation period is 10 or 11 days, both male and female take part, sometimes a second clutch is undertaken.

CALL: Short, sweet warble. It is heard from April until July, also has a sharp *tack* note and a churring sound .

RING SIZE: Code E, which has an internal diameter of 2.9mm.

SHOWING REQUIREMENTS: Size and type, as large as possible, full bodied, nicely filled breast, gentle rise of shoulder to rump, full-well round head. Neat wings and tail carriage. Tendency for female to be larger than male. Current-year birds have more brown suffusion.

LEGAL REQUIREMENTS: Non-scheduled species. General Licence in force which states "any bird sold or shown must be ringed with a legible, individually numbered metal close ring, which is a ring or band in a continuous circle (without a break, join, or any signs of tampering since it was manufactured) and which cannot be removed from the bird when its leg is fully grown". The bird must have been bred in captivity etc.

SPECIAL NOTES: Old, local names include hay jack, hay chat, mock nightingale, nettle creeper and nettle monger.

Photograph by Dennis Avon

WILLOW WARBLER

Phylloscopus trochilus.

Related species: Chiffchaff and wood warbler.

DESCRIPTION: Slim and delicate warbler, almost identical to chiffchaff, tends to be yellower than chiffchaff with clearer eye stripe and less obvious eye ring. Length 11cm (4¼in).

STATUS IN THE WILD: Summer visitor, arriving in March and April and departing in August and September. About 3,000,000 pairs breed in the British Isles. Inhabits broad-leaved woodland, mixed woodland, willow scrub, larger parks and gardens.

HARDBILL OR SOFTBILL? Regarded as a softbill.

AVAILABILITY FOR BIRDKEEPERS: Not taken up by many keepers, so some work involved to find aviary stock. Specimens would cost about £70 each.

ADVANTAGES TO KEEPING: Delicate little warbler. Challenge for breeders. Makes nice show bird.

DISADVANTAGES TO KEEPING: Difficult to obtain pairs. Specialised feeding required. Warm quarters also needed during the cold months.

DIET: Insectivorous – mostly flies, but also bees, beetles, and aphids. Young fed on larvae.

HOUSING: An aviary 1.8m square (6ft x 6ft) would be suitable for a pair of these delightful little birds. Planted out with small bushes and grasses, and with twiggy perches.

BREEDING: Breeding is from April to July. The nest is situated on the ground among coarse grass, made of dead grass, moss, dead fern fronds and leaves, lined with horsehair, cow-hair and feathers and is built by the female. It is domed in shape, with an entrance hole at the front. Four to eight eggs are laid, these are spotted and marked in a rusty-red shade. They are incubated by the female for 13 days. The young are tendered by both parents for between 13-16 days whilst in the nest and for a similar period after fledging. In home-bred conditions, domed wicker finch nest baskets would be taken up by the birds, if placed low down among the foliage of the flight. Obviously, the pair must be in a high state of condition to attempt breeding. Offspring can be fed on small mealworms, buffalo worms, pinkies, wax moth larvae and as many other tiny insects as can be supplied.

CALL: Alarm call, a plaintive *hweet*, note of anxiety a double *loo-ee*. Song, though simple, is wonderfully sweet, a cascade of pure descending notes.

RING SIZE: Code A.

SHOWING REQUIREMENTS: Cage desk or box type, no smaller than 18in long, 15in high and 12in wide, painted black outside, including wire front and white inside. Decorated out to imitate habitat of species, with two springy perches. Exhibit: As large as possible, of elegant build, nicely filled head and body, neat wing and tail carriage. Autumn plumage maybe somewhat duller. Shown singly or in pairs.

LEGAL REQUIREMENTS: Protected at all times. Not listed on any schedule, but can be shown or sold under current legislation, if ringed and bred in captivity from legally held stock.

SPECIAL NOTES: Local and other names: Willow wren, Peggy-whitethroat, oven bird, Jinny wren, Scotch wren, yellow wren, haybird, huckmuck, and ground wren. A close sitter.

Photograph by Tony Tilford

CHIFFCHAFF
Phylloscopus collybita.
Related species: Willow warbler, wood warbler.

DESCRIPTION: The olive-green upper body, yellowish on the rump, and with underparts tinged with grey on the breast and suffused with yellow, closely resembles the plumage of the willow warbler. The eye stripe is whitish and short. The bill and eye are brown, the legs dark, almost black. In the young birds the upperparts are browner, the underparts more yellow, and the breast is duller. Length 11cm (4¼in).

STATUS IN THE WILD: Summer visitor, with over 900,000 pairs. Chiffchaffs arrive as early as March. Some birds thought to arrive from Europe to winter here.

HARDBILL OR SOFTBILL? Known as a softbill.

AVAILABILITY FOR BIRDKEEPERS: Some are propagated each year. Interest lies with specialists. Sale birds are offered at around £60 each.

ADVANTAGES TO KEEPING: If special needs are met, they are reasonably easy to breed and maintain. They are hardy and very interesting.

DISADVANTAGES TO KEEPING: Not advisable for the faint-hearted or beginners. Keepers of birds must put the interest of any bird first.

DIET: Insects, including small beetles, flies, moths and caterpillars, spiders and aphides. Aviary stock will take any small invertebrates available on the open market!

HOUSING: The species requires a small planted aviary, suitable for a single pair. The birds will require plenty of ground cover, such as nettles and brambles. Best kept indoors in a roomy cage with springy perches in cold spells.

BREEDING: Nest often in yew tree and evergreen bushes; also in thick cover and bramble undergrowth in woods, near the ground. The nest is rather bulky, made of leaves, moss and stalks, domed with flattened entrance hole at side, lined with feathers. Eggs number three to nine, white sparsely marked with purplish spots. Laying begins in early May. The incubation period is about 13 days. The species is usually single brooded.

Captive pairs require natural, nesting material. Purchased live food could include mini mealworms, buffalo worms, small crickets and wax moth larvae. Domed foreign bird wicker nest baskets may be taken up by the birds; well worth trying, if used must be altered slightly to allow ringing.

CALL: Simple song of two notes - *chiffchaff*, sometimes a third note between the two.

RING SIZE: Code A.

SHOWING REQUIREMENTS: Show cage can be box or desk type, made of wood, with wire front, no smaller than 16in long, 13in high and 8in wide. Painted black outside and white inside. White utensils. Cage decoration carefully constructed to set birds off, to include two springy perches. Exhibit must be in fine fettle, with bright eye. Shown singly or in pairs.

LEGAL REQUIREMENTS: Fully protected, not listed on any Schedule of the Wildlife and Countryside Act 1981. General Licence in force allowing species to be shown if ringed and bred in captivity.

SPECIAL NOTES: Local and other names: least willow wren, lesser pettychaps, and choice and cheap. The chiffchaff's middle note described as *hedededet*!

Photograph by Tony Tilford

WOOD WARBLER

Phylloscopus sibilatrix.

Related species: Willow warbler and chiffchaff, collectively known as leaf warblers.

DESCRIPTION: Species slightly larger than the willow warbler or chiffchaff, has longer wings. Upperparts greenish, yellowish neck and breast, white belly. Yellow stripe over eye, legs also yellow. Juvenile similar to brightly coloured adult. Sexes are similar. Length 12.5cm (5in).

STATUS IN THE WILD: Summer visitor, arrives on its breeding grounds in May, leaves at the end of summer to overwinter in equatorial Africa. About 17,200 pairs, mainly in the west. Bird of the tree tops. Oak and beech woods favoured. About 30 pairs increasing in Ireland.

HARDBILL OR SOFTBILL? A tiny softbill.

AVAILABILITY FOR BIRDKEEPERS: Sometimes available at about £80 each.

ADVANTAGES TO KEEPING: Species suitable for very experienced keepers and makes an interesting show bird.

DISADVANTAGES TO KEEPING: Needs specialised all-round care, especially during the cold months. It's difficult to locate legal aviary pairs.

DIET: Insects, these include small beetles, moths, and caterpillars, also aphids and other invertebrates. Some berries taken in autumn.

HOUSING: Small, partly sheltered, fully-planted aviary with bushes and climbers. Wood warblers will take to domed wicker nests if placed well hidden in the undergrowth.

BREEDING: Prefers hilly terrain. Breeds in woodlands or well grown parkland. Nests on the ground within cover, a domed structure with side entrance hole. Made of dead leaves, stems, bark fibre, bracken and grass, lined with fine grass and hair, built by female, between May and June, usually single brooded. Eggs number six or seven, short, smooth and glossy, coloured white, profusely speckled with deep brown markings, varying from chocolate to reddish brown. Incubated by female for 13 days. The nestlings are downy, mouth bright, deep yellow, gape flanges pale yellow. Young fed by both parents for 11-12 days and for quite some time after fledging. Aviary pairs need specialised soft foods, together with insects, which can include wax moth larvae and buffalo worms.

CALL: Alarm note, a soft *duik* or *vit-vit-vit*. Song is a descending trill. Song flight around its territory among the branches, flies with shallow wing beats, keeps singing until it lands and finishes with a trill. Often alights by the female with quivering wings and fanned tail. More than one type of song.

RING SIZE: Code B, which has an internal diameter of 2.4mm.

SHOWING REQUIREMENTS: Show cage box or desk type, no smaller than 18in long, 15in high and 12in wide, painted black outside, including wire front and white inside, door on right. Decorated out with foliage to give impression of bird's habitat. Exhibit to be as large as possible, of elegant build, nicely filled head and body, neat wing and tail carriage. Distinct yellow legs, shown singly or in pairs.

LEGAL REQUIREMENTS: Protected at all times. Not listed on any Schedule. Can be sold or shown if bred in home conditions and ringed under current legislation.

SPECIAL NOTES: Local and other names: Wood wren, sits closely.

Photograph by Sergey Yeliseev

GOLDCREST

Regulus regulus.

Related species: Firecrest.

DESCRIPTION: Olive-green above and creamy buff beneath. The forehead, chin and throat are buff. A black line from the forehead passes on either side of the chrome-yellow crest, the rump in the male is deep orange. The wing has two white bars and a dark band. The legs are brown, and the eye almost black. The young are duller in colour and have no yellow in the crest. Length 9cm (3½in). This and the firecrest are the smallest European birds.

STATUS IN THE WILD: Common species, resident and partial migrant. About 860,000 pairs. Breeds widely in the UK and Republic of Ireland.

HARDBILL OR SOFTBILL? Softbill.

AVAILABILITY TO BIRDKEEPERS: Very rare in captivity.

ADVANTAGES TO KEEPING: Exhibition birds would do well on show bench if nicely displayed.

DISADVANTAGES TO KEEPING: Would employ the dedication of a talented specialist to keep this species in good health and vigour.

DIET: Chiefly small insects and their larvae, including small beetles, flies, etc. plus spiders and various blights on trees.

HOUSING: A sheltered aviary containing small conifers would be ideal, and planted out with honeysuckle and hop to entice insect life. A shallow pool could be included; this would also bring in insects.

BREEDING: Usually the nest of the goldcrest is affixed to the lower side of a branch of a tree such as a yew, Scots pine or fir, less frequently on the upper side; also in ivy or furze bushes. It is built of green moss and spiders' webs, lined with feathers and is of the cup-shaped design. The eggs which number seven to ten, sometimes more, are white or light buff in ground colour, with fine brownish spots tending to form a cup at the larger end. They are laid towards the end of April. Incubation is between 15-17 days, believed to be by the female alone. The species is usually single brooded. The nestlings have down on their heads, short and sparse and of a blackish-grey shade. The mouth is orange, gape flanges pinkish-white. Young are tendered by both parents. Their eyes open on the seventh or eighth day, they leave the nest between 16-21 days.

In captivity small wicker baskets fastened beneath suitable branches, would encourage nest building. Their natural food should be supplemented with small mealworms.

CALL: The song comprises of two notes repeated five or six times ending with a rapid trill, quite sweet and very quiet to the ear. It has several call notes, one of which sounds like *se-se-s*. The bird sings from February until November.

SHOWING REQUIREMENTS: Cage no smaller than 18in long, 15in high and 12in wide, painted black outside including wire front, white inside, decorated with sprigs of conifer and two springy perches. Any exhibit must be in good health and condition, with bright eye and confident in its movements. Shown singly or in pairs.

RING SIZE: Code A.

LEGAL REQUIREMENTS: Fully protected, non-scheduled bird. Can be sold or shown under terms of General Licences if ringed and bred in captivity.

SPECIAL NOTES: Local and other names: Gold-crested wren, crowned kinglet and woodcock pilot. The latter derived from the fact that, as a winter visitor, it precedes that bird by a few days.

Photograph by Tony Tilford

FIRECREST

Regulus ignicapillus.

Related species: Goldcrest.

DESCRIPTION: Above the eye is a broad almost- white stripe, and below a narrower one, whilst through the eye, dividing the white face, is a conspicuous black line, or eye stripe. The ear-coverts are slate-grey, and there is a slight moustachial streak. On the side of the neck is a yellowish patch, and the upperparts are greener and the lower whiter than in the goldcrest. Length 9cm (3½in).

STATUS IN THE WILD: Autumn visitor to Great Britain, chiefly on eastern side, also resident with about 50 breeding pairs. Found in coniferous and deciduous woodlands. The firecrest has extended its range over recent times in Wales, the New Forest, South-east Kent and on the Suffolk coast.

HARDBILL OR SOFTBILL? Softbill.

AVAILABILITY FOR BIRDKEEPERS: Very few available, simply due to lack of interest.

ADVANTAGES TO KEEPING: Delightful species, offering a real challenge to the specialist breeder.

DISADVANTAGES TO KEEPING: Only suitable for the very experienced keeper.

DIET: Chiefly small insects and their larvae, small beetles and flies, also spiders and aphides.

HOUSING: A small outside flight with a shelter is ideal. Very small mesh would be appropriate, to prevent mice coming in or the birds getting out. Plenty of foliage would bring in insects, ivy, honeysuckle, and small conifers would suit the inmates.

BREEDING: The species sometimes places its nest like the goldcrest under branches of conifer, but also against tree trunks, in ivy or in bushes. It is built of down or moss, according to locality, and is lined with feathers. The clutch of eggs number seven to eleven, their ground colour is pinkish or reddish, with a tinge of yellow and lightly marked. The breeding period is from April to May. Incubation period is 14-15 days by female alone. The nestlings have down on their heads. They are tendered by both parents for nearly 3 weeks in the nest and for about the same period after fledging. In captivity, small wicker baskets fixed under branches would attract the birds. Live food should be as varied as possible.

This could include small fly maggots and mini-mealworms.

CALL: Song is a high pitched crescendo of rather similar notes; *see-see-see-see-see-see-scirr*.

RING SIZE: Code A.

SHOWING REQUIREMENTS: Softbill Cage No.5, length 18in, height 15in, width 12in, painted black outside and white inside, with white food and water containers. Cage interior, decorated to suit the exhibit, with two springy perches. Shown singly or in pairs.

LEGAL REQUIREMENTS: The bird is listed on Schedule 1, Part 1 of the Wildlife and Countryside Act 1981 and is specially protected at all times. Captive bred and close-ringed specimens can be sold or shown under the terms of a General Licence.

SPECIAL NOTES: It is most unlikely that many examples of this species will be seen on the show bench in the near future.

Photograph by Tony Tilford

SPOTTED FLYCATCHER

Muscicapa striata.

Related species: Other flycatchers are from a different genera.

DESCRIPTION: Recognised by its habit of perching on posts and making short excursions into the air in pursuit of flies. Upperparts mostly ash-brown, with dark brown streaks, bristles on gape. Bird gets its name from dress of young, which unlike mature birds are mottled or spotted on upperparts with buff. Sexes very similar. Length 14cm (5½in).

STATUS IN THE WILD: Summer visitor, wintering in tropical Africa. In Britain, about 150,000 pairs. Has declined in numbers over recent years, possibly due to problems encountered in its winter quarters.

HARDBILL OR SOFTBILL? Regarded by the fancy as a softbill.

AVAILABILITY FOR BIRDKEEPERS: A few bred each year, so occasionally available.

ADVANTAGES FOR KEEPING: Interesting subject to study.

DISADVANTAGES TO KEEPING: More suited to the specialist with required knowledge of its dietary needs, and accommodation. Somewhat delicate.

DIET: Insects, chiefly flies, also moths, butterflies, wasps, bees, small beetles; most caught on the wing.

HOUSING: A small, partly sheltered aviary about 6ft x 3ft x 7ft would suit a breeding pair. This should be planted with flowering bushes, ivy and honeysuckle. Posts and perches should be positioned at each end of the aviary for song and exercise. Open nest boxes inside shelter, about 5ft up, and in foliage, would encourage breeding. Insects are required all through the year, these should be supplemented with a good quality insectivorous mixture. Insects should include flies, wax moth larvae, small mealworms and buffalo worms. Flies (from maggots) rising from a container into the flight would induce natural hunting - a brood could be reared this way.

BREEDING: The species nest in ivy on walls, or branches of fruit trees, and on projecting beams or trellis etc. Will use open nest box. Nest is slight, built of oak flowers, mosses, cobwebs, and lined with hair. Eggs number four to five, the ground colour ranges from blueish-green to greyish, with spots of reddish-brown. Laying begins in mid May. Incubation period is between 12-14 days, both sexes take part. Sometimes two broods are reared.

CALL: A weak chirp and a harsh call note.

RING SIZE: Code B.

SHOWING REQUIREMENTS: Show cage desk or box type, size 18in long, 15in high and 12in wide. Painted black outside and white inside, with door on right. Suitably decorated to give an impression of habitat, perhaps a wall with clinging ivy and two thin perches. Exhibit to be of good feather, with bright eye, well trained. Shown occasionally. Singly or pairs.

LEGAL REQUIREMENTS: Not listed on any Schedule of the Wildlife and Countryside Act 1981. Can be shown under terms of General Licence if bred in captivity from legally held stock and if close-ringed.

SPECIAL NOTES: Arrives in early May, leaves September or October. Local and other names: Beam bird, rafter, chanchider, cherry-sucker, bee-eater, post bird, and cherry chopper. Sits closely and flies away without demonstration when disturbed.

Photograph by Dennis Avon

PIED FLYCATCHER

Ficedula hypoleuca.

Related species: Collared flycatcher and red-breasted flycatcher.

DESCRIPTION: The adult male has upperparts black, the forehead is white, rump greyish, wings black, with large white patch, the tail is black, the outer three feathers have most of their outer web white, except the tips. The female is olive brown above, buffish beneath, the throat and belly white, tail as in male, but not so bright. The young have whitish or buff patches on wings. Legs, toes and claws are black, eye dark brown. Length 13cm (5in).

STATUS IN THE WILD: Summer visitor, wintering in West Africa. In Britain about 40,000 pairs located in north and west. Inhabits hilly and wooded districts with rapid streams.

HARDBILL OR SOFTBILL? Deemed a softbill within the fancy.

AVAILABILITY FOR BIRDKEEPERS: Available in small numbers, individuals cost about £70 each.

ADVANTAGES TO KEEPING: Endearing subject, make very attractive show birds especially when shown as a pair, due to their plumage differences.

DISADVANTAGES TO KEEPING: Keeper needs some softbill keeping experience. Birds require inside accommodation during the winter.

DIET: Mainly insects, chiefly flies, but also small beetles, butterflies, moths and their larvae, earwigs and ants, also worms and grubs. Birds catch some prey in the air.

HOUSING: Best suited to an elaborate aviary, consisting of plenty of bushes, climbers, and grasses, with running water, also with old timbers and convenient perches. Tit-like nest boxes fixed at least 4ft up for their use.

BREEDING: The species nests in natural holes in trees and stumps, also in old buildings and loose stone walls. The nest is loosely constructed of moss, strips of outer bark of honeysuckle and roots, lined with hair and sometimes a few feathers. The eggs number five to seven in a clutch, colour pale blue, they are laid in May. The incubation is by the female alone for a period of 12-13 days, fed by the male; beginning with the last egg. The young are tendered by both parents, but mainly by the female for 13-16 days, and for a similar period when the chicks have fledged. In home-bred conditions, their insect diet should include fly larvae (maggots), mealworms, buffalo worms and wax moth larvae.

CALL: The song, a very delightful descending cadenza, uttered rapidly, resembling the redstart. Usual call note, *whit* or *wet*.

RING SIZE: Code B.

SHOWING REQUIREMENTS: Show cage; length 18in, height 15in, width 12in, painted black outside, including wire front, with white interior. Food and water vessels inside. Floor covering optional, but to catch the judges eye, should be nicely decorated out to give a semblance of natural habitat. Exhibits must be as large as possible, in good health and excellent feather, correctly trained to show no nervousness. Size and type: 35 points, colour and markings: 35 points. Feather quality and condition: 15 points and steadiness and staging 15 points. Total 100.

LEGAL REQUIREMENTS: Unscheduled species. Protected at all times. Can be sold or shown under complicated terms of General Licence if ringed and bred in captivity.

SPECIAL NOTES: Often returns to the same nest site year after year. Other name: Coldfinch. A close sitter.

Photograph by Sergey Yeliseev

BEARDED TIT

Panurus biarmicus.

Related species: No close relatives.

DESCRIPTION: The bird is recognised by its rounded, fawn-coloured tail. Its upperparts are deep tawny, the underparts greyish white with a rosy tinge, the tail coverts are black. The male has a blueish-grey head with black moustache from eye to beak. Its outer tail feathers are tipped with white. The female lacks the moustache and head tawny, passing into greyish white. The back is more or less lined with black. Young birds are more golden, with blackish backs. Length 16.5cm (6½in).

STATUS IN THE WILD: In recent years there has been a growing emphasis on protection. This together with milder winters, has enabled the species to increase its numbers. Resident with about 400 pairs.

HARDBILL OR SOFTBILL? In aviculture, the bearded tit is classed as a softbill.

AVAILABILITY FOR BIRDKEEPERS: Available as birds are being bred in British aviaries. Aviary specimens also available from European sources.

ADVANTAGES TO KEEPING: Delightful to observe.

DISADVANTAGES TO KEEPING: Species needs specialist attention.

DIET: Insects in summer, mainly seeds in winter.

HOUSING: Can be kept in colonies or in pairs, need quite large, sheltered quarters, with reeds and pools. Reeds cut and tied in bundles, placed in strategic positions will also serve as nest and roosting sites.

BREEDING: In the wild, the nest is made among thick sedges or reeds and close to the ground. It is made of pieces of dead reed leaves and is lined with flowering heads of reeds and feathers. It is cup-shaped. Aviary birds utilise the conditions available. Keepers should provide a near natural setting for them. Eggs number five to seven and are white with short streaks and specks of brown. Laying begins in early April. The incubation period is 12-13 days. Both sexes take part.

CALL: The species has no song. The usual call is a disyllabic *ping-ping*, extremely distinctive once learned. When alarmed, bird utters a scolding sound.

RING SIZE: Code E, which is 2.9mm internal diameter. It should be placed on the leg on the fifth day.

SHOWING REQUIREMENTS: A show bird should be as large as possible, nicely rounded head, gentle rise from shoulder to rump, with neat wings and tail carriage. The latter of good length and graduated. Desk or box-type cages should be at least 18in long x 15in high x 12in wide. Can be shown singly or in pairs.

LEGAL REQUIREMENTS: Listed on Schedule 1 of the Wildlife and Countryside Act 1981. Birds protected by special penalties at all times. Can be sold or shown under the Act and its regulations.

SPECIAL NOTES: The bearded tit or bearded reedling is not a titmouse at all, but belongs to an Asian family, the parrotbills. Its bill however, is tit-like.

Photograph by Tony Tilford

WILLOW TIT

Parus montanus.

Related species: Marsh tit, coal tit, Siberian tit, sombre tit, blue tit, great tit and crested tit.

DESCRIPTION: Similar in size and appearance to marsh tit, but looks less smart. Adult has black cap extending down to mantle. Black bib quite extensive, with poorly defined borders. Tail is roundly ended. Length 11.5cm (4½in).

STATUS IN THE WILD: Resident in Britain with 60,000 pairs (England and Wales). Absent from the Fens, north Scotland, north Wales, Isle of Man and Ireland. Despite its name, the willow tit prefers damp, scrubby areas of elder, alder and birch.

HARDBILL OR SOFTBILL? Regarded as a softbill.

AVAILABILITY FOR BIRDKEEPERS: Some available most years.

ADVANTAGES TO KEEPING: Durable little bird, active, easy to breed and ideal show bird.

DISADVANTAGES TO KEEPING: Lack of interest in the species among fanciers.

DIET: Many insects, spiders and other invertebrates during breeding season, seeds and berries at other times.

HOUSING: Aviary no smaller than 1.8m long x 1.8m high x 0.9m wide (6ft x 6ft x 3ft), planted out with a few berry bushes, and fitted with twiggy perches. Tit type nest boxes fixed about two feet above the ground. Can be filled up with chipping as birds like to excavate their own cavity.

BREEDING: Cavity and nest made by female, lined with wood fragments, sometimes sparsely lined with hair or feathers. The breeding begins in April. The species is single brooded. Usually six to nine, white, variably spotted and speckled eggs are laid, these are incubated by the female alone, fed by the male; beginning with the last egg, for 13-15bdays. Young very similar to marsh tit. They are tendered by both parents for 17-19 days.

CALL: A buzzy *eez-eez-eez* song, which is rarely heard, consists of a liquid warble.

RING SIZE: Code A.

SHOWING REQUIREMENTS: Show cage box or desk type, No smaller than 18in long, 15in high and 12in wide. Painted black outside, including wire front and white inside, with door on right. Food and water vessels inside cage. Pleasantly decorated out to suit inmate(s), with bark and ferns etc. Exhibit size and type: As large as possible, full, nicely rounded head on well filled body. Neat wing and tail carriage, latter with inverted V end. Colour and markings: Upperparts grey-brown, wings and tail glossy black extending into nape area, the crown area is dull not glossy, bib slightly more expansive than marsh tit, cheeks and underparts whitish, nicely suffused buff upper breast and flanks. Sexes alike. Note: Typical tit species, active action, but to move with confidence. Shown singly or in pairs.

LEGAL REQUIREMENTS: Protected at all times. Not listed on any Schedule of the Wildlife and Countryside Act 1981. Can be shown under General Licence.

SPECIAL NOTES: Apparently some gardeners have persuaded the species to breed in nest-boxes filled with expanded polystyrene, which can then be removed by the birds to a level of their liking.

Photograph by Tony Tilford

MARSH TIT

Parus palustris.

Related species: Willow tit, coal tit, Siberian tit, sombre tit, blue tit, great tit and crested tit.

DESCRIPTION: Almost identical to willow tit with one or two subtle exceptions. The head, except cheeks and throat are glossy blue-black, sides of head dull white, upperparts greyish olive brown; wings and tail mostly ash brown; underparts dull white with buff on flanks. Willow tit has dull black head, calls and breeding behaviour also differ. Length 11.5cm (4½in).

STATUS IN THE WILD: Resident in Britain, about 140,000 breeding pairs. Tends to occupy open woodland, especially damp woods, copses, parks and gardens.

HARDBILL OR SOFTBILL? Known as a softbill.

AVAILABILITY FOR BIRDKEEPERS: Often available, as a few are home-bred each year. Cost about £60 each.

ADVANTAGES TO KEEPING: Easy to maintain due to diet, hardy and interesting to study.

DISADVANTAGES TO KEEPING: Not of high potential as a show bird.

DIET: Consume both insect and vegetable matter. Small insects of many kinds, including small beetles, seeds and berries also taken. Frequent visitor to bird table, where sunflower seeds are favoured.

HOUSING: Small, well planted aviary, with some shelter will suffice a pair of these acrobatic little birds. A sheltered bird table placed therein, with scattered food items would be an attraction.

BREEDING: Usually breeds in a natural hole in a tree stump or in the trunk of a tree, such as willow or alder. Sometimes birds will enlarge a hole in order to nest in it. Nest boxes are also used occasionally. The nest is built of green moss, with a thick lining of hair or down. The eggs number seven to eight, they are white, spotted chiefly at the large end with red-brown. The species begins to lay at the end of April. Incubation is by female alone, fed on the nest by the male, for 13-17 days. The nestlings have down on their head and back, the mouth is buffish yellow. The gape-flanges are pale yellow. Young are tendered by both parents. Female broods young for 9-10 days, they remain in the nest for several further days. After fledging are tendered by both parents for a further week. In captivity nest boxes should be affixed to old stumps, quite low to the aviary floor. Live food of as many varieties as possible will sustain the chicks until they are self sufficient.

CALL: Song *chit-a-bee-be-be-be*. Usual call, a harsh *tchee tchee*. Song period is chiefly January to July.

RING SIZE: Code C.

SHOWING REQUIREMENTS: Size and type: As large as possible. Full, nicely rounded head on well filled body. Neat wings and tail carriage, latter with inverted V end. Upperparts: grey brown wings and tail. Crown glossy black extending into nape area. Black, well filled bib, cheeks and underparts whitish, nicely suffused buff upper breast and flanks. Sexes alike. Show cage: Length 18in, height 15in, width 12in, painted black outside, white inside, decorated with a woodland effect, and two springy perches. Shown singly or in pairs.

LEGAL REQUIREMENTS: Not listed on any Schedule. Fully protected. Can be sold or shown under terms of General Licence if ringed and bred in captivity.

SPECIAL NOTES: Other names; black cap, little black-headed tomtit, willow bitter, and coalhead. Sits closely, and hisses and bites when disturbed.

Photograph by Tommy Milner

BLUE TIT

Parus caeruleus.

Related species: Willow tit, marsh tit, coal tit, Siberian tit, sombre tit, great tit and crested tit.

DESCRIPTION: The azure blue crown, and dark blue line that passes through the eye and encircles the white cheeks to the chin, give the blue tit a very distinctive appearance. The nape, wings and tail are blue; the back is yellowish green; the underparts mostly sulphur-yellow with a dark line down the belly, the legs blueish grey and the eye is dark brown. The male appears to be of a slightly brighter hue than the female. The chicks are much paler when they emerge from the nest. Length around 12cm (5in).

STATUS IN THE WILD: Resident in Britain, with about 4.5 million pairs.

HARDBILL OR SOFTBILL? Known to the fancy as a softbill.

AVAILABILITY FOR BIRDKEEPERS: Very few available due to lack of interest within the hobby. If you wanted one, specimens would cost from £50 each.

ADVANTAGES TO KEEPING: Very hardy, easy to keep and maintain due to their varied diet and very interesting to observe.

DISADVANTAGES TO KEEPING: Limited reasons for keeping the species within the fancy, due to lack of interest and negative attitude in relation to show birds.

DIET: Insects and their larvae of all kinds, also spiders, seeds of trees and plants, such as great reed mace during the winter months. Regular to bird tables, with a liking for peanuts and scraps.

HOUSING: Best kept outside in a small flight, with growing plants, and with a shelter provided, perhaps in the form of a nest box.

BREEDING: Nests in holes in trees and walls etc, nest-boxes readily taken. The nest is made of moss and some grass, lined with softer material such as hair, down or feathers. Eggs number between 8 and 11; their ground colour is white, sometimes quite unmarked, but as a rule, spotted sparingly or freely with red-brown. The blue tit is single-brooded. If housed in captivity, nest-boxes would be required, livefood to include small mealworms, buffalo worms and wax moth larvae. A bird table should be set up within the enclosure, where peanuts could be offered.

CALL: Alarm call *tsee-tsee-tsee*. Song very clear, pure notes followed by a series of deeper trills.

RING SIZE: Code C, which has an internal diameter of 2.5mm.

SHOWING REQUIREMENTS: Size and type: as large as possible. Full, nicely round head with good rise, on well-filled body. Neat wing and tail carriage, latter full with inverted V end. Typical tit species - active action but to move with confidence. Shown singly or in pairs.

LEGAL REQUIREMENTS: Unscheduled under Wildlife and Countryside Act 1981, but fully protected. Can be sold or shown under General Licence if ringed and captive-bred.

SPECIAL NOTES: A tight sitter, hisses like a snake when disturbed. Local and other names include Tom tit, blue Tom tit, Billy biter, willow biter, blue bonnet, blue cap, blue mope, hickwall, nun, and titmal.

Photograph by Tony Tilford

GREAT TIT

Parus major.

Related species: Willow tit, marsh tit, coal tit, Siberian tit, sombre tit, blue tit and crested tit.

DESCRIPTION: The head, neck, and a streak of varying width from the chin to the centre of the otherwise white under tail-coverts are glossy blue-black; the cheeks and ear-coverts are white. A pale, often white, nape spot shades into yellow and then into olive-green on the back and mantle; the rump, tail and most of the wing are blue. There is a very conspicuous white bar on the wing, and the outer tail feathers are white-edged. The underparts, except for the black streak, are sulphur-yellow. The bill is black, the legs and feet lead-blue, and eyes dark brown. The sexes are alike. The young are duller, with the black replaced by dark brown, and the white suffused with yellow. Length 14cm (5½in).

STATUS IN THE WILD: Resident, comprising about 2 million pairs.

HARDBILL OR SOFTBILL? Softbill.

AVAILABILITY FOR BIRDKEEPERS: Usually available. Purchase price about £60 each.

ADVANTAGES TO KEEPING: Easy to breed, hardy species and interesting to observe.

DISADVANTAGES TO KEEPING: Not particularly popular- fewer kept than coal tit or long-tailed tit.

DIET: A regular visitor to bird tables. Insect food comprises of beetles, moths and their larvae, especially those of the destructive winter moth, larvae of flies, bees and earwigs, also aphides, scale insects, spiders, worms, corn kernels, and various nuts.

HOUSING: An outside, vermin proof and sheltered aviary, measuring 1.8m x 0.9m x 2.1m high (6ft x 3ft x 7ft), would be suitable for a pair of these beautiful birds. It should be suitably stocked with climbing plants and nettles, to attract insects, together with suitable perches. The birds would either roost in nooks and crannies or in any nest box provided.

BREEDING: The species normally breed in holes in trees or walls, and readily takes to nest boxes. The nest is built of moss and a few grasses, the cup is lined with feathers and down. The eggs in a clutch number seven to eleven typically spotted with red or brown. The eggs are covered up during laying. Nest boxes placed at various heights would be eagerly taken up by the birds. Ideally the top (roof) should be hinged for access by the keeper. Their usual food can easily be supplemented by the numerous types of invertebrates available on the market.

CALL: The great tits' familiar ringing call is expressed as *teacher, teacher, teah*. The alarm is *sha-sha*. It also has a single note not unlike the chaffinch.

RING SIZE: Code E.

SHOWING REQUIREMENTS: Cage should be no smaller than 18in long, 15in high and 12in deep. Exhibit should be as large as possible, of strong appearance, full, well rounded head with good rise and front cushion, well filled breast and gentle rise of shoulder to rump, neat wing and tail carriage, latter full with inverted V end.

LEGAL REQUIREMENTS: Fully protected, not listed on any Schedule of the Wildlife and Countryside Act 1981. Legislation allows sale and exhibition.

SPECIAL NOTES: Sometimes known as oxeye, pickcheese, bee biter, Tom Collier, and 'sit-ye-down'. Sits closely and hisses when disturbed.

Photograph by Tony Tilford

COAL TIT

Parus ater.

Related species: Willow tit, marsh tit, Siberian tit, sombre tit, blue tit, great tit and crested tit.

DESCRIPTION: The head, throat and neck are glossy blue-black, setting off the white of the nape and sides of the face; the back and wings are olive brown shading to brownish fawn on the rump; there is a double white bar on the wing. The underparts are white, shading through buff to pale reddish on the flanks. The bill is black, the legs are lead coloured and the eye dark brown. The young are duller, the black head having no sheen, and the wings, nape and cheeks are tinged with yellow. Length 11.5cm (4½in).

STATUS IN THE WILD: The coal tit is resident in the British Isles, with about 900,000 pairs. Commonest in conifer habitats.

HARDBILL OR SOFTBILL? Softbill.

AVAILABILITY FOR BIRDKEEPERS: Kept by a few keen breeders. Specimens fetch about £50 each.

ADVANTAGES TO KEEPING: Specimens add colour and charm to any collection of small softbills.

DISADVANTAGES TO KEEPING: None known.

DIET: Largely insects, including beetles and their larvae, larvae and eggs of moths, larvae of flies, also spiders, aphides, beech mast, seeds of some conifers, seeds of thistles and nuts including peanuts from bird tables.

HOUSING: Small, outside aviary is preferred with a shelter, suitable for one pair, ideal if nicely planted out with small conifers. Those in tubs are fine, and climbers such as hop and honeysuckle.

BREEDING: These birds begin their nesting activities in April, the eggs being laid towards the end of the month. In the wild they frequently build in a mouse hole in a bank, sometimes in a stump, tree or wall. The nest is made of mosses with a very warm layer of down or hair. Eggs usually number eight to eleven, their colour is white, with reddish brown spots, sometimes forming a well marked area. The species is single brooded.

In captivity, their needs should be simulated, natural sites and nest boxes would be used. Added food could consist of mini mealworms, buffalo worms and wax moth larvae.

CALL: Sings in every month of the year. Contact call is a high pitched *see* or *tsee*. Song is of repeated phrases.

RING SIZE: Code B is recommended, placed on the leg about the fourth day.

SHOWING REQUIREMENTS: Cage painted black outside including front, white inside, with door constructed in right end; size no smaller than 18ins long, 15ins high and 12ins deep. Tastefully decorated to mimic habitat of exhibit, and with two springy perches. Exhibit to be as large as possible, full, well rounded head, set on well filled, compact body. Neat wing and tail carriage. Bright eye, active, and to move with confidence. Often seen at shows. Can be shown singly or in pairs.

LEGAL REQUIREMENTS: Fully protected, not listed on any Schedule. Can be sold or shown under General Licence.

SPECIAL NOTES: Local and other names - cole mouse, coal titmouse, coalhead. Sits closely and hisses when disturbed.

Photograph by Tommy Milner

CRESTED TIT

Parus cristatus.

Related species: Blue tit, great tit, coal tit, marsh tit, willow tit, Siberian tit and sombre tit.

DESCRIPTION: The upperparts of this rarity are buffish brown, darker on the wings and tail; the under side from dull white to light brown. The head is crowned by the crest in which the black feathers have white margins, giving it a speckled appearance in front, but streaked towards the nape, where the feathers are elongated and pointed. From the eye to the nape a black line runs to join another which curves round the white cheeks, below this, but separated from it by a white band, is a black collar, forming in front a gorget and extending to the chin. The bill is black, the legs lead blue and the eyes brown. Juveniles have shorter crests. Length 11.5cm (4½in).

STATUS IN THE WILD: 900 pairs are resident in Scotland, absent elsewhere in Britain.

HARDBILL OR SOFTBILL? Softbill.

AVAILABILITY FOR BIRDKEEPERS: Specimens could be acquired from European keepers.

ADVANTAGES TO KEEPING: I have watched these birds in the wild and they are delightful.

DISADVANTAGES TO KEEPING: None known.

DIET: Chiefly insects, caterpillars of moths, also aphides, small seeds, berries of the juniper, and nuts from bird tables. Will store seeds of pine cones for later use. Join other tit flocks, usually seen in small numbers.

HOUSING: A small, sheltered flight or aviary would suit a single pair. Small potted conifers, old, dead stumps, and climbers such as honeysuckle would give the inmates hunting opportunities.

BREEDING: In the wild crested tits excavate nesting holes in stumps. Captive birds would use nest boxes affixed to stumps. The nest is made of moss lined with hair, often deer or hare in the wild, but dog hair would be ideal in home-bred conditions. Eggs number five or six in a clutch, quite heavily marked at the larger end. Laying begins at the end of April. Incubation is carried out by the female alone for between 13-15 days. The species is single brooded.

CALL: High pitched double note, similar to other tits, and a *purring choor*, repeated as a song.

RING SIZE: Code E.

SHOWING REQUIREMENTS: Size and type large as possible, well filled head and body, nicely raised crest, neat wing and tail carriage. Excellent condition with bright eye. Typical tit species, active action, but to move with confidence. Cage: No smaller than 45cm long x 38cm high x 30cm wide (18in x 15in x 12in). Painted black outside and white inside. Decorated to mimic habitat of species and with two springy perches. Shown singly or in pairs.

LEGAL REQUIREMENTS: Listed on Schedule 1 of the Wildlife and Countryside Act 1981, and specially protected. Can be sold or shown on General Licence.

SPECIAL NOTES: In Scotland, inhabits the remnant fragments of old Caledonian pine forest in the Highlands, especially Speyside.

Photograph by Tony Tilford

LONG-TAILED TIT

Aegithalos caudatus.

Related species: No close relatives in Britain.

DESCRIPTION: A long tail and pink and black plumage in essence, describes the species, the head is white striped with black, the eyelid is orange-red; the back is black and mixed rose, the underparts white, with striations on throat and breast, rest grey, wings and tail chiefly black. The sexes are alike. The young lack the rose colour. The tail makes up more than half of the bird's total length. Length 14cm (5½in).

STATUS IN THE WILD: Resident in Britain with about 250,000 pairs.

HARDBILL OR SOFTBILL? Softbill.

AVAILABILITY FOR BIRDKEEPERS: Pairs available from time to time, more bred in aviary conditions now than ever before. Cost about £60 each.

ADVANTAGES TO KEEPING: Delightful species, present challenge to an experienced keeper. Makes nice show bird.

DISADVANTAGES TO KEEPING: Difficult to keep in good condition, unless keeper is prepared to understand its needs and provide them.

DIET: Almost entirely insects, small beetles, small moths etc., also spiders, scale insects, centipedes and buds. Sometimes visits bird table for titbits such as peanuts. Practically never comes down to the ground for food. The species forage numbers of trees in rotation, depending on the season.

HOUSING: A small, well planted aviary is essential, nicely planted out with insects in mind.

BREEDING: Built in thorn bushes, brambles, thickets, gorse and hedgerows, the nest is a beautiful structure, dome shaped, with an entrance hole high up on one side, built chiefly of moss, hair, cobwebs and completely covered with lichens, this fits in well with the surroundings. The interior is lined with hundreds of feathers. The eggs usually number eight or nine, white, sometimes unmarked, but generally with fine spots. They are laid in late March, early for such a small bird. The incubation period is 15-17 days. A second brood is sometimes undertaken. Aviary stock require a great variety of invertebrates when young are being reared.

CALL: Wandering flocks keep in touch with their *tzee, tzee, tzee* calls, as they forage through the trees. There is also a harsh alarm note. The song is a thin trill.

RING SIZE: Code B, which has an internal diameter of 2.4mm.

SHOWING REQUIREMENTS: Size and type: As large as possible, cobby-bodied, long tailed. Nicely rounded head, full breast with good rise of shoulder to rump. Neat wing and tail carriage, latter nicely graduated. Typical tit species. Active action but to move with confidence. Show cage box or desk optional, size no smaller than 18in long, 12in wide and 15in high, painted black outside including the wire front and white inside. It should be tastefully decorated out to give a natural look to the observer and judge. Two springy perches are essential. Shown singly or in pairs.

LEGAL REQUIREMENTS: Fully protected at all times. Not listed on any schedule, but can be sold or shown due to terms of General Licences providing bird is close ringed and bred in captivity from aviary bred stock.

SPECIAL NOTES: Other names: Bottle brush, mufflin, poke pudding, bottle tit, mum ruffin, and many more. Sits closely with tip of tail protruding from the entrance hole.

Photograph by Tommy Milner

NUTHATCH

Sitta europaea.

Related species: No close relatives in British Isles.

DESCRIPTION: The bird is blue-grey above, whitish throat, and creamy yellow or rusty below. There is a black stripe that runs through the eye to nape and sides of head, white below it. The flanks are chestnut, outer tail feathers have white area. Sexes are similar. Agile and beautifully balanced in its climbing technique. Length 14cm (5½in).

STATUS IN THE WILD: Resident in Britain with about 50,000 pairs. Bird of old woodlands and parks where big trees exist.

HARDBILL OR SOFTBILL? Judged as a softbill.

AVAILABILITY FOR BIRDKEEPERS: Frequently bred in home conditions, available at a cost of about £80 each.

ADVANTAGES TO KEEPING: Hardy, easy to breed and delightful to watch.

DISADVANTAGES TO KEEPING: Stores surplus food around the aviary.

DIET: Insects, these include small beetles, especially wood boring and tree haunting species, earwigs, flies, and larvae of wasps within oak apples, also acorns, beech mast, hazel nuts, yew berries, seed and food such as peanuts from bird tables.

HOUSING: Flight about 1.8m square x 2.1m (6ft x 7ft) high, would suffice, with plenty of rotten boughs stacked up around the inside walls. Strong perches, and tit type nest boxes, with access hole larger than usual, enabling birds to mud it up to their specifications.

BREEDING: Usually builds in a hole in a tree or wall, sometimes uses a nest box. The nest cavity is partly filled with bark flakes, Scotch pine is a favourite, or with birch bark, dead leaves of beech or oak. The eggs number five to eight and are white, sometimes unmarked, but generally with chestnut brown blotches or spots. They are laid towards the end of April. The incubation, which is carried out by the hen, is between 13-17 days, beginning with the completion of the clutch. The young are cared for by both parents for 23-25 days in the nest. Generally single brooded. Young require a variety of invertebrates, these can include mealworms, buffalo worms, crickets, fly maggots and wax moth larvae.

CALL: The nuthatches loud mellow call sounds like *be quick* or *tewit, twit, twit*. Song a soft whistling *vivivivivi* or *peey-peey-*

peay.

RING SIZE: Code G.

SHOWING REQUIREMENTS: Show cage 18in long, 20in high (at least), and 12in wide. Painted black outside, including wire front and white inside, with door on the right. It should be nicely decorated with imitation bark, and two twiggy perches. There should be no hiding places. An exhibit should be as large as possible, short, thick-set body and neck, large wedge-shaped head, nicely cushioned forehead, neat wings and tail carriage, latter short and square cut, strong beak and feet. Woodpecker like in action. Often climbs with head facing downwards.

LEGAL REQUIREMENTS: Fully protected. Not listed on any Schedule of the Wildlife and Countryside Act 1981. Can be sold or shown under terms of General Licence, providing it is ringed and bred in captivity from lawfully held stock. Proof of this in writing, must accompany sale or exhibit.

SPECIAL NOTES: Other names include woodcracker, nutjabber, nuthack, mud stopper. Sits very closely and hisses like a snake when disturbed.

Photograph by Tommy Milner

TREECREEPER

Certhia familiaris.

Related species: Short-toed treecreeper.

DESCRIPTION: The crown is dark brown, spotted and streaked with pale brown, back of neck, back and rump tawny-brown, mixed with ash-grey. The wing coverts are brown, tipped with ash-grey, quills variegated with brown and black, the tail is tawny-brown. The chin, throat, breast and belly greyish-white. Legs, toes and claws light brown, eyes brown. Length 12.5cm (5in).

STATUS IN THE WILD: Resident in Britain with about 245,000 pairs. Favours woodlands, parks and gardens.

HARDBILL OR SOFTBILL? Softbill.

AVAILABILITY FOR BIRDKEEPERS: Available from time to time. Sale birds are offered from £70 each.

ADVANTAGES TO KEEPING: Interesting subject, suitable for keeper with advanced knowledge of its demands.

DISADVANTAGES TO KEEPING: Obtaining true pairs.

DIET: Insects of many kinds and their larvae, also spiders.

HOUSING: Partly sheltered accommodation with plenty of old tree branches stacked around in vertical lots, replenished from time to time.

BREEDING: Will use hole in a tree, or built behind loose bark, from April to June. Nest consists of fine twigs, grass, wool, feathers and rabbit fur. Six to nine eggs are laid. These are smooth and non-glossy, they are white, spotted and speckled with reddish-brown and sometimes dullish purple. Incubation is carried out by the female alone, beginning with the last egg, for 14 days. The nestlings are downy with yellow mouth and yellowish-white gape flanges. They are fed by both parents for 14-16 days in the nest and for sometime afterwards. On leaving the nest they are weak flyers but good climbers. In home conditions a knowledgeable keeper will provide nesting sites of strong bark, cut in half, then reassembled, with the top hinged, the whole then fixed to a dead branch, allowing for a space between large enough (about 2in) for the birds to build their nest and keeper access, for inspection and closed ringing purposes. Multitudes of tiny insects and their larvae will be required if chicks are to be reared, the tiny fly maggots, 'pinkies', wax moth larvae and buffalo worms are recommended for this task.

CALL: A thin, high *tsut* or *tsu*. Song penetrating *tsip-tsee-tsee-tsee*, ending with a flourish.

RING SIZE: Code A.

SHOWING REQUIREMENTS: Exhibit should be as large as possible, of slim appearance, slender downward curved bill, nice curve of head to broadish shoulders, neat wing carriage, tail, broad, stiff, slightly forked and separated. Sexes alike. Current-year birds more suffused grey, their spots more pronounced. Cage at least 18in long, 24in high and 15in wide, painted black outside including wire front and white inside, fitted with bark at the back for exhibits to climb, moss covered floor. Shown singly or in pairs.

LEGAL REQUIREMENTS: Fully protected, General Licence in force for lawfully held, closed-ringed stock, to be exhibited.

SPECIAL NOTES: Local and other names: Creeper, tree-climber and common creeper. Sits very closely.

Photograph by Tommy Milner

RED-BACKED SHRIKE

Lanius collurio.

Related species: See special notes (below)

DESCRIPTION: Adult has back red, crown and nape grey, with conspicuous black band running through the eye and across the forehead, rump ashy grey. Central feathers of tail black, outer black and white, underparts white, with rosy buff tinge on breast; wings mostly dark brown, beak strong and hooked. The female less coloured, back dull brownish chestnut, underparts dull white, with buff tinge on breast, barred with black markings. Young have back barred with black on red or reddish grey. Length 18cm (7in).

STATUS IN THE WILD: Virtually disappeared from Britain as a breeding bird during my lifetime. Very rare breeder. Now mainly seen in autumn on the east and south coast.

HARDBILL OR SOFTBILL? Softbill.

AVAILABILITY FOR BIRDKEEPERS: Available from European sources, some could be dubious so beware! Has bred in British aviaries.

ADVANTAGES TO KEEPING: Will breed in spacious aviary. Interest in species growing. Can be seen on show bench from time to time.

DISADVANTAGES TO KEEPING: Finding surplus birds.

DIET: Entirely animal and very varied, including carrion, mice, shrews, voles, small birds and their young. Larger part of diet is insects including bees, flies, beetles, earwigs and grasshoppers.

HOUSING: Aviary as spacious as possible, fully planted with bushes, including thorn or bramble and climbers.

BREEDING: Usually breeds in bramble thickets or high hedge. Nest is bulky, with a mossy foundation, as well as grasses, neatly lined with hair and fine roots. Eggs four to six, ground colour from pinkish to pale greenish, brownish- olive, or white, and the markings being red-brown. They are laid in the latter part of May. Incubation period 14-16 days, by female alone. Single brooded (will replace lost clutch). Home-kept stock may use wicker basket and will raise chicks on mealworms, crickets, locusts, dead mice, etc.

CALL: Described as a series of warbling notes. The bird is a great mimic. Alarm call is *chack*. The call note of the male to the female is *chec-uck*, the call of the female to the male for food is something like *chi-ee-i* or *chee-ay*. Song period is from end of April to June.

RING SIZE: Code J.

SHOWING REQUIREMENTS: Show cage, box or desk type, no smaller than 18in long, 15in high and 12in wide. Nicely decorated out, and with two springy perches. Size and type: As large as possible, narrowish shape, hooked bill, square tail. Colour and markings: Cock chestnut back, black mask, wings and tail, the latter edged white. Eye stripe to be as prominent as possible. Hen, red-brown above, pale below with dark, wavy markings. Shown singly or in pairs.

LEGAL REQUIREMENTS: Specially protected. Listed on Schedule 1 of the Wildlife and Countryside Act 1981. Can be sold or shown under current legislation.

SPECIAL NOTES: Other names: Jack Baker, murdering pie, Whisky John, butcher bird, flusher and cheeter. In former times was a regular summer visitor. Winters in Africa. Related species: Great grey shrike, (page 301) lesser grey shrike (page 218) and woodchat shrike (page (217).

Photograph by Tony Tilford

CHOUGH

Pyrrhocorax pyrrhocorax.

Related species: No closely related species in Britain. Alpine chough nearest.

DESCRIPTION: Black, with blue, violet and green gloss. Bright red feet and curved bill that is straight at first in young, and reddish or orange until first moult. Length of adult 40cm (16in).

STATUS IN THE WILD: Resident in British Isles, about 1,100 pairs, the majority of which live in Ireland, and Western Isles. A few breed in Cornwall.

HARDBILL OR SOFTBILL? Deemed to be a softbill by the fancy.

AVAILABILITY FOR BIRDKEEPERS: Available through advertising. Only a small number of zoos and private keepers have kept it, though it does appear on the show bench from time to time.

ADVANTAGES TO KEEPING: Charming, intelligent and interesting.

DISADVANTAGES TO KEEPING: Require extensive accommodation, noisy.

DIET: Chiefly insects, especially beetles and their larvae; also worms, crustacean, spiders and molluscs, also lizards and small mammals.

HOUSING: The birds require a large aviary, at least 5m (16ft) square and 4-5m (13-16ft) high. The interior may either be constructed partly to imitate a cliff face, with a high wall with ledges and cavities, or may be a partly built structure with open windows, and ledges suitable for nest sites. The birds will also need well-cited perching facilities enabling them to fly from one to the other.

BREEDING: Nests from April, usually in holes in the roof or sea caves, or in crevices of cliffs, occasionally in buildings, especially those that are in ruin or disused. The nest is an irregular mass of sticks, heather stems and furze, lined thickly with wool and hair, and these items should be made available in home-bred conditions. The eggs usually number four to six in a clutch, (sometimes as few as two), which may be white, creamy, or pale greenish, spotted and blotched with yellowish brown. Some clutches are distinctly reddish. Eggs can be artificially incubated and chicks hand-reared.

CALL: The usual cry of the chough is *kchare* or *ch-e-e-e-o*, other notes are *kchouf*, hence its name, and *kquouc*. Its song is a chattering warble.

RING SIZE: Code S.

SHOWING REQUIREMENTS: Size and type: As large as possible, of strong appearance, standing somewhat erect. Long, slim, down curving beak, with nice curve from forehead into nape. Good cushion on forehead. Gentle curve from nape over shoulders to tail. Tail short, broad and wedge-shaped. Wings very long and cross over tail, and extend beyond it. Species must be exhibited in a show cage with plenty of space for it to move about and with two sturdy perches.

LEGAL REQUIREMENTS: Specially protected. Can be shown under General Licence if ringed and bred in captivity from legally held stock.

SPECIAL NOTES: When shown, always creates attention by its calls and antics. Local and other names: Red-billed chough, Cornish daw, Cornish chough, Cornish kae, chouk daw, red-legged crow, killigrew, hermit crow and cliff daw. Gregarious.

JAY

Garrulus glandarius.

No related species in Britain.

DESCRIPTION: The jay has a reddish-fawn back, white rump and black tail. There is a patch of alternating, white, blue and black on the wing. The underparts are pale brownish buff, turning to rufous on the flanks. The erectile crest is whitish, striped with black. The bird is very conspicuous in flight. Length 34cm (13½in).

STATUS IN THE WILD: Resident in British Isles with about 170,000 pairs. Habitat; mixed woodlands, wooded parks and gardens.

HARDBILL OR SOFTBILL? Softbill.

AVAILABILITY FOR BIRDKEEPERS: Often available, price for a specimen would be in the region of £70.

ADVANTAGES TO KEEPING: Not too difficult to breed, very hardy. An interesting and intelligent species.

DISADVANTAGES TO KEEPING: Can be noisy at times. Need secluded accommodation.

DIET: Young birds and eggs, mice, frogs, insects and their larvae, (chiefly beetles), gall insects, worms, snails, slugs, also grain, nuts, acorns, beech mast, peas, potatoes and fruit. Will visit bird tables.

HOUSING: Flight or aviary large enough to enable the birds to fly about and stretch their wings, with strong perches and some shelter.

BREEDING: In the wild, nesting sites vary and can be in undergrowth, in trees, especially oak, or in conifers from 5ft to 50ft above the ground. The nest is neatly built, and smaller than one would imagine, cup-shaped, made with twigs and stems with a little earth mixed in, the inner lining fine roots and hair. The eggs usually number four to six. Their ground colour is pale, sage green to olive buff, closely speckled with darker olive, and sometimes a black streak at the large end. They are laid from the end of April to early in May, at this time the parents are quiet and secretive. Incubation takes about 16 days, and is carried out by both sexes, beginning with the first egg. At first the nestlings are naked, mouth pale pink, gape flanges pinkish white, they are tendered by both parents. In their early stages of development, the female broods while the male brings the food. Later both forage for food. The young leave the nest at about 20 days. In captivity, all their needs must be met. Large wicker baskets set in cover will suffice as nesting sites, coconut fibre, grass and mud will be used by the birds to make their nest. Hand rearing may be undertaken when the pin feathers appear.

CALL: Loud, raw screaming calls. Song is varied, low chatter.

RING SIZE: Code P.

SHOWING REQUIREMENTS: Size and type: As large as possible, of strong, somewhat stout appearance, broad, nicely rounded, well cushioned head. Broad tail, square cut finish. Wings set nicely on back. Show cage; length 20in, height 15in, width 12in or larger. Painted black outside, white inside, with two strong perches, and two white coloured vessels placed inside for food and water. Shown singly.

LEGAL REQUIREMENTS: Listed on Schedule 3 of the Wildlife and Countryside Act 1981. Birds which may be sold alive if ringed and bred in captivity. Law allows the bird to be shown . General Licence in force enabling species to be killed or taken by an authorised person.

SPECIAL NOTES: Local and other names: Jay piet, jaypie. Not a very close sitter.

Photograph by Dennis Avon

MAGPIE

Pica pica.

No related species in Britain.

DESCRIPTION: Easily recognised by its black and white plumage with green and blue reflections, and very long wedged-shaped tail. Length 46cm (18in).

STATUS IN THE WILD: British resident, with about 800,000 pairs. Likes open country with hedgerows and fields, villages, parks and gardens.

HARDBILL OR SOFTBILL? Softbill.

AVAILABILITY FOR BIRDKEEPERS: Quite a few young birds are available in the spring, at a cost of about £70 each.

ADVANTAGES TO KEEPING: If room is available, they are quite easy to breed, intelligent and interesting, and they make nice show birds.

DISADVANTAGES TO KEEPING: Can be noisy, especially at feeding time or when a predator is in vicinity.

DIET: Insects, chiefly beetle and moth larvae, birds and birds' eggs, small mammals, worms, carrion, fruit and berries.

HOUSING: Good-sized aviary, suitable for a pair or single bird, no smaller than 1.8m (6ft) square and 2.1m (7ft) high, furnished with strong perching and some shelter.

BREEDING: Usually breeds high up in a tree, also in thorny hedgerows and bushes. Nest bulky, built of sticks, thickly lined with earth, on which a layer of roots are placed. A framework of sticks, usually thorny in nature, forms a dome over the nest, with an entrance hole near the top. The eggs are five to seven in number, greenish blue in colour, spotted and freckled with greyish brown. They are laid in April, the incubation period is about 18 days. In home-bred conditions, various baskets can be tried, fixed high in the aviary to encourage nesting. An old magpie's nest still situated in its original position, cut down and secured in the flight is a better option, and will be rebuilt by the birds. Handfuls of dead sticks about 1ft long, should be scattered over the aviary for their use. Old pigeon nests are ideal, together with a bowl of mud and coconut fibre. The young can be raised on commercial live foods, or home grown fly maggots, road kills, dead day old chicks, and dead rats and mice etc. As a staple diet, poultry pellets will be consumed, together with some fruit and meaty items.

CALL: In spring the birds gather in numbers and chatter in various tones. A kind of song comprises of chatter and piping calls. The alarm note resembles *ka,ka,ka,ka.*

SHOWING REQUIREMENTS: Size and type: As large as possible, heavy build, full bodied, stout at shoulder. Broad, well cushioned head, long graduated tail. Wings set nicely on back. Show cage: Length 36in, height 24in, and width 16in. Box or desk type cage, painted black outside including the wire front, white inside, with two sturdy perches and two white food and water containers. Floor covering optional. Shown singly.

LEGAL REQUIREMENTS: Listed on Schedule 3. May be competitively exhibited or sold if ringed and bred in captivity. May be killed or taken from the wild, under complicated General Licence.

SPECIAL NOTES: Other names: Pyet, Madge, Mag, Maggie, pianet and hagister.

Photograph by Dennis Avon

JACKDAW
Corvus monedula.
Related species: Carrion crow, hooded crow, rook and raven.

DESCRIPTION: The general plumage of the small jackdaw is black glossed with blue on the head and upperparts, duller beneath, the nape, back of neck and ear coverts are distinctly grey, being clearest after the moult in autumn. The young are browner, and the grey is little in evidence until the autumn. The bill and legs are black and the eyes blueish or grey white. Length 33cm (13in).

STATUS IN THE WILD: Resident and partial migrant in the British Isles, with about 600,000 breeding pairs.

HARDBILL OR SOFTBILL? Classed as a softbill.

AVAILABILITY FOR BIRDKEEPERS: Usually available, fairly easy to buy at about £60 each.

ADVANTAGES TO KEEPING: Easy to breed, either with single pair or in a small colony. Intelligent and hardy.

DISADVANTAGES TO KEEPING: Require suitable quarters. Can be noisy.

DIET: Mainly insects and worms, but also young birds and frequently eggs, slugs, wheat, and fruit, also nuts. Will scavenge.

HOUSING: Generously sized aviary required, with solid perches, and nesting boxes in situ for breeding purposes.

BREEDING: Usually nests sociably in tree holes, rocks, ruined building and cliffs. Nest built of sticks, lined chiefly with wool, also hair and grass, even bits of rubbish. The clutch of eggs usually number four to six, their colour, pale greenish blue, shading to blueish white, spotted brownish black and ash grey. Laying begins late in April. Incubation period is 17-18 days. Only one brood is taken in a year. Captive birds need suitable nesting material such as old pigeon nests scattered on the aviary floor, these sticks will be collected by the birds. Food should include eggs, (domestic quail's eggs will be relished), dead baby mice, pigeon mixture, poultry pellets etc. When young are in the nest, their food could include large mealworms, locusts and crickets, soft pet food can also be offered.

CALL: The jackdaw has two or three notes that may be heard following each other in a lively sequence as it flies; a *jack* or *ka* or *ky-ah* are common.

RING SIZE: Code R.

SHOWING REQUIREMENTS: An exhibition bird should be as large as possible, of strong, somewhat cone shaped appearance, broad, nicely rounded, well cushioned head. Tail broad, square finish; wings set nicely on back. Females and current year birds have duller grey mantles.

Show cages, no smaller than 24in long, 20in high and 16in deep. Painted black outside, white inside, with two strong perches; floor covering optional.

LEGAL REQUIREMENTS: A General Licence exists, allowing authorised persons to kill or take the species. Separate General Licences allow its exhibition and sale, if ringed and bred in captivity.

SPECIAL NOTES: Very fond of bright objects such as rings, which sometimes turn up in their nest.

Mingles with rooks when foraging for food, especially during the autumn and winter months. Other names: Daw, kae, and Jack.

Gregarious and close sitter.

Photograph by Tommy Milner

ROOK

Corvus frugilegus.

Related species: Carrion crow, hooded crow, jackdaw and raven

DESCRIPTION: Beak is large, strong, arched towards the point, and black. Around the base of the bill in the adult, the skin is bare, and light grey. This feature readily distinguishes it from the carrion crow. The eyes are dark brown. The plumage is black, glossy and rich purple on the upperparts. The legs, toes and claws are black. Length 45cm (18in). Female slightly smaller and less brilliant.

STATUS IN THE WILD: Resident in the British Isles with about 1,350,000 pairs.

HARDBILL OR SOFTBILL ? Regarded as softbill.

AVAILABILITY FOR BIRDKEEPERS: Low, since there are few in captivity. Colour-variant specimens are in greater demand than "normals".

ADVANTAGES TO KEEPING: No doubt of interest to zoos, as any small rookery would be of interest to the public, especially during the breeding cycle.

DISADVANTAGES TO KEEPING: A pair would need a spacious aviary, to enable flight; not always possible for the average fancier.

DIET: Mainly vegetable matter such as corn, root vegetables, berries and seeds and nuts. Specialist at extracting invertebrates from below the soil surface, taking many harmful insects and their larvae, worms, slugs, spiders and some carrion. On balance they are beneficial.

HOUSING: Large aviary, no smaller than 15ft square with strong perches, and sheltered area. Nest sites in the form of tall, strong branches, erected closely in groups with large wicker baskets affixed at the top .

BREEDING: Breeds in open cultivated country or grassland with groups of trees or broken woodland. Nests are built amongst the highest branches of tall trees in rookeries of various size. The material used comprises of twigs knitted and plastered together with mud and clay, the cup is lined with straw, hay or wool. Birds often steal sticks from a neighbour's nest. Four or five pale green ground coloured eggs are laid in February, March, April and May, these are blotched or spotted with greenish or smokey-brown. The female incubates for 16-20 days, being fed on the nest by the male. Nestlings are downy on back and thighs, dark smokey-grey. Mouth is orange at first, becoming pinkish-red. Gape flanges pink coloured tinged with yellow. Both sexes feed the young for 29-30 days in the nest, and for a few days afterwards. They are single brooded.

CALL: A variety of harsh notes, including *caw* or *coah*.

RING SIZE: Code U.

SHOWING REQUIREMENTS: Show cage, desk or box type, no smaller than 36in long, 24in high and 16in wide. Painted black outside, including the sturdy wire front, white interior and with two sturdy perches. Only colour variant varieties likely to be exhibited.

LEGAL REQUIREMENTS: Listed on Schedule 2 Part 2 of the Wildlife and Countryside Act 1981. May be killed or taken under terms of General Licence. May be shown under terms of General Licence if bred in captivity and ringed.

SPECIAL NOTES: Local and other names: White-faced crow, and craa.

Gregarious and a close sitter.

Photograph by Frank Stark

CARRION CROW

Corvus corone.

Related species: Hooded crow, rook, jackdaw and raven.

DESCRIPTION: The plumage is black with a green or purple sheen, a greener gloss than that of the rook. The bill, legs and feet are also black. The eyes are dark brown. The female is smaller than the male. The young are duller. In flight the wing fingers are less spread than those of the rook, and the tail much squarer than that of the raven. Length 47cm (18½in).

STATUS IN THE WILD: Resident in Britain. There are about 800,000 nesting pairs. It is absent from most of Ireland.

HARDBILL OR SOFTBILL? The species falls into the category of softbill.

AVAILABILITY FOR BIRDKEEPERS: Usually some available. Normally coloured birds cost about £50 each, colour variants cost much more.

ADVANTAGES TO KEEPING: Intelligent and interesting species.

DISADVANTAGES TO KEEPING: Quite a large aviary is required, their harsh calls could annoy neighbours.

DIET: Carrion, small mammals, wounded birds, eggs, reptiles, fish, amphibians, mollusc, worms, nuts, acorns and insects. In captivity, will consume poultry pellets, meat from road kills or shot animals such as wood pigeons and rabbits, nuts and giant mealworms.

HOUSING: An aviary of good proportions, to allow the bird to fly, as high as possible, furnished with old branches, and a small pool if possible. Wooden platforms situated near the roof would encourage nest building.

BREEDING: A single pair nest in trees, well away from rooks, or on cliff edges on the coast. Captive birds require plenty of twigs and sticks. Old pigeon nests are a source of such material. Earth, hair, and coconut fibre would be used by the birds to line any nest.

The eggs usually number four or five, occasionally six, colour is greenish, ranging to clear blue, usually thickly flecked with brown and ash grey. Laying begins in April. Incubation period is between 18 and 21 days, and is carried out by the female alone. Nestlings are downy and smokey grey, mouth pink, gape flanges are pink, they are fed by both parents for 4 to 5 weeks, and are single brooded.

CALL: The call is a loud, hoarse 'kwarrp'. The anger note consists of a rapid, high pitched screech.

RING SIZE: Code U.

SHOWING REQUIREMENTS: None set in stone, but essential for exhibition birds to be in high condition, and stand well, with tightly held wings. Shown singly. Show cage No 8. Length 30in, height 24in and width 16in, larger cages also allowed.

LEGAL REQUIREMENTS: Can be sold or shown if bred in captivity and close ringed under General Licence. Can be killed or taken by authorised person under separate, complicated General Licence.

SPECIAL NOTES: Virtually of no interest to the hobbyist in normally coloured birds, interest in mutations however.

Photograph by Frank Stark

126

HOODED CROW

Corvus cornix.

Related species: Carrion crow, rook, jackdaw and raven.

DESCRIPTION: Except for the head, throat, wings, tail and thigh feathers, which are black and mostly glossy, the plumage is ash-grey, the dark shafts giving it a streaky appearance, where black feathers mingle with the grey on the lower throat the streaky appearance is most marked. The bill and legs are black, the irises dark brown. There is only one moult in autumn, as in other crows. The male is the larger bird, otherwise the sexes are alike. Length 47cm (18½in).

STATUS IN THE WILD: In the British Isles it is resident in Ireland, North Scotland and Isle of Man. Its range overlapping that of the carrion crow in Scotland, where interbreeding may take place. In England it is a winter visitor from Northern Europe, chiefly to the east coast. A bird of the moorlands and wilder places. About 450,000 pairs in the British Isles.

HARDBILL OR SOFTBILL? Softbill.

AVAILABILITY FOR BIRDKEEPERS: Very few available within the fancy due to lack of interest in them. Would cost about £70 each if there was a market for them.

ADVANTAGES TO KEEPING: Intelligent bird, reasonably easy to breed.

DISADVANTAGES TO KEEPING: Requires large aviary, not always feasible. Loud calls.

DIET: Carrion, small mammals, from rabbits downwards, wounded birds, eggs, reptiles, fish, amphibian, mollusc, crustacean, worms, insects, especially beetles, also vegetable matter, walnuts, acorns, and maize, as well as small seeds. They will also scavenge.

HOUSING: Requires large flight or aviary, big enough to fly about in, and exercise satisfactorily, planted with one or two trees. For nesting; additional sites in the form of platforms should be erected for their use.

BREEDING: Like the carrion crow, but in treeless areas, often nests on or near the ground. Both sexes build the nest, the eggs number four or five, these have a greenish colour, occasionally blue, covered with flecks of brown and grey. Laying begins in April, rarely in March. The incubation is 19-20 days. Chicks have plentiful smoke-grey down, mouth bright pink, with pink gape flanges. Young leave the nest after 4-5 weeks. After fledging, juveniles follow their parents; dependant on them for food for many weeks. Single brooded. Captive birds will consume road kills, dead day old chicks and dead mice.

CALL: Hoarse crowing call, often repeated three times.

RING SIZE: Code U.

SHOWING REQUIREMENTS: Wooden cage, either box or desk type, no smaller than 36in long, 24in high and 15in wide. Painted black outside, including a substantial wire front. White inside, door on right end. Two strong perches, and two white vessels inside for food and water. Floor covering optional. Exhibition birds should be in excellent condition, and feather. Very rarely shown. Judge will assess overall presentation.

LEGAL REQUIREMENTS: May be killed or taken by authorised persons under terms of a General Licence. Can be sold or shown if ringed and bred in captivity under terms of separate General Licence.

SPECIAL NOTES: Local and other names: Hoddy, dun crow, grey crow, bunting crow, Royston crow, Norway crow, Kentish crow, scarecrow. Known to drop crustaceans from height over beach to break shells in order to eat contents.

Photograph by Frank Stark

RAVEN

Corvus corax.

Related species: Jackdaw, rook, carrion crow and hooded crow.

DESCRIPTION: The feathers are black as are legs, feet and beak. Most of its plumage is glossed with blue and green. Wedge shaped tail. The bill is curved and hooked. The sexes are alike; the young are duller. Length 64cm (25in).

STATUS IN THE WILD: Once widespread, now inhabits remote uplands, sea coasts, moors and cliffs. Frequents western and northern Britain and much of Ireland. Ravens with territories stay in them all year round. Young birds disperse and non-breeding birds form sizeable flocks.

HARDBILL OR SOFTBILL? A softbill within aviary terms.

AVAILABILITY FOR BIRDKEEPERS: Sometimes available.

ADVANTAGES TO KEEPING: Specialist keeper/zoos.

DISADVANTAGES TO KEEPING: Noisy, requires large accommodation. Very little interest in it within bird clubs.

DIET: Like other crows its food is varied; small birds, mammals such as rats and young rabbits, molluscs, vegetable matter and carrion. Sometimes small lambs are taken.

HOUSING: A large aviary which allows plenty of flying space. Strong perches at both ends and protected nesting platforms.

BREEDING: The nest is a massive structure of sticks, heather stems and roots, stuck together with earth, built on a ledge, rocky outcrop or ancient tree. The cup is lined with softer material such as rabbit fur, wool and grass. The eggs are laid in February or March and number 3 to 7, these are blueish-green, blotched and streaked with brown and black. Incubated by female for 3 weeks. The nestlings have greyish-brown down, purplish-pink inside mouth, yellowish flanges. Fed by both parents. Pairs often tumble and roll in mid-air during display flights. Leave nest after 5-6 weeks.

CALL: Has a deep croak. This short deep bark is different from any other corvine utterance. When perched upon a rocky crag the whole body lunges forward with each call. Captive birds have been heard to utter a whole range of sounds.

RING SIZE: Educated guess, size Code V.

SHOWING REQUIREMENTS: Rarely shown, cage must be of a size that adequately houses the exhibit. Show-bird to be tame, and in good feather condition.

LEGAL REQUIREMENTS: Protected at all times. Can be sold or shown if bred in captivity from legally held parents and correctly close-ringed.

SPECIAL NOTES: Bird often soars and wheels at a great height, its wings motionless. Flight feathers extended like fingers. Sometimes used as a prop for educational purposes in schools and television shows.

Other names: Corbie, corbie crow, great corbie crow.
Sits lightly.

Photograph by Frank Stark

NUTCRACKER

Nucifraga caryocatactes.

No closely related species in Britain.

DESCRIPTION: Large crow like bird with blackish-brown plumage, boldly spotted above and below with silvery white. White under coverts and white tip to tail, this creates striking under-tail pattern. Has powerful bill to crack open hard-shelled nuts. Legs and feet greyish. Sexes are alike. Young birds similar to adults. Size about 34cm (13½in).

STATUS IN THE WILD: Rare irruptive species to Britain in autumn and winter. Huge influx in 1968-9, to southern and eastern England from Russia; attracted to gardens and almost fearless of people. Normally lives in cool forests of spruce and pine. Is a vagrant here.

HARDBILL OR SOFTBILL? Fancy agrees, this is a softbill.

AVAILABILITY FOR BIRDKEEPERS: Sometimes available at large auctions. Cost about £250 a pair.

ADVANTAGES TO KEEPING: Makes wonderful aviary subject, fancy or zoo. Very interesting species.

DISADVANTAGES TO KEEPING: Hides food around enclosure, especially at end of the year.

DIET: Very dependent on conifer seeds, and hazel nuts, also consumes insects. Hold nuts with the feet, or wedge them in convenient hollow. Prepares food stores in autumn to last through until the spring.

HOUSING: Need quite large aviary, with plenty of old branches and some green cover. Fir branches should be affixed high up in the flight, with the larger wicker baskets firmly fixed among them as spring approaches. This will encourage the birds' breeding activities.

BREEDING: Breeds in conifers and mixed woodland, usually near the trunk and quite high up. Nest consists of a cup of twigs, moss, lichen and a little soil mixed together, and is lined with a thick layer of grass. The breeding season begins in mid-March in the south of its range and April or May in the north. The species is single brooded. The eggs number three to four very pale blue or greenish blue, finely spotted and speckled with olive brown and grey. The incubation is by the female alone, beginning with the first or second egg, for 17-19 days. The young are fed by both parents. They leave the nest at about 21-28 days, but remain dependant on their parents

for a further few weeks. Aviary stock would need appropriate nesting material. A plentiful supply of invertebrates would be required to produce healthy chicks, these could include large mealworms, crickets and locusts.

CALL: Utters a far-carrying *Kraak*.

RING SIZE: Code P recommended.

SHOWING REQUIREMENTS: As large as possible, of excellent condition, with bright eye, and steady. Show cage; 24in long, 20in high, 16in deep, painted black outside and white inside, door on right. Two strong perches. Floor covering optional. Scale of points: size and type 35, colour and markings 35, feather quality and condition 15, steadiness and staging 15. Total 100.

LEGAL REQUIREMENTS: A General Licence exists which permits the competitive exhibition of certain captive birds of species which have occurred as vagrants in Britain providing they have been bred in captivity from parents lawfully held in captivity. Rings optional.

SPECIAL NOTES: The species has two forms, the thin billed and the thick billed. Both live in the far north, and both occur in Britain.

Photograph by Sergey Yeliseev

STARLING

Sturnus vulgaris.

Related species: Spotless starling and rose-coloured starling (page 202).

DESCRIPTION: In spring, male is very glossy and colourful, has blue base to beak. Female has pink patch on bill. Juvenile are mouse brown on fledging, by late summer have glossy wing feathers and spotty body feathers, head moults last. Length 21.5cm (8½in).

STATUS IN THE WILD: Resident and partial migrant. About 3,000,000 pairs breed in Britain.

HARDBILL OR SOFTBILL? Softbill.

AVAILABILITY FOR BIRDKEEPERS: Invariably available. Many imported here from Europe. Cost can be high, especially for colour variant stock, of which there are many forms.

ADVANTAGES TO KEEPING: Attractive birds, easily catered for, will breed quite freely and ideal for showing.

DISADVANTAGES TO KEEPING: None really, prefer to nest in a colony.

DIET: Mostly insects and larvae in the breeding season; also seeds, fruit, nectar, and scraps.

HOUSING: An aviary 1.8m long x 0.9m wide x 1.8m high (6ft x 3ft x 6ft) suits a single pair of these attractive birds, more than one pair is ideal when breeding, as they like their own kind nearby. Sturdy perches necessary, and nest boxes, with access for ringing, are essential when breeding.

BREEDING: Nest in hole in trees, rocks, buildings, creepers on trees, or nest-boxes. Male builds a rough nest in spring, he then sings and displays to attract the female, if compatible female will line nest. Five to seven pale blue eggs, sometimes white, make up the clutch and are incubated by both birds, the male sits occasionally during the day, the female for most of the day and all night, the clutch hatches after 12-15 days. The chicks are downy, mouth bright yellow. Gape flanges pale yellow, they are fed in the nest by both parents for about three weeks. They are dependant on their parents for food after leaving nest. Usually double-brooded.

CALL: A wide range of whistles, chuckles and grating notes. Will imitate other birds and sounds around. Call is a repeated *tcheer*.

RING SIZE: Code M which has an internal diameter of 4.4mm.

SHOWING REQUIREMENTS: Size and type - as large as possible, cone shaped of strong upright appearance, short tail, head wedge-shaped but with nice rise and well rounded back skull. Good wing and tail carriage. Faults - poor wing carriage, eye defects, deformities, poor presentation, insufficiently trained. Show cage 20in long, 15in high, and 12in wide, desk or box type, painted black outside, including wire front, and white inside, with two sturdy perches, floor covering optional.

LEGAL REQUIREMENTS: Protected species. Listed on Schedule 3 of the Wildlife and Countryside Act 1981, may be shown or sold if closed-ringed and captive bred under current legislation.

SPECIAL NOTES: Local names - sheep starling, stare, sheep stare. A close sitter. Mutations include, opal and phaeo, both recessive and cinnamon which is a sex linked mode of inheritance. Species form huge flocks in winter before roosting.

Hebridian race

Photograph by Frank Stark

GOLDEN ORIOLE

Oriolus oriolus.

No related species in Britain.

DESCRIPTION: The handsome male is golden yellow with black lores, wings and central tail feathers. It has yellow and whitish tips and edges on the closed wing, and the tail-feathers are also partly yellow, the black forming a graduated wedge. The bright yellow is replaced by greenish yellow on the back and head of the female, and her lighter underparts have dark brown streaks; her wings and tail are also browner. The young resemble the female, but at first are spotted on the back with pale-yellow, and later more olive in colour, whilst the flanks are distinctively yellow. The bill is brownish red in the young, this becomes dull red in the adult, the legs are slate grey, and the eye crimson. Length 24cm (9½in).

STATUS IN THE WILD: A summer visitor from Africa with a few pairs nesting in south-east England. They arrive in May. Some arrivals are non-breeding, first year males.

HARDBILL OR SOFTBILL? Softbill.

AVAILABILITY FOR BIRDKEEPERS: Birds available from Continental breeders. The cost of a pair would be substantial.

ADVANTAGES TO KEEPING: No specimens were registered when recent changes were made to Schedule 4. Anyone taking up the species would be a trailblazer.

DISADVANTAGES TO KEEPING: Ascertaining true aviary pairs and promoting species as a worthwhile aviary bird.

DIET: Chiefly insects in early part of the year, beetles, tree-haunting species such as cockchafer, larvae of moths, flies, caterpillars, grasshoppers, bumble bees, also spiders. Later in the year fruit is taken, such as cherries, mulberries, currants, ivy and yew, also small snails.

HOUSING: A good-sized outside flight with shelter, nicely planted out with small trees and shrubs, including some evergreens.

BREEDING: On the Continent, the species tends to prefer parks, gardens and oak woodland. Here in Britain, it often nests in hybrid poplar plantations where it constructs its hammock-like nest, around a horizontal fork by weaving fibre, and sedges around it. The cup is lined with grass-heads, and often bits of paper. The eggs which number four or five in a clutch have a white or creamy ground colour, with a few black spots with a slightly purple tinge. Incubation is carried out by both sexes, but mainly by the female, for 14-15 days. Nestlings are attired in a thick, but short down. Their mouths are bright pink and the gape flanges whitish. They are fed in the nest by both parents for 14-15 days and for some time thereafter. The species is usually single brooded.

CALL: A loud, clear and very musical whistle of four or five varied notes. Sounds like *peeloo-peeloo*. The call rings through the woods and carries for quite some distance. There is also a harsh, jay like *krass* and a mewing call.

RING SIZE: Code M.

SHOWING REQUIREMENTS: Softbill show cage, which must be no smaller than 18in long, 15in high and 12in wide. The interior could be decorated out, just furnished with two sound perches. The exhibit should be in excellent condition. Shown singly.

LEGAL REQUIREMENTS: Specially protected. General Licences in force enabling bird to be shown or sold if ringed and bred in captivity.

SPECIAL NOTES: I have had the privilege of watching these birds feeding their young at their nest, a wondrous sight. The species is not rare within its full range.

Photograph by Tony Tilford

HOOPOE

Upupa epops.

No related species.

DESCRIPTION: Distinguished by its conspicuous crest - fan shaped when erect. Long, slender and slightly curved bill, and rich cinnamon buff plumage, relieved by black tips to crest, rump and alternating bands of black and white on wings and tail. Rump and belly white. Female rather smaller and duller. Young have shorter bill. Length 26-28cm (11in).

STATUS IN THE WILD: Regular spring visitor to Britain. Has bred here in distant past, also as recently as 1977 when four pairs raised chicks. Most breeding has taken place in southern counties of England.

HARDBILL OR SOFTBILL? Softbill.

AVAILABILITY FOR BIRDKEEPERS: Keepers seeking pairs are usually successful. Cost significant.

ADVANTAGES TO KEEPING: Ideal zoo bird. Brings prominence to successful breeders.

DISADVANTAGES TO KEEPING: Species requires large aviary accommodation, in which to fly about. This is not always possible, even for those who would like to keep these birds. Nest, when chicks are being reared, tends to smell. Rearing costs can be high.

DIET: Mainly insects, including beetles and larvae, locusts and grasshoppers, earwigs, moths, flies, ants, also spiders, centipedes, earthworms and woodlice.

HOUSING: I have witnessed the breeding in home-bred conditions of this species. The birds were kept in a large aviary, with a pond. Nest boxes were placed on posts. This type of accommodation with a shelter is essential. This breeder kept his hoopoes inside a brick shed during the winter months.

BREEDING: The nest is always in a hole of some kind; often in a tree, or building, height from the ground varies considerably. The nest is scanty, made of straw and feathers, and with the excrement of animals, making the site very offensive. Eggs, usually five to nine, elongated in shape and dull in texture, often greyish white or yellowish, becoming stained as incubation progresses. Laying begins about the end of April or May. Incubation period is around 20 days, by female. Captive birds, when breeding, will consume locusts,

dead day old mice, crickets, larvae and mealworms.

CALL: The bird owes its name to its unusual note, *poo-poo-poo*, which is uttered with its head bowed to a branch, its crest depressed and neck inflated. The neck is re-inflated after each treble call. The alarm call is a harsh chattering, and a mewing call is sometimes heard.

RING SIZE: Defined by General Licence, which includes one that cannot be removed when the foot is fully grown.

SHOWING REQUIREMENTS: Cage to be no smaller than one of 24in long, 20in high and 16in deep. Painted black outside, including the front, and white inside, with two sturdy perches. Door on right hand end. Exhibit to be in excellent health and feather condition, with bright eyes, sound bill and feet. Shown singly.

LEGAL REQUIREMENTS: Specially protected. Listed on Schedule 1, Part 1, of the Wildlife and Countryside Act 1981. Can be sold or shown within the terms of a General Licence if ringed and bred in captivity.

SPECIAL NOTES: In former times bird was shot on sight for the taxidermy trade. In King Solomon's time it was thought that the crest of the hoopoe was made of gold.

Photograph by Tony Tilford

COMMON QUAIL

Coturnix coturnix.

No related species in the British Isles.

DESCRIPTION: Smallest of our game birds, brown barred with black above and creamy below. The flanks are pale chestnut streaked with black and white, and the head of the male is marked with a black chin and throat band. Female has chin and throat buff and is slightly larger. Length 18cm (7in). Haunts cultivated land, cornfields and rough pastures.

STATUS IN THE WILD: Summer visitor to Britain, with about 300 pairs, fluctuates from year to year.

HARDBILL OR SOFTBILL? Assigned to softbill classes at caged bird shows, exhibited at specialist game events.

AVAILABILITY FOR BIRDKEEPERS: Usually available from World Pheasant Association sources, and private keepers.

ADVANTAGES TO KEEPING: Having a small native game bird such as this would bring advantage to any collection.

DISADVANTAGES TO KEEPING: Foot sores may occur from time to time, due to hard surfaces or cocks frequently patrolling the perimeters of their flight; to avoid this problem, grass or sandy floors should be provided, and the outside of the aviary should be boarded up to about 9in from the ground.

DIET: Seeds and green leaves of many plants, corn, small snails, insects and their larvae. Captive specimens require plenty of calcium, feeding poultry layers pellets or turkey starter crumbs have the nutrients needed, including calcium, also grit is desirable at all times.

HOUSING: Quail dislike wet conditions, in particular puddles or muddy patches on the floor of their accommodation. This should always be dry. Flights can be small, built with ½in x ½in wire panels, with an enclosed roof. One pair per flight is desired, this will prevent fighting. A false roof made of fine net, effectively positioned will prevent damage to the inmates if they decide to explode upwards, as is their trait.

BREEDING: In the wild often nests in growing corn, rough meadows or in other field crops. Nest in a hollow scratched out in the ground and scantily lined. Eggs, laid on successive days, number seven to twelve, oval, smooth and glossy, yellowish ground colour, varying much in markings laid in latter part of May. Incubation by female beginning on completion of clutch, for 16-20 days. Sits tightly. Nestlings are downy, pale yellowish buff below, becoming orange on sides of head. Orange buff above, with dark forehead, spot and two dark parallel lines over crown, blackish-brown dark bars on wings. Young all hatch within short period, and leave nest within a few hours, are cared for by female for about 19 days. They feather rapidly, can flutter at 11 days and fly at 19 days. Usually single brooded. In home-conditions, eggs should ideally be incubated by the mother, chicks are far better suited to the natural environment when parent reared, than are those that are hatched in an incubator.

CALL: A repeated and rapidly uttered *quip, quip, quip*. Also sounds like *wet-my-lips* and *pickwerwick*. Most frequently heard at dawn and dusk.

RING SIZE: Ringing recommended (see legal requirements).

SHOWING REQUIREMENTS: Exhibits should be in good feather and general condition and have bright eyes. Cage in British section, should be painted black outside, including the front and white inside, decoration optional.

LEGAL REQUIREMENTS: Specially protected at all times. Listed on Schedule 1 of the Wildlife and Countryside Act 1981. Article 10 Certificate required for movement, sale and transfer. Birds must be ringed or micro-chipped in these instances.

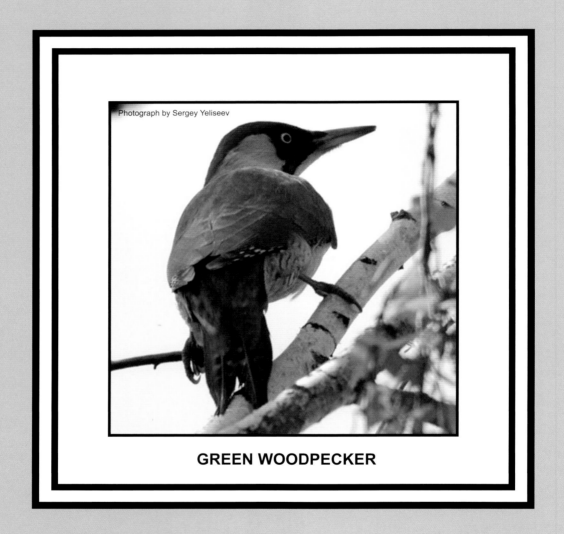

Photograph by Sergey Yeliseev

GREEN WOODPECKER

CHAPTER THREE
Hardbills

Cock Blue Blackbird

Photograph by Dennis Avon

HOUSE SPARROW
Passer domesticus.
Related species: Tree sparrow and Spanish sparrow.

DESCRIPTION: The male has a rufous brown head with a grey area on top. A black stripe runs across the eyes and a broad black bib runs down over the chest. The ear coverts and the entire underparts are greyish, and there is a whitish area under the tail. Females are a duller shade of brown, with a pale stripe behind each eye and a fawn bar on each wing. Length 14cm (5½in).

STATUS IN THE WILD: Resident with about 6,000,000 pairs. Breeds around or near human habitation, usually in association with agriculture.

HARDBILL OR SOFTBILL? Hardbill.

AVAILABILITY FOR BIRDKEEPERS: Readily available, good number bred in Britain each year, popular aviary bird in Europe.

ADVANTAGES TO KEEPING: Very interesting species with a host of mutant colours to choose from. Not an easy species to breed.

DISADVANTAGES TO KEEPING: Very difficult to tame or train for the shows, tends to crouch in cage.

DIET: Varies according to locality. Town birds consume quite a lot of scraps. On farms, chiefly corn, seeds of weeds, also many insects taken especially when young are being reared, these include beetles and aphides. Also takes seedlings and fruit buds. Common visitor to bird tables.

HOUSING: Can be kept in a colony or in pairs, in outside accommodation. Will readily use nest boxes, these need to be placed under cover, and built to allow access for ringing.

BREEDING: Builds either in a tree or bush, where its nest is domed, or in a building, or under the eaves of a house. Nest made of straw, grasses and rubbish, lined with feathers and wool. The eggs usually number three to five, variable colours, often greyish white, with numerous flecks of dark or light ash grey. Laying usually begins in May. Incubation chiefly by the female for 13-14 days, beginning with the completion of the clutch. Young fed by both parents for about 15 days. Several broods are undertaken in the year. After the breeding season, flocks, consisting of old and young birds forage for food, always remaining in the vicinity in which they were bred.

Chicks can be fed exclusively on live food, such as mealworms, wax moth larvae and buffalo worms. Soaked seed, and egg food will also be taken.

CALL: Chirps, repeated as a song.

RING SIZE: Code E, these should be fitted on the fourth day.

SHOWING REQUIREMENTS: No. 3 hardbill cage. Exhibit must be in excellent health and of good feather. Most importantly, the bird must perch correctly, not crouch; and have a confident and tame bearing. Many are exhibited in Europe, especially at the world show.

LEGAL REQUIREMENTS: Can be sold or shown within the terms of a General Licence if ringed and bred in captivity.

SPECIAL NOTES: The house sparrow has been domesticated by hobbyists to the extent that numerous mutations have been developed, these include cinnamon, agate and satinette, all sex-linked: and phaeo, both in single and double factors, masked or blackfaced, a single factor, also a double form of masked, all these are dominant, and finally two recessive mutations, namely opal and albino.

Photograph by Tommy Milner

TREE SPARROW

Passer montanus.

Related species: House sparrow and Spanish sparrow.

DESCRIPTION: Smaller and neater than house sparrow, has dark chestnut crown and nape. The cheek shows a conspicuous black patch below and behind surrounded by areas of white. Back and rump yellowish-brown. Tail dark brown, wing has two wing-bars. Underparts whitish, palest on belly, and washed buff on flanks. Beak black, legs pale brown. Sexes alike, although female is a little smaller and her plumage less brilliant. Juvenile duller than adult. More bouncy flight action than house sparrow. Lives in small woods with old trees, ivy covered objects and parks. Length 14cm (5½in).

STATUS IN THE WILD: Resident British bird with about 285,000 breeding pairs. The demise of the elm, with its many holes and cavities, and lack of certain foods have reduced species numbers dramatically in recent times.

HARDBILL OR SOFTBILL? Hardbill.

AVAILABILITY FOR BIRDKEEPERS: Generally available, in an assortment of colours. Normal coloured birds cost about £50 each, mutants much more.

ADVANTAGES TO KEEPING: Interesting species, willing breeder, can be maintained in a colony setting.

DISADVANTAGES TO KEEPING: Never found fame as an exhibition bird, very timid nature.

DIET: Mainly feed on the ground on seeds of small weeds, usually feed in groups. Invertebrates also taken, especially during the breeding season.

HOUSING: Flight as small as 0.9m x 0.9m x 1.8m (3ft x 3ft x 6ft) is adequate for single pair. Larger aviary if colony preferred, fitted out with plenty of perches and nest boxes.

BREEDING: Will use nest box, tree hole, cliff, quarry, wall, thatched roof, haystack, rocks or hedge. Nest, a domed structure or untidy cup of plant stalks and twigs, lined with down and feathers, constructed by both sexes, from April onwards, double or treble brooded. Usually four to six eggs, smooth and slightly glossy, dark brown, heavily marked. Incubation is by both sexes for 11-14 days. Nestlings are naked. Mouth pink, gape flanges pale yellow, they are tendered by both parents for about a fortnight and for a further period after fledging. In home conditions, plenty of tit type nesting boxes, accessible by the keeper, should be put up in sheltered positions and left all year. Nesting material can include grasses and feathers. The chicks will require a varied supply of invertebrates such as small mealworms, wax moth and buffalo worms.

CALL: Flight call a hard *tek-tek-tek*. Song similar to house sparrow, but shorter in length.

RING SIZE: Code D, which has an internal diameter of 2.7mm. Chicks should be close-ringed on the fourth day.

SHOWING REQUIREMENTS: Exhibit needs to be clean cut, smart in appearance and tame. Hardbill show cage No. 2. Shown singly.

LEGAL REQUIREMENTS: Not listed on any schedule of the Wildlife and Countryside Act 1981. Protected at all times. Can be exhibited within terms of a General Licence, if close-ringed and bred in captivity from legally held stock.

SPECIAL NOTES: Also called mountain sparrow. Mutations include cinnamon, opal and cinnamon-opal, all recessive.

Photograph by Tony Tilford

CHAFFINCH
Fringilla coelebs.

Related species: Bramblefinch and blue chaffinch.

DESCRIPTION: The head of the male is slate-blue on the crown and nape, pinkish chestnut on the cheeks, the back is chestnut and the rump greenish. The breast is deep pink, lighter on the belly, shading to white, with white patches on the shoulders, conspicuous in both sexes. The wings are crossed with yellowish white. In spring and summer the bill is lead-blue, in winter a pinkish horn shade. The legs and eyes are brown. The female has only a faint touch of pink on the breast and is yellowish brown above, with a greenish rump, and paler beneath. In winter the colours of the species are of a duller shade. Young resemble the female. Length 15cm (6in).

STATUS IN THE WILD: Resident and winter visitor. Our commonest finch, with about 7,000,000 breeding pairs.

HARDBILL OR SOFTBILL? Regarded by the fancy as a hardbill.

AVAILABILITY FOR BIRDKEEPERS: Usually available, from £30 per specimen.

ADVANTAGES TO KEEPING: Relatively easy to breed, hardy and long lived, with a joyful song. Will hybridise with some other species, in particular the brambling.

DISADVANTAGES TO KEEPING: None.

DIET: Seeds of many weeds and garden plants, seeding buds of fruit trees, grain and fruit. Invertebrates of all description. Almost wholly insectivorous during the breeding season.

HOUSING: Usually kept outdoors when breeding. A small flight or aviary will suffice for a single pair. If planted with flowers and bushes so much the better, sheltered in some respects against inclement weather.

BREEDING: In the wild will nest in hedgerows, bushes or trees from between 3 to 12 metres from the ground. In an aviary set-up, birds require prepared and covered nesting sites, wicker baskets are often used. The nest is a very neat, compact open cup, made of grasses, moss, roots, wool etc, externally decorated with lichens, birch bark and cobwebs, so these items should be made available for their needs. Eggs usually four or five, sometimes only three in a clutch. Their ground colour is greenish or brownish stone, occasionally clear blue, with spots or streaks of dark purple-brown.

Incubation is about 12 days. The species is double brooded as a rule.

CALL: Familiar call is *spink*, *pink* or *twink*. The short, often repeated song is a cheerful ditty of descending phrases, accelerating towards the end.

RING SIZE: Code C.

SHOWING REQUIREMENTS: Cage, hardbill No 3. English pattern or No 3 Scottish type which is slightly smaller. An exhibit should be as large as possible, thick set with bold appearance. Wing markings well displayed. Steadiness is essential, as is condition and staging.

LEGAL REQUIREMENTS: Listed on Schedule 3 of the Wildlife and Countryside Act 1981, can be sold or shown if aviary bred and close-ringed.

SPECIAL NOTES: Numerous colour variants in existence, as species is close to domestication. These include cinnamon and opal, both recessive. Agate, pastel and a second cinnamon type which are all sex-linked.

Photograph by Dennis Avon

138

BRAMBLEFINCH

Fringilla montifringilla.

Related species: Chaffinch and blue chaffinch.

DESCRIPTION: The breeding male has a blue-black bill, a glossy blue-black head and neck, often with some of the white bases of the feathers showing as flecks or markings, especially on the nape. The wing has a chestnut-buff patch on the lesser coverts, followed by two white wing bars, and the black quills are margined with white. The chin, belly and rump are white, the throat and breast ruddy buff. After the moult the black is obscured by broad, brown tips, which gives it a barred effect. Also brown tips and edges dull the back and underparts, the bill is yellowish with a dark tip. The female has none of the black and chestnut of the male, and is browner. The young, at first resemble the female. Length 14.5cm (5¾in).

STATUS IN THE WILD: Winter visitor in varying numbers from Scandinavia. Has occasionally bred in Britain.

HARDBILL OR SOFTBILL? The bramblefinch is treated as a hardbill.

AVAILABILITY FOR BIRDKEEPERS: Popular aviary and exhibition bird. Cost about £40 each.

ADVANTAGES TO KEEPING: Easy to breed and maintain, long-lived and will readily hybridise with the chaffinch.

DISADVANTAGES TO KEEPING: Can be noisy in early spring especially during darkness when, although home-bred, desire to migrate.

DIET: Largely on beech mast in the wild, in winter, also corn, berries, and various kinds of nuts, seeds, insects and their larvae. Home-bred stock require some live food to supplement their seed intake, especially when rearing their young. In the wild these are raised exclusively on invertebrates.

HOUSING: Can be kept in a birdroom, in roomy cages or in outside quarters.

BREEDING: In the wild, the bramblefinch usually nests in birch or conifer at varying heights. Nest much bulkier than that of the chaffinch but similar, built of grasses and bents and covered with lichens or birch bark, lined with hair and feathers. In captive conditions will build their nests using grass, moss, coconut fibre, dog hair and feathers, wicker baskets will often be used. Usually five to six eggs are laid, not unlike the chaffinch, but often darker and greener. Laying begins in mid May. Incubation lasts for 11-12 days, and is carried out by female alone. Chicks are covered in white down at first. They leave the nest on about the 12th day, being fed by both parents for a further fortnight.

CALL: A sharp or rasping *wheeze*. Song is rather sweet and melodious with several flute-like notes followed by a long drawn out *zweee* or descending mixed rattle.

RING SIZE: Code D which has a 2.7mm internal diameter.

SHOWING REQUIREMENTS: Type - full head well cushioned at front, well filled, bold-fronted body of strong upstanding appearance. Cocks tend to be slightly longer than hens. Current year birds will usually have some lightness around their eyes.

LEGAL REQUIREMENTS: Specially protected on Schedule 1 of the Wildlife and Countryside Act 1981, also listed on Schedule 3, birds which can be sold or shown under the Act or its regulations.

SPECIAL NOTES: Other name, brambling. No subspecies.

Photograph by Tommy Milner

GREENFINCH
Carduelis chloris.

Related species: Goldfinch, linnet, twite, mealy redpoll, lesser redpoll, siskin, pine siskin and Arctic redpoll.

DESCRIPTION: Plumage yellowish-green, with bright yellow primaries and base of tail. Bill stout. Female duller with browner head and mantle. Young striped with brown above and below, rump brown. Length 14.5cm (5¾in).

STATUS IN THE WILD: Resident and winter visitor with about 700,000 breeding pairs in Britain.

HARDBILL OR SOFTBILL? Hardbill.

AVAILABILITY FOR BIRDKEEPERS: Always available.

ADVANTAGES TO KEEPING: Very easy to breed in cage or aviary. Popular show bird, and eager hybridiser, with canary and other finches. Multitude of mutant colours to enjoy.

DISADVANTAGES TO KEEPING: Prone to what is called in the fancy, as 'going light syndrome' a wasting disease, caused in most cases by the protozoan parasites, lankesterella and coccidia isospora, transmitted through the droppings. Also occurs in other hardbill kinds. This syndrome can be satisfactorily treated with sulphonamides, (sulpha) drugs. This medicine can be obtained from a veterinary surgeon.

DIET: Wheat, turnip seeds, oats and seeds of numerous weed species, also beetles, aphides and ants. Young fed chiefly on insects and their larvae.

HOUSING: Can be kept in outside accommodation or in roomy cages within a bird room.

BREEDING: The wild bird breeds in bushes and hedgerows, the nest is built of twigs and moss, and with pieces of wool and bents, lined with bents, roots and hair. Eggs usually number four to six in a clutch, occasionally seven or only three, they are pale purplish white or pale greenish, with a few red brown spots and streaks, chiefly at the larger end. Laying begins in late April, generally early May. Incubation by the female. Two, sometimes three broods are reared in a season. In home-bred conditions, may use wicker or plastic nest pans suitably placed. Coconut fibre often utilised. Adults should be treated for the wasting disease, before breeding activities begin, and for a further period as the chicks are developing. Soaked seed and fresh greens like groundsel and chickweed should be offered to the birds throughout the rearing period, mealworms can be added, as these are often taken. Fresh grit and cuttlefish bone should always be available.

CALL: Song, a coarse *wheeze*, which usually has three phases. Sings from February to August.

RING SIZE: Code E, usually fitted on the sixth day.

SHOWING REQUIREMENTS: An exhibit should be as large as possible, with broad, well rounded head with good rise and cushioned at front, set on full neck with nicely rounded, really short, thick set body of strong appearance. Set well across the perch. Shown in No.3 show cage.

LEGAL REQUIREMENTS: Fully protected. Listed on Schedule 3 of the Wildlife and Countryside Act 1981, and can be sold under the Act and shown under ringing regulations, if close-ringed and bred in captivity.

SPECIAL NOTES: Fully domesticated, and in a range of variant colours, including cinnamon, lutino, satinette, agate, Isabel, pastel, pied, dark-eyed clear and many others. Local and other names: Green linnet, green chub, green grosbeak, green bird and green linnie. Sits very closely.

Photograph by Tommy Milner

SISKIN
Carduelis spinus.

Related species: Greenfinch, pine siskin, goldfinch, lesser redpoll, mealy redpoll, Arctic redpoll, twite and linnet.

DESCRIPTION: Both sexes have black wings with broad, yellow wing-bar across tips of greater coverts and inner primaries. Adult male, green above and yellow below, with black forehead, crown and chin. Tail is forked and black-edged along the base, with brilliant yellow markings. Belly and undertail coverts white, the latter streaked black. Yellowish tapered pointed bill, legs dark brown. Females lack the black crown. Juvenile similar to female. Length 12cm (4¾in).

STATUS IN THE WILD: Resident and partial migrant. In Britain about 360,000 pairs. Inhabits spruce and mixed woodland. Visit birch and alder in winter, also bird tables. Gradually extending its range.

HARDBILL OR SOFTBILL? Hardbill.

AVAILABILITY FOR BIRDKEEPERS: Readily available. Cost varies for each bird, this depends on type and mutation. About £70 for pair of normals.

ADVANTAGES TO KEEPING: Popular cage bird. Will hybridise with canary and other finches. Domesticated.

DISADVANTAGES TO KEEPING: Can become overweight. Strict diet advisable - fatty seeds should be avoided.

DIET: Conifer seeds in summer, especially spruce, larch and pine, alder, birch and deciduous species in winter. Evidence that species first attracted to bird tables by the red bags of peanuts. Feeds similar to tits. Bill ideal for extracting seeds.

HOUSING: Can be housed in sizeable, well lit, indoor cage or small outside aviary suitable for one pair, or large, mixed aviary.

BREEDING: The wild bird nests in conifers, the nest is difficult to locate. It consists of a neat cup of twigs and grasses, bound together with moss and lined with wool and plant down. The eggs are light blue and spotted, there are usually three to five in a clutch, laid in late April. Incubation commences with the second to last egg, carried out by the female for 11-14 days. The chicks are fed by the male for the first few days while the female broods, then both parents feed the chicks. Food is regurgitated. Double brooded. Home-bred pairs require clean nesting material, this can include coconut fibre; small wicker nest baskets will be used by the birds. Sheltered sites are necessary, with some privacy provided in the form of conifer sprays fixed around the nest site. In addition to finch mixture, egg food, sprouted seeds, and insects should be added when breeding, also chickweed and dandelion relished.

CALL: Include *dluee* and *tsuii*, often given in flight. Song, a sweet twitter with wheezy ending.

RING SIZE: Code B.

SHOWING REQUIREMENTS: No.2 hardbill show cage. Exhibit to be as large as possible, with nicely rounded, full head and cobby body.

LEGAL REQUIREMENTS: Listed on Schedule 3. Can be sold or shown if bred in captivity from legally held stock and close-ringed.

SPECIAL NOTES: Local and other names aberdevine, (name used by bird catchers of yesteryear) and barley bird. Close sitter. Mutations include brown (dark-eyed) agate, brown-agate (Isabel) all sex-linked. Single factor pastel and double factor pastel, both dominant.

Photograph by Tommy Milner

GOLDFINCH
Carduelis carduelis.

Related species: Linnet, greenfinch, siskin, pine siskin, twite, mealy redpoll, lesser redpoll and Arctic redpoll.

DESCRIPTION: The goldfinch is easily recognised by the crimson, white and black head, and a bright golden wing bar on the wing. The wing and quills are black with white tips, the underparts mostly grey-brown and the back brown. Juveniles, known as "grey pates", lack the fancy pattern on the head, which is brownish. Length 12cm (4¾in).

STATUS IN THE WILD: Resident with 300,000 pairs.

HARDBILL OR SOFTBILL? Hardbill.

AVAILABILITY FOR BIRDKEEPERS: Readily available. Cost about £60 each, though some mutant varieties may cost much more.

ADVANTAGES TO KEEPING: Beautiful and charming bird, easy to keep and breed. Will hybridise with other finches, and is a desirable exhibition finch. Quite domesticated.

DISADVANTAGES TO KEEPING: None that I know.

DIET: Mainly weed and flower seeds, especially thistles and chickweed, also small cone seeds. Insects include small beetle larvae and aphids.

HOUSING: Can be bred in cage or aviary. Cages, each to accommodate one pair, should be no smaller than 60cm long by 50cm high and 46cm deep (24in x 20in x 18in). The nest-site within the cage can be in the form of a fixed, open wicker basket surrounded by foliage. In an outside aviary or flight, one pair, with no other inmates, is ideal. Nest sites can be constructed under shelter and out of the direct sun.

BREEDING: In the wild, the goldfinch usually breeds in gardens, shrubberies and hedgerows. The beautiful nest is constructed with moss, cobwebs, lichens, fine grasses, down and hair. The clutch usually numbers four or five, occasionally six, blueish white eggs with a few streaks and spots of purplish brown and some ashy shell marks. Laying begins in late April or May. Incubation is by the hen for 12-13 days. The species is double-brooded. Home-bred pairs should be fed on a good British finch mixture, with sprouted seed plants. When chicks are self-supporting they should be separated, to allow the adults to bring up a second round.

CALL: High-pitched *deed-lit*. Song is a high-pitched rapid twitter.

RING SIZE: Code C.

SHOWING REQUIREMENTS: Size: as large as possible. Type: nicely rounded full head with well-filled cone shaped body and upstanding appearance. Points as follows: Size, 10; Type, 25; Colour, blaze and markings, 45; Feather quality and condition, 10; Steadiness and presentation, 10: Total 100 points. Show cage No. 2 English, or No 2 Scottish, which is slightly smaller.

LEGAL REQUIREMENTS: Fully protected, listed on Schedule 3 of the Wildlife and Countryside Act 1981. Ringing regulations allow goldfinches to be sold or shown if ringed and captive-bred from legally held stock.

SPECIAL NOTES: The goldfinch is the jewel in the crown of the British fancy. Other names: Gold spink, draw water, thistle finch, goldie, King Harry, redcap and proud tail. Many mutations exist.

Photograph by Tommy Milner

LINNET

Carduelis cannabina.

Related species: Goldfinch, greenfinch, siskin, pine siskin, twite, mealy redpoll, lesser redpoll and Arctic redpoll.

DESCRIPTION: A mainly brown finch, males in wild state have red forehead and breast when in breeding attire, duller in winter and in captive surroundings. Female lacks the red, is streaked however, and dark brown above. Juveniles more heavily streaked. Species often form flocks in with other finches, such as goldfinches. A bird of the hedgerow and open country. Length 13.5cm (5¼in).

STATUS IN THE WILD: Resident in these islands, with a breeding population of around 650,000 pairs.

HARDBILL OR SOFTBILL? Hardbill.

AVAILABILITY FOR BIRDKEEPERS: Readily available, many are home-bred each year. A pair would cost about £70.

ADVANTAGES TO KEEPING: Kept since time immemorial for their song. A delightful little finch. Excellent for showing, easy to breed and renowned for its readiness to hybridise.

DISADVANTAGES TO KEEPING: Of very nervous disposition, also prone to 'going light'. Sulpha drugs will help to prevent the onslaught of this disease.

DIET: Mainly the seeds of many species of weeds, also turnip, rape, cabbage, flax and hop. Insects also taken, these include beetles, moths and their larvae. In winter grain and berries eaten. Home-bred stock require a basic finch seed diet from a commercial supplier, together with wild seeds.

HOUSING: Linnets can be housed and bred in cage or aviary. Cages inside the bird room should be roomy; outside flights can be as small as 3ft square and 6ft high.

BREEDING: The wild linnet often breeds in colonies in gorse thickets, or in single pairs in gardens and hedgerows. The nest generally is not far off the ground, and is built of stalks, bents, moss and twigs, lined with hair, wool or feathers. The eggs usually number four or five, but seven have been recorded, they are pale blueish-white, with a few spots and streaks of purplish-red, and are laid in April. The incubation period is 11-12 days. Two or more broods are raised in a season. Captive pairs will use small wicker baskets. As the birds come into condition, dandelion heads should be offered, later on sow thistles will be enjoyed by the stock, commercial wild seeds should be added when chicks are being fed.

CALL: Flight call *ge-ge-ge*. Song quite pretty, beginning with a series of calls and developing into trills and fluting.

RING SIZE: Code C, which has an internal diameter of 2.5mm.

SHOWING REQUIREMENTS: No. 2 Hardbill show cage. Shown singly. Size: as large as possible. Type: Nicely rounded full head, well filled in cone shaped body of strong bold appearance. Colour and markings: Rich nutty brown throughout, distinct throat markings, well defined even ticking giving well filled chest and carried well down flanks. Well defined whites in wings and tail. Hen darker brown with plentiful heavy working on head, chest and flanks. Less distinct whites in wings and tail.

LEGAL REQUIREMENTS: Protected at all times, listed on Schedule 3 of the Wildlife and Countryside Act 1981. May be sold or shown if ringed and bred in captivity under current legislation.

SPECIAL NOTES: The name grey linnet refers to the young before their first moult. Also called whin linnet, red linnet and linnie among others.

Photograph by Dennis Avon

TWITE
Carduelis flavirostris.

Related species: Mealy redpoll, lesser redpoll, Arctic redpoll, linnet, siskin, pine siskin, goldfinch, and greenfinch.

DESCRIPTION: The general plumage of the male in summer is pale reddish-brown, shading to white on the belly and under-tail coverts. The rump is rose-red. The brown wings are crossed by a white wingbar and some of the feathers have white margins - these are very noticeable in flight. The bill is pale yellow, legs and eyes brown. After the autumn moult the plumage appears duller. The female and young lack the rose-red rump, the young are greyer. Length 14cm (5½in).

STATUS IN THE WILD: Resident and partial migrant. Winters mainly along north and east coasts. About 68,500 pairs breed in British Isles. Inhabits almost treeless countryside, open heather and gorse moorland in north of England and in Scotland.

HARDBILL OR SOFTBILL? Regarded as a hardbill.

AVAILABILITY FOR BIRDKEEPERS: Regularly available. Popular aviary bird. Cost about £60 per bird.

ADVANTAGES TO KEEPING: Easy to cater for, sought after show bird. Will hybridise with linnet, greenfinch, redpoll and canary.

DISADVANTAGES TO KEEPING: Plain species, less likely to catch the eye of the judge, although outstanding examples may do well.

DIET: Weed seeds.

HOUSING: Usually kept in small outside flights or in spacious cages within a birdroom.

BREEDING: Breeds on rough pastures and heather moors, and areas of moorland scrub on hillsides. The nest is bulky, made of grasses and plant stems; lined will wool, hair and feathers, built by female. The season begins in late April to early May. Single or double brooded. Five to six eggs form a clutch, smooth and lightly glossy, similar to linnet. Pale blue with varied specks, spots and scrawls in dark purple or reddish brown. Incubation by female alone, beginning before completion of clutch, for 12-13 days. The nestlings are tendered by both parents for 15 days whilst in the nest and for several days after fledging. In home-bred conditions will make use of nest pans or wicker baskets, will feed chicks on soaked seeds, and green food such as chickweed. May take small mealworms etc.

CALL: A nasal *chwee*. Song is a rattling twitter, slightly slower than linnet. The flocks fly with linnet-like indecision, dancing and wheeling over the countryside and twittering as they go.

RING SIZE: Code B, which has an internal diameter 2.4mm.

SHOWING REQUIREMENTS: As large as possible. Nicely rounded full head, cobby body. Sexes similar. Cocks have plum coloured rump. No.2 hardbill show cage. Seed mixture on floor. Points awarded, size 10, type 25, colour and markings 35, feather quality and condition 15, steadiness and presentation 15, total 100.

LEGAL REQUIREMENTS: Protected at all times. Listed on Schedule 3 of the Wildlife and Countryside Act 1981. Can be sold or shown under current legislation if bred in captivity from legally held parents and correctly closed-ringed.

SPECIAL NOTES: Local and other names. Mountain linnet, twite finch and heather linnie. Sits closely.

Photograph by Dennis Avon

LESSER REDPOLL

Carduelis cabaret.

Related species: Arctic redpoll, siskin, pine siskin, linnet, mealy redpoll, goldfinch, greenfinch and twite.

DESCRIPTION: Small, dark-brown finch with a crimson forehead and crown. Mantle and back streaked with dark brown, lower back greyer than mantle, rump tinged with pink, chin black, underparts buffish white, breast dark pink. Two buff bars on wing. Female has no pink on breast, but has the crimson forehead. Young have no pink on head, breast or rump and are speckled brown. Species slightly smaller than the Mealy (Page 146).

STATUS IN THE WILD: Resident and partial migrant. About 230,000 pairs in British Isles. Inhabits moorland and heaths, among birch, alder and willow, also conifer plantations and gardens.

HARDBILL OR SOFTBILL? Treated as a hardbill.

AVAILABILITY TO BIRDKEEPERS: Depending on quality or rarity of colour £30 to £100 each.

ADVANTAGES TO KEEPING: Delightful little variety, easy to cater for, and an important show bird domesticated in a range of colours.

DISADVANTAGES TO KEEPING: None that I am aware of.

DIET: Chiefly seeds of alder, birch, bullrush, and weeds of many species, also insects.

HOUSING: Outside flight, large or small, or inside the birdroom, where two broods are often taken.

BREEDING: The wild bird nests in hedgerows, willow or conifer. Often in colonies. The nest of twigs, coarse bents and stalks are lined with white down, hair or feathers. Captive pairs will use coconut fibre, moss and grasses in small wicker type baskets. Four to six dull, deep blue eggs with some spots are laid from mid-May, incubation 11-13 days. Food includes British finch mixture, soaked seeds and egg food, small mealworms, wax moth larvae, and any other invertebrates when young are in the nest. Millet spray can be offered, and greenfood, such as dandelion, chickweed, shepherds' purse and sow thistle.

CALL: Trilling, unmusical song often delivered in flight.

RING SIZE: Code B, internal diameter 2.4mm placed on leg at fifth day stage.

SHOWING REQUIREMENTS: No. 2 hardbill show cage.

Nicely rounded full head of good width, on short, cobby thick-set body, set well across perch. Warm, rich nutty brown throughout, with plentiful, well defined flank markings, reasonably well-defined bib and crimson poll, devoid of too large a white split on chest. When colour fed, to show rich pink flushes on breast and rump; hens more profuse working carried well into chest. No pink flush on chest.

LEGAL REQUIREMENTS: A separate species to mealy redpoll say scientists. Now unscheduled. Such birds can be shown or sold under General Licence.

SPECIAL NOTES: Several colour mutations are available, including cinnamon, agate (silver,) cinnamon-agate (Isabel) all sex linked, phaeo, recessive and cobalt which is dominant.

Photograph by Sergey Yeliseev

MEALY REDPOLL

Carduelis flammea.

Related species: Lesser redpoll, Arctic redpoll, siskin, pine siskin, linnet, twite, goldfinch and greenfinch.

DESCRIPTION: Slightly larger than lesser, with bright crimson, occasionally orange or even yellow forehead. Nape and sides of neck pale 'frosted' grey or pale greyish-buff, dark streaked. Mantle and scapulars pale tawny-brown, streaked with black. Rump greyish-white. Tail very dark. Face greyer than lesser more black on chin of males. Throat and chest pink. Winter plumage slightly paler. Length 13cm (5in).

STATUS IN THE WILD: Winter visitor to Britain in varying numbers, breeds in Scandinavia and far north.

HARDBILL OR SOFTBILL? A top hardbill.

AVAILABILITY FOR BIRDKEEPERS: Readily available, domesticated, birds larger than wild counterparts. Cost about £50 each, varies.

ADVANTAGES TO KEEPING: Willing breeder, many colour variants, surplus readily sought.

DISADVANTAGES TO KEEPING: Often not long-lived. Prone to becoming overweight.

DIET: Mainly seeds of weed and tree.

HOUSING: Can be kept in small outdoor flights or within large indoor cages.

BREEDING: The standard of home-bred strains is similar to exhibition greenfinches, for both size and type, these modern strains are line-bred. Pairs must be watched during the breeding season, especially the cocks, which if overweight may become infertile. They might also interfere with eggs or even young chicks, so should be removed when the clutch is laid, can be returned to the breeding cage when the chicks are about 12 days old. Food required is a good finch mixture and rearing egg food when required. Dandelion heads will be readily dissected by the birds and fed to the chicks and is an excellent food.

CALL: A distinctive metallic twitter, varying in pitch from soft to harsh. The alarm call is a sharp goldfinch-like *eeeze*. The song is a short rippling trill. In the wild, is given in flight displays, song otherwise delivered from song perch.

RING SIZE: Code C, with an internal diameter of 2.5mm. Determined by separate General Licence, first issued in 1985.

SHOWING REQUIREMENTS: Size, as large as possible.

Type, full head of good width on short thickset body, set well across perch. Colour and markings: Rich silvery grey-brown with plentiful heavy, well defined flank workings. Reasonably well defined bib and crimson poll. When colour fed will show rich pink flush on breast and rump. Hens more profuse working carried well into chest. Lack pink flush on chest. Faults: Poor colour, lack of working, eye default, deformities, poor presentation, insufficiently trained. Current-year birds difficult to sex and carry profuse working and well-defined dark bib. Lack pink flush on breast and rump. Hardbill show cage, size 2. Shown singly.

LEGAL REQUIREMENTS: Fully protected. (Listed on Schedule 3 as redpoll). Can be sold or shown under current legislation.

SPECIAL NOTES: Various beautiful colour variants exist, including cinnamon, agate (silver) cinnamon-agate (Isabel), and cobalt.

HOARY (OR) ARCTIC REDPOLL

Carduelis hornemanni.

Related species: Mealy redpoll, lesser redpoll, goldfinch, greenfinch, linnet, twite, siskin and pine siskin.

DESCRIPTION: Generally much paler than the redpoll, in some races almost white. The rump of adult bird is always unstreaked. Bill yellowish-white. The male has pale buff-brown streaked upperparts and pale, usually white underparts, with faint streaks on flanks. During the breeding season may have pink flush on breast, also shows black bib and red forehead. Length 11.5cm-14cm.

STATUS IN THE WILD: Breeds on Arctic tundra. A very rare autumn and winter vagrant to Britain, mostly from Greenland and Lapland, noted in Fair Isle, mainland Scotland, north-east England and Norfolk.

HARDBILL OR SOFTBILL? Hardbill.

AVAILABILITY FOR BIRDKEEPERS: Occasionally available from continental sources. A few kept in British collections.

ADVANTAGES TO KEEPING: For specialists, a real opportunity for a challenge, as this is a different species to the lesser and mealy. It should be kept in a similar manner to these.

DISADVANTAGES TO KEEPING: The difficulty in obtaining stock. Persistent enquiries should bring results.

DIET: Mainly seeds of trees such as birch, alder and willow. Young are fed mainly on insects until they fledge.

HOUSING: Outside, small, partly sheltered aviary, to contain a single pair with no other inmates; to contain perches, water and food vessels, the latter undercover. Inside, roomy flight cages, with twiggy perches would suit for all year care.

BREEDING: In the wild state, breeding begins in late June, and a single brood is taken. The nest is a cup of grasses and twigs, sometimes roots, and is lined with feathers, hair and plant down. The eggs usually five in a clutch, sometimes four to five, are similar to those of other redpolls, but larger, and a little paler in ground colour. The incubation period is 11 days, the young leave their nest at the 11th or 12th day in captivity. Wicker baskets would be used by the birds, if given a little cover. Two or three such sites should be provided in each aviary for choice, and more than one clutch of eggs may be expected in a season, if sufficient food is available, due to our warmer conditions. From a diet of hard seed, the type of food should be increased as spring comes, to include soaked seed and a few small mealworms. Nesting material can include moss, coconut fibre and plant down. An increased supply of mealworms, together with buffalo worms, and wax moth larvae will sustain the chicks, together with any invertebrates that can be collected. The chicks can be removed when they can fend for themselves, this will allow the old pair to pursue a second brood.

CALL: Call is very similar to that of the mealy redpoll, but with some differences, it is a little more metallic and coarser.

RING SIZE: Code C size, seems about right.

SHOWING REQUIREMENTS: No standard set. Exhibit should be as large as possible with nicely rounded head of good width and with a cobby, thick-set body. The rump should not be streaked. Hardbill cage size No.2, English or Scottish, both applicable.

LEGAL REQUIREMENTS: It is not listed either on Schedule 3 of the Wildlife and Countryside Act 1981 or its ringing legislation. It can however be shown under terms of a General Licence.

SPECIAL NOTES: In recent years some well known fanciers have included this species in their collections, and no doubt as more birds become available its path towards domestication will begin.

Photograph by Frank Stark

BULLFINCH
Pyrrhula pyrrhula.
Related species: No close relatives in British Isles.

DESCRIPTION: The male has the head, chin, the secondaries and tail glossy blue black, the back is blue-grey and the underparts including the cheeks are brick-red shading to white. The wings have a conspicuous white bar. The bill is blackish, the legs and eyes brown. The grey on the upperparts of the female is less pure and the underparts are browner. The young have no black on the head. Length 15cm (6in) some foreign races are larger.

STATUS IN THE WILD: In evidence throughout Britain, as a resident, also a winter visitor. About 200,000 pairs in the British Isles.

HARDBILL OR SOFTBILL? Hardbill.

AVAILABILITY FOR BIRDKEEPERS: British race usually available in small numbers, females are more sought after than males due to their use in the breeding of mules and hybrids. Irish home-bred hens, due to their dark shades, are highly sought after. Multitudes of larger northern and Siberian birds are bred in a variety of colours on the Continent. Prices vary considerably, depending on specimen.

ADVANTAGES TO KEEPING: Delightful bird, easy to breed and highly desired as a show exhibit.

DISADVANTAGES TO KEEPING: Prone to gapes, usually curable.

DIET: Mainly buds in spring, also seeds of ash, sycamore, birch, lilac and heather and those from dock. Also berries of rowan, buckthorn, blackberry and mistletoe. Insects occasionally taken.

HOUSING: Bullfinches can be bred in outside flights or in large cages.

BREEDING: In the wild bullfinches nest in evergreens in gardens and woodlands, thick bushes and hedgerows. Home-bred pairs in cage or aviary need cover. Wicker baskets are ideal for their nests of twigs, hair and roots. Coconut fibre can be used. Early conditioning is advisable, egg-food and soaked seed should be offered, with livefood.

Usually four or five smooth and slightly glossy eggs are laid in April or May. They are pale blue in colour, with fine spots, blotches and scrawls, most marking on the larger end.

Incubation by the female alone takes 10-13 days. Two broods are normal.

CALL: The ordinary note of the bullfinch is a soft flute-like *pee-ew* or *whe-on*. The song is a series of short, low notes.

RING SIZE: Code D.

SHOWING REQUIREMENTS: Shown singly. Broad, full well-rounded head with good rise, and well-rounded, short, thickset body of strong, upstanding appearance. Cage: Size 3 or B in England or Wales type; length 12in, height 10in, width 5in. No.14 gauge wires and ¾in apart, centre to centre. Drinking hole 1in in diameter. Bottom rail 1½in high. Top rail shaped 1in, in at the outside, sloping to ½in at the centre. Scotland standard; No. 3 11in long, 10in high, 5in deep. Both these cages can be used anywhere in the UK.

LEGAL REQUIREMENTS: Listed on Schedule 3 of the Wildlife and Countryside Act 1981 and can be sold or exhibited if ringed, under the Act or its regulations. All sub-species come under UK and EU law.

An unringed northern bird can be sold if a colour variant. Licence WLF026837, with documentary evidence of captive breeding. Normal unringed birds can also be licenced.

SPECIAL NOTES: Local names include beechfinch, horsefinch, pink, twink, olph, nope, red hope, alp, hoop. Sounds like Trumpton!

Photograph by Frank Stark

Northern bird

SERIN

Serinus serinus.

Related species: Citril finch and canary.

DESCRIPTION: A tiny finch, size of blue tit, male is streaky greenish-brown above with bright yellow head, breast and rump. Blackish-brown wings have pale fringes to wing coverts showing as pale wing bars. Tail forked, black eyes, short, grey bill, legs brown. Female has similar pattern as male but browner above with duller yellow parts. Juvenile resembles dull female. Length 11.5cm (14½in).

STATUS IN THE WILD: Is extending its range and has spread across Europe from Spanish and Italian base, many sightings in British Isles. Breeds in the Channel Islands, south and south-east England in small numbers. Birds leave Britain and temperate Europe to return to their Mediterranean home to winter.

HARDBILL OR SOFTBILL? Hardbill.

AVAILABILITY FOR BIRDKEEPERS: Many bred on near continent, birds available from there at about £200 per pair. In Britain kept widely and bred in numbers.

ADVANTAGES TO KEEPING: Smart, little show bird, will readily hybridise.

DIET: Mainly small seeds from plants such as the daisy, cabbage family, catkins and weed seed.

HOUSING: Can be successfully kept like siskin or greenfinch, either in small outside flight, one pair to each, or in roomy birdroom cages. The species require the same feeding regime as other finches; suitable canary mixture, grit and cuttlefish bone, with added greenfood and soaked seed when breeding, together with live food as some pairs will relish this.

BREEDING: The nest is built high in a deciduous tree, occasionally in an evergreen well concealed towards tip of a thin branch, the cup of which consists of grasses, roots, and moss lined with feathers and hair, is constructed by the female from March to May. The eggs number four or five and are pale blue, spotted and scrawled with reddish-brown. They are incubated by female alone for 13 days. Chicks are downy, down is sparse and rather long, mouth bright pink. Gape flanges pink. The chicks are fed by both parents for 14 days in the nest. Dependant on parents for a week or so afterwards. The species is double brooded.

CALL: A flight note *tirrillillit* and *tsoo* etc, are the most common calls. Song a rapid jingling of high pitched notes.

RING SIZE: Code B, which has an internal diameter of 2mm.

SHOWING REQUIREMENTS: Size 2 hardbill cage or Scottish No. 1, (legal but seldom used). Painted black outside, Leyland emerald within. Exhibit, no standard laid down (one is needed) but must be as large as possible with bright eye and colour, good feather and condition.

LEGAL REQUIREMENTS: Listed on Schedule 1 Part 1 of the Wildlife and Countryside Act 1981, birds protected by special penalties at all times. A General Licence exists enabling exhibition of species if ringed and bred in captivity.

SPECIAL NOTES: Smallest European finch.

Photograph by Tony Tilford

Male

Photograph by Tony Tilford

Female

SCARLET ROSEFINCH

Carpodacus erythrinus.

Related species: None in British region.

DESCRIPTION: A medium-sized finch with large, stubby bill. All ages and all plumages show two wingbars. Mature adult male distinctive with red head, breast and rump; wings brown with wing-bars tinged pink and underparts white. Immature male and adult in winter have less intensive colour, female and juvenile have brown plumage with underparts pale and streaked. Length 14cm (5½in).

STATUS IN THE WILD: Rapidly expanding westward. Has bred in Highland region of Scotland and eastern England. Singing males are becoming more common. Found in Shetland in spring months and along east coast of British Isles. Uncommon passage migrant.

HARDBILL OR SOFTBILL? Regarded as a hardbill.

AVAILABILITY FOR BIRDKEEPERS: Very rarely available in the UK though breeders of these birds exist in Europe.

ADVANTAGES TO KEEPING: These pretty little finches would no doubt be accepted on British bird hardbill benches and make a wonderful addition. Rosefinches are not new to British aviculture - plenty of specimens from various species are being bred.

DIET: Seeds and other plant material, with some insects.

HOUSING: An outside aviary, partly sheltered, measuring 1.8m x 1.8m x 2.1m (6ft x 6ft x 7ft) planted out with shrubs and climbers, would suit a pair of these delightful finches. A shallow pool would also be of benefit to them. Wicker baskets need to be affixed within the shrubbery to induce nest building. A good finch mixture with a few added mealworms would act as a staple diet.

BREEDING: In the wild, breeds in swampy areas or by water, in swampy woodland with undergrowth, copses, scrub thickets and cultivation with bushy cover. Nest built in a shrub or low tree, from ground level up to 9ft. Loosely built structure of plant stems and grass, lined with roots and hair made by the female alone. The breeding season begins in mid-May. Single brooded. Five to six eggs are laid in a clutch, they are smooth and glossy, light blue in colour, but deeper colour than other finches, sparingly marked at the large end with spots. Incubation is by the female only for 12-14 days. Young are tendered by both parents. In home-bred conditions, birds will require a multitude of insects and spiders when rearing their chicks, mini mealworms, buffalo worms, fly maggots and wax moth larvae would be readily consumed.

CALL: Male has a distinctive, far carrying musical song.

RING SIZE: Code E, which has an internal diameter of 2.9mm.

SHOWING REQUIREMENTS: No. 3 hardbill show cage. Exhibit should be as large as possible, with good feather and bright eye. Good wing and tail carriage. Confident when in exhibition arena.

LEGAL REQUIREMENTS: Listed on Schedule 1 Part 1 of the Wildlife and Countryside Act 1981, birds protected by special penalties at all times. Can be sold or shown under current legislation if ringed and bred in captivity.

SPECIAL NOTES: Other names are common rosefinch and scarlet grosbeak.

Photograph by Sergey Yeliseev

HAWFINCH

Coccothraustes coccothraustes.

No related species.

DESCRIPTION: A huge beak with horny pads inside. Its plumage is generally orange and tawny-brown, with blue-black quills and black throat and lores. The inner primaries are very distinctive, those from the 6th to 9th are notched, curled and shaped like a billhook and are used in courtship. The female is paler. Length 18cm (7in).

STATUS IN THE WILD: Resident and partial migrant. In Britain about 4,000 pairs, mainly in south-east.

HARDBILL OR SOFTBILL? Hardbill, only equalled by the corn bunting in length.

AVAILABILITY FOR BIRDKEEPERS: Usually available from UK and Continental breeders at £70-£100 each.

ADVANTAGES TO KEEPING: Once quite uncommon in captivity, their ecology is now better understood and experienced fanciers can breed them without much trouble. A hardy species.

DISADVANTAGES TO KEEPING: There is no profit in bird keeping, and to raise hawfinch chicks in any number is expensive.

DIET: Kernels and seeds of sloe, hawthorn, hornbeam, beech, bird cherry, cherry, plum, laurel, ash, maple and sycamore, maize, cotoneaster and sunflower also green peas, larvae of moths and other invertebrates.

HOUSING: An outside aviary is ideal, but no smaller than 9ft x 6ft x 7ft high, and as these birds are rather shy, it might be either wholly boarded or partly boarded up all round, with a wire roof partly covered to allow light, sun and rain to penetrate or one of wire if the birds are very tame. The flight should be planted out with climbers, such as honeysuckle and hop, these will attract insects.

BREEDING: In the wild the bird breeds in orchards, old wooded gardens, blackthorn, hornbeam or forest trees. Nest usually placed on horizontal bough, made of a foundation of twigs, the shallow cup is lined with roots, hair, fibre, bents lichens and roots. The eggs number four or five, ground colour blue to greyish-green, boldly streaked with blackish-brown. Laying begins in April or early May, often later with home-bred stock. The incubation is carried out mainly by the female for 10-12 days. Young are fed by both parents, they leave the nest at between the 10 to 14 day stage.

As a staple diet, aviary stock should be offered sunflower, safflower, hemp and British finch mixture seeds, and berries when in season, also small pine cones and chickweed. Live food should be offered all year round, increased at breeding time, especially when young are in the nest.

CALL: Sharp *tsik*, the song is a jerky tinkling mixture of call-like notes.

RING SIZE: Code K.

SHOWING REQUIREMENTS: Hardbill cage No. 4 England or C Scotland, which is slightly smaller. Size of exhibit: As large as possible. Short body, very thickset at shoulders and through body. Broad, bold head, with good rise and plenty of back skull. Well defined, clean-cut nail shaped bib.

LEGAL REQUIREMENTS: Fully protected. Not listed on any Schedule of the Wildlife and Countryside Act 1981. Can be sold or shown under terms of General Licences if ringed and bred in captivity.

SPECIAL NOTES: Other names: Grosbeak haw, grosbeak, common grosbeak, and black-throated grosbeak. Sits closely.

Photograph by Dennis Avon

COMMON CROSSBILL
Loxia curvirostra.

Related species: Scottish crossbill, parrot crossbill and two-barred crossbill.

DESCRIPTION: Male and female common crossbills differ greatly in their coloration. Both sexes are robust with blunt looking head and short forked tail and crossed mandibles. The male is red with an even redder rump, whereas the female is greener above and yellowish below. Length 16.5cm (6½in).

STATUS IN THE WILD: Resident, large numbers in Scotland, England and Wales, beginning to colonise Ireland. Inhabits conifer forests. Population irruptions from northern Europe land in Britain from time to time and swell numbers. At least 1,000 pairs in Britain.

HARDBILL OR SOFTBILL? Hardbill.

AVAILABILITY FOR BIRDKEEPERS: Strains of home-bred birds have been built up both here and overseas, making it relatively easy to obtain stock. A specimen would cost about £100.

ADVANTAGES TO KEEPING: Early breeders and easy to propagate, make nice show birds, and will hybridise with other finches such as canary, greenfinch, goldfinch, linnet, redpoll, bullfinch and serin.

DISADVANTAGES TO KEEPING: Will destroy aviary or cage woodwork with their strong beaks.

DIET: Seeds from cones of pine, larch, spruce, Scots pine, also berries of hawthorn and rowan, apple pips, ivy berries and insects especially aphides and larvae.

HOUSING: Can be bred in large, indoor cages or in outside accommodation. Outside flights can be made in various forms. One such suggestion is to arrange a series of aviaries each measuring 1.8m x 0.9m x 2.1m (6ft x 3ft x 7ft) each completely enclosed with timber boards, and with wire roofs, constructed on each side of a passageway, with safety door, and a hatch in the door of each compartment to enable feeding and observation. Crossbills should be kept as a colony, but with each pair apart from its neighbour.

BREEDING: The common crossbill nests in conifers, generally Scots pine, usually on the outskirts of forests, or in a single tree and at varying heights, but generally fairly high, the nest is built on a foundation of fir twigs on which is loosely fixed a cup of grasses and wool, rather flattened and lined with grasses, rabbit's fur and feathers. Eggs usually number four to six in a clutch, and are greyish white, occasionally pale blueish or pinkish, with a few bold streaks of purple, red or black. Laying begins in February or March, sometimes January when snow is on the trees. Incubation is by the female and lasts for 12-13 days. Often two broods are reared. Home-bred birds should be provided with natural materials, nest sites comprising of Scots pine branches should be secured in suitable locations. Females should be introduced into breeding quarters first, around the middle of January, males a little later. Nesting baskets should be made of solid material such as shaped wire netting, and placed among the foliage, two to each flight. Before chicks hatch a prepared diet must be available, made up of soaked seed and chickweed, together with pine cones and mealworms. Chicks can be weaned at about the six week stage.

CALL: Similar to the greenfinch, with repeated phrases. Both sexes sing.

RING SIZE: Code J.

SHOWING REQUIREMENTS: Hardbill cage size 4, Scottish cage slightly smaller. An exhibition specimen should be as large as possible, with a short body, very thick-set throughout, bold, wide head and neck. Shown singly.

LEGAL REQUIREMENTS: Specially protected at all times. Can be sold or shown under terms of General Licence.

SPECIAL NOTES: Also known as shell apple and red crossbill, a close sitter.

Photograph by Tommy Milner

SCOTTISH CROSSBILL

Loxia Scotica.

Related species: Common crossbill, parrot crossbill and two-barred crossbill.

DESCRIPTION: Scottish crossbill has a larger, blunter bill than common crossbill and has a larger body. It is Britain's only unique species. It is a bird of the Highlands of Scotland, breeding in the ancient pine woods. The male is red, the female dull green. Young birds resemble the female, but with greyer tones. Length 17cm (7in).

STATUS IN THE WILD: Resident in its Scottish homeland with about 1,000 breeding pairs.

HARDBILL OR SOFTBILL? Hardbill.

AVAILABILITY FOR BIRDKEEPERS: Not as many specimens are kept as one would have thought, but a few pairs are maintained by ardent enthusiasts.

ADVANTAGES TO KEEPING: Early, easy breeder. Wonderful show bird will hybridise with canary and some other finches.

DISADVANTAGES TO KEEPING: Requires robust accommodation, due to its strong bill, with which it can destroy wooden batons etc. Legs can get infested with scaly mite, this condition is easily treatable.

DIET: Pine seeds, berries and other seeds.

HOUSING: Two terraces of flights, each 6ft x 3ft x 7ft high, with 3ft wide passageway between, will suffice. Safety door fitted to wired passage, and doors to flights provided with feeding hatch. Good light is essential, so any covering should be of see-through material.

BREEDING: The nest is usually located on an outer branch of a pine tree, some considerable height from the ground. The base of which is constructed of twigs, this supports a cup-shaped nest made of grasses and mosses. It is lined with feathers, and is built early in the year, usually February or March. Three to five, pale blue eggs are marked with purple and are incubated by the female for 14-15 days; starting with the first egg. Both parents feed the chicks for 17-21 days whilst in the nest and for some time after, until they have developed the crossed mandibles that enables them to find their own food. This is at about the 6 week stage. The species is single brooded in the wild. Within home-breeding conditions, pairs will breed more than once in a season. Several pairs in a collection will stimulate breeding. Nest pans of 6in in diameter fixed among Scots pine branches will be used. Some birds will take mealworms. Main diet should consist of hemp, safflower, sunflower seeds and pine nuts, together with chickweed, soaked seed and red-band pigeon conditioner. Grit and cuttlefish bone should also be offered.

RING SIZE: Code J.

SHOWING REQUIREMENTS: As large as possible. Short body, very thickset throughout, bold, wide head and neck. Even, bright colour. The plumage being of the highest possible standard. Points: Size 15, type 25, colour and markings 30, feather quality and condition 15, steadiness and presentation 15. Total 100. Hardbill No.4 cage.

LEGAL REQUIREMENTS: Listed on Schedule 1, Part 1 of the Wildlife and Countryside Act 1981. Can be sold or shown within terms of current legislation.

SPECIAL NOTES: The crossing of the bill can be right or left. This determines which is the stronger foot and leg. Gregarious. Spends life high up in conifers.

Photograph by Ron Summers

PARROT CROSSBILL

Loxia pytyopsittacus.

Related species: Common crossbill, Scottish crossbill and two-barred crossbill.

DESCRIPTION: The largest - at 18cm (7in) of the crossbill species, but superficially very similar to the common crossbill. The species shows a larger and heavier bill, the mandible tips of which cross. The head and neck also appear proportionately larger. The male has red plumage with dark wings. Female has yellowish-green plumage with dark wings. Juvenile have grey-brown streaked plumage.

STATUS IN THE WILD: Breeds in northern Europe, but prone to invasions beyond regular range. Irruption in 1962-63, for example, brought small numbers of the birds to England and Scotland. Now breeds in goodly numbers in Scotland, notably in the Abernethy forest.

HARDBILL OR SOFTBILL? Hardbill.

AVAILABILITY FOR BIRDKEEPERS: Widely kept by enthusiasts, both here in Britain and on the continent. Prices vary, but in excess of £100 for a single bird.

ADVANTAGES TO KEEPING: Grand bird, easy to breed in home conditions. Will hybridise with a variety of hardbill kinds, including the canary.

DISADVANTAGES TO KEEPING: None evident.

HOUSING: Suggested facilities for home-kept pairs involves the construction of wooden aviaries in parallel lines with wire netting roofs, and with a wire-covered passageway between them with safety door. Flight doors with feeding hatch and observation keyhole are advised.

BREEDING: In the wild, the parrot crossbill breeds in pine forests often near clearings. Often breed in loose social groups. The nest is built 3m -13.7m (10 - 45ft) high in a conifer, and is a more substantial structure than that of the common crossbill. It is a cup similarly built of a solid foundation of twigs or grass, pine needles and moss, lined with fine grass, bark, lichen and feathers. Laying begins in late March, but at times from December to June. Usually single brooded in the wild. Eggs two to four, smooth and glossy, pale with variable markings. Incubation by female, fed by male for 14-16 days. Nestlings fed on pine seeds regurgitated by adults. In aviary conditions, nests will be built in clumps of collected fir branches. Food could consist of safflower,

sunflower, hemp, Chinese pine nuts, and chickweed.

CALL: Utters *chip chip* flight call, lower pitch than common crossbill. Song consists of greenfinch like elements, lower pitch than common crossbill.

RING SIZE: Code J.

SHOWING REQUIREMENTS: (General points) Size: As large as possible. Short body, very thickset throughout, bold wide head and neck. Colour and markings: even, bright colour. The plumage to be of the highest possible standard. There are three distinct phases in the colour cycle. Juvenile: grey green with heavy lacings. Second season cocks: copper red when colour fed. Older mature cocks: yellow, sometimes with copper streaks. Hen similar to above, but of rich olive-yellow green hue devoid of smokiness. Show cage, hardbill size 4. The parrot crossbill has in recent times, become a popular show bird.

LEGAL REQUIREMENTS: Listed on Schedule 1 of the Wildlife and Countryside Act 1981. Specially protected. Can be sold or shown within terms of General Licence.

Photograph by Ron Summers

TWO-BARRED CROSSBILL
Loxia leucoptera.

Related species: Common crossbill, Scottish crossbill and parrot crossbill.

DESCRIPTION: Adults of both sexes have slender bill with overlapping mandible tips and two striking white wingbars. Male has pinkish-red plumage, female yellowish-green. Juvenile shows double wingbars but has grey-brown streaked plumage. Length 15cm (6in).

STATUS IN THE WILD: Bird of conifer and larch forests of northern Scandinavia and eastern Russia. A rare wanderer to Britain, especially to Fair Isle and along east coast from July through to winter. Worth searching crossbill flocks during irruptions where a specimen or two may be discovered.

HARDBILL OR SOFTBILL? Hardbill.

AVAILABILITY FOR BIRDKEEPERS: Available at high cost from continental sources.

ADVANTAGES TO KEEPING: Beautiful species, highly regarded as a show bird; often seen at main events.

DISADVANTAGES TO KEEPING: Will chew through wooden cages etc. Some difficulty in securing pairs.

DIET: Mainly larch seeds and seeds of true conifers, also berries.

HOUSING: Colony nester, small flights, partly protected from the weather and damage-proof positioned in a block, or in large indoor flight-cages. If only one pair is available, mirrors placed nearby might help to stimulate breeding.

BREEDING: Breeds in conifer/larch forests, often nests in cedars. The nest is built close to the trunk, and consists of a cup made on a foundation of twigs, grass, lichens, moss and leaves, inner lining of roots, lichens, hair and feathers. The breeding season begins in late March. Usually single brooded. Eggs number one to four in a clutch, smooth and glossy, spotted or marked in dark purple, they are incubated for 14 - 16 days. The nestlings are downy, mouth bright purplish-red. Young leave the nest after about 3 weeks and depend on their parents for a like period thereafter. Nest sites for home-bred pairs can consist of wicker baskets affixed amid conifer sprays. Pairs should be introduced into their breeding quarters in mid-January. Diet with which to feed the chicks should consist of soaked seed and chickweed. Often double-brooded in aviary conditions.

CALL: Utters chattering call in flight. Rattling and buzzing song, occasionally a trumpet-like call.

RING SIZE: Code J.

SHOWING REQUIREMENTS: As large as possible; short, very thickset throughout, bold, wide head and neck; both sexes to portray highly conspicuous white wing bars. Points: Size 15, type 25, colour and markings 30, feather and condition 15, steadiness and presentation 15. Total 100. Show cage, hardbill no 4.

LEGAL REQUIREMENTS: All four species of crossbill, fall within Schedule 1 of the Wildlife and Countryside Act 1981, birds protected by special penalties. Can be sold or shown under current regulations made under the Act.

SPECIAL NOTES: Also called white-winged crossbill.

CORN BUNTING
Miliaria calandra.

No related species in genus.

DESCRIPTION: In summer both sexes are medium brown streaked with dark brown on the head, back and breast. Eye-stripe, chin and throat paler. Coverts have pale edging; as do the wing and tail feathers. A streak runs downwards from the base of the bill. The bill is brown and the eyes hazel. In winter the plumage is darker overall. Young birds have more and deeper spots and are buffer in tone. A bulky bird which often sits in a conspicuous position on a post, over-head wire, or bush to sing. Length 18cm (7in).

STATUS IN THE WILD: Dry, open countryside is its habitat. Resident in Britain with some 20,000 pairs, but declining.

HARDBILL OR SOFTBILL? Hardbill.

AVAILABILITY FOR BIRDKEEPERS: Occasionally kept and bred by small number of enthusiasts.

ADVANTAGES TO KEEPING: Interesting subject, song very welcome. Makes nice exhibition bird.

DISADVANTAGES TO KEEPING: None that I know of.

DIET: Chiefly cereals and weed-seeds, also insects such as small beetles and their larvae, plus caterpillars, and sycamore buds, ivy berries also eaten.

HOUSING: A flight 1.8m (6ft) square or larger, furnished with perches, including 'singing posts'. Can be kept outside all year.

BREEDING: Wild birds usually nest low down in gorse, bushes, open fields or in corn, and sometimes on the ground. The nest is of grasses and bents, with a few hairs for lining. The eggs, usually three to five, have a greyish white or pale white to light sienna ground-colour. They are boldly streaked and spotted with brown-black, or rarely without markings. Laying begins in late May or later, occasionally double-brooded. A captive environment should reflect these breeding conditions if possible, with suitable nesting materials. A wicker basket will sometimes be used. The chicks are fed on insects, small mealworms, buffalo worms, cleaned fly maggots and wax moth larvae will also be offered to the chicks in home-bred conditions.

CALL: Song a series of little crackling notes, often described as like the jangling of a bunch of keys. Usual call is a *tsick*

which, rapidly repeated forms part of its song. Song period is from January to October, occasionally later.

RING SIZE: Code J.

SHOWING REQUIREMENTS: Cage size No. 4 for hardbills. Size, shape and head: large as possible, thick, defined neck with bold head. 15 points. Markings: Bold, well defined, with rich, deep nutty brown profusion. 15 points. Colour: Sound throughout but brown above, sandy-buff underneath. 15 points. Steadiness: 35 points. Quality and condition: 10 points. Staging: 10 points. Total: 100 points. Hens similar to above , but slimmer. Hens are invariably better coloured and marked. Difficult to sex.

LEGAL REQUIREMENTS: Not listed on any Schedule. Can be sold or shown within current legislation from legally held stock.

SPECIAL NOTES: Local and other names: common bunting, bunting lark and ebb. Sits closely.

Photograph by Dennis Avon

YELLOW BUNTING

Emberiza citrinella.

Related species: Reed bunting, black-headed bunting, yellow-breasted bunting, rock bunting, ortolan bunting, Cretzchman's bunting, little bunting, rustic bunting and cirl bunting.

DESCRIPTION: The breeding-plumage male has a bright lemon or canary yellow head, throat and underparts, and orange-rufous to chestnut back, mantle and rump. The head and throat are streaked with dusky brown, the back and flanks with rich brown. The bill is brown above and blueish horn beneath. Legs and irides brown. Female is a browner yellow, more striated on the head and underparts, and with a less distinct moustachial stripe. At first, the young are like the female, but after the first moult the males show yellow on the head, though for a year the streaks are pronounced. Length 15-16.5cm (6-6½in).

STATUS IN THE WILD: Resident in Britain, with about 800,000 breeding pairs.

HARDBILL OR SOFTBILL? Hardbill.

AVAILABILITY FOR BIRDKEEPERS: Good; since numbers are bred each year. Prices from £70 per pair to much more from dealers.

ADVANTAGES TO KEEPING: Most popular of its tribe, makes an excellent show bird.

DISADVANTAGES TO KEEPING: Nervous species, need to be well trained.

DIET: In summer, insects form the main diet, but in winter its preferences vary according to food supply. Flocks wander about seeking in fields and from farmyards.

HOUSING: Aviary or flight must be large enough to accommodate fast nuptial pursuits before nesting, male chasing female. Perches fitted at both ends are essential, and covered nest area also required.

BREEDING: The nest is built in April, of grass and moss lined with hair. It is either on or near the ground, typically in a hedge bank. Three to five brownish or purplish white ground-coloured eggs are laid. These are profusely lined with irregular fine or fairly thick markings. Two or more broods are reared in a season. They are laid at daily intervals. Incubation is usually carried out by the female, fed by the male, for 11-14 days. The young are tendered by both parents. Eyes open at five days. They leave the nest at 9-14 days, before they can fly properly, to avoid predators. They are able to fly at 16 days. Will readily nest in protected, wicker baskets at low level. Chicks can be fed on small mealworms, waxworms and buffalo worms.

CALL: From an elevated perch, male utters his well-known song, a single chit repeated several times, followed by two notes, the first sharp, the last drawn out. It all sounds like "a little bit of bread and no cheeeeese". (Scottish version "may the de'il take you!")

RING SIZE: Code E.

SHOWING REQUIREMENTS: No.3 hardbill show cage. Nicely rounded full head, well-filled body of good length and strong, bold appearance.

LEGAL REQUIREMENTS: Protected at all times. Schedule 3 species, can be sold or shown under regulations.

SPECIAL NOTES: Local and other names: yellowhammer, yellowyowley, yoist, yellow voiding, yeldrocko, yellow yelding, writing lark and scribbling lark.

Photograph by Dennis Avon

CIRL BUNTING
Emberiza cirlus.

Related species: Yellow bunting, black-headed bunting, yellow-breasted bunting, rock bunting, ortolan bunting, Cretzchman's bunting, little bunting, rustic bunting and reed bunting.

DESCRIPTION: More compact than yellow bunting, both sexes have olive-brown rump and white outer tail-feathers; male has black stripe through eye, edged above and below with yellow, black throat with greenish breast-band below it; female is a drab version of male. Length 16.5cm (6½in).

STATUS IN THE WILD: Resident. About 300 pairs in south-west England, plus a few in Jersey.

HARDBILL OR SOFTBILL? Harbill.

AVAILABILITY FOR BIRDKEEPERS: The species is bred in numbers in aviaries in Europe; fewer by specialist bunting keepers in the UK.

ADVANTAGES TO KEEPING: A challenge becoming popular again as a cage bird, with some notable examples staged.

DISADVANTAGES TO KEEPING: Not easy to breed, but may improve as keepers gain experience.

DIET: Corn and seeds of many species of weeds and grasses; also insects, including small beetles, grasshoppers and moth larvae. Young fed on insects.

HOUSING: Small, outside aviary suitable, planted out with small bushes and climbing plants such as hops and to include "singing posts".

BREEDING: In the wild, the nest is usually built higher up than that of the yellow bunting, sometimes against trunks of trees, in bushes and hedges also on the ground in banks. Nest has plenty of moss in its foundation, sometimes leaves; bents are also used. It is lined with grasses and horsehair. The eggs number three to four and have a greenish-blue ground colour and blackish markings. The species begins laying in May. Incubation is by the female for 11-13 days. Two or three broods are undertaken. The young are fed by both parents for about a fortnight, and for about the same period after fledging. Captive pairs should be provided with nesting material such as grasses and coconut fibre. Live foods should include mealworms, buffalo worms, and wax moth larvae. Wicker baskets, if suitably placed low down in cover, may be used by the birds.

CALL: Described as a metallic rattle on one note, similar to the song of a lesser whitethroat.

RING SIZE: Code E.

SHOWING REQUIREMENTS: An exhibition bird should be as large as possible, good length of body and thickset. Steadiness is very important, as is condition and staging. No. 3 hardbill cage is applicable. Shown singly.

LEGAL REQUIREMENTS: Listed on Schedule 1, Part 1, of the Wildlife and Countryside Act 1981, and is specially protected. General Licence exists enabling it to be shown or sold, if ringed and bred in captivity from legally held stock.

SPECIAL NOTES: DEFRA pays farmers to retain stubble in winter for cirl buntings and other birds to feed on. There is also a scheme under which volunteers hand-rear birds for release, under licence.

Photograph by Tony Tilford

REED BUNTING

Emberiza schoeniclus.

Related species: Yellow bunting, black-headed bunting, yellow-breasted bunting, rock bunting, ortolan bunting, Cretzchman's bunting, little bunting, rustic bunting and cirl bunting.

DESCRIPTION: Males have a complete black hood extending from the nape to upper breast, and broken only by a white moustachial streak. The lower nape is white, forming a collar between head and the chestnut and black-striped back and wing. The tail is broadly edged with white and the white underparts are finely streaked on the flanks. The female is a heavily streaked brown and buff bird with a light outline extending from the eye around the ear coverts, and bordered below by a black moustachial streak. Length 15cm (6in).

STATUS IN THE WILD: Resident in British Isles, about 350,000 pairs.

HARDBILL OR SOFTBILL? Hardbill.

AVAILABILITY FOR BIRDKEEPERS: Frequently bred in home conditions, usually available at a cost of £70 per pair.

ADVANTAGES TO KEEPING: Hardy species, breeds freely. Makes interesting show bird. Interesting study subject.

DISADVANTAGES TO KEEPING: Duller than yellow bunting, so always in its shadow at the shows.

DIET: Seeds of marsh weeds and grasses, also grain in autumn, and insects, including water-beetles, larvae of moths, water boatmen, dragonflies etc.

HOUSING: An outside, partly sheltered aviary of about 6ft long, 3ft wide and 7ft high, would suit a pair of these delightful birds. Some greenery is essential - reeds growing in tubs would help.

BREEDING: Breeds in a variety of situations, mainly wetland, among reeds and other dense vegetation. The nest is constructed on or near the ground, in grass or rush clump, or in a bush a few feet up. A cup of grass and moss, lined with finer grasses, hair and reed flowers, it is built by the female. Home-kept pairs will readily use small wicker baskets in which to build, coconut hair is often utilised. The breeding season begins in late April to June. It is double or treble brooded. Four or five eggs make up a clutch, they are smooth and glossy, pale purplish or lilac-grey, with blackish markings. The chicks are tendered by both parents for 10-13 days in the nest and for sometime afterwards. Livefood is required all through the year, especially at breeding time, when mealworms, clean fly maggots, buffalo worms and wax worms are all welcome.

CALL: Song, *te,te,te,te*. Alarm note, a sharp twitter. Sings out in the open from a bush, reed or some other vantage point.

RING SIZE: Code C. Internal diameter 2.5mm.

SHOWING REQUIREMENTS: Hardbill show cage No. 3. Exhibit, as large as possible, nicely rounded, full head, well filled cone shaped body of strong, bold appearance. Tendency for cocks to be larger than hens. Buffs are of less intensive colour. Rarely wins specials at events due to its inconspicuous attire.

LEGAL REQUIREMENTS: Listed on Schedule 3 of the Wildlife and Countryside Act 1981. Can be sold or shown under the Act.

SPECIAL NOTES: Local and other names: Reed sparrow, passerine bunting, black bonnet, chink, water sparrow, black-headed bunting. Sits closely. Its eggs, smallest of the buntings found in Britain.

Photograph by Dennis Avon

159

ORTOLAN BUNTING

Emberiza hortulana.

Related species: Yellow bunting, black-headed bunting, yellow-breasted bunting, rock bunting, reed bunting, Cretzchman's bunting, little bunting, rustic bunting and cirl bunting.

DESCRIPTION: The male has a greenish head and breast with a yellow moustachial streak. The upperparts are brown streaked with black, it has white outer tail feathers, and rich orange underparts. Female and juvenile darker and more heavily streaked above, the yellow throat pattern can usually be seen. Length 16.5cm (6½in).

STATUS IN THE WILD: Spring migrant to Europe from Asia. Occurs in Britain on Fair Isle in spring, Norfolk and Suffolk coasts in autumn, also south coast of England. Bird of open country with low vegetation, agricultural land, hedgerows and gardens.

HARDBILL OR SOFTBILL? Regarded as a hardbill.

AVAILABILITY FOR BIRDKEEPERS: Available from continental sources, occasionally found at bird sales. Cost substantial.

ADVANTAGES TO KEEPING: Perhaps a ready breeder in suitable conditions. Would make nice addition to bunting ranks at the shows.

DISADVANTAGES TO KEEPING: Availability is the biggest issue.

DIET: All kinds of insects and their larvae, also seeds of grasses, cereals and weeds.

HOUSING: A pair should occupy a roomy, planted flight, with small bushes and grasses, allowing the birds to forage. These should be kept in good growth by watering.

BREEDING: The nest is placed on the ground among grass or low bushes and consists of a cup of grasses lined with hair and built by the female in May or June. Small wicker baskets would be used in aviary conditions. The species is single brooded. Eggs number four to six. These are smooth and glossy, very pale blueish, pinkish, purplish or grey; sparingly, but evenly marked with spots, small blotches and scrawling. The incubation is by the female alone for 11-14 days. The nestlings are downy, pale buffish grey. They are fed by both parents for 10-15 days in the nest, and for a similar period after fledging. Home-bred chicks will require plenty of invertebrates, these could include, mealworms, wax moth larvae and cleaned fly maggots.

CALL: A thin *zit* and stronger *tseu*, the song is rather melancholy with several *tseu* notes.

RING SIZE: Code D advised.

SHOWING REQUIREMENTS: No. 3 hardbill show cage. As large as possible, with nicely rounded full head, well filled cone shaped body of strong bold appearance. Shown singly.

LEGAL REQUIREMENTS: Not listed on any Schedule of the Wildlife and Countryside Act 1981, but appears on an Annex, and subjected to a General Licence, for vagrant species which permits the bird to be exhibited if bred in captivity from lawfully held parents. Rings optional in law, but recommended.

SPECIAL NOTES: France is traditionally associated with the eating of ortolan. The practice has been made illegal there since 1999, but the habit is said to persist. Ortolans are caught in nets and then placed in dark boxes where they gorge themselves on oats and millet, this increases their weight fourfold, they are then drowned in Armagnac, plucked and roasted... need I go on?

Photograph by Sergey Yeliseev

SNOW BUNTING

Plectrophenax nivalis.

Related species: No others in genus.

DESCRIPTION: Breeding male has white head and underside, black wings with large white patches and black bill. Female has less bright plumage and browner underparts. Winter male has pale brown back and brownish cap and cheek. Juvenile darker than parents. Length 16.5cm (6½in).

STATUS IN THE WILD: About 12-17 pairs breed on Scottish hills. Several thousand spend winter along east coasts of Scotland and England.

HARDBILL OR SOFTBILL? Recognised as a hardbill.

AVAILABILITY FOR BIRDKEEPERS: Specialist breeders are able to locate aviary pairs fairly easily, most of them bred by European fanciers, although a few are now being raised within British collections. Birds cost about £200 a pair.

ADVANTAGES TO KEEPING: A challenge for any enthusiast.

DISADVANTAGES TO KEEPING: Has sombre colours in winter, so not as attractive as a summer bird from an exhibitors' point of view.

DIET: Insects, especially flies and caddis, also seeds of dwarf trees and grasses.

HOUSING: Small outside aviary with pool and grassy mound, rocks with crevices for nesting, also perches including 'song' post.

BREEDING: Males show off their bold pied plumage in elaborate courtship displays. The nest is hidden in rocks, and is constructed of grass and moss and is lined with feathers. The eggs four to six are laid in May; and are off-white, blotched brown. The female alone incubates for 10 -15 days. Both parents feed the young for about a fortnight, the female brooding for the first few days. Chicks often leave the nest for short periods before fledging. Double brooded. Home-bred pairs will need every available insect, together with small mealworms, clean fly maggots, buffalo worms and wax moth larvae in order to raise a family.

CALL: A rapid trilling, sung from perch or in flight. Tinkling calls.

RING SIZE: Code G.

SHOWING REQUIREMENTS: Bird exhibited in hardbill show cage size 4 or C, the largest of the hardbill series of cages. Standard not too defined, but exhibit must be as large as possible, with bright eye, and good tail and wing carriage, and to move from perch to perch in a confident and unstressed manner.

LEGAL REQUIREMENTS: Listed on Schedule 1 Part 1 of the Wildlife and Countryside Act 1981. Birds protected by special penalties at all times. Can be sold or shown under current legislation.

SPECIAL NOTES: Breeds further north than any other small bird.

Photograph by Tommy Milner

LAPLAND BUNTING

Calcarius lapponicus.

Related species: No others in genus.

DESCRIPTION: The male in breeding condition is unmistakable. The head has striking black, white and chestnut markings and black-tipped yellow bill. The underparts are white, back brown with bold streaks. The female in breeding condition is similar to the male, but has the black on the face replaced by brown feathering. Both male and female of the species lose bold markings on the head as winter approaches. Juveniles resemble female. The bird crouches low and runs rather quickly and jerkily. Length 15cm (6in).

STATUS IN THE WILD: Regular winter visitor to east coast of England. Has bred in Scotland. Visits treeless country and rough ground; preferably near the sea in Scandinavia and Arctic tundra. Bird winters around Baltic and North Sea coast.

HARDBILL OR SOFTBILL? Hardbill.

AVAILABILITY FOR BIRDKEEPERS: Available from time to time, cost about £70 each.

ADVANTAGES TO KEEPING: Opportunity for experienced keepers to take up this bird and breed a strain for sale or show.

DISADVANTAGES TO KEEPING: Stock difficult to find, but now that no Schedule 4 paperwork is involved prospect for finding stock may become easier.

DIET: Chiefly insects, and seeds of various grasses and plants.

HOUSING: Aviary 1.8m square x 2.1m high (6ft sq x 7ft) suitable for one pair, interior to mimic bird's habitat, with rocks, sand, grasses and tussocks.

BREEDING: Nest made of moss and bents, rather bulky, lined with fine grasses and feathers, built in a depression on the ground at side of a tussock. Eggs in a clutch number five to six, laid at daily intervals, coloured greyish to brownish, usually thickly clouded and blotched with chestnut, sepia or brown, with a few dark streaks and spots. They are laid late in May and June. Incubation is by both birds, but mainly by the female, commencing at the completion of the clutch for 10 to 14 days. They leave the nest after 8-10 days, 3-5 days before they can fly.

CALL: There are two distinctive flight calls, a musical *tew* and a short rattling *trrrk*, sometimes heard in quick succession, both rather quiet. Song is a rapid trill, all too seldom heard in Britain.

RING SIZE: Code E.

SHOWING REQUIREMENTS: Species was exhibited in small numbers in distant past. Its return would be welcomed by the fancy. Hardbill cage No.4. length 14in, height 12in, with 6½ inch No.14 gauge wires, 1in apart, centre to centre. Drinking hole 1¼in in diameter. The bottom rail is 2in high. Top rail 1½in high at the outside, sloping to ¾in at the centre. Top, bottom, outside back and sides black, with the inside and front wires and both rails Georgian green. Floor covering seed only. Two perches. Exhibit: size, as large as possible 10 points, shape 10 points, markings well defined 10 points, colour 30 points, steadiness 20 points, quality and condition 10 points, staging 10 points. Total 100 points. Shown singly.

LEGAL REQUIREMENTS: Specially protected. Species can be sold or shown under current legislation, if ringed and bred in captivity.

Photograph by Bozena Kalejta-Summers

KEEPING HOUSE SPARROWS

I first began keeping house sparrows (*Passer domesticus*) in the late 1960's, and have bred one or more examples of the bird every year since then. The house sparrow needs no lengthy introduction, as it is a familiar bird to both town and country folk. It is very domesticated as its Latin name implies. Numbers have fallen in the wild, in recent times; this is thought to be due to modern agricultural practices, and the bird's tendency not to migrate far from its local area. Crops are rotated nowadays in such a manner that stubble is buried by the plough almost immediately after harvesting. This process of planting autumn-sown crops subjects the house sparrow to a scant winter and starvation.

It is reasonable to suppose that sparrows followed Man out of Africa into Europe. They are weaver-like in habit and before dwellings appeared in their natural habitat or in the absence of caves, weaved their bulky nests in any available bush or tree, near to where humans had camped. House sparrows still build their nests in areas where habitation is scarce. They use grasses to form the shape and feathers to fashion the inner chamber as a nursery for their young.

In this species, the cock bird is the more gaudy. In breeding conditions he is indeed a handsome fellow, dressed in chestnut streaked with black, a black bib and a crown of uniform dark ash-grey. The female is somewhat sombre in appearance. My house sparrows were at one time kept in a large planted aviary, every year I enjoyed studying them immensely. Wooden nest-boxes were placed on shelves near the top of the aviary. The birds did well in this environment, behaving in a way one would expect a wild colony to, taking part in courtship chases and bickering over nesting material. All the pairs went down to nest at the same time. At least three clutches of eggs were laid by each pair in a season, starting in April and ending by the end of July.

One main disadvantage encountered with the colony system is the lack of control over the selection of the pairs. In order to comply with the law which requires a keeper to inform a potential buyer of a bird's ancestry, observation is necessary to ascertain which cock bird is fathering which chicks, an almost impossible task. I kept records as accurately as possible, and observed each numbered box. However, the cock entering a given box is not always the father of the chicks within. Another, less severe problem is the difficulty in catching a bird up quickly, especially in a large aviary. The aviary has become somewhat dilapidated lately, and no longer used for house sparrows. I now house them in smaller flights.

A significant number of young house sparrows in my collection have gone light, in the same way as young greenfinches. In the past years I have lost several good birds, especially variants. Now, I use sulpha drugs and have surmounted the problem. Over the years, I have kept and bred many variant house sparrows, including melanistic, pied and cinnamon. On one occasion, many years ago, a policemen friend of mine had a jet black (melanistic) cock house sparrow frequenting his garden. I remember quickly building a small portable aviary into which we finally enticed the bird, in order to add it to my collection. Although black house sparrows are uncommon, I have known a few colonies in the wild containing several individuals of that hue.

My favourite variety of variant house sparrow is the cinnamon, which is referred to as brown on the Continent. My first cinnamon house sparrows were given to me by Tommy Sharland of Ipswich. The best bird was a superb visual cinnamon cock which I exhibited on a number of occasions including the National Exhibition. I also bred equal numbers of split cocks and visual hens from it. Sometime later another East Anglian fancier gave me a cinnamon hen. I was able to breed split cocks from it. Unfortunately, the variant hens bred from them proved difficult to get through the moult. It was not until 1989, that I finally overcame this problem.

The year 1990 proved to be a very good year for my house sparrow project, with several visual cinnamon hens being bred to maturity. One pair, consisting of a split cinnamon cock and a normal hen produced no fewer than three visuals in one nest, all of which survived. The young were reared on a varied diet, including insects caught by the birds themselves, mealworms and moistened soft-food. The young were cared for by the adults for 14 days, then for a further fortnight after they had fledged.

In late summer, it is usual for nest-boxes to become infested with earwigs. Sometimes, when this occurs, a pair will revert to building a natural nest in a bush. Two of my pairs did this in 1990, one built a domed nest in an elder bush, another couple using an old teapot I had nailed to a post. These "outside" nests had eggs laid in them before the domes were completed. Each roof was built around the cups on the nests during the incubation stage. It must have been like lying in bed when someone is painting the ceiling! During the 1990s I added many other colour variant varieties to my collection and have bred many youngsters from them, these include black-faced or black-masked, phaeo-melanin, satinette, fawn, opal and Isabel. My present strain consists mainly of phaeo-melanins.

The house sparrow is not an easy subject for the beginner. Success usually comes with experience and an understanding of the bird's behaviour. However, they are well worth keeping and have a future in the Fancy, especially with the establishing of new strains of the variant varieties.

Phaeo-melanin cock house sparrow

THE CHAFFINCH – BREEDING

The cheerful song of the chaffinch can be heard from mid-February until well into July. During the breeding season the male sings almost without interruption, each song lasting for only a few seconds. Mid February is also the time when I pair my birds up and introduce them into their respective planted aviaries.

A good-sized flight is beneficial to a breeding pair, in fact, the larger the enclosure is, the better it will be for the birds, enabling sexual display flights to be performed unhindered and encouraging a varied insect life to thrive on and around the growing foliage. This food is essential to supplement any provided by the keeper.

Sexual display flights begin in early March, with the cock's rapid chase of the hen. The birds commence building operations towards the end of April; the hen is seen carrying material to a favoured spot. If the chosen location is not protected from the weather, or has an unstable foundation, I rectify the problem without disturbing the birds too much.

A canary nest pan or an open wicker basket affixed at the site or as near to it as possible, will usually be accepted by the birds, and if the correct nesting materials are supplied, a beautiful, snug nest will be made, identical to any made by a wilding. A plentiful amount of nesting material is provided for the birds as soon as they approach breeding condition: various mosses, lichens, cobwebs, hair, feathers and vegetable down are the main materials used.

I always secure a number of nesting receptacles in suitable places in each flight, prior to the birds' occupation. I screen them to some extent with fresh conifer branches. In the larger aviaries the birds often construct their nests in a bush or a small tree, entwining fibres around the platform branches to ensure a firm foundation. The plants growing within my aviaries include elder, leylandi, honeysuckle and box.

The hen constructs the nest, although on rare occasions the cock will assist. The male's usual role is to guard the nest with the only weapon he has – his song. With this he defends the territory from other birds.

INCUBATION

Three to six eggs are laid in early May, and these are reddish-brown with almost black irregular streaks. Incubation is carried out by the hen alone for a period of 12 days. The young are downy; their mouths are deep red with orange upperparts and the gape flanges are white.

They are fed by both parents for about two weeks before they fledge and for up to five weeks after leaving the nest, their heads swaying from side to side to stimulate their parents to bring food for them. The young birds are almost as big as their parents by the time they become self-supporting. Each chick is close-ringed at six days old.

Insects of many kinds are caught and fed to the young; the adult birds search every nook and cranny for this vital source of food, small crickets, mini mealworms, buffalo worms and wax moth larvae are made readily available for the birds. Home-grown, clean blowfly maggots are also supplied to the birds and some egg-food is also consumed.

First and second year birds tend to produce only one round of chicks but as they age two broods often becomes the norm. One advantage is their spider-like mentality; the urge to reproduce is so strong they persist in raising a family, even if set-backs have occurred.

Pair of breeding chaffinches

Cock chaffinch bred by Bernard Howlett in 1989

WHITE CHAFFINCHES

In the mid 19th Century, Robert Browning wrote his poem Home Thoughts from Abroad, with its memorable lines: While the chaffinch sings on the orchard bough in England – now!

That poem not only enlightened me to the song of the chaffinch but inspired me to write my own book of poems.

The chaffinch is a beautiful bird. The handsome male has a slate-grey head, pink breast and chestnut mantle. His wings are dark with brilliant white patches, very noticeable in flight. The female is less colourful, with much paler pink on her breast, and a yellowish brown mantle and head. I have always kept chaffinches and have enjoyed show bench success with them. Then came the opportunity to breed mutations….

In August 2006 I met a fellow keeper in a car park in Lincolnshire. He had with him eight very rare split white recessive chaffinches. All these birds were siblings, bred from a visual white cock. They consisted of four cocks and four hens, all raised since 2001.

None were closed-ringed. Their breeder had refrained from ringing them because of their rarity - he did not want to disturb their nests in case they were ejected by their parents. During this period some of the stock were closely bred together, and though white chicks appeared, only one survived. Their breeder thought a lethal gene of some kind was to blame. The lone, white survivor had been passed on to another fancier. The original white cock had died. I was asked to take the birds on, in the hope of producing a robust white strain.

If the mode of inheritance was indeed recessive, I knew that the eight siblings would be carriers of the white father. If I continued to pair them together and they were recessive would the "lethal gene" continue to manifest itself, or was there another explanation for the early deaths of these young, white birds?

I decided to introduce new blood into the stud by using my own, normal strain and specimens from friends. I could then introduce eight healthy pairs, each containing a split and a normal bird, into my flights. If a lethal gene were present, it would perhaps, be weakened - I hoped!

"Lethal" traits can indeed disrupt the metabolism and cause death. By out-crossing the "affected" birds, I aimed to dilute any lethal gene. Eventually I would be able to propagate viable white chaffinches and therefore promote a white strain, alongside my lovely normal one.

I colour-banded the eight rare birds with plastic split coloured rings - pink, red, white, purple, yellow, green, black and blue. All their spouses were already closed-ringed.

On November 26th I discovered that the hen fitted with the white split ring had died. There were no signs of any outward injury, and the bird was in good bodily condition. I put the death down to possible "night fright" or age.

2007 was a disastrous year – pairs bred but not one youngster was raised. I was losing my way with the stud.

In 2008, two chaffinch chicks from the project were raised, both cocks, which each had a 50 per cent chance of being a carrier. The young birds, which were housed in quite a large aviary, were fed mainly on mini-mealworms and buffalo worms. In 2009/10, more were bred, but due to age some of the split stock had been lost.

By April 2011, I only had one carrier left, the cock with the yellow split ring. I paired this bird, the best of the original group, to an exhibition hen. The end of April saw the cock keeping close contact with the hen in their large, planted aviary, and he was also beginning to sing.

It was early May before I saw any hint of breeding, when I noticed the hen was pulling feathers from her breast. There were plenty of feathers around for her to use, together with moss. I thought then that it would be only a matter of time before nesting began. I had fixed several wicker baskets around the large aviary and by early June the pair had built a nest in the elder bush. By the 11th, three eggs were being incubated. The hen incubated the clutch well, but all the eggs failed to hatch. I still await the first white chaffinch to emerge.

GREENFINCHES CHARM AND CHALLENGE BEGINNERS

Greenfinches are so tame and endearing that they are an obvious choice for anyone wanting to take up bird keeping.

My main interest lies with the breeding and exhibition of British softbills, particularly blackbirds and song thrushes, but I have always kept greenfinches and am very fond of them. They are confiding in habit and easy to breed and maintain. There are also many colour variants for newcomers to choose from. Understanding their genetics is challenging and another inducement to breeding them.

At the present time there are many colour mutations, including cinnamon, Ino (lutino), cinnamon-ino (satinette), agate, cinnamon-agate (Isabel), pastel, cinnamon-pastel (brown-pastel). I am presently breeding pieds, black-eyed and plum-eyed clears and phaeos.

Although I occasionally show them, my main reason for keeping them is for study purposes and their therapeutic qualities. Just having them around to watch and study helps me cope with the irritations of life.

All my greenfinches are housed outside for most of the year - usually a pair to each flight. The only occasions when birds are brought into the birdroom is when I wish to prevent youngsters from going light, or when I collect birds to make up pairs for a new breeding season.

PAIRS SECURED

The calendar year therefore begins with all the pairs secured in their respective aviaries, having been selected in autumn when all their quarters were cleaned out and repaired as required.

Birds receive a quality British finch mixture, supplemented with small sunflower seeds. This is maintained throughout the year, with greenfood, eggfood and soaked seed added during the breeding season. Some birds will take mealworms, and this should be encouraged.

The breeding season often lasts for months, from early April to early September, with some pairs producing two or even three rounds, depending on how fit they are. Only young, fit birds are used for breeding, each pair is administered a daily dose of a sulpha drug over a five-day period before breeding begins, the solution being 3ml of drug to one pint of water. This is repeated from the day chicks hatch with the solution mixed with eggfood. Some losses are inevitable among any bird species, the greenfinch is no exception, but great strides have been made in recent time to improve their health, with good results.

I use canary nest pans, placed under cover for the birds. These are soon taken up. The hens build sturdy nests with moss, horsehair, coconut fibre, and other plant material. It is essential to have nesting material available at the time the birds require it, as otherwise eggs will be laid on the cold floor of the nest-pan. Clutches of greenfinch eggs are variable, with 3-5 the average, which are incubated by the hen alone for about two weeks. Both parents feed the chicks on regurgitated food. I use soaked seed, dandelion, chickweed and other herbs, and any seeding grasses or plants available. Rape, in its green stage, is much relished by the birds and seems to be particularly good for them. Some breeders insist that greenfood is unnecessary and they may be right as some young birds are reared completely without it. My greenfinches are small birds compared to those within the top strains. At the present time I only occasionally show specimens of the species, and they are usually variant varieties. I do regret not having large show birds of all colours in my collection, and even at this late stage I am attempting to redress the issue. I have mentioned clear and phaeo birds. Clear greenfinches are used to breed clear mules with Norwich hens, the larger the greenfinch, the better the mule. Another type not so far covered in this article is the cinnamon pied. I also have these in my collection, a nice looking mutation. I exhibited a phaeo at the South East Ipswich show in October 2012, the first ever seen in Britain - or so I understand.

NOTE: At the 2013 World Show staged at Hasselt, Belgium, I exhibited two phaeo hens, one of which was awarded 93 points and the GOLD MEDAL (bird on far right not shown).

Photograph by
Dennis Avon

**Juvenile Lutino
greenfinches bred by the author**

Note: further breeding from Bill's birds have
produced a strain of phaeo melanin greenfinches.
(See page 321 for World Show winner)

Photograph by
Dennis Avon

**This is the Continental-bred "White
Greenfinch" now owned by the author.**

I bought eight pairs of Greenfinches from Bill Roberts
which I thought contained a pied gene, but I failed to breed a
Pied specimen from them. It was always the ambition of Syd
Evans of Port Talbot to breed an Albino colour variant Greenfinch. This variant is now being bred on the Continent, so it is
possible that they will be available in the UK soon.

I recently acquired a bird that was bred on the Continent
which I believe is a pure Greenfinch and not a Mule. It is
virtually pure white as the accompanying picture shows. I am
trying to contact its breeder to find out more about it. It has
lime-yellow suffusion on the shoulders, and its rump is bright
lime-yellow. Its wings and tail show faint traces of yellow-green.
Its eyes are dark red and it has the call of a Greenfinch.

Undoubtedly similar specimens exist in Europe. If it is a
pure Greenfinch it could well be termed an Albino. I have never
seen a bird like it before and would welcome readers' views
about it. I have paired it to a Normal cock and put them into an
outside aviary. The pair seem compatible so I hope to be able
to breed a strain of Albinos from them. **1993**

AGATE GREENFINCH

Photograph by
Dennis Avon

Photograph by
Andrew Calvesbert

**Phaeo melanin hen
greenfinch from
my rare strain**

TWO YOUNG ISABEL GREENFINCHES
OWNED AND BRED BY BERNARD HOWLETT

Photograph by Dennis Avon

BREEDING THE SISKIN

Hundreds of siskins of various colours are bred each year, both in this country and in Europe. Many are bred inside bird rooms – but they are easy to breed outside, too.

During April 2006, I released a pair of normal coloured siskins into a large, planted aviary. The birds had been bred in 2004 and raised young in 2005. They settled down well, and were fed on a good seed diet. Flowers and seeds of plants growing within the aviary provided them with an added source of nourishment.

16th May. The little hen was seen carting nesting material to a small wicker basket which I had attached to the aviary wire, at a height of 2.65m (8ft 6in). Growing up towards the site was an elder bush, which had been trimmed back in the autumn.

24th May. Four eggs had been laid and incubation had begun. Although I had a ladder in the aviary, I used another one to lean against the outside so that I could inspect the nest from time to time.

4th June. I discovered that some of the chicks had hatched.

7th June. Using the interior ladder, I climbed up through the elder bush (which in the intervening period had grown alarmingly) and was able to closed-ring three chicks. The fourth chick was too small to ring. I decided not to ring it at all but to make a note to this effect in my records. Although the parent birds appeared a little agitated while the ringing was in progress, they quickly returned to their parental duties.

13th June. All four chicks had grown well.

19th June. Three chicks left the nest on 19th June their smaller sibling followed a few days later. The young were fed by both parents on soaked seed, egg food and mini-mealworms.

20th June. I discovered the hen sitting on a new nest. This was on a ledge 2.8m (9ft) up, under a beam. I had no idea that a second nest was being built. To my delight three eggs had already been laid. A fourth followed and incubation began. Meanwhile, the four first-round young were flying about in the enclosure, exploring every nook and cranny. The smallest had now caught up well and was recognisable only by the absence of a ring. They were fascinating to watch - all seemed to be on a journey of discovery, nibbling at anything in reach, especially elder and honeysuckle leaves, devouring the many insects which were available within the large aviary or had settled on the perimeter wire.

I placed a feeder filled with peanuts in the aviary, a

a height of 1.2m (4ft). Immediately the cock bird flew down to taste the new source of food, soon to be followed by some of the youngsters.

30th June. The four second-round chicks had hatched. I closed-ringed them all at the last possible moment of growth - about the eighth day - so that even the smallest was officially banded. I became concerned about the apparent fragility of the nest. It had not been well constructed and I was worried that, as the chicks grew, some might fall out. I kept a strict watch and luckily, all flew successfully towards the end of the month.

At that time I had eight young siskins, plus their parents, flying around the aviary in the hot July sun. Their contact calls and their calls for food seemed unceasing.

1st August. My attention is drawn to the apparent absence of the female adult. I thought little of it, since the aviary looked like a jungle, and with three well placed feeding stations it was easy to miss an individual bird.

4th August. I re-find the little hen sitting on her original nest, high up in the elder bush.

From my vantage point I could see well-grown chicks inside it.

Again I climbed the internal ladder to the site. I had great difficulty in reaching the nest through the branches of the elder bush. In due course I managed to ring three of the four chicks, the fourth was too small, so I left it unringed and made a note to that effect.

With 14 siskins to feed, I increased the quantity of soaked seed and egg food for the birds. Seeding plants continued to be available for them, growing within the enclosure.

14th August. Three of the four third-round chicks left the nest, and were observed flying about in the branches. There was no sign of the fourth chick in the nest or elsewhere.

Some of the older chicks lose their drab juvenile feathers and begin to colour up. The young cocks, in particular, display yellow wing-bars and a hint of a black cap.

2nd September. The young from the third round stop calling for food.

6th September. Cocks from earlier nests begin to sing for the first time!

After the breeding season, wild siskins forage for food in small flocks.

I left the family in the aviary for some time, but as winter approached, I removed the youngsters, leaving the old pair in situ.

Male Siskin - not one of my birds

Photograph by Dennis Avon

LUTINOS IN THE FOREST

On a warm spring day, in the late 1970s children were playing in a Norfolk wood, when a phenomenon of gigantic proportions so far as aviculture was concerned made itself manifest. Three little yellow birds were found struggling to fly, thinking they were escaped canaries, the children caught them up and took them to the house of a well-known canary breeder, but unfortunately the gentleman was not at home. The children returned later, but by this time the three little orphans were near death's door. The bird man, on examining the young birds, immediately identified their species, they were yellow buntings, lutino yellow buntings. Two died, but the third was saved by the man's dedication and care. It moulted out into a very nice specimen.

The lone lutino, a hen, was transferred to a yellow bunting expert, into a large, especially prepared aviary for it and for its prospective mate. The rare hen built a nest on the floor, but no eggs were laid. The pair proved incompatible, the cock being very aggressive.

The lutino hen was again transferred, this time to a Midlands fancier, who also tried to breed from it, but was unsuccessful. Being a lutino mutation, with red eyes, eyes not geared to see well in strong light was no doubt a factor in its failure to breed. Had the lutino thrived and bred, a strain could have been developed giving the fancy a wonderful addition. It may be many years before such a rare yellow bunting is raised again.

I have been keeping the yellow bunting for many years and have bred them on several occasions. Best results have been with single pairs, each housed in large aviaries. They have built their nests in wicker baskets and in various boxes. Three eggs seem to be the usual clutch. Young birds leave the nest in my experience early on, before they can fly, this is a self-preservation measure.

I have done well on the show bench with hand-reared, colour-fed birds, often winning a special. The most important wins have been at the World Show where both silver and bronze medals have been awarded.

MALE YELLOW BUNTING

Photograph by Tony Tilford

CHAPTER FOUR

My Mules and Hybrids

BLACKBIRD HEN

Photograph by Dennis Avon

MY MULES AND HYBRIDS

My expertise with British birds has been with softbills and in particular, blackbirds and song thrushes. My most important mules and hybrids have been in the production of the greenfinch mule, canary x bullfinch, bramblefinch x chaffinch and song thrush x blackbird hybrids. I have however bred other crosses, these include greenfinch x chaffinch, goldfinch x redpoll, linnet x greenfinch and linnet x canary.

My most important mules have been clear or nearly clear mules, produced from black-eyed clear or almost clear greenfinches, crossed with Norwich hens. Six such birds have been produced within the last few years, the best being the first of these bred in 2006, a nearly clear and good shaped hen (see show record page 254). One was bred in 2007, two smaller birds, one absolutely clear, bred in 2008, both were close-ringed with the intention of sending them to the World Show, but I was told they were too big for the event so not sent, another was bred in 2009, none in 2010 and one in 2011, this too is a very nice example.

All have been bred in double-breeders, some have been parent reared and some have been fostered out to small canaries or with reliable greenfinches in outside flights.

The best results have been with over-year birds. The birds are paired in April and are left together throughout the breeding season with no problems encountered. Fertility tails off later in the year. Usually yellow canary hens are used.

The birds are reared on moist egg food, soaked seed and green-stuff, usually chickweed, dandelion and sow thistle. Colour food is supplied via their drinking water with unpredictable results I'm afraid! The greenfinches are predominately recessive in their make-up, but when paired to a canary some form of dominance obviously occurs. The straight greenfinch pairs produce, not only clear birds, but non-clears, these are virtually green, some have a yellow tail feather or one elsewhere, and all have white toe nails, which appear to grow at a faster rate than in absolutely normal birds.

I exhibit clear greenfinches, especially yellows which are a beautiful buttercup yellow, from time to time, entering them in the 'any other colour greenfinch class'. I have been asked on more than one occasion, "What bird is that"? At the time of writing I am trying very hard to improve the size of the greenfinches and the mules they produce.

**Clear or nearly clear greenfinch mules. Bottom right
clear yellow greenfinch. (No photo of first bred mule)**

BREEDING THE BRAMBLEFINCH X CHAFFINCH

The bramblefinch (Fringilla montifringilla) and the chaffinch (Fringilla coelebs) are closely related species, as their Latin names indicate. They should therefore readily hybridise in an aviary environment, and in fact a good number of such hybrids are bred each year.

During the spring of 1991 I attempted to breed from a cock bramblefinch and a hen chaffinch. Three chicks hatched and indeed fledged, but none survived the weaning period. However, I achieved success in 1992 when I bred a cock hybrid, which is illustrated.

WINTER VISITOR

The bramblefinch is a winter visitor and passage-migrant to these shores. It has bred in Britain on a number of occasions, being first confirmed as a British breeding species in Sutherland in 1920. A few pairs now breed in Scotland each year. During the season the head and mantle of the cock is black, the breast and shoulders are orange-buff, and the rump is white. This makes the bird very conspicuous when in flight. The hens and juveniles are duller in colour.

The chaffinch is mainly a resident bird in Britain, and this population is joined in the autumn by birds from continental Europe. Together with other finches including bramblefinches, sparrows and buntings, they form flocks and forage among wood and agricultural areas for food which includes beech mast and other seeds.

The cock chaffinch has a blue-grey head and neck, pink breast and cheeks, a chestnut back, white shoulder patches, white wing-bars, and white outer tail feathers. The hen is yellow-brown above and paler below while juveniles resemble the hen.

During October 1990, I placed a cock bramblefinch, bred by myself in 1988, and a hen chaffinch, which I had also bred that year, in a planted aviary. Inhabiting the flight were a pair of blackbirds.

By May 1st 1991 the chaffinch was carrying nesting material to a canary nest-pan, which was situated in an elder bush. On May 20th the first of four eggs were laid. The blackbirds also had eggs and the two clutches were due to hatch about the same time. The finches' eggs hatched out on June 3rd and the chicks grew rapidly on a diet of mealworms and other insects.

On June 8th there were three chicks in the nest which I close-ringed and by June 18th all three had left the nest. They varied in size, but all looked reasonably perky as they perched among the foliage. At this time the weather became very cold and wet, and conditions were appalling for the time of year, and consequently the chicks did not survive.

In retrospect I could have transferred the whole family to inside quarters, but the weather closed in so quickly the damage which also affected many wild birds, was done in a single night. No attempt was made by the pair to raise a second clutch that year.

During mid-November, the pair was transferred into a small aviary some distance away from the main blocks. This aviary was situated in a sheltered position and backed onto a shed. Honeysuckle and clematis grew over it; during the summer months these climbers are in full flower and attract many insects to the location.

In late March 1992 I arranged fir branches in two corners of the flight where I had previously placed nest pans. By the end of April the hen chaffinch was gathering nesting material from the floor: various mosses, hair and a few feathers were used to construct the nest.

By May 3rd the hen was incubating a clutch of eggs, but after a few days eggs began to disappear from the nest, I suspected mice were taking them: although the aviary including the floor, was covered in ½" wire netting, these small rodents can make their way into an enclosure without much difficulty. Two eggs remained in the nest but these were clear.

By June 1st the cock bramblefinch was displaying to the hen chaffinch, and soon after this the hen refurbished her old nest. Meanwhile I had taken steps to eradicate the mice. The first egg of the second clutch was laid on June 8th but only two eggs were laid. One of these disappeared during the first week of incubation, and again I suspected mice.

The hen sat tightly on the remaining egg, which hatched on June 22nd. The chick grew rapidly, being fed by both parents on mealworms and many kinds of insects caught within the flight including flying ants which had a nest close by. I close-ringed the young hybrid for identification purposes on June 27th and it left the nest on about August 12th. However it did not begin to fly about the aviary until August 19th remaining in its early days close to the floor. The hybrid resembled the hen chaffinch and I was not able to identify the sex of the bird until some weeks later.

I transferred the bird, a young cock, to the birdroom at the end of August to prepare it for the shows. I added a little colouring agent to the drinking water, prior to bringing it inside and continued to colour feed until it moulted out.

By early October the hybrid was much paler than the bramblefinch cock; this was to be expected, as colour deepens with age. It had an orange breast like the bramblefinch and white shoulder patches similar to those of a cock chaffinch, the rump was more grey than white.

Since 1992 I have bred the bramblefinch x chaffinch hybrid on a number of occasions and for most of that time have had an example of one in my show team. In 2011 I exhibited a cock hybrid of this cross at the World Show in France.

Photograph by Dennis Avon

THE BIGGEST ASPIDISTRA IN THE WORLD

My team of softbills secured the Best British Birds awards on numerous occasions before the 2005/06 show season only to be beaten by a Northern mule or hybrid at local events. To redress the situation I decided to add specimens of these large birds to my exhibition team.

I had in mind a lightly variegated yellow Norwich canary cock of good size and substance, and a buff bullfinch hen - the progeny of a Northern type bullfinch cock and an English bullfinch hen - to be paired together in the spring of 2005. I hoped they would produce some exhibition birds of the type I required. Both these birds were bred in 2004.

The hen bullfinch had been raised in an outside aviary, one of four chicks. It was the smallest and not doing well. It was placed inside, under a small canary that already had two chicks of the same age - five days. The canary accepted the bullfinch chick and reared it to maturity.

The Norwich cock had spent the winter with other cock canaries in a small aviary within the bird room. The young bullfinch however, spent that season alone in a double breeding cage. The birds were not placed together until the middle of March 2005. The cage measured 0.9m (3ft) in length, 0.6m (2ft) in height and 0.45m (1ft 6") deep. The two birds seemed uninterested in each other. They were given a diet comprising a bullfinch mixture, soaked seed, egg food and mealworms, mountain ash berries were added, together with chickweed and dandelion.

Two nest sites were placed in the cage, a canary nest-pan affixed to the back wall and a wicker nest basket was fitted to the front wires; conifer was placed around both sites to afford privacy.

At the beginning of May, the bullfinch was seen collecting lengths of coconut fibre and placing them in the wicker basket, where she made her nest.

The first of the four eggs appeared on May 7th. Incubation started on the 10th. The canary cock still appeared to pay little attention to the hen.

On May 15th the bullfinch hen was alarmingly off the nest and paying no attention to it. She appeared in good health. The eggs were cold so they were removed and placed under a small canary which was sitting on clear eggs.

On May 24th a young canary x bullfinch hatched out. The canary hen took to the chick and began to feed it on soaked seed and egg food, supplemented with dandelion heads and chickweed. Mealworms were offered but not taken. As the youngster feathered up, bright orange feathers appeared over the top of its rump. It turned out to be a very good yellow buff cock, as it showed both feather types. It left the nest after a fortnight and was removed at 28 days.

The bullfinch laid four eggs again. They were removed and replaced with dummy ones. The precious eggs were placed under a canary hen on May 23rd. Once again, the bullfinch hen left its nest after five days. The canary sat on and hatched one egg of the four on June 5th. The chick grew well, but did not show the orange colouring early on. It turned out to be another cock: a buff, not so brightly coloured as its brother. It also proved to be slower in maturing. It was 15 days in the nest and was not removed from the canary until it was 32 days old.

During this time, the bullfinch hen obliged again with four eggs. These were removed on June 12th and replaced with dummy eggs, but this time the bullfinch hen sat for the full incubation period. Her eggs had been placed under a canary hen that had a canary cock in the cage with her. Only one egg hatched on June 25th. This youngster grew fast. It had two foster parents to feed it and there was a huge supply of sowthistle available at that time, As soon as it began to feather up the orange patch above its rump was vivid, almost red. This third canary x bullfinch was an outstanding yellow cock bird.

The bullfinch laid three more eggs. She sat for the full incubation period but the eggs were infertile. The three youngsters were housed separately in double breeding cages to moult out.

Carphyll Red was administered through the drinking water from mid-July and I continued it almost up until the day of the first show. The staple diet consisted of a bullfinch mixture soaked seed and egg food, along with mountain ash berries, broccoli and cress, together with a few mealworms. I told no one of the breedings, so the yellow canary x bullfinch cock's first showing, at the Lancashire BB&HC event at Lowton in November 2005, took the fancy by storm. It was the largest unflighted yellow canary x bullfinch cock ever seen on the British show bench, according to Terry McCracken. It won best unflighted hybrid and best mule or hybrid in show, among other awards.

The bird was, in canary x bullfinch terms, the "biggest aspidistra in the world". The win was not too popular in some quarters, but it is in the record books and cannot be expunged.

Individuals who never usually speak to me from one year to the next came out of the woodwork to interrogate me. The most popular question was "How much northern blood is holding that bird up?" I replied: "A little".

Twenty-five percent was the precise amount. This complies with the show standard set down by the leading lights of the fancy, in other words, dark mules and hybrids - the larger the better: compatible in size with that of their parents. These may not be compatible with native finches, but with the parents of the bird(s) in question - which is what mine were.

After my canary x bullfinch's first outing, an elderly gentleman phoned me to say: "The knives are out. That bird will never win again. They say it's northern." I thought Aberdeen was northern, my birds were bred in Norfolk. He went on to say the bird would make a nice pet.

During the season it became obvious that the fancy was divided over the northern debate. I found five top judges in favour of them. Several of the main shows saw northern exhibits win top awards. Fanciers were split over the merits of my bird, some said it should have been wrong-classed every time, others said it should have won at every event and I had been robbed!

Its up to the fancy to come to terms with the situation, one that will become worse if nothing is done. Long ago mules were far more colourful and

numerous than hybrids. Some idiot decided to redress the balance and henceforth the canary x bullfinch has been called a hybrid. Nowadays the situation has changed. Hybrids with their numerous variant forms are more colourful than ever, so the canary x bullfinch should be returned to its proper category, that of a mule.

In the mule classes, anything goes - large, northern goldfinches are routinely used, and classes are provided for miniature mules. The northern classes should be done away with and classes provided within the mule section for native and northern birds.

I exhibited the bird on many occasions after this first outing and I touch on each one of these in the following text; this will duplicate, in some way, with show reports which appear in the exhibition pages of this book.

Pictures taken by the author in his bird room

Staffordshire British Bird & Mule Club, 8.1.06. Entered as northern; annexed best northern exhibit.

National British Bird & Mule Club, gained award for best northern.

Eastern Federation of British Bird Fanciers, best current-year bird in show.
St Neots 7.10.07, best mule or hybrid.
Diss 2.12.06, best in section.

2007 South East Ipswich Members' Show - best in Show.

Stafford British Bird & Mule Club, 14.1.07, best northern.

National British Bird & Mule Club, best northern bird at the event.

12.10.08 Bingley Hall Bird Show of the Year, won best mule or hybrid, Judge Sean Fitzpatrick, not thought to be a northern enthusiast. Many fanciers were upset at my win.

Yorkshire British Bird & Hybrid Club, best northern, entered in normal class and won it, there was no northern class. There was however a special for best northern left in the schedule by mistake. There was an objection to the win by Terry Ball and the decision was revoked, but when I pointed out that a special was in the schedule for northern birds, it was re-instated, I didn't bother to tell Mr Ball.

Diss, best in section.

2009 National British Bird & Mule Club, best northern exhibit.

Staffordshire British Bird & Mule Club, best northern exhibit.
I disposed of the other two canary x bullfinches.

BREEDING THE SONG THRUSH X BLACKBIRD HYBRID

In 1985 I bred my first softbill hybrid, a lovely song thrush x blackbird cock. That February, I released a song thrush cock and a cinnamon blackbird hen, bred the previous year, into a planted aviary. The birds seemed compatible at once.
Nesting began on April 20th and two eggs had been laid by May 5th, but three days later the nest had been deserted. By May 15th, the hen had tidied up the old nest and had laid three eggs. On May 28th, to my dismay I found a dead, partly

hatched chick on the floor of the enclosure. Another egg was chipping in the nest and a third appeared clear.
A hybrid hatched from the egg that had shown signs of chipping. The hen continued to brood, only leaving the nest to feed herself and the chick. The song thrush cock would visit the nest at times and peer in, sometimes with a mealworm in his beak, but I never saw him feed his mate or youngster.
In the nest, the hybrid resembled a young blackbird, as it had a large head and gape, but it looked similar in colour to a song thrush. I watched it take its first flight at 4pm on June 11th. It was a nice moment in my avicultural life.
The hen refurbished the nest and began laying her third clutch of eggs. She fed the young hybrid frequently on a variety of foods including mealworms and earthworms, and it grew rapidly. By June 14th 1985, it was a lovely large bird, dark in colour, with well defined spots on its breast. Its primaries and tail were dark brown, and the legs, toes, and nails very dark indeed.
No further young were reared that year. Over the next three years however, the pair produced several more hybrids. Every year the activity followed a similar pattern. The only variation was when a young bird was fostered out satisfactorily with a pair of blackbirds.
In 2001, I had near success. I had paired a split cinnamon song thrush to a cinnamon blackbird hen and they produced two hybrids: one a cinnamon, perhaps the first colour variant ever to be bred. However, both chicks were lost almost immediately after hatching.
By May 30th 2002, the hen of this pair was sitting on a clutch of eggs, and, by June 6th, two young hybrids were growing well in the nest, one a normal, the other a cinnamon. But by June 8th the parent had virtually stopped feeding them. I had no choice but to foster them out, and unfortunately the cinnamon youngster developed a problem and died.
The remaining hybrid, a cock, became a lovely specimen. No further chicks hatched that year.
The softbill hybrids were excellent show birds. The best two, whose photographs are printed, won numerous specials and beat many good hardbill mules and hybrids. I showed the first at the 1985 National Exhibition, in a class for 'other current year hybrids between two British birds.' There were no classes for softbill hybrids back then, but this bird changed all that.
In 2003, I sent the 2002-bred hybrid to the World Show in Amiens, France. There it gained 88 points - three short of a medal in a class where all other entries were hardbill crosses.

Photograph by Dennis Avon

1985

During early spring of 2010, I paired a good quality cock song thrush to a hen blackbird, both a year old. They settled down well in their flight and by April 19th a nest had been made and the first egg laid; a full clutch followed, these all failed to hatch. By May 14th a nest was underway, and after a few days, incubation of the second clutch. On June 1st the cock bird was singing, but with a mealworm in his mouth. On June 3rd, I viewed the nest from above without entering the enclosure, and discovered young within it. On June 7th I was able to close-ring three chicks. I decided to ring the hybrids because I hoped to exhibit them in the World Show in January 2011. These birds were eventually hand-reared. No other youngsters were bred that season.

After the moult, all three were trained for the shows. All proved to be cocks, the best of which was exhibited about my area, and did well. All three were entered in the World Show in France, one was withdrawn, the other two, unfortunately, were entered in the wrong class, so were not judged. It turned out that no class was available for this cross. The best of the three will be shown locally.

The parent birds remained together all winter, and by April 14th 2011, were building once more. I checked the nest on April 23rd, and found that it contained 4 eggs. Three chicks hatched and were being satisfactorily reared; one died shortly after ringing, the other two died when being hand-reared, a sad business.

By May 21st the hen was laying her second clutch of 4 eggs, three of which hatched, and grew rapidly, being fed mainly on mealworms. Two were ringed on June 11th, the third was too big to be ringed, this bird died shortly after fledging. The smallest of the three died shortly afterwards. The remaining youngster made it to the perches and is a nice specimen. A third round was taken, three chicks hatched, two of which were ringed. Again three chicks were reared, giving me six to train for the 2012 show season.

The cock parent bird is obviously not split, so was replaced in 2012 by a carrier. Three clutches were laid but all the eggs were clear.

Photograph by Dennis Avon

2002

CHAPTER FIVE

Thrush Breeding Programme

Photograph by Dennis Avon

**Winner
Cinnamon Blackbird Hen**

BREEDING REDWINGS AND FIELDFARES

October 1989, and relevant to this date.

This chapter provides an account of the programme, from a position where some of the six common thrushes were absent in the Fancy, to one where they were all being bred. **There Is Some Duplication In These Pages Of Text**, but I hope it shows what a struggle it was to obtain legal stock and prosper, when legislation was against keepers: It is very difficult nowadays for any individual to get a licence to take British birds from the wild. This is in spite of Section 16 (1) (e) of the Wildlife and Countryside Act 1981, which allows the granting of a licence for the purpose of aviculture.

As far as the authorities are concerned, licences will not normally be issued to take species included in Schedule 3 Part 1. Birds in this schedule are those assessed as having a self-sufficient captive-bred population, so the principal reason for the issue of any licence will be for replenishment. For other species, such as those on Schedule 4 Part 11, consideration will normally be given to applications which form part of a co-ordinated breeding programme. It is the responsibility of the various clubs to organise such schemes.

Under the Protection of Birds Act 1954-1967, it was comparatively easy to obtain such a licence as the application in those days was submitted to the Home Office. I was granted various licences in the 1970's to take birds from the wild for the purpose of aviculture. These species included blackbird, mistle thrush, song thrush, redwing, fieldfare, meadow pipit, pied wagtail, blue tit, great tit, goldfinch, chaffinch, greenfinch, reed bunting and tree sparrow.

COLOUR VARIANTS

I bred from many of the specimens taken; indeed some of their descendants adorn my collection today. Some of my colour variant strains have been propagated from examples taken on licence under former legislation.

When the new Act was introduced many keepers disposed of species which could no longer be readily exhibited, such as the redwing, fieldfare, hawfinch and nightingale. Although disposing of these birds at that time amounted to short-sightedness on the part of those fanciers involved, it was quite understandable. Many such keepers were devastated by the sweeping and complex restrictions which had suddenly befallen their hobby. Consequently the rarer species such as those mentioned became scarce in aviculture, some even becoming extinct.

FOUR WAYS

There are only four official ways open to fanciers to obtain stock and the scarcer the species, the more difficult it is to acquire. These four ways are: 1. Captive-bred. 2. Imported. 3. Wild disabled. 4. Wild taken under licence.

In November 1988, not being able to obtain redwings and fieldfares by any of the first three methods above, I applied for a licence from the appropriate Government department to take two pairs of each from the wild. Although I was not a member of a co-ordinated breeding scheme, I considered that I had the right in law as an individual to apply. To my mind there are too many pitfalls to be considered when several people are involved in a legal act, such as carrying out the directives of a licence.

With my application I furnished the authorities with sensitive data as to the species of birds I kept, their quantity and ring numbers, together with aviary sizes etc. In reply they wrote to me stating that after consulting their scientific advisers, the Nature Conservancy Council, they were unable to issue a licence in this instance. Three reasons were given, these I relate here together with my comments relating to them, which I hope may be of interest.

1.	The NCC was concerned that the application was not part of a co-ordinated breeding scheme.

2.	Taking and breeding the birds may stimulate a demand for them.

3.	 No conservation purpose would be served by the taking of the birds from the wild.

I found their reasoning quite bewildering as it seems that my application had been met with scant regard. My comments are that firstly, it appears that if I were part of a co-ordinated breeding programme, my application would have been dealt with more favourably. This in effect takes away an individual to be considered, which I feel is wrong. Secondly, "taking and breeding" these cannot, I feel, be a proper reason for refusing a licence. I readily agree that there would be a demand for the progeny, but that would be a good thing. Only a small number of fanciers, in any event, would be interested and they would almost certainly be of a high repute.

Finally any gene pool is useful, especially relating to redwings and fieldfares which breed mainly in the contaminated lands of the North, where nuclear fall-out and acid rain are features of their endangered environment and habitat. (see p182)

Photograph by Dennis Avon

FIELDFARE

181

Another point worth mentioning is the fact that I did not, in any case, apply under Section 16 (1) (c) of the Act which refer to conservation but, as stated, under Section 16 (1) (e) which refers to aviculture; so reason 3 appears not to be applicable in my case. Reason 1 and 2 I would submit, are not compatible which each other.

It would appear from my enquiries that the redwing and fieldfare are now probably totally absent as breeding birds in British aviculture. However they have a history as aviary birds and were kept by a number of fanciers in the past. Grand specimens often appeared on the show bench at local shows and at national events. Many keepers had breeding pairs including the late Harry Blaxall of Ipswich. Both the redwing and fieldfare have been recorded as being bred by members of the British Bird Breeders' Association. There is nothing sinister in wanting these aviary birds to come back into the field of aviculture.

Parliament itself recognises the redwing and fieldfare as aviary birds; hence their inclusion in the 1981 Act, and are in fact geared to cater for them in a regulation scheme. Official Government close ring lists include these species, stipulating that any chicks bred, be ringed with code K and code M rings respectively. There is no doubt that perseverance on behalf of keepers will achieve their eventual return to the hobby.

OFFICIAL RELUCTANCE

One theory put forward as to the reluctance of officials to licence the capture of wild redwings and fieldfares is that fragile colonies breeding in the north of Scotland would be at risk in some way. It is an offence with special penalties to interfere with rare breeding birds. This fact would deter any would-be offender in the future, as it does now.

The Government recently announced the break-up of the NCC. What effect this will have on aviculture remains to be seen, but it is hoped that it will not prove to be detrimental in any way and perhaps decisions will be made on a regional basis in future. The British Bird Council has undertaken breeding programmes in the past, notably with crossbills and snow buntings. It is hoped that such programmes involving redwings and fieldfares will be undertaken in the future. I would enjoy being involved in their rehabilitation.

(Note: On 26th April 1988 one of four nuclear reactors at Chernobyl in the Ukraine exploded, contaminating a wide area of northern Europe. The repercussions of the fallout are still being felt today). (See Page 180).

Photograph by Dennis Avon

WILD DISABLED REDWING

FIELDFARE FROM THE ISLE OF MAN

Autumn 1989, and relates to this time.

Following my article on breeding redwings and fieldfares in Cage & Aviary Birds October 7th issue I received a letter from the honorary secretary of the Isle of Man Cage Bird Society, Roy Howarth. In it he explained that Nick Pinder, the curator of Curraghs Wild Life Park had approached him in August 1989 and asked him to find an aviculturist willing to take on a permanently injured fieldfare (Turdus pilaris) which had been cared for by the park since October 1988.

Fortunately, after making unsuccessful enquiries to try and find a fancier who could use the bird in a breeding programme, Roy Howarth read my article. He was writing to offer me the bird, and I was delighted to accept.

ISLE OF MAN

The Isle of Man is a foreign country to residents of the UK when it comes to the red tape and various laws which have to be complied with before a bird can be exported. Nick kindly undertook this assignment and also obtained the necessary documents for the lawful transfer of the bird. This involved an application to our DoE on November 8th for permission to import the bird which was duly agreed. A CITES import licence was also needed to be granted to allow Curraghs Wild Life Park to send the specimen to me.

On receipt of both these documents, he applied for and obtained an Isle of Man export licence which was granted on December 5th, under the Endangered Species (Import and Export Act 1981), through the Isle of Man Department of Agriculture, Fisheries and Forestry. These documents were accompanied by a letter issued on behalf of the Isle of Man Government setting out all details of the transaction.

At this point, Roy contacted me again to tell me the paperwork was in hand and he would be arriving at my address with the bird on December 7th.

Everything had gone smoothly and no quarantine was required when the bird arrived in England. When I heard this news, I immediately informed the DoE of the situation by recorded delivery, keeping a copy of the letter as a safeguard. When Roy and Betty, his wife, finally arrived at my door with their precious cargo, a flock of wild, chattering fieldfares flew overhead.

The fieldfare is one of the most beautiful thrushes in the world and the Manx cock bird was no exception. Its blue-grey head, nape and rump, chestnut back, dark tail and speckled brown breast all contributed to its beauty. Roy explained the bird had been found after its broken wing had partially healed. Consequently, the wing had failed to return to its former position and had dropped slightly. Otherwise the bird was healthy and active.

REGISTRATION FORM

As soon as the fieldfare arrived, I informed the appropriate authorities by letter. They acknowledged my correspondence and sent me an application form to register this Schedule 4 bird. I completed and returned it together with the registration fee of £7.

A DoE inspector subsequently visited my home and I fitted a Government split ring on the bird in his presence. A registration document was then issued which contained all the relevant details together with an identification number that I was allocated. The bird is housed with a hen blackbird (Turdus merula), a near relative to the fieldfare. The fieldfare behaves like a mistle thrush (Turdus viscivorus) on the ground and in flight. However, its eggs resemble the blackbird or ring ouzel (Turdus torquatus).

Hopefully a mate for the cock bird can be found. I would be grateful if anyone with a hen fieldfare in captivity would contact me so a breeding programme can be set up. Then once again, these beautiful birds can grace the collections of British bird fanciers.

In the meantime I will endeavour to breed a pure strain of fieldfares using a near relative as a mate, such as a blackbird. With good fortune, this may be possible.

Each hybrid from pairing a fieldfare with a blackbird would acquire 50% of the required genes and would be a F1 hybrid. If any of the F1 hybrids proved to be fertile, it should follow that F2, F3 and F4 hybrids would also be fertile. Then it would be possible to transfer all the required genes and breed near pure fieldfares in a relatively short space of time.

If the project goes well, but I want to cut out the need for registration and ringing, breeding the birds to a purity just short of 100% would produce normal looking fieldfares, with similar plumage and behaviour, but which were still hybrids in law and Schedule 4 Part 11 hybrids do not have to be registered.

The fieldfare has settled down well and is at present being fed on fruit and a good insect mixture, together with a few mealworms and poultry pellets. It has become quite vocal, emitting a loud 'chattering' from time to time. This chattering invariably coincides with the movements of flocks of wild fieldfares overhead. They forage the East Anglia countryside at this time of year in search of earthworms, snails, haws and other wild fruits.

I would like to publicly thank Roy and Betty Howarth and Nick Pinder for everything they did to ensure the bird reached me. I also wish them luck with their impending Wildlife legislation, which I understand they are helping to fashion.

FIELDFARE FROM THE ISLE OF MAN

Photograph by Dennis Avon

THREE THRUSHES
NEW BREEDING PROGRAMME

Written on July 14th 1990 and relates to this date.

I have recently taken on the title of breeding co-ordinator for the British Bird Council in respect of three thrush species, the mistle thrush (Turdus viscivorus), the fieldfare (Turdus pilaris) and the redwing (Turdus iliacus) and hopefully the ring ouzel (Turdus torquatus) will be included in the scheme.

The purpose of the project will be to obtain several pairs of each species and distribute them among fanciers participating in the scheme and so establish aviary strains. Later on, an application can be made to the Secretary of State to have these birds added to Schedule 3 Part 1 of the Wildlife and Countryside Act 1981, so they can be exhibited alongside the blackbird and song thrush. At the moment, I would be pleased to hear from any BBC member willing to take part in the programme either to facilitate breeding or help. There may be considerable numbers of mistle thrushes presently available in members' aviaries and a few ring ouzels may be owned by British aviculturists. However, fieldfare and redwing numbers are low at present for those in captivity in

this country.

Experienced breeders will know that Schedule 4 species, such as the fieldfare and redwing, have to be registered with the Government, paperwork maintained and fees paid. Registered keepers will occasionally be visited by DoE inspectors either to deliver split rings or on 'spot' checks. None of this will apply to the mistle thrush or ring ouzel as these species are not listed on Schedule 4.

Breeders should realise it can become very expensive when the rearing of young thrushes is undertaken, unless supplies of worms are freely available. At least two pairs of a species should be considered so they can be kept in sight and hearing of each other to stimulate breeding. These points should be considered by less experienced members contemplating taking part in this project. Other similar co-ordinated programmes are already showing signs of success, so there is every reason to suppose the thrush project will also benefit if an interest is shown in it.

The mistle thrush is the largest of its genera and a very robust bird. It is a common resident and is also partially migratory. The species nest from late February and breeds readily in controlled conditions so long as the pair are compatible. Enormous quantities of livefood are required when the young are raised. These thrushes become very tame and confiding in captivity and before the law prevented them being shown, fine examples adorned the benches at most major shows.

The fieldfare is a winter visitor to British shores; it is a handsome bird, dressed in blues and greys with a yellowish breast covered in spots.

The redwing is a nocturnal migrant to Britain and arrives in September and October. I vividly remember, one autumn night in the late 1960's as I walked along a north Suffolk street a flock of these delightful little thrushes descended, landing on the pavement all around me. It was an amazing experience. The redwing is slightly smaller than the song thrush.

The ring ouzel is a summer visitor to the British Isles and a bird of passage in spring and autumn. It enjoys a moorland habitat and an aviary should be laid out to imitate its natural environment. This is pleasing to the eye and strikingly familiar to the birds. The ring ouzel is about the size of a blackbird, but can be at a glance distinguished by its crescent of white feathers below its throat, a truly beautiful bird.

All these thrushes are easy to maintain, but aviaries no smaller than 9ft x 4ft x 7ft should be used. A staple diet of softbill food or poultry pellets, will suffice. Fruits and mealworms are also relished when available. Vitamins and minerals should be added to the food or drinking water on a regular basis.

Photograph by Tony Tilford

AVIARY BIRD - post article

Thrushes build bulky nests of grasses and mud, so ample supplies of materials should be made available at breeding time. They will utilise makeshift building sites, such as wooden boxes or bunches of heather, if natural ones are not available.

If sufficient interest is shown in a particular species, then an application will be made to the Government for a licence authorising the taking of specimens from the wild. This coming winter would be a good opportunity to obtain fieldfare and redwing. As far as the mistle thrush and ring ouzel are concerned, a decision about whether more specimens are needed from the wild will be made when current aviary-bred numbers are known.

LICENCE APPLICATION

If a licence application is refused, steps will be taken to import aviary-bred specimens in from overseas. Several breeders of fieldfare and redwing exist in Europe and it should not prove difficult with the necessary paperwork, to bring birds in.

I will endeavour to keep concise records of the programme as it develops and keep Government and members informed of its progress, in the same way as Ron Phillips reports on the crossbill project.

I will also be available for advice and to help in any way I can with queries. I would therefore be obliged to hear from any BBC member who wishes to take part in the scheme and from continental breeders.

SETBACK TO REDWING AND FIELDFARE BREEDING PROGRAMME

Written in 1990 and relates to this time

The first of this year's young aviary-bred thrushes will now be leaving their nests in collections up and down the country. Among these will be mistle thrushes and ring ouzels, two of the species now re-established in British aviculture.

Very little progress is thought possible however, with the redwing and fieldfare, which make up the quartet of targeted species catered for within the Thrush Breeding Programme. This is because only a handful of specimens are available to programme members, and all of these are wild-disabled birds.

Both redwing and fieldfare are listed on Schedule 1 of the Wildlife and Countryside Act 1981 (birds which are protected by special penalties), and on Schedule 4 (birds which must be registered and ringed if kept in captivity).

When the Act became law, keepers of these birds disposed of their stock for a variety of reasons. Hasty decisions were made, which many now regret. It was thought at the time that these species, and others on Schedule 4, would never again appear on the show bench. In reality a licence to display specimens can usually be obtained. Birds listed on Schedule 4 do appear on the benches as before and will continue to do so, with only the formality of the issuing of a licence being required.

Keepers were also reluctant to become involved with registration forms and payment of fees for their redwings and fieldfares. This, again, is actually a small price to pay, and easily rewarded by the interest these birds generate. Rings are provided free by the authorities, so any extra cost is insignificant.

The mistle thrush and ring ouzel are also protected species, but they are not included on Schedule 4. Therefore there is no paperwork to contend with, and no fees to pay. Keepers of these species retained their stock and continued to breed from them.

The mistle thrush (Turdus viscivorus) is a large grey bird with dark, round breast markings. Its song is loud and ringing. It prefers broad-leafed woodland and parks and is a resident in the UK and throughout Europe. Mistle thrushes are early nesters.

The ring ouzel (Turdus torquatus) is similar in size and colour to the blackbird, but has a broad, white throat patch, more obvious in the male than in the female. Its song is made up of a few fluty notes. Ring ouzels are upland birds and have a liking for rocky, heather moorland with a scattering of small trees. It is a spring and summer visitor to these shores.

The redwing (Turdus iliacus) is easily identified by its facial stripes which are obvious against its dark head. Its flanks and underwing are russet-brown. The song is simpler and briefer than that of the song thrush. The redwing prefers open country, parks and gardens. It breeds in northern European countries and winters in southern ones, including Britain, where it searches for hedgerow berries.

The fieldfare (Turdus pilaris) is a large thrush with a distinctive grey head and rump, and a faint song. Fieldfares breed in continental Europe, and prefer light woodland. They are winter visitors to the UK.

In November last year, I made an application to the authorities, on behalf of the British Bird Council, for a licence to take redwings and fieldfares from the wild. The application was turned down. Apparently it was carefully considered and scientific advice was taken from English Nature. The authorities came to the conclusion that to issue a licence to take individual birds of these two species could not be justified, despite the low number in captivity.

This is a setback and will frustrate the programme to some extent. It is the third time such an application has been turned down, so this is obviously not an avenue worth pursuing.

There must be several fieldfares and redwings held in captivity, unbeknown to the fancy. Some of these will be in care, having been found injured on roads or elsewhere. It is hoped that these birds will be brought into the programme so that progress in captive breeding can be made.

Ironically, the registration and ringing laws, which help to protect these birds, cost far more than can be afforded by the taxpayer and a review is under way. It is likely that these two common species will lose a degree of protection in the future, making them more appealing to the fancier.

Photograph by Tony Tilford

REDWING

BBC AIM TO HAVE THRUSHES ADDED TO SCHEDULE 3

Written on November 24th 1990 and relates to this date.

During the past summer, the British Bird Council instigated a breeding programme; the species involved being the mistle thrush (Turdus viscivorus), the fieldfare (T.pilaris), the redwing (T. iliacus) and the ring ouzel (T.torquatus). This was done in the hope that after breeding strains had been developed, these species would be added to Schedule 3 Part 1 of the Wildlife and Countryside Act 1981, thus allowing them to be exhibited once more if aviary bred and close ringed.

I became the programme's co-ordinator at the outset, and in Cage & Aviary Birds (July 14th) my first report on the subject was published. The response was encouraging, in the sufficient number of bird keepers that wrote showing an interest in that project. Letters came from all over Great Britain, and were mostly from experienced fanciers, although a few more were from beginners and one from a junior.

One writer has a wealth of experience with the ring ouzel, and another with the redwing. The knowledge of these two particular keepers will be of great importance as the programme gets underway. This initial response from fanciers has made that possible.

It was hoped that sufficient specimens of all species would be already available in aviaries and that these would form the nucleus of the scheme, but unfortunately this is not the case. It appears that these species are almost extinct as aviary birds in Britain.

When the Act became law, many keepers were disgusted with the depletion of species which could be lawfully exhibited if aviary bred and close-ringed, so much so that they discarded birds that were not included in Schedule 3 Part 1.

In the Act, the fieldfare and redwing are placed on Schedule 1 Part 1, (birds which are protected by special penalties) and on Schedule 4 (birds which must be registered and ringed if kept in captivity). The mistle thrush and ring ouzel were not placed on any schedule, so they also became available to exhibitors.

In my view these four species should have been included on Schedule 3 Part 1, alongside the blackbird and song thrush, as they have been avicultural subjects for generations. The reason the fieldfare and redwing were finally placed on Schedule 4 was although they are primarily winter visitors, they are also rare as British breeding birds,

and it was thought by the legislators that their fragile colonies would be vandalised unless they were specially protected.

There are only four lawful ways of acquiring stock. These are 1, captive-bred; 2, imported; 3, wild disabled; and 4, wild birds taken under licence. All these four methods must be examined and assessed. It is important that the breeding project makes head-way next spring, so time is not lost. In order to achieve this it is imperative that breeding pairs of all four targeted thrushes become available very soon.

I have already taken steps in this direction by completing an application form in order to obtain a licence to take 12 fieldfares and 12 redwings from the wild; hopefully during the winter. This application form has been submitted to the DoE. They will probably consult their scientific adviser, the Nature Conservancy Council, and reply this month. It is difficult to guess what their decision will be. They were in fact helpful with the crossbill and snow bunting, so I am guardedly optimistic.

Meanwhile, a member of the British Bird Council will be visiting fanciers in Europe soon, in order to locate aviary bred fieldfares and redwings, with a view of importing some into this country for the benefit of project members. Aviary stock will settle down quickly in new surroundings and will also have a taming influence on any birds that are collected from the wild on licence.

It is not envisaged that any application will be made for a licence at the present time to take wild mistle thrushes or ring ouzels, as it is hoped that surplus birds will become available from aviary stock, in fact, two wild disabled mistle thrushes, both hens, are available to breeders at the moment. One of these birds is presently kept in the Northampton area, the other near Chester. If any project member is interested in using these birds within the scheme, this would be helpful. Also I have a registered male fieldfare and would be glad of a hen to make up a breeding pair.

List of members of the British Bird Council's Thrush Breeding Programme.

R.Windle, A.Robinson, B.Fisher, C.A. Francis, R. Hastings, R.Baglow, H.Warman, R. McCluskey, R. Gill, V. Carr, R.Costellow, R. Mitchell, J. Raven, S. Robinson and B.A. Howlett (co-ordinator).

Fieldfare owned by the author (photograph: Dennis Avon).

FROM Mr BELL - see page 194

NESTING MISTLE THRUSHES HUNGRY AND COSTLY

The mistle thrush (Turdus viscivorus) is a relatively common resident in Britain. It is also partially migratory; many British birds leave in late August or September, while birds from Europe arrive from September onwards.

Its fondness for mistletoe berries has given the bird the name it has borne since mediaeval days. Another local name for the bird is storm cock, this originates because of its habit of singing from a high tree during a storm.

The colour of a mistle thrush is ashy-brown above while back, rump and upper tail coverts are washed with buff, the latter only on the margins. The lesser wing coverts are coloured like the back, the medium and greater coverts are dark brown, the former tipped and the latter edged with dull white, inclining to buff on the inner greater coverts.

DARK BROWN

The bastard wing, primary coverts and quills are dark brown edged with ashy-whitish. The tail feathers are light brown with ashy margins, all but the centre tail feathers have a white spot at the end of the inner web, increasing towards the outermost feathers where it is very large.

The head is grey, the eye-lid is white, the feathers below the eye and ear coverts are buff, the feathers tipped with black forming a line on the

upper ear coverts. Cheeks, throat, and under surface of the body are clear ochreous buff, spotted with triangular tips to the feathers, forming a line above and below the cheeks.

The throat is scarcely spotted, and the tips to the feathers of the breast and sides of the body rounded. The lower abdomen, thighs and undertail coverts are buff-white without spots and the undertail coverts are edged with dusky-brown. The auxiliaries and underwing coverts are white, the quills ashy below, white along the inner web.

The bill is dark brown, yellowish at the base of the lower mandible, feet and claws are yellowish-brown and the iris is dark brown. The female is similar to the male in plumage, but less richly spotted.

The mild, clear song of the mistle thrush is usually uttered from a high vantage point. It is not dissimilar to the blackbird's (Turdus merula), but lacks its beauty and mellowness. Usually, it is one of the first song birds to sing, I heard one singing on a Christmas day one year on the Norfolk-Suffolk border where I live.

SONG CONDITIONS

However, this songster is also one of the first to lose its volume. The song continues until April, but from then, although it can be heard almost every month of the year, it is weak compared to its early power. The mistle thrush song cannot be confused with its smaller relative the song thrush (Turdus philomelos), for it has none of the latter's repetitive notes.

At times, the bird sings as it flies, but the usual flight call is a grating churr. This harsh note is modified and intensified when excited by alarm, such as when angered by any intruder near its nest. Any potential enemy, including man, may be savagely attacked.

A suitable aviary for a pair of mistle thrushes should be as large as possible, one measuring 9ft long x 4ft wide x 7ft high will suffice. It is important that the selected pair are compatible to each other. If not, they should not be housed together, for they will undoubtedly attack each other, causing injury or death.

New pairs should be gradually introduced to each other and a close watch maintained on their progress. Their aviary should be as secluded as possible, preferably well away from the aviaries of the other thrushes. This will give them security and the knowledge that their new territory is relatively safe from intruders.

In a planted enclosure, the birds select their own nesting site and provided suitable material is available, build a perfectly sound nest.

Open boxes can be provided if desired. Attempt to keep any site chosen for the nest protected from inclement weather.

The bulky nest of the mistle thrush is similar to the blackbird, but a little larger. Supply the birds with fresh, dry grasses, mosses and mud, the latter provided in an old pan or similar container.

The nest is constructed in about three days, a little mud is used as a base, and the bulk of the nest is fashioned with the dry materials. The shape of the nest is obtained by the hen sitting inside and moving around. Mud is used to line the inner structure, and soft grasses to line the nest ready for the eggs and young.

LIVE-FOOD

The eggs usually number four or five and are sub-elliptical, smooth and glossy; pale blue, pale greenish-blue or tinged with buff; with spots or blotches of reddish-purple or pale purple. The markings are usually evenly distributed. Two broods a season are often reared with incubation undertaken by the hen. The chicks hatch after 13 days and are fed by both parents for a fortnight and for some time after they have left the nest.

An enormous amount of live-food is required to bring up the young, this can be quite costly. Once the nest building starts the amount of live-food given to the adults should gradually be increased; when the young begin to hatch mealworms, earthworms, slugs, snails etc should be made available to allow the young to grow quickly. Supplementary foods should be added if the birds will take them, such as moist biscuits, or brown bread. Vitamins and minerals are essential to promote healthy growth.

BUFF CENTRES

The mistle thrush young are very spotted underneath, throat is white without spots, upperparts are streaked with buff centres to the feathers, which have black tips. The wings are broadly edged with buff and have triangular spots of the same colour at the ends. Young birds can be recognised after the autumn moult by their larger buff tips on their medium wing coverts.

THRUSH BREEDING PROGRAMME CREATES FURTHER INTEREST

Written April 27th 1991, and relates to this date.

Since my last report which appeared in the November 24th edition of Cage & Aviary Birds, the thrush breeding programme has created further interest among enthusiasts, but has also had set-backs.

The application made to the authorities for licence to take 12 redwing and 12 fieldfare from the wild was refused. The DoE took advice on the matter from the now defunct Nature Conservancy Council, who stated they were concerned at the possible depletion of a very small British breeding population. As to what this has to do with the application to take the birds outside the breeding season from Norfolk and Suffolk is difficult to comprehend, but this was their main reason for refusing the licence.

They also felt that no fully organised breeding scheme had been set up. This may have been my fault, although I gave them all the information, which I considered relevant, but this did not satisfy them. Obviously we would have been quite happy to agree to any likely condition, such as aviary size etc., and would have been glad to organise the programme in any way asked of us.

Further representations are being made to the authorities through the good officers of the British Bird Council. Since the application was made the NCC has been split up into three separate organisations, one each for England, Scotland and Wales. The English one is called English Nature and is based in Peterborough. Maybe they will be more helpful than their predecessors, since there are no fieldfare or redwing breeding populations in England.

PAIRS PUT DOWN

The only species of the four that are targeted, fieldfare, redwing, ring ouzel and mistle thrush, likely to make any progress this spring will be the latter. Several breeding pairs have been put down to nest, and it is hoped that there will be a surplus of young birds at the end of the year for distribution among programme members.

One fancier, not involved directly with the project, but a BBC member nevertheless, writes that he has some lovely mistle thrushes and they were carrying bits of straw and hay as early as the first week in March, so it is hoped that he will be successful.

I noted with interest that a fieldfare and a redwing were among the exhibits benched at the recent World Show, these birds are available on the continent and I am attempting to make contact with the breeders there, in the hope of importing birds in.

It is ironic that these species can be exhibited legally in Europe, but are banned from the show bench here. One day perhaps, a system uniform to all the countries of the EEC will be developed to supersede present legislation, a system whereby many more common bird kinds will be added to the meagre list of species which can be exhibited in this country at the present time.

SECTION 4

Under the terms of Section 4 (2) (a) of the Wildlife of Countryside Act 1981, any person can legally take in a wild bird if it can be shown that the bird has been disabled, other than by the takers unlawful act, and was taken solely for the purposes of tending it and releasing it when no longer disabled. If the bird taken is one of the registered species listed on Schedule 4 of the Act, such as the redwing or fieldfare, then it should be registered with the DoE.

DISABLED BIRDS

Some of these disabled birds remain with their benefactors indefinitely, a few can never be released due to their injuries, and could be used in a breeding programme in the same way as raptors stricken down by accident often are. No doubt there are disabled redwings and fieldfares in the caring hands of Licenced Rehabilitation Keepers and others which could be used in such a project, if only they were made available to the aviculturists through the legal machine.

Many years ago now, my old friend Richard Baglow of Dunfermline bred the redwing from injured birds he had rescued from the ravages of winter and nursed back to health. He told me that they were not at all easy to breed; it took him about three years before any young were raised. He was awarded a bronze medal for his wonderful achievement. His success must give heart to all members of the scheme to emulate his work.

RARE SPECIES

For thrush diversity, there are several rare species on the British list, listed on a section 16 licence, which can be shown if aviary bred. Two of these, the Siberian thrush and the eye-browed thrush have recently hit the headlines in a big way, a specimen of the former was best Foreign bird at the National Exhibition for R.Taylor, and S.J Jerrard of South Yorkshire bred the latter in 1990.

Some of the more forward British Bird clubs, including my own club, the Eastern Federation of British Bird Fanciers, are now putting on classes at their annual shows to cater for Section 16 licensed British birds, which I feel is very good news. I have

a pair of Siberian thrushes, these are in good fettle and may breed this year. The exhibition of these rare British thrushes will add greatly to the interest of the aviculture in general, and to British birdkeepers in particular.

If any BBC member wishes to join the thrush project, or if any reader can help in the search for legally held redwing, fieldfare or ring ouzel, I would be very glad to hear from them.

Eye-browned Thrushes (T. obscurus)... at home in the stunted landscape of eastern Siberia.

Photograph by Dennis Avon

THRUSH BREEDING PROGRAMME MAKES SOME PROGRESS

Written on October 12th 1991, and relates to this date.

The thrush breeding programme was set up by the British Bird Council a year ago. Its aim, to breed strains of redwing, fieldfare, ring ouzel and mistle thrush in aviary environments, in such numbers as to make them viable once again as exhibition birds. This goal still remains.

The first year has seen some progress, but only minimal, partly due to the lack of initial stock. It was not possible to take the redwings or fieldfares from the wild due to a refusal by the authorities to grant the necessary licence; also numbers of ring ouzels and mistle thrushes were fewer in captivity than first assumed. Progress has been slow, and will be so for some time yet. Eventually these birds will become available in numbers for those dedicated fanciers now waiting. It is hoped that this small band of enthusiasts will continue to be patient. A further attempt to obtain a licence is contemplated. Of the four species, two, the redwing and fieldfare are winter visitors to our shores, although a few pairs breed here annually. The bulk however, hail from Scandinavia and so far as the redwing is concerned, also from Iceland. We now have three redwings within the programme, these I will refer to later in this article. We also have one fieldfare, a cock bird.

The redwing is the smallest of the European common thrushes and is easily identified by the creamy-white eyestripe and the conspicuous reddish flanks and underwing, from which it derives its name. The fieldfare, which is the same size as the blackbird, has a blue-grey head and rump and a chestnut back, in flight resembles the mistle thrush.

The ring ouzel winters in Africa and visits these shores to breed in the spring. It has a liking for hilly and moorland habitats, especially where there is a scattering of trees. It is easy to identify from the blackbird by its white gorget. One member of the programme hopes to obtain several pairs in the near future, no other details are available at this time.

The mistle thrush is widely spread throughout Europe and there is great deal of movement, especially during the spring and autumn. In the main the species is resident here all through the year, and is one of the first to sing. It is slightly larger than the blackbird. Just a few pairs are kept, some by non-programme members.

DISABLED

During early spring I received a telephone call from Tony Maddox, that British bird stalwart, who lives near East Leigh, to the effect that he was aware of the existence of three disabled redwings which were being cared for nearby. The carers had indicated their willingness to pass the birds on as they alas, are not fit enough to be returned to the rigours of the wild.

Tony kindly made the initial arrangements with the carers and with the DoE, and the necessary paperwork was instigated. Some weeks later I met Tony and collected the three birds. All were as healthy as could be expected, bearing in mind the injuries and ordeal each had suffered.

I learned that two had been involved in road accidents during freezing conditions and a third had been savaged by a cat. Obviously they had received a great deal of loving care. All the birds were able to use their legs normally, and one could fly a little.

On my arrival home with the redwings, I placed them into a prepared, roomy, indoor aviary, and supplied them with plenty of fir branches on which to perch and in which to find some seclusion. They settled down well on a varied diet. The DoE were kept informed of the proceedings and one of their wildlife inspectors visited my establishment in

possession of three official metal split rings, which I applied to the birds in his presence.

The birds have now been registered, and are, I believe, the only ones listed on the register. No doubt there are other redwings in captivity, some with carers, which must be released when fit, or registered with the authorities if permanently disabled. I mention this as undoubtedly some are being kept illegally, probably through ignorance of the legislation. It is hoped that more of these unfortunate birds will find good homes with members of the Thrush Breeding Programme as time goes on.

There appears to be two cocks and a hen redwing. The sexes are similar in this species so identifying them is difficult especially in the case of injured specimens. I intend placing a pair outside in a planted, covered, aviary in the spring, and house the odd bird with a song thrush for company, until a mate of its own kind is found. The three birds have moulted out well and are now more mobile than before.

Following my last report on the progress of the programme which appeared in Cage & Aviary Birds in April, I was contacted by a very caring lady, Anita Brown, a former teacher, who has dedicated her life to the caring of sick, injured and orphaned birds and runs a centre known as Bird Aid, based at Chingford, London. Birds from all over the capital and elsewhere are brought to her in need of help. She explained that a fieldfare caught up in fishing line and found dangling from a tree by the line and badly injured, had been cared for by her.

According to a veterinary surgeon the bird was too disabled to be released. Anita offered me the bird together with a mistle thrush, which had been rescued from a cat. I accepted both birds which were conveyed to my address by friends of Anita Brown; unfortunately the fieldfare died whilst in my charge. This brought home to me the responsibilities involved in taking on a bird, which had been brought back to health, by a carer. It was an unexpected loss and made me think whether it was wise to take on such charges and perhaps let the former carers down.

DISABLED BIRDS

The mistle thrush, however, has made very good progress, so much so that I may be obliged to free the bird as the law demands in situations where wild disabled birds recover. I therefore hope to free it in a local park in the early autumn.

I would like to hear from anyone who has any of these four species of thrushes, so that figures and other data can be kept and a register maintained.

All aviculturists are asked to help. By pooling information and the exchange of stock, strains of these birds will be built up that much faster if information is widely known. I can be contacted via the British Bird Council.

PATIENCE THE ORDER OF THE DAY IN YEARS AHEAD

Written April 25th 1992, applicable to that date.

The year will usher in the second breeding season for enthusiasts involved with the Thrush Breeding Programme. Members of the British Bird Council with an interest in these species, were invited, in the latter part of 1990, to participate in the scheme. A satisfactory number of bird owners from many parts of Britain indicated their willingness to take part. Stocks still prove very difficult to come by, so it seems patience will be the order of the day for some time to come.

Of the targeted species, the mistle thrush, will be re-established on the avicultural map within a comparatively short time. Several fanciers are waiting for pairs of this particular bird, so much hard work needs to be accomplished during the coming months in order that surplus stock becomes available to fulfil outstanding needs. Anyone with mistle thrushes is asked to make every effort to breed with them this year.

The rearing of the mistle thrushes can be very expensive. It is unlawful to sell them or barter with them, but no doubt on the transfer, any cost accrued by a breeder in rearing a particular specimen could be legally recouped on transfer to a new keeper. This would obviously alleviate the expenses incurred by the breeder to some degree. It is wise for every new keeper taking charge of an unscheduled bird, such as the mistle thrush, to obtain a declaration form from the breeder to the effect that the specimen was aviary bred and supplied absolutely free of charge. A conservative estimate of the cost in rearing a bird of this size would be in the region of £12.

PROGRESS

It is hoped that some progress will be made this year with redwings. Only a few, all wild specimens, are kept within the scheme; the sexes are alike in the species, so a true pair may not exist in captivity. However, it will be considered as progress if the sex of each of these birds can be identified. The redwing is a popular bird with programme members, and again, several are waiting for stock.

Every winter many of these birds are injured on our roads, maimed by cats or other forms of accident. Any carer tending an injured bird such as a fieldfare or a redwing and is unable to release it into the rigours of the wild, due to its injuries, is asked to consider transferring it to the Thrush Breeding Programme where it can be assured of a good home within the membership of the project. The fieldfare is proving a difficult bird to encounter in captivity. A wild-disabled specimen, a cock, is kept at the present time housed with a hen blackbird, they are compatible and the possibility of producing hybrids is quite good. Whether any such youngster bred will prove fertile, so the experiment to breed pure fieldfares can be continued, is a matter for conjecture; we will have to wait and see how things develop.

DISABLED BIRDS

It is a pity that aviculture is forced to resort to breeding from disabled birds and from pairs of mixed birds, in order to establish gene banks when during the winter months, fieldfares and redwings arrive here in their thousands, outnumbering our resident blackbirds and song thrushes.

The ring ouzel, the last of these four targeted thrushes, has also aroused considerable interest. Here again, aviary birds are extremely rare. As with the mistle thrush, they are non-scheduled, so if any fancier residing in ring ouzel country would like to take a small number from the wild, I would be obliged if she/he would contact me. The authorities are more likely to be sympathetic to such a request for a licence than to applications involving Schedule 4 species.

REDWING

Photograph by Sergey Yeliseev

READERS CAN HELP IN THRUSH BREEDING PROJECT

Written in 1992.

For generations, British bird fanciers enjoyed a virtually unrestricted hobby. These enthusiasts bred a multitude of native species in cage and aviary, and exhibited strong teams of their best birds at shows up and down the country. The Wildlife and Countryside Act 1981 brought about sweeping changes in the law. Only species listed on Schedule 3 Part 1 to the Act, some 18 common kinds, can now be sold or shown at competitive exhibitions provided the specimen is "bred in captivity" and ringed in accordance with regulations. "Bred in captivity" requires that the parents were lawfully in captivity when the egg was laid.

Many fanciers were displeased with the new situation particularly because fewer species could be exhibited. A great proportion of the birds not included in the new law were discarded. The actions taken by some of these keepers was wholly understandable but, in retrospect, very short-sighted. Many vanished altogether when strains were broken up.

The fieldfare and redwing were placed on Schedule 4 of the Act (birds which must be registered and ringed if kept in captivity). The mistle thrush and ring ouzels were not placed on any Schedule, so they too became unavailable as exhibition birds. It was felt by the Fancy that the legislators had got it wrong with respect to these four thrushes which, most fanciers thought, should have been placed on Schedule 3 Part 1.

The Schedule can be amended by Order made by the Secretary of State with species being removed or added. The data forthcoming from breeding results would play an important part in any decision. In the light of this, the British Bird Council decided in 1990 to set up a special breeding programme for these four species. The purpose of the project is to obtain several pairs of each kind and distribute them among interested fanciers participating in the scheme.

It was hoped, that over a period of time, new strains would become established and as a species become viable once more, an application would be made to the authorities to have it added to the list of birds which can be shown.

These aims still remain.

I became programme co-ordinator and within a short time was able to enlist a satisfactory number of enthusiasts willing to take part in the project. It was hoped at the outset, that sufficient numbers of each of the targeted species would be available in captivity to form the nucleus of the programme. A nation-wide search was undertaken which revealed only a few pairs of mistle thrushes existed in captivity; no pairs of any of the other three species were located.

This revelation was the worst possible scenario, and meant that much more work had to be undertaken than was first envisaged.

There are only four lawful ways of acquiring stock – through captive breeding, importing, taking wild birds on licence and acquiring wild disabled. It was obvious that all these avenues had to be considered in order to obtain stock.

An application was made to the authorities for a licence to take a small number of fieldfares and redwings from the wild, but this was turned down. It is understood that numbers of these species are kept in captivity on the Continent, and it is hoped that keepers overseas can be contacted with a view to supplying birds.

Following an appeal to Rehabilitation keepers and other carers of the injured and wild birds, a small number of wild disabled redwings and one fieldfare were transferred to the programme.

It is hoped that other wild disabled specimens which, due to injuries, cannot be returned to the wild, will also find their way to good homes with members of the project.

Some progress was made in 1991 with the mistle thrush, several youngsters were bred and it is hoped that many more will be reared this year, enough possibly to put this species firmly back on the avicultural map. It is also hoped that some progress will be made with the redwings. It is not yet known, however, if a true pair exists in captivity.

Of the four species, the redwing and the fieldfare are winter visitors to the UK, although a few pairs breed here. The bulk however, hail from Scandinavia, with some redwing also from Iceland.

The redwing is the smallest of the European thrushes and is easily identified by the creamy-white eyestripe and the conspicuous reddish flanks and underwing from which derives its name. The fieldfare, which is the same size as the blackbird, has a blue-grey head and rump and a chestnut back.

In flight it resembles the mistle thrush.

The ring ouzel winters in Africa and visits Britain to breed in the spring. It has a liking for hilly and moorland habitats, especially where there is a scattering of trees. It is easy to identify from the blackbird by its white gorget.

The mistle thrush is widely spread throughout Europe and there is a great deal of movement, especially during the spring and autumn. In the main, the species is resident here all through the year, and is one of the first to sing.

It is slightly larger than the blackbird.

Any reader in possession of healthy specimens of these four thrushes is invited to pass them on to the programme.

SLOW PROGRESS BY THRUSH BREEDING PROGRAMME

Written February 1st 1993 and relevant to that date.

No significant progress is likely on the Thrush Breeding Programme until several strong, unrelated and compatible pairs of the four target species are available.

Last year, like 1991, was one of slow progress for the Programme, set up by the British Bird Council in 1990 to promote the breeding in captivity of four Turdus species – the mistle thrush, redwing, fieldfare and ring-ouzel, in the hope that aviary strains would evolve.

However, only a few birds have been bred, all from the mistle thrush.

As last spring approached, five wild, disabled mistle thrushes arrived at my home, sent by bird lovers from Cheshire, London, Northampton, Hampshire and Wales. Some had been nursed back to health, others were sent by their carer.

One very large mistle thrush had been with Dorothy Jones since 1989, when she was given a fledgling by the RSPCA. It was in a bad way, having lost an eye. She nursed it back to health and it is now a magnificent specimen.

WARM BATH

Mrs Jones wanted to find a breeder close to her, but her search failed, so she sent it to me with the instructions that a warm bath should be provided every morning. There seems to be far more to being a co-ordinator than envisaged.

On March 30th one of the cock mistle thrushes was singing softly from its aviary, so I decided to place the one-eyed hen, which according to Mrs Jones had laid in 1991, with him. The pair settled down reasonably well together. By April 18th the hen was busy building a nest in an open, wooden-box. The pair seemed compatible, but this was short-lived. She then became more interested in a cock song thrush in an adjoining aviary than her own hapless suitor.

On April 28th the first of four eggs were laid and although the hen mistle thrush sat tightly during the incubation period, the eggs failed to hatch, all being clear. A second clutch was laid, but these also proved infertile.

Meanwhile a second true pair of mistle thrushes had been sorted out and I placed them in an aviary within earshot of the first pair, but out of sight. This pair also built a nest and two eggs were laid, but again these failed to hatch, and there was no other attempt to nest.

Although the season had been disappointing, important knowledge was gained and will be useful when the birds are paired up this year.

Following my article in the June/July issue of Bird Keeper, I received some good news from Gordon Bell, North Yorkshire, relating to the programme. He said he found an injured fieldfare in March last year at Cowlan Crossroads, Sledmere, Driffield, Yorkshire. (See photo page 188).

It had a rancid, broken wing, having apparently collided with overhead power cables. The badly damaged wing could not be saved and was removed in order to save the bird's life.

Mr Bell, who breeds small foreign finches and grass parakeets, spent months caring for the fieldfare, digging up masses of garden worms for it and providing it with mealworms and fruit. The bird a mere skeleton when found, gradually put on weight and recovered well.

Mr Bell offered it to the Programme, indicating that he was short of space, and my article had "answered his prayer" in finding it a home. I immediately accepted the offer, and the fieldfare duly arrived at my premises in late May.

The fieldfare is listed in Schedule 4 of the Wildlife and Countryside Act 1981 and its possession has to be registered with the Department of the Environment. I informed them immediately and the usual procedures were carried out. The bird was ringed with an official metal split ring in the presence of a Wildlife Inspector and is now registered in my name.

Already owning what I believed to be a cock fieldfare, I compared it with the new arrival and noticed several differences. The beak of the new arrival was darker, like a hen Blackbird, and it was not so brightly coloured.

Although ornithologists state that they are identical I believe I may have a true pair and intend to keep trying to breed from them.

The two birds are housed together and appear compatible. Their aviary will be furnished with fir branches in the spring, together with suitable low nesting sites, which I hope will be to their liking.

FULLEST PRAISE

Dorothy Jones, Gordon Bell, and others like them, who care for wild birds which become injured on our roads, or by cats and other means, deserve the fullest praise for their work. Disabled birds can often be assigned to breeding programmes where they can live for years and in some cases, reproduce.

Since my last article on the Programme, I have been able to co-ordinate the transfer of several birds between its members. I have also dealt with a number of letters from the public seeking advice on how to look after birds, some of which have been found as fledglings or injured in some way.

One golden rule is to leave alone any young bird which is fit, but has apparently been abandoned by its parents. Invariably parent birds are aware of the location of their offspring, and will continue to feed them when the coast is clear. Finders of badly injured birds who feel they cannot adequately treat them should seek expert advice.

MISTLE THRUSH SENT TO AUTHOR BY DOROTHY JONES (photograph; Dennis Avon)

MISTLE THRUSH BREEDING PROGRAMME MAKES GOOD PROGRESS IN 1995

The mistle thrush, one of the four species of thrush being catered for within the British Bird Council's Thrush Breeding Programme, is making good progress this year with healthy numbers now being kept by fanciers.

No significant progress has been achieved with the other three targeted species in the programme, namely redwing, fieldfare and ring ouzel. However, following my advert for ring ouzels I have made contact with a number of keepers of this species. I began the breeding season with three pairs of mistle thrushes, mainly wild, disabled stock. One pair was successful, rearing three strong youngsters.

The breeding pair, a disabled cock and an aviary-bred hen, was placed in a planted aviary which measured 10ft x 3ft x 7ft, towards the end of March. By mid-April a nest had been built by the hen inside an open wooden box at the front of the flight. This was lined and ready for the first egg by April 20th. Four eggs were duly laid and these incubated by the hen alone.

During the evening of May 12th, both birds were at the nest. I watched as the cock fed the hen and she in turn fed the newly hatched chicks. Some of this early food was regurgitated matter, or at least food which had been mashed up by the cock in some way. I took an early opportunity to view the contents of the nest and was delighted to see four chicks covered in down.

This was the first time I had bred mistle thrushes since 1988. When, during the late 1970s and 1980s, I owned a nice strain of these large, bold birds.

I was able to close-ring three chicks with BBC size M rings on May 15th. The fourth had disappeared by this time; I imagine it had died in the nest and had been discarded by the parents. Mistle thrushes can become extremely aggressive when their nest is approached, but on this occasion the pair remained quite calm as I ringed the chicks.

The young mistle thrushes grew rapidly and fledged from the nest ten days later. They were constantly fed by both parents for a further fortnight, after which they were able to fend for themselves.

The hen had built a second nest and laid again, but due to interference from the young birds, nothing came of it. To achieve a successful second round they should be removed from the flight when they are self-supporting.

I was pleased to read the list of successful breedings by members of the Association for the Study and Propagation of European Birds in Aviaries (ASPEBA) in 1992. Among the young birds bred by its members were fieldfares and redwings. I spoke at length with the association secretary Frank Meaden about these particular breedings as I felt it would be of great value to exchange notes and stock. Mr Meaden verified my suspicions that these birds were bred by association members abroad.

ANONYMOUS

I fully understand that it is the right of an individual to remain anonymous, but I also feel it would be sad for aviculture if the various societies held back from exchanging information.

I sincerely hope that the ASPEBA fieldfare and redwing keepers will feel able to share their remarkable achievements with the Thrush Breeding Programme in the future and I look forward to hearing from them.

On December 1st 1992, Lord Strathclyde announced a review of the operation of UK wildlife sales and other matters relating to the Wildlife and Countryside Act 1981, EC regulations and miscellaneous controls, and a re-appraisal of Schedule 4. Its finding and government response will be announced in 1994.

When I was invited by the authorities to submit comments on the subject, among my recommendations was the removal from Schedule 4 of the fieldfare and redwing.

Any BBC member wishing to join the Thrush Breeding Programme, or any member of the public who has wild, disabled redwings, fieldfares or ring ouzels in their possession - or comes across such birds - would be of interest to the Programme. The Programme is at present unable to take in anymore mistle thrushes, unless a colour variant is offered.

Photograph by Dennis Avon

SATINETTE BLACKBIRD

Photograph by Dennis Avon

CINNAMON BLACKBIRD

Blackbirds and song thrushes are well established and not part of the thrush breeding programme.

CINNAMON SONG THRUSH

Photograph by Dennis Avon

197

Baby song thrushes 12 days old

PROGRESS WITH THRUSHES

1998 – An update.

Before the Wildlife and Countryside Act 1981 came into force most species of British Birds were kept and bred without much hindrance from regulations. Among these were all the large thrushes, namely the blackbird, song thrush, mistle thrush, ring ouzel, fieldfare and redwing.

Unfortunately, as the new legislation began to take effect; the birds listed on Schedule 3 (those which could be sold or shown if ringed and bred in captivity from legally-held stock), were seen by softbill keepers as the most attractive kind to develop. Of these thrushes, only the blackbird and song thrush were so listed.

Breeders got rid of the other four kinds of thrush mentioned for a number of reasons, but mainly due to confusion and fear over the new laws. Most of these fanciers have since regretted their actions, and wish they had maintained their strains of these delightful birds.

These events resulted in the near disappearance of the mistle thrush, ring ouzel, fieldfare and redwing from British aviaries, so in 1990 the Fancy set up a Thrush Breeding Programme aimed at increasing the numbers of these species to pre-Act levels. I became its co-ordinator, and within a short time a good number of enthusiasts were supporting the scheme. A nation-wide search was undertaken for aviary-bred and wild disabled specimens, with mixed results. A few pairs of mistle thrushes and ring ouzels were located, but only disabled specimens of the fieldfare and redwing were found. During the next few years good progress was made with the mistle thrush and ring ouzel, but due to injuries and lack of compatible pairs, no breeding occurred within the fieldfare and redwing stock. Applications to take the wild specimens of the fieldfare and redwing on licence were turned down by the authorities. Both these species are mainly winter visitors to these shores from the north, but a few pairs of each kind breed in Scotland, so fall into the category of rare breeding birds. This is perhaps the reason why any attempt to lawfully take wild specimens was disallowed. Of the millions which invade the countryside each year, three or four pairs of each species taken from the wild would not, I think, have had any detrimental effect on their numbers.

In recent times the importation of continental aviary-bred birds of any species has notably increased. Among the species to come into the UK were a few fieldfares and redwings, so the task of breeding strains is now more realistic than at any time since the 1981 Act became law.

The current status of each of the six species is briefly outlined below -

BLACKBIRD: Now well established with numerous aviary strains in existence. Many wonderful colour variants available, these include albino, cream, cinnamon, opal, grizzle, blue and pied.

SONG THRUSH: Possibly the commonest kept of all native softbills. Quite domesticated; with cinnamon and cream mutations becoming well developed. This species is now in decline in the wild. Aviary-bred stocks are on the increase.

MISTLE THRUSH: Plenty of pairs now within captive collections. Quite a number are bred each year. It is the largest of our common thrushes. A cream specimen has turned up and an attempt is being made to breed a strain of this mutation.

RING OUZEL: A bird of the mountains, it is somewhat difficult to breed in captivity. However some are propagated from time to time. Some were bred in an East Anglian aviary last year.

FIELDFARE: A few exist in captivity now, notably a beautiful breeding pair, which it is hoped will raise young soon.

REDWING: A handful were imported recently. I have a single bird, a hen, I would very much like a mate for this bird. The redwing is the smaller of the larger thrushes native to these islands.

The Thrush Breeding Programme has now been going for quite a few years and with pleasing progress being made with all six species, the likelihood of all of them being bred in satisfactory numbers is now well within reach.

To conclude this chapter of the Thrush Breeding Programmes, this was closed down by the BBC in 1995. I set up my own project and began keeping breeding and showing redwings and fieldfares soon after. Stock began coming in from Europe, birds also became available from Norman Woodhouse, a distinguished breeder of British Birds; these events are documented in Chapter 1 of this book.

The British Bird Council obtained a licence in the autumn of 1998 to take 60 redwings; only 4 birds were taken, a disaster, and an opportunity missed

SATINETTE SONG THRUSH

Photograph by Dennis Avon

199

Photograph by Dennis Avon

HEN BLACKBIRD

DETR GRANTS LICENCE TO TAKE REDWINGS

Report in Cage & Aviary Birds October 3rd 1998.

The British Bird Council (BBC) received a major boost for its redwing breeding programme when the Department of Environment, Transport and the Regions (DETR) granted a licence to take up to 60 redwings.

The announcement was made by the BBC's chairman Chris Boyce at September's delegates' meeting. It was Mr Boyce in fact who was instrumental in getting the DETR to approve the licence. The opportunity came about when BBC member John Naylor applied for the licence but was turned down. Mr Naylor then approached the Council and Chris Boyce wrote to the Rt. Hon. John Prescott, Deputy Prime Minister and Secretary of State for Environment, Transport and Regions, explaining the merits of Mr Naylor's case.

"The intention is to obtain 20 pairs of redwings from the wild for distribution to members as part of a co-ordinated plan to establish a viable captive breeding population," explained the BBC administrator Roger Caton. He continued: "Redwings are difficult to sex, therefore DNA tests will have to be carried out to determine their gender. The costs of these tests and other expenses like registration fees will be met by the BBC".

"The birds will be taken during November, December and January. A special committee has been set up to control all aspects of the operation with John Naylor as the breeding programme co-ordinator. Participation of the scheme will be limited to members of the BBC with proven track record of breeding large softbills. Anyone who feels that they have the necessary credentials and would like to take part should apply in writing to John Naylor at: The British Bird Council, 1st Floor, Facet House, Facet Road, King's Norton, Birmingham, B38 9PT."

I did not apply, having my own birds by that time. The number of redwings caught during the duration of the licence was four, all cocks, this can only be described as a fiasco. The council had let everyone down, including Prescott. No apology was ever issued by the BBC and no one 'fell on his sword'. The individuals mentioned in the report have to live with their failure.

FROM STRENGTH TO STRENGTH

January 30th 1999

The 1981 Wildlife & Countryside Act was a blow to the Fancy, as it curtailed the number of British Bird species that could be shown from the many to just a few. Although the Fancy was shaken it was not downhearted, and soon some class numbers began to rise as new colour variants emerged from the birds that remained outside the legislation.
It is possible that had it not been for the 1981 Act, the production of new variants in the country would not have gained the momentum it did. Gradually common sense prevailed and the Government, which had been duped to a large degree by the opponents of birdkeeping in drawing up these draconian laws, began its now famous series of U-turns. After a few years of allowing the display of non-scheduled birds, a General Licence was issued to permit their competitive exhibition once more.
A further such licence came into force concerning vagrant species. I recall Jimmy Rutter judging the Eastern Federation of British Bird Fanciers show, when at about midday he called: "Bring over the pastor". It was not that Jimmy was hungry for his lunch, but the fact that there was a rosy pastor (rose-coloured starling) on show which he wanted to see. (see photograph page 202)
With the exception of northern goldfinches and bullfinches, which are sub-species of our own stock, true vagrants such as the aforementioned starling were not attracted to the British Bird show benches but have found a home among the exotics of the Foreign Bird section.
With the issuing of a licence to take wild redwings, the protectionists, who furiously objected to such a move, have again been snubbed. Three "new" species – the redwing, fieldfare and serin – are being bred for exhibition once more.
So where do we go from here? I predict an end to compulsory ringing and scrapping of the schedules, as we know them. The policing of the hobby will be far more scientifically orientated, with DNA profiling coming into its own. The trend to sideline the protectionists in this important field of conservation will continue.
Ironically, the Fancy is stronger now than it has ever been. The biased and scientifically bankrupt attitudes of its opponents have been defeated by the sense of democracy. Long may such happy circumstances continue.

Letters regarding the Redwing licence issue

Redwing Licence

I APPRECIATE Bernard Howlett's desire to provoke discussion (strength to strength, January 30), but it does the Fancy no good to exaggerate or mislead. He is not a member of the British Bird Council and does not have any detailed knowledge of the recent licence issued to take Redwings from the wild.
The licence was issued for the purposes of aviculture, not exhibition. None of the birds taken under licence will be used for exhibition. They will be used for a concerted breeding programme to try to ensure the species' widespread availability in the future.
The protectionists have not been snubbed, we merely have different views on the subject of aviculture and exhibition, but we both have common ground in having the interests of the birds at heart.
The council is aware of only a handful of Redwings in this country and even fewer breeding. To suggest that three "new" species are now being bred for exhibition is to mislead the Fancy. We are a little way from this yet.

CHRIS BOYCE
British Bird Council chairman,
Birmingham

Redwing Rules

I APOLOGISE for not making it clear in my article (Strength to strength, January 30) that the Redwings bred for exhibition will be from independent stock.
I am fully aware of the limitations written into the licence for taking birds from the wild. They are the reasons why I and others have declined to take part.
Redwings form part of my present show team and I hope to breed hybrids and colour variants from them within a few years.

BERNARD HOWLETT
Diss, Norfolk

ROSE-COLOURED STARLING
(reference page 201)

Photograph by Tony Tilford

NO EXAGGERATION

I did not exaggerate or mislead, in my 'From Strength to Strength' article. I had resigned from the BBC earlier as I found the organisation to be an albatross around my neck, (I have always considered myself to be a 'free spirit'), and I had been promised redwings from another source.

For years the minor authorities had turned down licences, Prescott had over-ruled them, their reasons for not issuing licences were pathetic, the 'protectionists' were undoubtedly putting pressure on these government light-weights; they, the 'protectionists', being anti-birdkeeping.

I had detailed knowledge of the licence because someone within the inner circle of the BBC had phoned me to put me fully in the picture, he asked me to join the programme.

COMPROMISE

Exhibition is part of aviculture. Many thought Boyce had made a compromise, which was not in the interest of the Fancy. He and his team captured only four redwings. Boyce and the rest of them finished up with 'egg on their faces', (allegedly)! No BBC resignations were forthcoming following the debacle.

THE BRITISH BIRD COUNCIL'S WEBSITE STATES:
'A redwing breeding programme was set up with a licence from DEFRA to take 60 birds from the wild'. Yes, good, but what happened?
We have a right to know! I will finish the announcement for Mr. Boyce ... 'to take 60 birds from the wild, but we messed up'.

Photograph by Dennis Avon

HYBRIDISING PAIR

Howlett vs Caton

Satinette Blackbird Hen

HOWLETT vs CATON

During the summer of 1994, Roger Caton, who at that time answered questions for Cage & Aviary Birds as British Bird Expert, answered a query from a fancier about bullfinches as follows:-

Bullfinches and Rosefinches

Q What are the scientific names for Red-cheeked Bullfinches and Long-tailed Rosefinches? Also, where do they originate and what are their feeding and breeding requirements? If I want to exhibit Mules or Hybrids from these species or from British Finches in a show, do I have to be a member of a bird club and would the birds have to be fitted with close rings? - P.A.

A The Red-cheeked Bullfinch (*Pyrrhula pyrrhula griseiventris*) originates from Korea and Japan. Its diet is the same as other Bullfinches with the emphasis on buds and berries. In captivity they should be fed on British Finch mixture with plenty of soaked or sprouted seeds and wildfood.

The Long-tailed Rosefinch (*Uragus sibiricus*) originates from southern Siberia and Mongolia. In captivity they will do well on a similar diet to that recommended for the Bullfinch, with the addition of seeding grass heads and weed seeds with plenty of livefood.

None of these birds need to be ringed either for sale or show. Any Mules or Hybrids bred from them would have to be exhibited in Foreign Bird classes.

11th June 1994

I disagreed with his views and wrote a letter to Cage & Aviary Birds as follows:-

Advice on Bullfinches was incorrect

I WOULD like to comment on the answer given to the query about Bullfinches and Rosefinches which was published in the June 11 issue.

I disagree with the advice given in the last paragraph of the answer which indicates that the Red-cheeked Bullfinch (*Pyrrhula p.griseiventris*) need not be ringed if sold or shown. This bird is merely a race of the common Bullfinch (*Pyrrhula pyrrhula*) – its Latin name makes this fact obvious – and therefore, under British law, must be aviary-bred from legally held stock and closed-ringed with an official ring, before it can be lawfully sold or exhibited. This is because the nominate species *Pyrrhula pyrrhula* is listed in Schedule 3 part 1 of the Wildlife and Countryside Act 1981.

There are nine or more races of the common Bullfinch scattered over its vast range across Europe and Asia. All originate from the same unique gene pool, and vary in colour and size due to local, long-term environmental and geographical influences. Where these races inter-breed, their offsprinbg are fertile; as any DNA test would show, they are one and the same bird – a fact of taxonomy and of law.

BERNARD HOWLETT

Diss, Norfolk.

20th August 1994

Roger replied to my letter with the following, written in Cage & Aviary Birds:-

Bullfinch owners within the law

READERS are bound to be confused by Bernard Howlett's comments in the August 20 issue, which disagreed with the advice I gave about the Red-cheeked Bullfinch (*Pyrrhula p. griseiventris*) not having to be ringed when sold or exhibited.

I always try to give a common sense answer to queries bearing in mind the law and, despite what Bernard says, these birds are not resident in or visitors to the British Isles in a wild state. Therefore it could be argued that they do not fall within the scope of the Wildlife and Countryside Act 1981.

When interpreting the legislation, I am sure the courts would consider what the intention of Parliament was when the Act was made law - and that was to give protection to British Birds.

This year quite a number of foreign Bullfinches have been legally imported and offered for sale in this country, and I would like to reassure anyone who has bought them that they are not breaking the law.

ROGER CATON

West Midlands.

17th September 1994

I replied to the latest letter from Roger Caton on
October 22nd 1994, my letter was as follows:-

NOTE: Since this chapter was written, the Azores bullfinch P. murina has been identified as a true species, making a total of seven species worldwide.

No exceptions in law over the Bullfinch issue

■ This cock Siberian Bullfinch was exhibited at a recent World Show.

WE ARE back to square one with the Bullfinch case. In the September 17 issue of CAGE & AVIARY BIRDS Roger Caton says we can sell and show foreign races of the Bullfinch without rings, while I still say we can't.

At least Mr Caton's remarks will be music to the ears of many fanciers including, for instance, those from Belgium and Spain; they will, no doubt, descend upon us in hoards with teams of unringed, aviary-bred local races of the common Bullfinch to exhibit at our shows.

I can just imagine a conversation between the "Old Bill" and a show manager somewhere in England, as they walk side by side along the rows of Bullfinch cages. The "Old Bill" asks: "What's this one then?", the reply being: "That's the Belgian Bullfinch (*Pyrrhula p. europoea*)". The "Old Bill" then points to another, and asks: "What's this one then?" The show manager answers that this one is the Spanish Bullfinch (*P. p. iberiae*). The "Old Bill" then remarks: "Shouldn't they all have rings on?" The show manager replies: "Oh no, officer, my understanding is that as they are all foreign, our law doesn't apply to them." The "Old Bill" takes out his notebook and his pen from his pocket, bends his knees, then straightens them again, and says: "Oh yes, it does."

The legislators, in their wisdom, have made no mention of race, so there are no exceptions in law; we are therefore obliged to go by the book. Of the six species of true Bullfinches in the world, only one -

the Common Bullfinch - is listed in the Wildlife & Countryside Act. The Red-cheeked Bullfinch is a sub-species of this bird. The law does not say that only the British race (*P. p. pileata*) is protected. It would be nonsense if it did, as many other races or sub-species on the Continent and elsewhere resemble

ours. There would be total confusion, and the law would not be enforced.

Far-eastern races of the Wryneck and the Dartford Warbler, for instance, have to be registered and ringed if kept in captivity in this country. It is the identity of the species which is relevant, not its race.

The other five species of Bull-finches are the Brown Bullfinch (*P. nipalensis*), the Philippine Bullfinch (*P. leucogenys*), the Orange Bullfinch (*P. aurantiaca*), the Red-headed Bullfinch (*P. erythrocephala*), and the Beavan's Bullfinch (*P. erythaca*). All these are completely foreign to this country, and we must never confuse our bird with any of them.

BERNARD HOWLETT
Diss, Norfolk.

Photograph by Sergey Yeliseev

DARTFORD WARBLER MALE

Mr Caton again replied to my letter as follows:-

IRRELEVANT BULLFINCH ISSUE

IN Bernard Howlett's letter (October 22 issue) he talks about all the various sub-species of Bullfinch. No doubt what he says is true but quite irrelevant in this case.

The difference of opinion arose over my answer to a query which stated that the Red-cheeked Bullfinch (Pyrrhula p. griseiventris) did not need to be ringed when sold or exhibited. Section 27 (1) of the Wildlife &

Countryside Act states "a wild bird means any bird of a kind which is ordinarily resident in or is a visitor to Great Britain in a wild state". As the species in question is found in Korea and South Japan and can easily be distinguished from our native Bullfinch, there does not seem to be a problem. In fact, I have seen these birds offered for sale in a local pet shop earlier this year.

ROGER CATON

West Midlands.

Meanwhile I had written an article, dated September 1994 in Bird Keeper magazine entitled "A Question of Race"

A QUESTION OF RACE

In essence the species of goldfinch (Carduelis carduelis) and, the species of bullfinch (Pyrrhula pyrrhula) and their subspecies found in the UK, no matter where they hail from in the world, must be close-ringed with British Bird Council or International Ornithological Association rings of the correct size, if they are to be sold or exhibited in this country. If they are ringed with any other band, they are deemed not to be ringed at all, and their keeper would require special dispensation to exhibit or sell them here.

The scientific name of a bird is part of the international language of science, enabling ornithologists or naturalists in one country to know what those in another country are referring to. The scientific name of a bird consists of two Latinised words, a generic name, indicating the name of the genus, which could be interpreted as a sort of a surname.

The first word always has a capital initial and is followed by a specific name, which could be linked to a sort of forename. This always has a small initial and indicates a species. These two names used together, form the full scientific name of a species for example, Turdus merula identifies the blackbird, whereas the song thrush, which comes from the same genus Turdus, has for its specific or forename philomelos. No other species have these combinations of names.

A species is a group or aggregate of birds, of the same kind, which are similar anatomically, have the same general appearance and are capable of interbreeding with other members of the same group. The species is the fundamental unit of classification. It is subordinate to genus, which groups similar species like the blackbird and song

thrush, for example, and superior to a sub-species, geographic race, or variety of which there may be several within the same species.

Third word

Where a sub-species or geographical race occurs, a third latinised word is added to the name; this does not mean that the bird referred to is of a different species or separate species, only that its race has been recognised.

For example, the race of the British goldfinch is known to taxonomists as "britannica", its full Latin name being Carduelis carduelis britannica and usually written Carduelis c. britannica. This sets it apart from other races of its species of which there are many. Two of the most popular in aviculture are the Siberian, which has the added name "major", and the Himalayan, one of the grey-headed races of our bird, which has the added name "caniceps". All these varieties are, however, of exactly the same species. They vary in some respects because of geographical isolation, diet and environmental factors, but all these races, in fact originate from the same, unique gene pool as any DNA investigation would prove.

The common bullfinch (Pyrrhula pyrrhula) has a wide range across Europe and Asia, its colour patterns varying enormously from one locality to another. The so-called blue bullfinch lives in the eastern regions of Russia and Mongolia and is often offered for sale in the UK. It is the same species as the common bullfinch, the bird that lives in Britain, and therefore cannot be legally sold unless bred in captivity and closed-ringed, from lawfully held stock, in accordance with the law. It has as its third latinised name "cineracea".

Although the hens of this race are similar to our bird, the cocks have no red on them at all. About nine different races of the common bullfinch Pyrrhula pyrrhula exist.

The Wildlife & Countryside Act 1981 lists in its Schedules only the common and latinised names of a species. No mention is made of race, so although our native goldfinch is the race britannica, no specific mention of it is made in the Act. This is because the nominate species Carduelis carduelis is listed and so far as science and the law is concerned, the listing embraces not only our local race, but also all other races of the species wherever they may hail in the world.

No specimen of a species listed on Schedule 3 Part 1 of the Act may be exhibited or sold in the UK unless aviary-bred and close-ringed and its breeding parents were lawfully held in captivity when the egg from which it was hatched, was laid. Any breach of the law, however trivial, obscure or technical, could lead to a prosecution being instigated, and as ignorance of the law is no excuse, proceedings could lead to a conviction. European Directive 79/409/EEC dated April 1979 underpins this legislation. Which essentially says that if a species is represented, in whatever form, in the wild, in a member state, every sub-species of that species is also subjected to national EC law, no matter where it comes from in the world.

....

The above article is slightly different, to that written in September 1994 and referred by Roger in his letter, (see below), as the European Court had not debated its case at that time. Note: ringing laws are changing in 2013.

Roger replied to this article.

Another view of the Law.

In his article "A Question of Race" (September issue of Bird Keeper) Bernard Howlett claims that the legislation applies to all sub-species of birds wherever they may be located in the world.

Section 27(1) of the Wildlife & Countryside Act defines a "wild bird" within the meaning of the Act as "any bird of a kind which is ordinary resident in or is a visitor to Great Britain in a wild state".

In my view the "Foreign Birds" referred to in his article do not fall into this category and therefore not covered by the Act. These birds have been imported and offered for sale quite legally for many years and I would like to reassure anyone who has bought them that they are not breaking the Law.

Roger Caton,
Pattington,
West Midlands
November 1994.

The fact was that these "sub- species" were of the same species that live in Britain, their Importation into the UK would only be legal if each were close-ringed with statutory rings, captive bred from lawfully held stock. They were illegal, and the keepers were breaking the law. (See European Court Case findings)

I wrote to Bird Keeper saying Roger Caton's letter of November 1994 was "an incitement to bird keepers to breach the law", etc. Peter Moss the Editor passed my letter on to Roger, who instructed solicitors to write to me concerning libel.
I withdrew my allegations and that was that.

Licence not necessary, says DoE

IS IT necessary to have a licence to sell or display the Bullfinch sub-species, such as *Pyrrhula pyrrhula griseiventris*? According to the Department of the Environment's Wildlife Division it is not.

Its the opinion of the Department that non-indigenous sub-species are not "wild birds" as defined by the Wildlife & Countryside Act 1981. As a result they are exempt from the sales and display provisions of the Act. The sub-species *griseiventris* is not recognised as being ordinarily resident or a visitor to Great Britain.

However, the onus is upon birdkeepers to prove that their birds are of a non-indigenous sub-species. This may well be difficult with birds whose different sub-species are not easy to tell apart.

February 25th 1995

Soon after this rather peculiar and erroneous outburst from the DOE was aired, Roger Caton graciously informed me of a decision made by the European Court of Justice to the effect that all sub-species of a species which naturally resides in an E.U. country are protected throughout the community. Full details of the Court ruling is described hereafter.

1979 COURT RULES ON GOLDFINCHES

Following the seizure at the home of a Dutch national in 1994 of a number of imported birds belonging to the sub-species Carduelis carduelis caniceps, of Grey-headed Goldfinch, the authorities in the Netherlands decided to stay proceedings and refer the case to the Court of Justice of the European Communities for preliminary ruling concerning the interpretation of European Community Law on wild birds. This judgement was given after hearing the opinion of the Advocate General.

In its order for reference, the Dutch court stated that the Black-headed Goldfinch (C.carduelis) occurs naturally in the wild and in several sub-species in the European territory of the Member States to which the treaty applies. However, the C.c.caniceps is, it stated, a sub-species which occurs naturally in the wild only outside the European territory in question, i.e. The Netherlands.

Since it was unsure whether The Netherlands' legislation under which the birds in question were seized correctly transposed the EC Directive on bird law, the Dutch National Court decided to stay its proceedings and refer a series of three questions to the Court of Justice. The first of these was of uttermost importance:

"Is national legislation which protects birds (within the meaning of Directive 79/409/EEC of April 2nd 1979, on the conservation of wild birds as amended) belonging according to the evidence, to a sub-species which, as such, does not at all occur naturally in the wild in the European territory of the Member States compatible with the wording and/or the Directive 79/409, and in particular with Articles 1. 1 and 14 thereof, if only because the (main) species and/or other sub-species do occur naturally in the wild in that territory or in the territory of the Member State in question".

The judges emphasised that, by the question, the national court was seeking to determine whether the Directive applied to a bird sub-species which occur naturally in the wild only outside the European territory of the Member States, where the species to which they belong or other sub-species of that species do occur naturally in the wild state within the territory in question.

Experts stated that, in avian taxonomy, the concept of species, includes by definition, all of a species' subdivisions such as breeds and sub-species. Consequently, a specimen belonging to a sub-species will always belong to the species comprising the sub-species in question.

Assuming that the scope of the Directive is to be defined on the basis of the taxonomic concept of species follows that, if a sub-species occurs naturally in the wild in the European territory of the Member States to which the treaty applied, the species to which the sub-species belongs must be considered to be a European species and consequently, all the other sub-species of the species in question, including those which are not European, will be covered by the Directive, concluded the judges.

The Court (Third Chamber) ruled in open court in Luxembourg that Council Directive 709/409/EEC April 2nd, 1979, the conservation of wild birds applies to bird sub-species which occur naturally in the wild only outside the European territory of the Member States if the species to which they belong or other sub-species of that species occur naturally in the wild within the territory in question.

I have always interpreted the law this way, and this is borne out in my various letters and articles, published in Cage & Aviary Birds and Bird Keeper on the subject. It has always saddened me to know that some fancies have found this issue irrelevant, when it is obvious that it is very relevant indeed.

GREY-HEADED GOLDFINCH

Photograph by Sergey Yeliseev

CHAPTER SEVEN

The Evolution of bird Fancy law

Normal Blackbird Hen

Photograph by Dennis Avon

THE EVOLUTION OF BIRD FANCY LAW

Add Birds to Schedule 3 (DATED 1991) and refers to that time.

This chapter outlines changes made after the Wildlife and Countryside Act 1981 until the present time, these include the law relating to General Licences and changes to Schedule 4.
At the present time officers representing the British Bird Fancy are attempting to persuade the Government to add the common crossbill (Loxia curvirostra) and the house sparrow (Passer domesticus) to Schedule 3 part 1 of the Wildlife and Countryside Act 1981 - birds which may be sold or exhibited if bred in captivity and close ringed.
So far no species have been added, or for that matter removed from this Schedule since the enactment of the legislation. The species on Schedule 3 Part 1 are those assessed as having a self-sufficient captive bred population. The common crossbill and the house sparrow have long achieved this criteria.

REMOVED OR ADDED

The Schedule of species which may be shown or sold can be amended by Order made by the Secretary of State for the Environment. Species can be removed or added. No prime legislation is required. Any data forthcoming from breeding records can play an important role in deciding on any change to the Schedule. When a species is added the rules about the correct type (and supply) of rings will apply.
There will not be any transitional arrangements. It is therefore, in the best interests of keepers to ensure that their birds are ringed with rings from an approved supplier, even if the birds are not currently listed on Schedule 3 Part 1. In the case of Schedule 4 birds like the crossbill, Government rings are issued to breeders as and when required. House sparrows, however, which are a Schedule 2 species, should be fitted with code E closed rings when chicks, in preparation for any change in their status.
Before the Act became law many crossbills and house sparrows were bred in numbers; it came as a surprise therefore, to many, when these birds were not included on Schedule 3 Part 1. Since 1981, an even greater effort has been made to breed strains of these species. Breeding programmes have been very successful. These birds are now well established in aviculture.
It is hoped that as the time is now right, the common crossbill and house sparrow will be added as indicated. Any delay will only tend to make a mockery of the sincerity of the legislators and bring the law itself into disrepute.

NO SPECIFIC NAME

So far I have referred only to the common crossbill, this is because no specific name indicating a species of crossbill is listed anywhere in the Wildlife and Countryside Act 1981. The crossbill is listed on Schedule 1 Part 1, birds which are protected by Special Penalties at all times, and on Schedule 4, and which must be registered and ringed if kept in captivity.
These entries refer to crossbills, and read crossbills, then in brackets, all species, and next to these words appear the scientific name of the genus, Loxia, so just the generic name for this group of birds is given. The law therefore encompasses all Loxia crossbills, of which there are four species. No doubt the common is the one the Fancy is interested in, but this will be a complicated issue for the Secretary of State to come to terms with.
I hope he will treat all species of crossbills in the future in the same way as, for example, the brambling is accommodated currently, which would leave them on Schedule 1 Part 1, but add them to the list contained in Schedule 3 Part 1. This would afford them that added protection, and for any new entry to read "Crossbill (all species) Loxia."
This action would give the Fancy four new species in which to invest freely. All of the four world species are on the British list, the common as aforementioned, the parrot crossbill (L. pytyopsittacus), the Scottish crossbill (L. scotica) and the white-winged crossbill, (L. leucoptera). Alternatively the white-winged, or two-barred crossbill as it is often called, could be designated elsewhere, maybe added to the General Licence, as it is a small bird with broad wing bars and therefore easily recognisable, as the other species resemble each other.
Taxonomy of the Scottish bird is somewhat uncertain. Some scientists insist that it is merely a sub-species of the common crossbill; others indicate that it is a separate species, and yet other experts claim the bird to be a sub-species of the Continental parrot crossbill. This uncertainty about the Scottish bird is probably the reason why the legislators declined to list the species of crossbills separately when the list was drawn up.
The documents in use in connection with the registration of these birds do not indicate the particular species kept, nor is a keeper asked to

supply this information, the name crossbill suffices. It is quite likely that all these species are kept within aviculture; undoubtedly there will be some of the Scottish type, and maybe some parrot crossbills. The white-winged crossbill however, may well be absent from the collections. Data is not within the knowledge of the authorities as to which species are kept and of their respective numbers.

The common, as its name suggests, is much the commonest and wide spread of all the crossbills, having a vast circumglobal range in the northern hemisphere. The parrot crossbill, which is a slightly larger bird has only a limited range and is confined to north Europe. Both birds are stocky looking, with large heads, thick necks and shortish tails, and the only visible difference in the field is the much deeper and more arched beak of the parrot crossbill.

SCOTTISH BIRD

The Scottish bird has a slightly deeper bill than the common, and there are subtle differences in its call.

The white-winged or two-barred crossbill is a circumpolar species, being found in northern parts of Europe and North Africa. It is a rare visitor to these shores.

There is nothing difficult to consider when identifying the other candidate for Schedule 3, the house sparrow. It is a bird familiar the world over, and known to town and country folk alike. The species is being bred nowadays in a host of colour variant varieties, many of which originate from the continent. The house sparrow is currently considered by the Government as a pest species. The Fancy as a whole and the British Bird keepers in particular, wait now with bated breath for the outcome of these negotiations. Progress is also being made with several other species. These include the redstart, black redstart, hawfinch, and mistle thrush. These too, and many more are waiting in the "wings" to become candidates for Schedule 3.

Note: These facts were written in 1991, since then, of course, many changes have been made.

Photograph by Tommy Milner

PAIR OF COMMON CROSSBILLS

DEPARTMENT OF THE ENVIRONMENT   LICENCE NO WLF010896
DIRECTORATE OF RURAL AFFAIRS

WILLIFE AND COUNTRYSIDE ACT 1981
LICENCE TO PERMIT THE EXHIBITION OF CERTAIN CAPTIVE BRED SPECIES OF BRITISH BIRDS

This licence, granted under Section 16(1)(f) of the Wildlife and Countryside Act 1981 by the Secretary of State for the Environment after consultation with English Nature, is valid unless previously revoked , in England and authorises **The East Anglian National Society** to exhibit the following species of birds:

Grey Wagtail	-	Motacilla cinerea
Pied Wagtail	-	Motacilla alba
Redstart	-	Phoenicurus phoenicurus
Black Redstart	-	Phoenicurus ochruros
Meadow Pipit	-	Anthus pratensis
Mistle Thrush	-	Turdus viscivorus
Fieldfare	-	Turdus pilaris
Redwing	-	Turdus iliacus
Hawfinch	-	Coccothraustes coccothraustes
Crossbill	-	Loxia curvirostra
Corn Bunting	-	Emberiza calandra
Tree Sparrow	-	Passer montanus
House Sparrow	-	Passer domesticus

This licence is subject to the following conditions:

1)   The bird must be bred in captivity and ringed with a close ring. A bird shall not be treated as bred in captivity unless its parents were lawfully in captivity when the egg from which it hatched was laid.

2)   That the birds mentioned above may not be sold

3)   That the licence is only valid for **31 October 1993**

4)   That the birds may only be displayed at **The Corn Exchange, Kings Lynn, Norfolk.**

5)   That any bird included on Schedule 4 of the Wildlife and Countryside Act 1981 must be properly ringed and registered in accordance with Section 7 of the above Act and the Wildlife and Countryside (Registration and Ringing of Certain Captive Birds) Regulations 1982 SI 1981 No 1221 as amended by the Wildlife and Countryside (Registration and Ringing of Certain Captive Birds)(Amendment) Regulations 1991 SI 1991 No 478.

Signed:

Authorised by the Secretary of State
for the Environment to sign in
that behalf

Date:

Department of the Environment
Wildlife Division
Tollgate House
Houlton Street
Bristol BS2 9DJ
Tel: 0272 218694

DEPARTMENT OF THE ENVIRONMENT   LICENCE NO WLF011386
DIRECTORATE OF RURAL AFFAIRS

WILDLIFE AND COUNTRYSIDE ACT 1981
LICENCE TO PERMIT THE EXHIBITION OF CERTAIN CAPTIVE BRED SPECIES OF BRITISH
BIRDS

This licence, granted under Section 16.(1)(f) of the Wildlife and
Countryside Act 1981 by the Secretary of State for the Environment after
consultation with English Nature, is valid unless previously revoked , in
England and authorises **Eastern Federation of British Bird Fanciers** to
exhibit the following species of birds:

Grey Wagtail - Motacilla cinerea
Pied Wagtail - Motacilla alba
Redstart - Phoenicurus phoenicurus
Black Redstart - Phoenicurus ochrurus
Meadow Pipit - Anthus pratensis
Mistle Thrush - Turdus viscivorus
Fieldfare - Turdus pilaris
Redwing - Turdus iliacus
Hawfinch - Coccothraustes coccothraustes
Crossbill - Loxia curvirostra
Corn Bunting - Emberiza calandra
Tree Sparrow - Passer montanus
House Sparrow - Passer domesticus
Nightinggale - Luscinia megarhynchos
Ring Ousel - Turdus torquatus
Blackcap - Sylvia atricapilla

This licence is subject to the following conditions:

1)   The bird must be bred in captivity and ringed with a close ring. A
bird shall not be treated as bred in captivity unless its parents were
lawfully in captivity when the egg from which it hatched was laid.

2)   That the birds mentioned above may not be sold

3)   That the licence is only valid for **6 March 1994**

4)   That the birds may only be displayed at **Assembly Rooms, Market Place,
Swaffham, Norfolk**

5)   That any bird included on Schedule 4 of the Wildlife and Countryside
Act 1981 must be properly ringed and registered in accordance with Section
7 of the above Act and the Wildlife and Countryside (Registration and
Ringing of Certain Captive Birds) Regulations 1982 SI 1981 No 1221 as
amended by the Wildlife and Countryside (Registration and Ringing of
Certain Captive Birds)(Amendment) Regulations 1991 SI 1991 No 478.

Signed: Department of the Environment
                                           Wildlife Division
Authorised by the Secretary of State   Tollgate House
for the Environment to sign in   Houlton Street
that behalf   Bristol BS2 9DJ
                                            Tel: 0272 218694

Date: 8 FEB 1994

213

FEWER RESTRICTIONS 1994

At the A.G.M. of the British Bird Council (BBC), which was held on March 20th, I had the privilege of being appointed as small softbill co-ordinator. Until that time I had the responsibility for the large softbills only, and this included the now well-established Thrush Breeding Programme. From now on, I will attempt to co-ordinate all softbill species, large or small, which BBC members keep. Much has been achieved in recent years. Many species of softbill have been bred in captivity in significant numbers, and are now genetically self-sustaining; these include the blackbird, song thrush, starling and dunnock. It is hoped that some 50 species will be in this position within a short period of time, but there is much work yet to be done.

Several areas are identified where work is urgent and essential, and these include:-

1)   The continuation of strain building with the seven Schedule 3 species. These are the four mentioned, plus three Corvid species - the magpie, jackdaw and jay.

2)   The development of bloodlines with the species now left on Schedule 4, such as the fieldfare, redwing, woodlark and black redstart.

3)   Controlled breeding with the many non-scheduled species, such as the mistle thrush, ring ouzel, blackcap and pied wagtail.

4)   The establishment of breeding strains of our vagrant birds which appear on a General Licence. These include the Siberian thrush, red-flanked bluetail or bush robin, Siberian rubythroat and rose-coloured starling.

The recent Government review of the Wildlife and Countryside Act and allied legislation has had some effect on the softbill situation. It has resulted in an Order being made on April 25th which removed all Category 3 birds from Schedule 4, some 40 species will no longer need to be registered with the authorities if kept in captivity. These are mainly waterfowl and similar; however the hoopoe, bee-eater, bluethroat, and a hardbill, the scarlet rosefinch, are included.

The hoopoe is well established while the bee-eater and bluethroat are scarce in captivity. Several fanciers have shown interest in the latter, and it is hoped that the keepers of bluethroat will make their birds available in a co-ordinated breeding programme.

The next review will take place in 1995, and at five-year intervals thereafter; these reviews will be carried out by the joint Nature Conservation Committee. It is important that progress is made within the Fancy with as many species as possible, and that breeding returns, for example, are submitted so that the law makers are aware of what is being achieved.

It is a fact that, as more specimens of a species are bred, so the law becomes more relaxed so far as that species is concerned. Schedule 4 and unscheduled species need to be bred in their hundreds before the authorities will consider adding them to Schedule 3. The crossbill with only some 250 specimens in captivity, for example, will have to quadruple its numbers before the authorities seriously consider any change to its status.

DATA NEEDED

Our aim must be to acquire stock from any legal source, such as from aviary breeding, customs, imports and disabled wild specimens from carers, and to build up as many species as possible, so they become self-sustaining.

To this end, it would be helpful if I could hold a register of birdkeepers' needs and details of softbill fanciers. Such an accumulation of data would be kept confidential.

As softbill co-ordinator I am prepared to devote time and energy to the work, but to be successful I must have input from birdkeepers as to their needs. Any fancier requiring advice, assistance in obtaining stock, or wishing to pass on suggestions as to what would be the best way forward in promoting softbills can contact me at anytime.

Note: (In 1995 - General Licence issued).

Photograph by Tony Tilford

BEE EATER

NEW BIRDS ON THE BLOCK 1995

British Bird shows around the country will have a different look about them from now on, with many new birds on the staging as a result of new legislation.

In the mule and hybrid classes, crossbill classes will again appear, they will include traditional birds and also perhaps, ghastly looking continental ones, where small and sometimes coloured canaries have been used.

In the hardbill classes, again the crossbill will play its part. Most exhibits will be of the Scottish species, some however may be of the common, parrot or white-winged kinds. All four species are kept in UK aviculture.

The hawfinch will make its return and do well, likewise the corn bunting. Breeders should enjoy showing their stock and richly deserve the right to do so.

The house sparrow has made good progress in captivity during the past decade; now many colour variant varieties have evolved. I have several, and hope to exhibit this species on a regular basis from now on. I hope the species will be taken more seriously than hitherto by judges; and look forward to winning a special or two with these birds.

Tree sparrows are rare in captivity in the UK. Some birds are bred in Northern Ireland and have official Ulster rings on them. These can now be considered for exhibition here, and may be the only ones available until new, local strains are formed.

I cannot see an early return of the snow bunting to the show bench, unless a serious programme of acquiring stock is undertaken.

Whether we shall see nightingales, or redstarts as good as those staged by Jim Walford and Colin Clarke in years gone by is questionable, but there will again be some big winners among these avicultural favourites, of this I have no doubt.

Like the snow bunting, the waxwing, redwing and fieldfare are scarce in captivity, but if aviary birds can be imported, these too, should find their way back on the benches before long.

There is one softbill which will match the best crossbills and hawfinches in the future and this is the ring ouzel. A huge cock bird in good condition and feather, well staged, will take some beating in the months ahead.

No doubt we will revert to the old policy of splitting the softbill section into two parts, small and large. This will be a good idea with specials allocated to both groups.

A good breeding season is now crucial. Cages re-discovered in the attic, will need to be refurbished as the new show season approaches, so that the new birds on the block can be competitively exhibited at shows up and down the land.

FIELDFARE

Photograph by Sergey Yeliseev

NEW LICENCE FOR EXHIBITING VAGRANT BRITISH BIRDS

Written in 1995, and should be read with this fact in mind.

A Licence no. WLF 100007 was granted by the Secretary of State under Section 16 (1)(f) of the Wildlife and countryside Act 1981, on January 1st 1995 to expire on the March 31st, 1996. It authorises, subject to certain conditions and expectations, the showing for competitive purposes of a captive live wild bird, of a species contained in the following list:

Rufous turtle dove, blue-cheeked bee eater, lesser short-toed lark, crested lark, brown thrasher, alpine accentor, rufous bush robin, Siberian rubythroat, red-flanked blue tail, rock thrush, White's thrush, Siberian thrush, hermit thrush, grey-cheeked thrush, veery, eye-browed thrush, dusky thrush, American robin, penduline tit, nutcracker, Spanish sparrow, trumpeter finch, pine grosbeak, summer tanager, rufous-sided towhee, fox sparrow, white-crowned sparrow, slate-coloured junco, pine bunting, rock bunting, Ortolan bunting, yellow-browed bunting, yellow-breasted bunting, Pallas's reed bunting, black-headed bunting, rose-breasted grosbeak and bobolink.

The bird must have been bred in captivity, and shall not be treated as such unless its parents were lawfully in captivity when the egg from which it hatched was laid. Documented evidence of captive breeding must accompany any bird competitively shown under this Licence.

The owner of any bird to be competitively shown under this Licence will, if requested by an official of the Department of the Environment, or police officer, make the bird available for a sample of blood to be taken from the bird to be shown. The blood sample will be taken by a qualified veterinary surgeon and may be used to establish the ancestry of the bird.

These species, although on the British list are vagrants or rare visitors to these islands. The previous licence, which was issued on July 29th 1983, and which this one replaces, made no mention of the requirement to present documented evidence of the breeding or of the blood testing. A total of 54 species was listed on the old Licence, whereas only 38 are listed on its replacement. The discarded birds are; bobwhite, roller, three-toed lark, black-throated thrush, lesser grey shrike, woodchat shrike, rose-coloured starling, rustic bunting, little bunting, chestnut bunting, red-headed bunting, blue grosbeak, indigo bunting and painted bunting.

The status of these 14 species is unclear and there is some question as to whether they are being ignored as British Birds or now fall within the species list which must be close-ringed if shown or offered for sale. I personally believe the 54 and the 14 all fall outside the ringing code.

Most of the species named on the new licence have virtually no following within British aviculture. A few, however are bred from time to time and exhibited. These include the Siberian rubythroat, red-flanked blue tail, rock thrush, eye-browed thrush, scarlet tanager, and black-headed bunting. I myself keep, breed and exhibit Siberian thrushes, so must remember to submit documented evidence

of breeding each time I exhibit a specimen from now on, and be aware that such a specimen may be subject to a blood test.

Note: 2011. Most of these species if shown would be entered in the Foreign Bird classes, but a few, such as the Siberian rubythroat, and rose-coloured pastor would be accepted on the British benches. Each licence has a time limit, but has been continually re-issued, giving it continuity.

Photograph by Dennis Avon

SIBERIAN THRUSH
On licence

Photograph by Sergey Yeliseev

ROLLER
Removed from licence

Photograph by Tony Tilford

WOODCHAT SHRIKE
Removed from licence

Photograph by Sergey Yeliseev

THRUSH NIGHTINGALE
No mention for this vagrant

DUSKY THRUSH
On licence

Photograph by Dennis Avon

LESSER GREY SHRIKE
Removed from licence

Photograph by Sergey Yeliseev

BRITISH BIRD KEEPING HAS GONE FULL CIRCLE

March 8th 1997

In its early days, British bird keeping was mainly the pastime of the working class. Birds were cheap and easy to come by. Linnets, goldfinches and even skylarks were numerous in captivity and prized to a greater extent than they are today.

In the 1960s, when I first began showing British birds, it was an exciting time and a great era for the hobby. In those days any lawfully held specimen could be exhibited. Rows of large, beautifully decorated cages of immaculately staged softbills graced the show halls; birds such as redstarts, blackcaps, stonechats, whinchats and wheatears were in prominence. In the hardbills sections classes of hawfinches, crossbills and corn buntings were on display.

When the Wildlife & Countryside Act of 1981 came into force, it restricted the number of species that could be shown to a mere handful, and although Section 16 (e) granted licences for aviculture (showing is part of aviculture) these were never applied for. On Schedule 3 Part 1 of the Act just 18 show species were listed: 11 hardbills and 7 softbills.

This had a dramatic, although short-term, effect on the hobby with the number of exhibits and classes at shows falling. Old favourites were missed and many strains of non-Schedule 3 birds were depleted or disbanded altogether. There was also a mood of anger and despondency among thousands of birdkeepers. The legislation was considered to be unnecessary and this feeling was proved right because today any lawfully held specimen of any species can again be exhibited if certain conditions are met. So the hobby has seen its fortunes turn full-circle. The future is now bright once more.

Since 1981, every effort has been made by the British Bird Fancy to return to, and to exceed, the former number of birds and classes staged on the show bench. In fact, this has been surpassed. Relevant factors include an immediate upsurge in the domestication of species and in breeding colour variant varieties.

The responsible attitude taken by the Fancy as a whole to promote the building of the line-bred strains of normal and colour variant serves as a shop window and indicates, to some degree, the extent of domesticity reached by the species involved.

Non-scheduled species and those listed on Schedule 4 can now be shown with the General Licence. Individual licences are also being issued authorising the exhibition of "unofficially" closed-ringed specimens of Schedule 3 species, and even non-ringed birds can be exhibited in some instances. The hobby is now, therefore, happily back to square one.

I am sure it was the intentions of the protectionists, who influenced the legislators at the time the Act was drawn up, to snuff out the keeping, breeding and exhibiting of indigenous species. Ironically, their biased attitude has had quite the reverse effect. Captive-bred birds are still, however, defined as wild, which in reality they are not, and with goods being freely transported throughout the Common Market, this definition cannot be justified much longer. Captive-bred birds are owned by birdkeepers and should be bought and sold with fewer restrictions. As the Fancy progresses along the lines of domestication of the stock, those who are not law abiding will become isolated, and any wild specimens in their collections will be inferior to the magnificent line-bred exhibits which are increasingly on view.

Today the British Bird Fancy is flourishing. People of all ages are now keeping, breeding and exhibiting captive birds. It is no longer a pastime just for the working man; it is an absorbing, but relaxing hobby for anyone from any walk of life.

Photograph by Dennis Avon

PAIR OF REDSTARTS

STATUS OF SCHEDULE 4 BIRDS WITHIN THE FANCY – 1997

Of the many species of birds listed on Schedule 4 of the Wildlife & Countryside Act 1981, about 20 kinds are of interest to the British Bird Fancy. Of these, only four - the chough, crossbill, black redstart and bearded tit - are bred in the UK on a regular basis. The following brief comments cover the species as they appear on the list.

Bunting: cirl, Lapland, snow. Of these buntings, only specimens of the snow bunting have been legally held in collections since the inception of the Act. In 1988, a few were taken under licence. No young were raised from any of these and all of the individuals taken at that time have since died.

Crossbills: (all species): About 200 pairs now exist within UK aviculture. Most specimens descend from lawfully taken Scottish stock from the wild many years ago. Recently, some birds, mainly common and two-barred have been imported from Europe.

Chough: A member of the crow family. Local along steep, rocky coasts - captive stock now number more than 80 individuals. More suitable for zoos and bird gardens than for the garden aviary.

Fieldfare: Winter visitor. A member of the thrush family. A handful of specimens of this species, all wild disabled, have been cared for in recent years. No breeding pairs were formed, and only one or two specimens are currently registered. A number of applications for licences to take wild specimens have been made. All have been rejected.

Firecrest: A member of the warbler tribe. To the best of my knowledge none are registered.

Golden oriole: About the size of a ring ouzel. Spring and summer visitor and bird of passage. Rumour has it that one or two exist in the UK collections, but I have not been able to find any evidence of this.

Black redstart: Summer resident in increasing numbers, and kept by specialised softbill enthusiasts who share some 13 pairs at the present time.

Redwing: Winter visitor and member of the thrush family. No legally held pairs exist at the present time. All applications to take wild specimens on licence have been refused. Four birds were legally imported in 1996, three of which have since died.

Serin: A tiny finch - none thought registered.

Shorelark: No evidence that any exist in confinement.

Red-backed shrike: Last specimen legally held died some years ago.

Bearded tit: A reed dweller. About 50 pairs thrive in collections.

Warblers: Cetti's, Dartford, marsh, Savi's. Of these four species only the Dartford had been bred in the collections within the country since 1981. About ten pairs are maintained at the present time.

Woodlark: A handful of specimens of this species are kept, all apparently disabled birds. None have been reared within a captive regime, since the Act came in force.

Wryneck: A few specimens have been imported in recent years, but none have been bred to date.

Schedule 4 birds must be registered and ringed if kept in captivity, including wild disabled specimens. Data is kept by the Department of the Environment.
There may be Schedule 4 birds which are not registered, kept by carers or others. Perhaps the law has not been explained to them that these specimens must be registered. I would advise any member of the public who has an unregistered bird to register it. It is important that pairs are brought together to breed.

It is hoped that interest will grow in this group of birds and that numbers will be built up of each kind. Importing legally held stock seems to be the obvious way forward to bring this about.

Since this article was written, slight changes may have occurred in some of the numbers given for these species.

IT IS TIME TO SCRAP SCHEDULE 4

Registration – a change for the better
October 26th, 2002.

Having been professionally involved in wildlife enforcement with the police service and DEFRA for more than 45 years, and an aviculturist for more years than that, I can comment with some experience on the department's consultation paper regarding Schedule 4 birds.
The criteria setting up the Schedule was wrong in the first place, it was based not on the world-wide distribution of a species, but on a species' ability to breed in Britain, often at the very extremity of its breeding range. For example, the fieldfare, an abundant winter visitor here, was found clinging on to a few sites in Scotland, hundreds of miles from its natural breeding grounds. Consequently it received a level of protection greater than that afforded the nightingale.

A weak government had acted primarily on the advice of the group of NGO's, who, by coincidence, had the greatest vested interest in rare birds. The higher the profile placed in law on a species, the better it is for these organisations. Rare birds make them rich, create jobs 'for the boys' and line pockets.

One eminent member of a bird protection group told me, when referring to a particular species: "We had to place the Cetti's warbler on Schedule 4, we just didn't want anyone keeping it in an aviary". So there you have it! This, of course, was a blinkered view, as specimens of both passerines and other species can be legally obtained abroad and registered here.

For example, aviary-bred red-backed shrikes that are nesting in the British aviaries at the present time are of European origin. By the way, the Cetti's warbler has never been in vogue. If it were to become so, stocks could be legally obtained overseas and imported. Believe me, I know.

The demand by aviculturists in Britain for large quantities of Schedule 4 listed passerines is just not there. Species like the redwing and fieldfare are already reaching saturation levels in captivity, and individuals can be purchased for as little as £25. I reluctantly brought an early end to my fieldfare's breeding endeavours this year, as I did not know what to do with any surplus stock.

All Schedule 4 listed species are protected by special penalties in Schedule 1 of the Wildlife & Countryside Act 1981. Schedule 4 was created specifically to protect these from birdkeepers. This second tier of legislation is no longer necessary. The vast majority of indigenous species listed on Schedule 4 have sustainable populations; they have not fallen in recent years. Those which do not, like the red-backed shrike, are on the very edge of the north/west range when they visit this country. Their decline is a natural one, it has nothing to do with bird keeping. The provision of suitable sites would further encourage these birds to breed here once again.

Schedule 4 should be totally scrapped. With the Countryside and Rights of Way Act 2000 facilitating DNA testing, and with a lack of evidence that Schedule 4 birds presently listed are being decimated by bird keepers, the retention of Schedule 4 is irrelevant in today's favourable climate. There is no credible scientific case for the inclusion of any species on such a schedule, because there is no significant threat. A self-regulatory scheme would be more appropriate. Money saved by ending this paper-chase could be better spent on additional enforcement efforts against offences relating to birds, such as targeting egg collectors.

Photograph by Sergey Yeliseev

CETTI'S WARBLER

These conservation organisations do a wonderful job looking after our wild birds, but there is one aspect of their activities, which has always disturbed me, and needs monitoring much more closely than hitherto.

This is the shady world of research, involving netting, ringing, tagging, nest disturbance and the like. How many of our wild bird are killed and injured each year in consequence of these dubious activities? The public has the right to know. Any unlicensed act should be brought before the court.

THE FUTURE

Unfortunately, Schedule 4 will not be scrapped; it will rise again like the Phoenix, emasculated, and in a slimmer form. This is made clear in the title of the proposed order. "The Wildlife and Countryside Act 1981 (Amendment and/or Variation of Schedule 4) Order 2002."

The species listed thereon, with one or two others, will perhaps be hen harrier, Montagu's harrier, honey buzzard, cirl bunting, chough, golden oriole, red-backed-shrike, Dartford warbler, and wood lark, primarily to pacify an audience unrelated to bird keeping.

As far as aviculture is concerned, the passerine species left off the list will automatically be catered for by an existing General Licence, thus continuing to receive an appropriate level of protection.

DNA IS PROOF OF ANCESTRY

The species currently listed on Schedule 4 can be loosely divided into three groups: raptors, passerines and hybrids. Two thirds of the raptor species listed are of foreign origin, while less than a dozen indigenous species are protected by international and domestic laws.

Of the British raptors, the peregrine, due to its success with around 1,500 breeding pairs, is running out of natural nesting sites. Some are now occupying urban locations and demands in some quarters would have them culled due to the amount of racing pigeons they kill.

The goshawk with about 200 breeding pairs was quite rare in 1981, but due to the falconers' releases, it is now spreading widely, albeit with Finnish and other foreign blood running through its veins. The sale price of captive-bred specimens of these two species, and all others, has dropped dramatically in recent years.

Of the passerines listed, only a few are of any great interest to bird keepers; these are chough, crossbill (all species), fieldfare, black redstart, redwing, bearded tit and serin. Little harm would befall their numbers in the wild if they were removed from Schedule 4. The rarest, the serin, with only a handful of pairs nesting in this country, would not be at risk, if removed, because of ample aviary-bred birds being available here and overseas.

Hybrids in their entirety should not appear on any future, updated, Schedule 4 list. We can discover the ancestry of individual hybrids, as we can with any captive bird, through DNA profiling. Therefore, in my view there is no sound reason to leave hybrids on the schedule.

Very few hybrids appear in the wild. Captive-bred hybrids are the product of Man's ingenuity, and are well protected by other, existing regulations.

COMMON CROSBILL
Photograph by Dennis Avon

YOUR BIRDS AND SCHEDULE 4 AS AT JANUARY 2004

The Department for the Environment, Food and Rural Affairs (DEFRA), is in the middle of a widespread consultation regarding Schedule 4, namely birds which must be registered and ringed if kept in captivity, and which species should be on the new list.

The conservationists would like it extended to include many more species, including non-avicultural kinds and all those that are currently listed on Schedule 1, birds which are protected by special penalties.

The list below shows the number of each species of perching bird of interest to the British Bird Fancy registered on November 5th, 2003:

Species	No. Registered
Cirl Bunting	29
Lapland Bunting	0
Snow bunting	3
Chough	65
Crossbill (all Species)	631
Fieldfare	88
Firecrest	0
Golden Oriole	0
Black Redstart	22
Redwing	50
Serin	18
Shorelark	0
Red-backed shrike	2
Bearded Tit	54
Crested Tit	3
Cetti's Warbler	0
Dartford Warbler	19
Marsh Warbler	0
Savi's Warbler	0
Woodlark	5
Wryneck	2

Numbers of these species in captivity will rise very slowly over the next few years, with perhaps the cirl bunting and the serin becoming well established. Strains will appear and examples will be exhibited. With luck, the number of red-backed shrikes will rise sufficiently to allow the showing of individual birds within five years, as the breeding o this shrike is within the grasp of specialists.

All these birds are also listed on Schedule 1, which leaves only seven 'new' species, which are of any interest to the Fancy to be added from it to Schedule 4, these being the avocet, bee-eater, bramblefinch, hoopoe, scarlet rosefinch and common quail. All these with the exception of the bramblefinch were listed on Schedule 4 originally, so it is unlikely that they will be re-instated. However, the bramblefinch could be a candidate for Schedule 4.

The avocet, bee-eater, hoopoe, and common quail are only bit players in our branch of the hobby. They are indeed kept, and bred, but examples are not exhibited at our shows.

This leaves just three species currently listed on Schedule 1 which if added to Schedule 4, would give the Fancy problems with paperwork and fees. These are the bluethroat, bramblefinch, and scarlet rosefinch - species that breed in Britain rarely. They fall neatly into the definition of a Schedule 4 bird, their candidature for Schedule 4 is a real possibility.

The bluethroat (Luscinia svecica) is of the same genus as the nightingale, but is a smaller bird. Its musical and varied song resembles both nightingale and the woodlark, although it is weaker and less rich.

The bluethroat is similar in form and actions to the robin, but is distinguishable from it by its much paler appearance. It has a distinctive pale eye stripe, some have red or white throats, depending on the race. The bird occurs regularly on migration in Britain, and has bred in the British Isles.

I have yet to see one on the show bench, and have no idea how many are kept, but it would make a beautiful addition to the softbill scene, and if placed on Schedule 4, it would stimulate interest in it, of this I have no doubt.

The bramblefinch (Fringilla montifringilla), is presently listed on Schedule 1 and Schedule 3 of the Wildlife and Countryside Act 1981, which covers birds that may be sold. Although it is protected by special penalties at all times, it may be sold or shown if ringed and bred in captivity from legally held stock. If the conservationists have their way it will be included on Schedule 4 when the new list is published. Several hundred home-bred birds will be affected and will need to be registered. No doubt there will be a period of licence for birds kept currently.

The bramblefinch also hybridises with other species, especially the chaffinch, so if hybrids remain on Schedule 4, these too will be subjected to regulation. There is just the nominate bird in this species, no sub-species are known. So, although it will be easy to identify it in its normal form, there are colour variants being bred, which may cause problems with identification.

Photograph by Tommy Milner

BRAMBLEFINCH

Although the bramblefinch is mainly a winter visitor to Britain, some do nest in the north, making it a prime target for the legislators to consider for inclusion on the new list.

The scarlet rosefinch (Carpodacus erythrinus), otherwise known as the common rosefinch and scarlet grosbeak, is an annual visitor to Britain in autumn and spring. It is the commonest rosefinch in Europe and is extending its range. The male has a reddish head and breast with brown upperparts and the female looks very like a female house sparrow. Immature birds resemble the adult female. Many rosefinches are bred in captivity, among these the Pallas's and long-tailed come to mind.

The scarlet rosefinch has little appeal as a show bird within the British bird fancy. Its inclusion on Schedule 4 would only tend to advertise it as a British bird, this may tempt breeders to breed more of them.

The recent review of bird registration has resulted in changes in the way the system will work in the future. These changes will be subject to new legislation in England and Wales and will come into force later this year.

The requirement to re-register birds every 3 years will cease. Once a bird is registered it will remain so until it is disposed of. Birds already registered will be deemed registered until disposed of.

There will be some changes to Schedule 4 once criteria for determining what birds should be included has been decided. We will have to wait some time before any new list appears.

PALLAS'S ROSEFINCH

Photograph by Sergey Yeliseev

A NEW BEGINNING FOR THE FANCY, DATED 18.02.05

General Licence No WLF 100094 issued by the Department of the Environment (DOE) came into force on January 1st 1995, and permits the competitive exhibition of most British Birds without the need for individual licences.

There are a number of conditions, but the licence will have the effect of bringing back to the show bench all species of birds and their hybrids, which have been absent for many years.

So long as the specimens are aviary-bred from lawfully held stock, and close-ringed, they will be eligible, making this licence the most important piece of legislation enacted for a decade, so far as the British Bird Fancy is concerned.

I strongly recommend that all societies, in particular national and area British Bird clubs, produce schedules for future shows which include all the species listed on the recent annual display licences.

Documentary evidence of captive breeding must accompany any bird competitively shown under the licence. Until legal advice is available, I suggest a signed note to the effect that any bird to be shown under this licence was aviary bred. This and ring number should be attached to the entry form and sent off with it.

The owner of any bird to be competitively shown under the licence will, if requested by an official of the DoE, or a police officer, make the bird available for a blood sample to be taken from the bird to be shown. The sample will be taken by a qualified veterinary surgeon. Such a sample may be used to establish the ancestry of the bird.

LONG-TAILED ROSEFINCH

Photograph by Sergey Yeliseev

An official is anyone authorised by the Secretary of State, and usually refers to members of the Wildlife Inspectorate. No doubt the show scene will be monitored by the authorities. Any test considered necessary could be taken at a keeper's address, a veterinary surgeon's premises, a show venue or elsewhere. It is important therefore, that only aviary-bred birds of authorised ancestry are entered at shows.

The Fancy has a new beginning; let it not be thrown away. Future exhibitions will become exciting places to visit with all the old favourites back on view. There should be something for everyone to enjoy.

Separate, similar licences are in force for England, Scotland and Wales, which expire on March 31st 1996. An annex attached to each refers to certain vagrant species.

DEFRA CONSULTATION

In 2006 DEFRA issued a consultation document to review regulations under Section 7 of the Wildlife and Countryside Act 1981, in England, Scotland and Wales, in respect of Schedule 4. This Schedule lists the birds that, if kept in captivity, must be registered and ringed or marked in accordance with regulations made by the Secretary of State.

The document was issued to interested parties, but many enthusiasts who do not keep Schedule 4 birds may be unaware of its contents. What follows is a listing of the species to the British bird fancy which DEFRA recommends should stay on the Schedule, in most cases this recommendation is based on the fact that the native populations of such birds are relatively small and the species are of avicultural interest.

Wryneck (Jynx torquilla) WCA Schedule 4: two birds registered (14)
In the wild, this is a rare woodpecker with only a single pair breeding in some years between 1994 and 2001.
The captive population is small, consisting entirely of imports (two recorded as captive-bred abroad). No captive-breeding in Britain.

Woodlark (Lullula arborea) WCA Schedule 4: 4 birds registered (20) total. The UK's wild population has varied between 850-1,500 pairs during 1997-2001.
The wild breeding population in Britain is relatively small. The same is true of the captive population, with few ever registered: nine disabled, five imports and seven captive-bred. The captive population does not appear to be self-sustaining.

Black redstart (Phoenicurus ochruros) WCA Schedule 4: 22 birds registered (243 total)
The British breeding population is small, and has varied in the last decade between 44 and 99 pairs. Of the 243 registered overall, 25 were registered as imports, the remainder captive-bred. Two hybrids with common redstarts have been registered.

Redwing (Turdus iliacus) WCA Schedule 4: 49 birds registered (164 total)
There is a small breeding population (three to six pairs) at five localities in northern Scotland. Abundant numbers visit in winter.
Of 164 birds ever registered, 104 are registered as captive-bred, 13 as of wild origin, 23 as wild disabled and 24 as imported. In the 1990s, a number of birds were permitted to be taken under licence from the wild for aviculture.

Fieldfare (Turdus pilaris) WCA Schedule 4: 79 birds registered (140 total) Britain has a small population of breeding fieldfares, numbering some two to six pairs. Large numbers visit in winter.
The captive population is small. Of all birds ever registered, one was wild origin, ten wild disabled, 37 imported and 99 recorded as captive-bred. The captive population does not appear to be bred to surplus.

Dartford warbler (Sylvia undata) WCA Schedule 4: 18 birds registered (979 total).
The wild UK population of this sedentary heathland warbler has varied between 900-1,900 pairs over the past decade.
The captive population, apart from seven imported birds, is recorded as being of captive-bred origin.

Bearded tit (Panurus biarmicus) WCA Schedule 4: 66 birds registered (626 total).
The British breeding population of this reedbed species is in the order of some 339-408 pairs. Of those birds registered, eight were described as having been imported and as being wild disabled.

Crested tit (Parus cristatus) WCA Schedule 4: 3 birds registered (8 total).
The UK breeding population of this species is of the order of 900 pairs, all of which are confined to the Caledonian Pine forests of the Scottish Highlands. The species is rarely kept in captivity. There is, apparently, no captive breeding under-taken.

Red-backed shrike (Lanius collurio) WCA Schedule 4: 2 birds registered (18 total).
The wild population of this species is close to extinction in the UK, with a maximum of only one to 13 possible pairs during the past decade and only a single confirmed pair in some years.
Of all birds ever registered, 14 were reported as being imported captive-bred birds and four as being captive-bred.

Snow bunting (Plectrophenax nivalis) WCA Schedule 4: 3 birds registered (54 total).
Britain has a small population of breeding snow buntings, which number some 70-100 pairs.
There is a small captive population. Of all birds ever registered, 10 are of wild origin, 2 wild disabled, 23 imported and the rest are recorded as captive-bred.

Cirl bunting (Emberiza cirlus) WCA Schedule 4: 28 birds registered (52 total).
The wild British population is some 500 pairs.
Of all birds ever registered, 29 are recorded as being wild origin, 15 as being imported and 13 as being captive-bred (some of which were imports).
While there is little evidence of illegal capture for aviculture, the species is in some demand and the wild population is small.

Serin (Serinus serinus) WCA Schedule 4: 22 birds and 4 hybrids registered (64 total). This finch has only bred rarely in southern England with breeding first reported in the late 1990s.
The captive population is small. Of all the birds registered, 43 are recorded as being captive-bred (some imported) and 1 wild disabled.

Chough (Pyrrhocorax pyrrhocorax) WCA Schedule 4: 64 birds registered (total 175).
The wild population of choughs is estimated at some 340 pairs, and has shown some range expansion in recent years.
The captive population is composed predominantly of birds registered as being captive-bred. A small number are registered as imports or as wild disabled.

Crossbills (Loxia supp) WCA Schedule 4: 491 common crossbills and hybrids, 32 parrot crossbills and 7 Scottish crossbills registered (2,603 total, all species). The relationship between the 3 species of crossbill found in the UK is complex and the subject of ongoing research.
Overall, the common crossbill does not readily meet the criteria for retention on the Schedule . The parrot crossbill and Scottish are scarcer in the wild and have only small captive populations. It is not clear that either is self-sustaining.
Although there is little evidence of illegal taking for aviculture, it seems appropriate to retain these species, and that hybrids between them could be produced, and retention of the genus on Schedule 4 is appropriate to facilitate enforcement.

Common crossbill (Loxia curvirostra). Population size varies. The species is commonly held in captivity and more than 2,500 birds have been registered, including hybrids with siskin (1 specimen) serin (5) redpoll (4) greenfinch (29), canary (23) and bullfinch (5).

Photograph by Sergey Yeliseev

COMMON CROSSBILL

Scottish crossbill (L. Scotica). Britain's only endemic bird. The current population estimate is 300-1,250 pairs. The captive population is also small, numbering some 7 birds (only 12 ever registered).

Parrot crossbill (L pytopsittacus). Parrot crossbills are rare breeding birds in the UK. Small numbers regularly breed in native pinewood in north-east Scotland with populations supplemented by irruptions (Summers & Pietney, 2003), and of all 58 birds ever registered, the majority are derived from imports, with the remainder as captive-bred.

Please note: Any bird, one of whose parents or whose ancestor in its recent lineage, was a bird of a kind specified in the list is included under the protection given by Schedule 4.

Some species may be downgraded, too.

As well as making recommendations about which species to keep on Schedule 4, DEFRA has also recommended that some species be deleted from the list. These birds are as follows.

Shore lark (Eremophila alpestris) WCA Schedule 4: No birds registered (4 total).
Has bred in Britain, not regularly. The captive population has always been small and the only 4 birds ever registered were all recorded as being imported in 1999. There is no recorded breeding in

captivity in Britain and the captive population is clearly not self-sustaining.

There is no evidence that illegal take for aviculture has occurred in the UK or that threaten continental populations. On balance, the species does not seem to require the protection of retaining on the Schedule as a deterrent.

Marsh warbler (Acrocephalus palustris) WCA Schedule 4: No birds registered (Total nil).
The population of this rare warbler has varied from 20-58 at up to 21 locations over the past ten years. While some nest robberies have taken place, there is no evidence or demand for illegal captive for aviculture.

Cetti's warbler (Cettia cetti) WCA Schedule 4: None registered (total nil).
In the UK, there were 678 wild singing males present in 2000. No birds have ever been registered.

Savi's warbler (Locustella luscinioides) WCA Schedule 4: No birds registered (total nil)
Appeared to recolonise Britain in the 1960's, but only 2 to 9 pairs of singing males have been recorded in the past five years. The species does not appear to be desirable in aviculture.

Firecrest (Regulus ignicapillus) WCA 4: No birds registered (total nil).
A rare breeding bird in Great Britain with up to 121 pairs at 39 localities recorded in 2001 – but as few as 19 pairs over the preceding ten years. No bird registered in captivity since species was listed on Schedule 4.

Golden oriole (Oriolus oriolus) WCA: Schedule 4: No birds registered (total 1).
Britain has a small population of breeding orioles (around 3-11 pairs) in 11 localities, with a strong south-easterly bias. There are no birds currently registered. The species does not strictly meet the criteria for listing.

Lapland bunting (Calcarius lapponicus) WCA Schedule 4: No birds registered (total nil)
A very rare, occasional breeding bird in northern Scotland with small numbers (200-500) of birds wintering. No birds at all have ever been registered as being kept in captivity and there appears to be little demand.

Note: The consultation opened in November 2006 and closed on Friday February 16th 2007.

ALL CHANGE FOR SCHEDULE 4

November 22nd 2007
The public consultation on the species listed on Schedule 4 of the Wildlife and Countryside Act 1881, and associated bird registration procedures closed on February 16th. Secondary legislation to amend the current registration requirements may be in place within months.

These amendments will not greatly assist the fancy or members who keep Schedule 4 birds. Most species presently listed will probably remain, with a few exceptions. Those thought to be axed from the Schedule are the shore lark, marsh warbler, Cetti's warbler, Savi's warbler, firecrest, golden oriole and Lapland bunting.

Of these only shore lark and Lapland bunting have ever been considered as show birds. The shore lark is highly colourful, especially in spring and summer when the male has a black and yellow head pattern and small, black 'horns'.

The Lapland bunting is known in avicultural circles by its American name longspur. The breeding male has a buff eye-stripe, chestnut nape, white underparts and black on head and cheeks.

In bygone days, and on rare occasions, specimens of both appeared at the shows. These days they are still kept and bred by fanciers on the Continent and will again appeal to keepers here – if the Schedule 4 paperwork is binned.

Among the Schedule 4 birds favoured by the British aviculturists, most are holding their own and numbers are being bred in captivity year on year. There is however, one exception: the redwing, which is again nearing extinction in captivity in Britain. This, the smallest of our six true thrushes, is in free fall. This has happened before when the Act became law. The late 1990's saw a mini revival but now another decline has set in and currently only about seven are left in British aviaries. To save it, it's urgent that keepers set up a breeding programme.

SCHEDULE 4 UPDATE. 2008

Following a thorough review, the new list of species of birds kept in captivity that need to be registered with DEFRA has been confirmed by wildlife minister Joan Ruddock (News, September 11th 2008).

The change to Schedule 4 of the Wildlife and Countryside Act 1981 was introduced on October 1st. As a result keepers of golden eagle, goshawk, honey buzzard, white-tailed sea-eagle, Montagu's harrier and osprey must continue to register their birds with the Wildlife Licensing and Registration Service (WLRS). In addition, peregrines and merlins must be registered – unless each bird is covered by a certificate under Article 10 of the Convention on International Trade in Endangered Species (CITES), which is issued by the UK CITES Management Authority (UKMA).

The 50-odd species – including hybrids on Schedule 4 have been removed and keepers are no longer required to pay a fee and register them (England and Wales only, Scotland followed).

In its whittled-down form, the list provides solid protection to those species whose conservation is most threatened by the illegal removal of birds from the wild for commercial purposes. It is notable that all of them are birds of prey.

Originally, Schedule 4 was all about conservation. It aimed to help the enforcement of wildlife legislation to act as a deterrent against the illegal taking of wild birds and to honour the UK's international conservation obligations.

In its first incarnation, it contained more than 80 species. During the 1990's many were removed, including bluethroat, sparrowhawk and buzzard.

In a further review in 2006, DEFRA issued a consultation document and invited comments from interested parties. Many factors were scrutinised, such as status in captivity, success rates in captive breeding, market demand and so on. Every species on Schedule 4 was assessed. Various options were considered, including doing nothing, adding species and removing all species including hybrids. The consultation ran between November 1st 2006 and February 16th 2007. After many months of waiting we now have a revised Schedule 4 list.

Some species that were removed from Schedule 4 on October 1st are of interest to British bird fanciers. They are: cirl bunting, Lapland bunting, snow bunting, chough, crossbill (all species), fieldfare, golden oriole, black redstart, redwing, serin, shore lark, red-backed shrike, bearded tit, crested tit, Cetti's warbler, Dartford warbler, marsh warbler, Savi's warbler, woodlark and wryneck.

All these species are listed on Schedule 1 of the Wildlife and Countryside Act 1981, which provides special protection for wild nesting birds and their eggs and young. They are also subject to the terms and conditions of General Licence WML-117, which is issued by Natural England. This reads as follows:

Any bird competitively shown under this licence must be ringed with a legible, individually numbered metal closed ring, which is a ring or band in a continuous circle (without any break, join or any signs of tampering since it was manufactured) and which cannot be removed from the bird when its leg is fully grown. For any bird competitively shown under this licence which is on Schedule 4 to the Act, the closed ring must have been issued by the Wildlife Licensing and Regulation Service (Animal Health) DEFRA 1/17 Temple Quay, Bristol, BS1 6EB.

1) The bird must have been bred in captivity. A bird shall not be treated as bred in captivity unless its parents were lawfully in captivity when the egg from which it hatched was laid. Documentary evidence of captive breeding must accompany any bird competitively shown under this licence.

2) The owner of any bird to be competitively shown under this licence will, if requested by an official of DEFRA or a police officer, make the bird available for a sample of blood to be taken from the bird to be shown. The blood sample will be taken by a qualified veterinary surgeon. Such sample may be used to establish the ancestry of the bird. If common sense prevails, the species removed from Schedule 4 will remain subject to the General Licence and be subjected to ringing requirements for unscheduled birds. It is important for fanciers to know the position. General Licence rings need not be unique or issued by statutory ring supplies. October 1st was a key date, especially for British bird fanciers. Many of the passerine species that were removed from the schedule are of little interest to the fancy, while those that are of interest are being bred in numbers both here and overseas. The burden of Schedule 4, which has besmirched keepers of those birds and their hybrids, has been lifted. A new era is ushered in.

SPARROWHAWK
scurge of bird keepers

Photograph by Tony Tilford

A WAKE-UP CALL FOR THE FANCY. 2011

Following a prosecution in Norfolk, in 2011 where a fancier was found wanting in relation to wildlife law it was found that it is more important than ever for keepers to comply with the regulations and in particular they need to adhere to the guidelines given by Natural England with regard to documentary evidence. These guidelines are found in General Licence 14 (which covers the exhibition of British birds) and General Licence 18 (which covers sales). The guidelines say:
'Persons intending to rely on the General Licence

must be able to demonstrate that birds are legally held and captive-bred, and are advised: to only purchase birds from breeders who are able to satisfactorily demonstrate that they are complying with the relevant regulations; to confirm, insofar as they are able, the bird's identification and age are correct; to check that the bird is correctly ringed, and to always obtain signed and dated written documentary evidence of captive-breeding from the breeder. Documentation should cite the bird's species, ring number and any other identification mark (e.g. microchips), hatch date, along with similar details for the parent birds, and the breeder's contact details'. General Licence 14, note (1); General Licence 18, note (k).

The terms of the General Licences for non-scheduled birds state: Any bird sold (GL18) or competitively shown (GL14) must be ringed with a legible individually numbered metal close ring, which is a ring or band in a continuous circle (without a break, join, or any signs of tampering since it was manufactured) and which cannot be removed from the bird when its leg is fully grown. The bird must have been bred in captivity.

A bird shall not be treated as bred in captivity unless its parents were lawfully in captivity when the egg from which it hatched was laid. (GL18, Condition 3).

The licence makes clear that documentary evidence must accompany any bird competitively shown or sold. The owner or keeper of any bird to be sold (GL18) or competitively shown (GL 14) under this licence will, if requested by an Official of DEFRA, or a Police Officer, make the bird available for a sample of blood to be taken from the bird. The blood sample will be taken by a qualified veterinary surgeon. Such a sample may be used to establish the ancestry of the bird. (GL 14 and 18, Condition 5).

The relevant open General Licence came into force on the 1st January 1995, with a time limit, but has been continually re-issued, giving it continuity. It had the effect of bringing back to the show bench species which had been absent for many years. I wrote about it in Cage & Aviary Birds on the 18th February 1995, everyone who was involved in selling their stock or exhibiting individual non-scheduled birds was aware of its contents. Many species of unscheduled softbill and hardbill were soon being displayed in numbers, show benches looked very different, as many new classes were added to show schedules in order to cater for them. Later on, exhibition standards for each new species were introduced. Today over a hundred softbills, many of them non-scheduled specimens are expected at some specialist event.

The "protectionists", for many years, for reasons unknown, were satisfied if a suspected bird displayed a legal ring. Not anymore: they are now interested in ancestry, and look for breeding records and details of parents, too. This makes it more important than ever for breeders and sellers to have such details. A closed, correct ring on a bird is not proof of aviary breeding in itself – records of captive breeding of a bird and of its lineage must be created.

THE CHALLENGE OF PROOF

This will no doubt be an easy task for breeders who, by habit, make the required records of their breeding. But for others, who have acquired stock without records from pet shops, from abroad or elsewhere, may find it difficult to prove a bird is legally held.

I understand some fanciers have been so worried, that they have released stock they cannot prove to be legally held. This is lawful under certain circumstances. Others, I understand, are inventing data, and this practice could put a keeper in jeopardy.

Successfully breeding a species over a five-year period, and building up a strain, has always been a benchmark for legitimacy. Unfortunately, only a handful of kinds fall into this category today. Although many species are bred, it is rare indeed for a strain of an unscheduled softbill species to be built up allowing for legally held specimens to be sold or shown.

"Protectionists" read Cage & Aviary Birds, they scrutinise the advertisements therein, they are aware of show reports, and they know a great deal about the birds and owners mentioned.

Information about ring issues can be ascertained by the police, who incidentally, have taken a great deal of interest in wildlife crime in recent years. They are also fully aware of keepers' addresses, and of their properties, which are pictured on various mapping sites. Cases against law-breakers are on the increase, and a keeper has to prove his/her innocence.

It is difficult to speculate how the King's Lynn Court Case will affect the sale or exhibition of birds at future shows. Numbers of the rarer species may fall. The British Birds in Aviculture (BBIA) has proposed a "Bird Passport", which is well designed and onto which all the relevant details of breeding can be recorded. The BBIA states that the British Bird Council is to adopt and publish a version of this "passport".

Everyone involved in the hobby has a duty to improve the situation in any way they can, in order to avoid ever more prosecutions. Ringing laws to be reviewed in 2013.

REDPOLL STATUS 2012

My understanding of the definition of a species had always been: "A group or aggregate of birds, of the same kind, which are similar anatomically, have the same general appearance and are capable of interbreeding with other members of the same group."

The British Ornithological Union (BOU) is responsible for maintaining the official list of British birds. In 2001, it decided to promote two subspecies of redpoll to full species rank: the mealy (Carduelis flammea) and the lesser redpoll (C. cabaret). The BOU stated that these two birds do not interbreed in the wild where they overlap.

As a result, the lesser redpoll is no longer listed on Schedule 3, Part 1 of the Wildlife and Countryside Act 1981 ("birds which may be sold alive at all times if ringed and bred in captivity"). No legislation has so far been provided to reinstate the lesser redpoll as an aviary bird.

However, some genetic studies have found no differences between the two. Indeed, there may be only one species of redpoll at the present time. Birds that live in the far north are paler and larger, with smaller types in the south. In time, evolution will separate them; they are on their way to becoming separate species but they are not there yet.

The lesser redpoll is a tiny finch about the size of a blue tit. It is streaky and brown, with patches of red on its head and sometimes on its breast. It is a resident breeder in the UK. The mealy redpoll is larger and paler, whitish below with black streaks, with two white lines on the folded wing. It is a winter visitor to the UK.

Recently, the NCA, BBC and IOA advised fanciers to show the previously named lesser redpoll as the "common" redpoll and retain the name mealy for the larger redpoll. Prosecutions could be successful when unscheduled redpolls are bought or sold, because specimens are still being taken from the wild. However, most aviary redpolls are now classified as hybrids and are not wild birds within the meaning of the law. Therefore any prosecution regarding these would fail.

Currently, the BOU lumps the following redpolls together as subspecies of the common redpoll (Carduelis flammea):

1) C.f. flammea (mealy redpoll)
2) C.f. islandica (Icelandic redpoll)
3) C.f. rostrata (Greenland redpoll)
4) Lesser redpoll (Carduelis cabaret) is treated as a separate species.
5) The Arctic (hoary) redpoll (Carduelis homemanni), with subspecies homemanni and exilipes, has long been recognised as a separate

species. However, I do not believe it is a true species, as it will hybridise with any redpoll variety in captivity and the young will be fertile.

BirdLife International and other authorities hold that the lesser and mealy redpolls are the same species. The NCA and others recommend fanciers to label small specimens as "common" and the large one as "mealy". However, the RSPB attributes the name "common redpoll" to the mealy - not the lesser! I believe they are right. The word "lesser' should continue to be used. It's the smaller bird, for goodness' sake. And after all, if the scientists are divided on the issue, a prosecutor would not be able to prove in a court that the "lesser' and "mealy" redpolls are different species.

In aviculture, though there are separate classes at the shows for lesser and mealies, the two interbreed and produce fertile offspring. When a new variant is discovered, such as the phaeo melanin (which is of recent origin) the mutation is transferred to the other type almost straightaway. All these birds are now hybrids, though they will remain in their well-tested hardbill class formats. I believe this is relevant to the argument, because when one species is paired to another, their offspring cannot produce fertile young. This is the point with which the BOU cannot justify their action.

This Government, and its predecessors, have pathetic records when making laws relating to wild birds. Failure to comply with European law with rings, and U-turns (remember the Schedule 4 debacle?) are in their DNA. They have been badly advised in the past and continue to be so.

NOTE: Non scheduled birds can be sold or shown under General Licence. This also applies to those bearing foreign rings. No individual licence is required for non scheduled kinds. Wildlife Law due to change in 2013.

Photograph by Dennis Avon

ISABEL LESSER REDPOLL

Exhibition Hen Satinette Blackbird

Photograph by Dennis Avon

HOWLETT vs BALDRY

March 7th 1998

Writing the article which follows these comments, brought some annoyance from Alan Baldry and others. Letters, which follow these notes, included one from the late Frank Meaden who commented on it, as did one S. Hissen an individual not known to me and Chris North another person unknown to me, made their thoughts known. Ron White and others tended to support me in one way or another. I was of the opinion that the fancy as a whole should have given itself time to breed strains of these species, before subjecting specimens to the exhibiting benches.

BRITISH BIRD NOTES

dated March 7th 1998. Refers to that date.

The common serin (Serinus serinus) a diminutive finch of only 4¼in length is undoubtedly a British bird but it has always been a rare visitor to our southern shores. Christopher Mathews' excellent article on the species (January 10th issue), portrayed the bird in great detail so much so that a reader could easily assume that the species is flourishing in UK aviculture, when sadly this is not the case.

Due to its rarity in Britain as a breeding wild bird, the serin is listed on Schedule 4 of the Wildlife & Countryside Act 1981. Birds that are listed must be registered with the authorities and ringed if kept in captivity. This also applies to any specimen whose parent or other lineal ancestor was a serin.

To the best of my knowledge no serin or Mules or Hybrids containing common serin blood are registered. In other words, no lawfully held specimens exist in the UK (unless very recently registered) at the present time (see date above) and this has been the situation for many years. If fanciers have unregistered birds, I hope they will register them because the Fancy needs serin stock. Serins are frequently bred within aviculture on the continent, so it is a mystery that none have been registered, as the importation of aviary-bred stock would appear to be fairly straightforward.

I would like to own pairs of serins. I would exhibit the species on the British Bird benches and would hope to experience no objection within the Fancy for doing so. The serin would make a lovely addition to the Hardbill classes and its mutations would also be of great interest to many fanciers.

The article on treecreepers by Frank Meaden (January 10th issue) also caught my attention. Mr Meaden said he found it difficult to peer into the nest of his breeding pair. He said: "It was impossible to count the clutch of eggs, even when using a dental mirror, and I had no intention of causing the birds undue stress or anxiety with further investigation… Had I wished to ring the chicks I could not have done so".

Mr Meaden's nest must have been unusually inaccessible. Some fanciers who keep this species are able to close-ring their youngsters, as specimens of this species are exhibited from time to time and will continue to be shown, I'm sure, in increasing numbers in the future.

Birds like the treecreeper, leaf warblers and others whose sexes are alike, should be shown singly or in true pairs. To be fair, judges must be satisfied beyond a reasonable doubt that true pairs are staged before considering awards.

For some judges the novelty of seeing non-scheduled 3 exhibits on the show bench has gone to their heads, leading to controversial decisions being made. This behaviour has been the main talking point among many top Softbill fanciers over the last two show seasons. It is hoped that the Fancy has seen the last of the "silly seasons" and in future common sense will again prevail, and due attention will be paid to high-class, line-bred exhibits of Type so that dedicated breeders are rewarded for all the hard work and effort they have put in to their breeding strains.

Softbills on show at South East Ipswich annual event (the author's cage has the rosettes).

Photograph by Andrew Calvesbert

Following my article 'British bird notes', these
letters were sent to 'Cage & Aviary Birds'

Missing the point

IN REFERENCE to Bernard Howlett's British Bird Notes (March 7 issue), I am pleased my article on Treecreepers (January, 10 issue) caught his attention. The nest of Treecreepers which I referred to in my article was inaccessible as it was concealed behind bark, so I did not interfere with them and did not ring the chicks. However, I was awarded a medal by the Avicultural Society for the first breeding of this species in the UK. This breeding incidentally, took place in 1968.

I am sure that some fanciers are able to close-ring Treecreepers but Mr Howlett missed the point. I had no wish to do this because I neither intended to sell nor exhibit the birds. If Mr Howlett manages to breed Treecreepers he will realise that ringing can cause problems.

Referring to Mr Howlett's article, when *Serinus canaria, S. serinus* and *S. pusillus* were being bred consistently in the UK, only one person, "Eddy" Ashwell of Southend-on-Sea, Essex, showed any interest. He had ambitions to breed a Black Canary, so I reared some *S. pusillus* x Canary Hybrids (1965-6) for his experiments. The other Serins were of no interest to anyone and when my work with them was exhausted I gave them away. So why would it be so wonderful to breed them again? Should Mr Howlett need any further information the Association for the Study & Propagation of European Birds in Aviaries data bank will be able to help.

FRANK MEADEN

Cambridgeshire.

Photograph by Dennis Avon

TREECREEPER

April 5th 1998

Negative vibes

I WAS horrified to read parts of Bernard Howlett's article "In search of the Serin" (March 7 issue), particularly when he referred to the "novelty" of certain species on the show bench.

Has Mr Howlett such a negative opinion of the Bird Fancy that he wants to kill off all the hard work done to encourage exhibitors to bring their Softbills to the show bench?

To criticise judges and breeders can only harm the Fancy which is already struggling to survive. These new Softbills have stirred the Fancy and enthusiasm is what we need, not negative responses.

S. HISSEN

Lincs.

WHEATEAR

Photograph by Dennis Avon

April 5th 1998

Leave it to the experts

REGARDING Bernard Howlett's British Bird Notes (March 7 issue), articles referring to the law should be left to the experts such as the British Bird Council and other governing bodies. If he restricted his articles to his breeding achievements they might be short!

CHRIS NORTH Yorkshire.

April 25th 1998

.... but I study wildlife law!!

Alan Baldry.

Judging Softbills

I FEEL I must write to express my frustration at Bernard Howlett's article (March 7 issue). The British Bird Fancy has strived to get Schedule 3 and 4 Softbills onto the show bench and an article such as Bernard's can undo all the good that has been achieved. He should accept judges' decisions and should not condemn them and other exhibitors for displaying birds better than his own.

I have shown small Softbills and have won many awards with them, and have beaten Bernard many times. None of the decisions, as far as I am aware, were controversial, and I do not reflect the "silly season" mentioned by Bernard. The "silly season" surely began in 1981 when all the non-Schedule species were removed from the show bench leaving very ordinary Blackbirds and Thrushes to move up the ranks, winning shows because of little or no competition. The dedicated small Softbill breeders got their act together by joining forces and through helping each other you now see well-staged Softbills, such as the Blackcaps belonging to J. & P. Jermy, that took the best Softbill award at the recent Eastern Federation of British Bird Fanciers' open show.

ALAN BALDRY

Cambridgeshire.

April 25th 1998

What is 'ordinary'?

WHAT did Alan Baldry (Letters, April 25 issue) mean when he said "ordinary" Blackbirds and Thrushes. Does a bird have to be rare or difficult to breed to do well on the show bench. Is this where I have been going wrong?

RON WHITE
Essex.

A very ordinary blackbird – National 2003 (still winning)

Showing Softbills

IT WAS pleasing to learn that we are once more able to show small British Softbills. But other fanciers I have spoken to think that judges are taken by the wonderful natural setting inside the cages rather than the birds themselves. It also appears that there are no standards laid down for the birds or the cages. As each Softbill cage and setting are to the exhibitor's own taste, this could constitute marked cages.

Mrs J. MARTIN
West Sussex.

Photograph by Dennis Avon

A very, very ordinary song thrush 1999

Views on Softbills well received

Photograph by Tommy Milner

TREECREEPER

DESPITE some of the letters published (April 25 issue), my article to which they referred (March 7 issue) was generally well received and I was warmly congratulated on it by several Softbill breeders.

There are no updated standards of excellence in respect of Schedule 4 and non-scheduled birds. This fact presents no real problems for experienced judges. Those, however, who rarely exhibit, or have little or no knowledge of exhibits such as Treecreepers, are asked to allocate points - and this is not easy when these birds are being shown.

I researched my article, as I do all my work, making notes on points raised by fellow fanciers, as I travelled around the country last winter, from Yorkshire to London. Several issues came up again and again, the most common of which was the showing of species such as the Treecreeper so soon after the regulations had been relaxed. They felt this was irresponsible and could undo all the good work we have achieved in recent years.

Quite a few exhibitors thought that the Fancy should adopt a firm approach in policing itself, and perhaps reduce the number of species that can be shown, at least in the short-term, to those that are viable in captivity and are bred in good numbers each year.

It was always on the cards that frustrated individuals would exploit the new situation and endanger the credibility of the hobby. They should remember that the Fancy has been given a reprieve, not a pardon.

BERNARD HOWLETT

Norfolk.

Pair of Blackcaps (not the birds mentioned in the letter).

May 30th 1998 (Page 234 bottom refers)

Everyone has their own opinion

I MUST reply to Alan Baldry's letter (April 25 issue) in which he said that Bernard Howlett should accept the judge's decisions. At a recent show at Portsmouth, he questioned the judge's decision and a couple of years ago in Yorkshire he disagreed with the judges.

Mr Baldry must realise that everyone is entitled to their own opinion. As far as the Blackcaps he mentioned are concerned, I saw both birds at the National Exhibition and Eastern Federation of British Bird Fanciers' show and both times the hen had a patch of feathers missing from her head. Surely this constitutes a major fault?

J. TOWNSEND

Hants.

Let's work together

I AGREE with Alan Baldry (Letter, April 25 issue) that the silly season started in 1981 with the Wildlife and Countryside Act. This will continue for some time until the smaller Softbills have been worked on as far as breeding and exhibiting is concerned, as has been the case with Hardbills and Softbill Colour Variants.

Some sort of standard should also be agreed for show cages as it has been in the Hardbill section. We also need to stop this constant bickering among ourselves for the good of our hobby. Let's all work together no matter what branch of the hobby we are in.

R. MITCHELL
Norfolk.

May 30th 1998

Mr. Ray Mitchell

Right to exhibit British Birds

I AGREE with R. Mitchell's comments (May 30 issue), following the recent correspondence in this magazine regarding Treecreepers and other small British Softbills, that bickering does the Fancy no good at all.

I also find Bernard Howlett's comments regarding people who show Small Softbills as frustrated individuals, amusing, and that there is no show standard for these birds. The show standard for these birds was revised just before the Wildlife & Countryside Act 1981 came into force, and as most judges know, they still apply today.

Under the new legislation I have the right to exhibit birds that I have captive bred, so I have invited Bernard Howlett and a representative of CAGE & AVIARY BIRDS to my aviaries, and those of other breeders, to see the birds that are currently nesting. These birds nesting at the time of writing include: Stonechats, Corn Buntings, Wheatears, Redstarts, Ring Ousels, Treecreepers and Mistle Thrushes. It should then be possible to report back to the Fancy what is fact, not fiction.

Hopefully it will put the debate to rest once and for all.

ALAN BALDRY
Cambridgeshire.
June 13th 1998

Aviary-bred close-rung Stonechat cock.

I declined Alan's offer. An independent observer did attend and viewed various birds breeding in his aviaries.

Photograph by Dennis Avon

Alan Baldry has exhibited some fine examples of the redstart over the years.

CHAPTER NINE

Exhibition and Records

Cinnamon Hen Blackbird

Photograph by Dennis Avon

AS THE SHOW SEASON DRAWS NEAR

Written September 2005, marginally updated in 2011.

As summer drifts into autumn, the thoughts of British bird exhibitors are turned towards the shows. There is much to do, however, before the first teams are assembled and staged.

Memories of last season soon flood back. The minutiae of those past events are mulled over, the highs and lows. "How did the team do?" "Could it have performed better?" Thoughts of improvements within a team and strategies for the future are foremost in the minds of many enthusiasts.

The moult is very important. It's no easy task to get the birds through it in pristine condition, using colour feeding where appropriate. After the moult a fuller assessment of the stock available, and of those worthy of being shown, becomes a little clearer.

Most teams are made up of adult and current-year birds. Some old favourites - birds that have won well over the years - may be past their best, and will probably need to be replaced by others coming on within the collection, or introduced into the team from elsewhere. Many of these individual specimens had been winning well over long periods, but have now lost their vigour.

I have been lucky with such birds. A cinnamon blackbird hen bred in 1992 was still winning in 1999. It won best softbill at the All British that year, aged seven. A canary x bullfinch cock bred by the late Basil Morris in 1998 won best exhibit in show at the 2005 All-British, when shown by his son. I was one of the judges on that day and the bird looked wonderful.

Flighted birds that have been previously trained for the shows, need little further training for on-coming events. They will usually behave well when reintroduced into a familiar training environment. Unflighted ones need special attention in training them for the necessary high standard, and these training techniques develop and evolve over time. A judge wants to see the specimen staged before him or her looking confident, moving from perch to perch in a leisurely way, not hurried, and looking towards the front of its cage, preferably towards the judge's eyes. It's a worrying time for the breeder/exhibitor. Great patience is required to steady the team for the shows and mishaps can easily occur.

When members of the show team are accustomed to their training cages, they should be introduced to people, outside noises and movement. This is where friends or family can assist. In my case, my grandchildren are allowed to move the cages around the birdroom, from time to time. A car trip round the block with the birds on board is also a good way of introducing the team to the journeying ahead. Loading and unloading gets them acquainted with the procedure that will have to be undertaken at each venue as the winter progresses.

Show cages need to be kept in good shape so an exhibit is not let down by an untidy or unsound cage. Most cages containing larger softbills are not decorated, but some are, especially song thrushes and virtually all small softbills. These are attractively staged in settings resembling a mini habitat, and decorating needs some thought to achieve the desired pleasing result.

My comments so far apply to any variety of British bird, mule or hybrid. (I send softbill and seed-eating bird teams to the shows I contest, and delight when I win a non-softbill special), but I'll concentrate in conclusion on softbills.

Most major clubs offer special awards for flighted and unflighted, normal and colour variant softbills. Often there are three cash awards for each category, so at least 12 birds are required of the relevant types. The most sought-after prizes however after the National, (now defunct), are those presented by Staffordshire British Bird & Mule Club. These are in the form of fine bone china vases and plaques, beautifully made and inscribed, portraying birds in full colour and in their natural surroundings, articles of beauty and very collectable, Gwyn Jones their creator, refers to his work as a "labour of love". (See page 273).

The birds most likely to win a major award are blackbird hens, song thrush cocks and hens and redstart and wheatear cocks. It will pay dividends to have all these in a team to contest all the prizes on offer. Each specimen should be of a type and of the condition laid down by the show standards. Besides these, a first-rate specimen of a different variety, would not only be a surprise, hopefully, to the judge, but might annex the best in show award. Some outstanding birds of old come to mind. The nightingale shown by Jim Walford of Barnett during the late Sixties and early Seventies was one of these, winning the best British awards on no fewer than three occasions at the National Exhibition. Some fancies thought this bird was a thrush nightingale, a close relative, but I was assured some years later by my friend Jim Theaker, who had inside information about the bird and confirmed that it was a nightingale. Another was a yellow (as opposed to buff) redstart hen benched by East Anglian exhibitor Peter Jermy of Norwich some years ago – a beautiful and eye-catching specimen.

Novice softbill exhibitors are thin on the ground at present, and it's important to encourage club members who have a liking for these colourful birds to try their hand at exhibiting. Song thrushes are reasonably priced and fairly easy to steady, and would make an ideal bird to start with.

As the new season draws near, everyone involved in the hobby is looking forward to a successful time.

HOW INSIDE INFO CAN PAY OFF

A good knowledge of adversaries' potential teams and inclinations is vitally important, much like it is in chess or soccer. The oppositions' strengths are worth understanding, so they can be negated so far as it is possible with the birds at one's disposal. One must resort to the grapevine to acquire the necessary intelligence.

There is no profit in staging mediocre specimens if an opponent has a quality bird entered in the same class at the show. It will only make his bird look better than it really is, and may prevent a better specimen of another kind, maybe one's own, from winning a decent prize.

However, if a bird staged is marginally inferior to the opponents, it may be worth staging so a little doubt enters the judge's mind. He may go elsewhere for a big winner, hopefully one of yours. It is a matter of judgement on behalf of the exhibitor.

Judges have their idiosyncrasies, likes and dislikes, and it's important for an exhibitor to know what they are. Although a judge is employed by a club to give an honest opinion on the day, each has a favourite variety, and seeing a good specimen that is familiar to them, may tempt them to give it a special when better show birds have been entered. On the other hand, staging such a bird may have the opposite effect. It is worth weighing up such a scenario.

Photograph by Dennis Avon

SONG THRUSH (CAGE DECORATION OPTIONAL)

Photograph by Bernard Williams

NORMAL HEN BLACK BIRD - a fine specimen

Photograph by Bernard Williams

CINNAMON HEN BLACKBIRD - shape is important

Photograph by Bernard Williams

HEN PHAEO MELANIN STARLING - outstanding colour

JUDGE THE BIRD, NOT THE CAGE

Written September 4th 1999

Wildlife law now authorises the whole range of native softbills to be exhibited. This has increased entry numbers and added interest to shows. Many beautifully staged birds unseen for many years, are being displayed again.

After the introduction of the new regime, everyone involved with the hobby went through a settling in period - one of becoming accustomed to the changing face of British bird events. Club officials had the pleasing task of adding extra classes to their schedules and arranging additional staging to cope with the increased entries, many of which are staged in large cages.

Exhibitors were set the task of assimilating the new rules and putting together show teams that reflect the new, liberal situation. Historically, most breeders of small softbills declined to show their wares, merely keeping them for study and interest. Therefore, at the outset there was a small but valuable pool of specimens available. As time went by, though, many exhibitors took up the challenge of breeding these birds for the first time, while others having lapsed, became rejuvenated and restarted dormant activities. Consequently some fine specimens have been raised.

However, those least prepared for the new challenge were, I feel, the judges. Many had never bred a softbill in their lives. Some, due to their young age, had never seen a nightingale or a fieldfare, for instance, on show. Some were thrown in at the deep end and mistakes were made, These, in my opinion, fell into two categories.

1.   Pretty little eye-catching birds were placed above examples of Schedule 3 pedigree strains.
2.   The cage decorations on which specimens perched tipped the scales in favour of quite ordinary birds.

I believe most of these teething problems have been ironed out and the majority of judges are up to the job, which will bode well for the future.

Top judges know who owns most of the birds staged before them. This knowledge must never have a direct bearing on the outcome. The top exhibitor may exhibit the best bird, but this can only emerge after careful, unbiased study and consideration of all the entries on display.

Cage decorations should have little bearing on the points allocated. This is because points allotted in such cases are virtually the same as for hardbills, which may come as a surprise to some readers. Points awarded to the staging aspect of a nicely presented redstart, for instance, should be eight or nine out of ten. In contrast to this, there are 40 on offer for colour and markings in this species. This I think puts the points system in perspective.

It should not matter to a judge who owns the bird placed before him or whether it is legally shown. These are the concerns of the exhibitor. A judge must judge the entries before him. Pretty bits of staging are perfectly adequate. The exhibit itself must surely attract the bulk of points.

SHOWING SOFTBILLS. 'THE FAB FOUR'

Over the past few years, the most popular species of softbill to appear on the show bench at the major events have been two medium-sized birds, the blackbird and song thrush and two small ones, the redstart and the pied wagtail. These four with their variants have made up most of the softbill contingent.

Probably the most popular has been the **blackbird**, hens in particular. A show specimen should be as large as possible, full bodied and strong. It should have a broad, nicely rounded head in proportion to a well-rounded body. The eyes should be set centrally in the head, and the wings carried well in a straight line with the tail.

A cock bird should be solid black all over, with a rich crocus-yellow bill and eye-ring The hen should be as dark as possible with a lightly speckled throat and mottled breast. Blackbird hens are rounder and slightly larger than the cocks and this often gives them an edge.

Colour-fed birds are welcome on the show bench. Among the colour variants is cinnamon, a sex-linked variety. Cinnamon show birds should be a rich 'ground-coffee' brown which should appear even throughout. Hens are a paler cinnamon.

The cream or satinette mutation is also sex-linked in its mode of inheritance. It is white with a light cinnamon suffusion throughout, which gives it a rich, creamy appearance. It also has the crocus-yellow beak and eye-ring, its eyes are deep red, its legs and feet deep pink and its nails clear.

A third colour variant often seen is the blue, a dominant variety. The single factor is blue and the double factor silver. Single-factor cocks should be a rich, blue-grey, with the usual yellow beak and eye-ring. Their legs and feet are dark, areas of pigment on the feet are often diluted.

Double-factor cocks are a light grey colour all over. They have fine, darker ticking and lacing which is just visible. Bill and eye-ring are the usual yellow and again the legs, feet and claws are dark with pigment somewhat reduced in places. Hens are similar with ticking and lacing more defined.

The beautiful **song thrush** is well regarded in the softbill community. Again, the hens tend to achieve more on the show bench than the cocks.

Show specimens should be as large as possible with a broad and nicely rounded head. They should be full-bodied with a strong appearance, a gentle rise over the back and neat wings and tail carriage. A normal coloured specimen should have rich, warm olive-brown upperparts. Below it should show a light sandy-buff breast, with colour running well down the flanks and a paler lower breast. Profuse, large well-defined dark brown spots are essential.

Two mutation forms are common within the fancy, both sex-linked. Cinnamons are a rich ginger brown colour. Their spots must be well defined, but are less prominent than in the normal bird. The cream or satinette is slightly less common. It is white with a light cinnamon suffusion. The eyes are deep red, the legs and feet lightish pink and the bill pale yellow.

The two small softbills that complete the "fab four" are both pretty and charming characters. The **redstart** is exhibited in a cage where height is important, so that it can show itself high on a well-placed perch perhaps one emerging from an old stump.

Exhibition specimens should be as large as possible, full bodied, but with a fairly upright stance. They should have a gentle rise to the shoulder, a straight back to rump, and neat wings and tail. The rump should be rich chestnut-red as should the tail and breast. In the cock bird, both head and mantle should be grey, the forehead white and well frosted, and the face and throat a rich black.

The hen redstart is a warm brown colour, with a rich chestnut rump and tail. Hens lack the white forehead and the black on the face and throat.

With the **pied wagtail**, the show cage needs to be longer than its height to give the exhibit room to display on and just above the cage floor. An exhibition bird should be as large as possible, cone-shaped, with a well filled breast tapering to the vent and a gentle rise at the shoulder to the rump. The tail should be a good length and neat and the wing carriage should also be neat.

The plumage is black, white and grey and all the markings should be crisp. The black apron should extend well down the breast and should be connected across the side of the neck and nape to the black cap, thus enclosing the white of the face. There are many tasks to complete before specimens of these species can be expected to win major prizes regularly. Individuals from a well-bred strain must be trained and staged in a professional fashion. Big, strong birds in immaculate feather and conditions are essential. They must be tame and perform well in a show cage before a judge.

It takes about five years to see a glimmer of progress in a strain of decent birds and then only if their ancestors were of good type, size and colour. Where a strict regime is applied to make sure that only birds with the required attributes are used, line-breeding will bring success year on year.

SHOWING NEEDS THAT EXTRA EDGE

If breeding a potential softbill winner is not tricky enough, staging it to win is even more of a challenge. Many keepers can breed a good bird, but having it in fine fettle and finger-tame often eludes them. The cage in which it is to perform can often let them down. Winners need to be well bred, in fine condition, tame and shown to their full potential. Only a few exhibitors have ever achieved this over time, and this is probably why so few take up the challenge of showing British softbills. Some find the law difficult to understand, the food requirements are too complex and the rigmarole involved in showing them to a high standard is too arduous.

Yet the fancy needs more softbill exhibitors. Softbill exhibitors are an endangered species, although simply exhibiting one or two birds is fine, the top champions tend to present a team of both flighted and unflighted birds, large and small, and one which has colour variants included in it, in order to compete for every special listed in the schedule.

Photograph by Bernard Williams

GWYN JONES GOT IT RIGHT AT THE 'ALL BRITISH' WITH HIS CINNAMON BLACKBIRD HEN IN 2003. (Page 252).

TOP SOFTBILLS AND SHOW STANDARDS

The chance of winning top awards with British softbills, on a regular basis at the major events depends upon a host of issues. Assuming everything has been done by the exhibitors in preparing birds for such achievements, a judge will choose one of four species, more often than not, for the supreme award.

These species are the blackbird, song thrush, redstart and pied wagtail. If a groomed specimen is not one of these, then its chances of winning the premier accolade are, mathematically, at a disadvantage.

This phenomenon is due to a plethora of reasons, the most obvious of which is the number of these birds being shown. They outgun any other.

Blackbirds and song thrushes have stolen a march on the rest.

They are nearing domestication, and like the greenfinch and redpoll of the hardbill world, differ, due to this, in several areas. They have been line-bred over a long period, have many colour variant varieties in their lines and have been shown nonstop throughout aviculture's history.

Not only do blackbirds and song thrushes win a majority of the specials available at the majors, these winners include normals and variants of both sexes. Blackbird colour variants include cinnamon, satinette and single and double factor blues. In the song thrush, both cinnamon and satinette exhibits often take the main prizes.

Redstarts and pied wagtails are attractive birds, and although strain building of these species is still in its infancy, judges see the better specimens as worthy winners. They contrast well with each other - the redstart is usually staged with its perches sited high in the cage, whereas the pied wagtail is provided with lower ones situated just above the cage floor. Exhibitors sense these species are best portrayed this way.

Regulations banned most small softbills from the shows for many years, so they have lost ground. Many species have a lot of catching up to do. Dedicated breeders are needed in order to make this happen.

Many of the small softbills exhibited at the shows are not bred by the exhibitors, but by fanciers who specialise in breeding these delightful birds for interest and commercial reasons. Most of them pay little regard to type. Unless more are bred by exhibitors who have a trained eye for a show bird and can spend time line-breeding both normal and variant strains, little will change.

However, line-breeding must be controlled. If not, problems can arise, such as double buffing. Cinnamon song thrushes, for instance, should be bred with the separation of spots in mind. A normal-coloured bird of type, with well-developed spots, evenly distributed over a light ground, has an advantage, when paired to a visual cinnamon whose spots are merged or submerged with a dark background, of producing nicely spotted birds that are a joy to behold. Many of today's song thrushes, especially cinnamons, have poorly developed spots amassed together, with virtually no separation between them.

NO MAN-MADE DESIGNS

The cultivation of quality strains of small softbills is pretty well non-existent at the present time. One only has to study individuals of certain species being shown to realise that there is no affinity between them - no man-made designs here! There is hope, however, that line-breeding and conformity of type will emerge among certain species, notably the dunnock, pied wagtail, redstart and wheatear. There is no doubt that many are being bred, but with type specimens available, any two birds of a species to make up a pair so that numbers can be increased is the priority at the present time. Real husbandry will come later, and with it type and mutant genes.

Providing fanciers are prepared to specialise in species of small softbills and give the necessary thought to strain building, it should be possible to bring them up to a good standard. Pairs containing the best available birds, with buff and yellow feather type taken on board, are the first steps along the road of strain building.

Depending on the species, their best show characteristics should be sought. For instance, black masks for redstarts and good, even aprons for pied wagtails - traits that are so often absent in today's birds.

Having mentioned the four most popular winning species, I must emphasise that any well-prepared specimen, from any one of more than 40 species available to the exhibitor, can win a major outright (and many specimens have done so). Some of these previous winners have been outstanding or extraordinary specimens of their kind. These include, among the larger birds, magpies, waxwings and starlings, while whinchats, wheatears, rock pipits, blackcaps and garden warblers have excelled among smaller varieties. I fear that some species are destined not to win big awards very often. It's not that they are inferior in any way, it's just that they don't inspire a judge very much. These include the tit family, the bearded reedling and, perhaps, the nuthatch. Numbers of these birds are shown every year and usually nicely presented. They are exhibited mainly to bring interest to any proceedings and to make up entries.

WIDER OPTIONS

What a difference it would be, and how fickle would the judges be, if a colour variant of one of these was bred and exhibited. I once heard of such a bird being reared - a white nuthatch. A white coal tit was also bred recently on the continent, also a dilute great tit.

It is only a matter of time before such variants turn up on the benches, especially now, when there is a better knowledge of genetics than there ever was, and the breeding and rearing of such birds has never been more favourable.

Although a rarity should be treated on its merits in the same way as any other exhibit, my experience tells me that any new, rare gem would catch the judge's eye.

Photograph by Bernard Williams

SHOW SCENE

STAGING BRITISH SOFTBILLS

Although only a few points are available in the exhibition standard for staging softbills, these can be important when a class winner or special prize is being decided.

Cages are of box or desk type and can be decorated at the exhibitor's discretion.

The golden rules are:

*ensure the cage, water and food pots are clean;
*paint all cages black on the outside, including the wire front, and white on the inside;
*make sure the door is on the right.

Two perches are recommended for each cage. These can be in various forms and situated at varying heights. The cages which are not usually decorated out (such as those for larger softbills) are invariably fitted with two dowel-type perches fixed to the back and some way apart.

Exhibitors usually decorate cages used for small softbills, where the selection of perches is influenced by the proposed exhibit. Springy perches are ideal for some kinds, such as leaf warblers. Others, such as wheatears, will show themselves off very nicely from a small post or rock situated at floor level.

Decorating material can usually be found in or around the garden, where mosses and heathers can be grown to supplement the natural vegetation.

Outside the garden, the law on wild plants (including mosses and lichens, often used in cage decoration) mirrors that which is afforded to wild birds. There are special penalties for unauthorised people who pick, uproot, or otherwise damage protected plants. Anyone wishing to gather mosses for cage decoration from the wild without a licence should check the law carefully before venturing out. Police powers of stop, search, seize and summons (or arrest) are almost identical to those for taking wild birds.

Most rare plants are listed on Schedule 8 of the Wildlife and Countryside Act 1981. These include 11 species of lichen (with names such as ear-lobed dog, river jelly, and starry breck) and 23 kinds of moss, including blue dew, rigid apple and triangular pygmy.

In todays climate, it might be sensible to consider the use of artificial floral decor when dressing show cages. In any florists' or garden centre shop can be found material so like the real plant that it will nearly fool the eye. The softbill fancy should take this opportunity to change gradually from natural to facsimile materials - no one would mind. These days it's not just synthetic vegetation that's available, but also rocks (for rock pipits), or bark suitable for treecreepers and nuthatches, or for use as a backdrop when displaying starts and flycatchers. These can be used without the fear of losing points.

Before decorating an exhibition cage, the use of a false floor should be considered, I often use one, I can fix perches to it without damaging the cage, or cut holes in it to secure plants in low containers. On the cage floor, I place a sheet of screwed-up, dampened paper, which gives it an impression of contour. It also helps to moisten the moss or other plant material that covers it. Potato or swede chunks, cut to shape, are placed at the back corners of the cage. Into these I push plant stems, including ivy. I cover these with moss to retain moisture for the duration of an event.

Finally, I place two white pots inside the cage, near the door for food and water. A third pot for special foods such as meal worms is acceptable, since the exhibit must be given every consideration.

For titmice, goldcrest and wren, I recommend small sprays of ivy (the wall-clinging variety), carefully positioned not to impinge on the birds, also consider some springy perches, too, cut from plants such as elderberry, elm or grape. A similar arrangement is also suitable for the dunnock.

Leaf warblers and nightingale are species that are constantly on the move. They must, I believe, be staged to stand out from their background when being shown. Laurel or copper beech sprays have the desired effect, especially if placed either side of the perches and fanned out towards the centre, at the back of the cage.

Wheatears, stonechat and whinchat require small 'flitting' perches, such as stumps or rocks, which are ideal to show off a specimen. A few sprigs of broom, heather or bracken will simulate a heathland. These can be pushed into the potato or swede blocks, between cage and false floor, or placed in pots.

For redstart, black redstart, pied and spotted flycatchers, it may be appropriate to suggest a woodland scene. Cages higher than their length should be used. The use of an old ivy-clad stump from a hedgerow, secured in an upright position in a cage, and a perch, either growing out of it or pushed in to it via a drilled hole, will ensure that an exhibit can alight and display in front of a judge.

Wagtails, pipits and other marsh-loving birds such as reedlings should have ornamental grasses, artificial rocks and small fern-like pot plants.

A properly trained exhibit is a confident one, and will display well, without the need to hide. The way a bird is presented can be a deciding factor between success and failure. Staging a bird correctly is therefore very important.

ROBB BROWN WITH HIS PAIR OF BLACKCAPS

Photograph by Bernard Williams

EXHIBITING BLACKBIRDS

Line-breeding - the use of birds displaying the required attributes each breeding season, many of which will be, by definition, closely related, is the key to achieving this. In a relatively short time, one will have a unique strain and the best individuals, if prepared correctly, will prove hard to beat on the show bench.

Of course keepers can have short-term results by buying their show teams in each year, but breeding one's own quality stock is far more rewarding and longer lasting.

Blackbird specimens assigned to the show team should be as large as possible, nicely rounded, not too long, with well rounded heads, a good wing carriage, and movement. In addition each bird should be endowed with the recognised desirable features unique to its kind. For instance, a mature normal cock blackbird of quality, should be glossy black with no hint of a white feather anywhere, a visual satinette hen should be as white as possible and so on.

The process of preparing young potential show birds should begin at an early stage, even in the nest, if a bird is big and fleshy at a few days old; it should if all goes well, turn out to be a nice bird. Youngsters leaving the nest can be assessed and if of potential for the show scene, can be isolated after weaning, and preparation for the bench can begin. Each young bird should be watched carefully during the moult, and well fed, with bathing water always available.

After the moult, the young pretenders can be trained for the shows, housed separately in show cages, in the bird room for short periods at first, and for longer periods of time as they become accustomed to their new environment. An old, tame, experienced bird caged near them, will give the youngsters confidence and take away much of the stress they may have. I have found it a good idea to sprinkle a few mealworms in each training cage, as in time the birds will look forward to the 'treat' and associate the cage with it, this will help each bird to settle down.

Only about four birds should be trained at any one time to maximise the attention given to each one. After a few sessions the training cages with the birds inside can be moved around the birdroom or placed in a vehicle to acquaint the potential exhibits to movement and routine, thus preparing them for the travelling and handling of their cages, which may lie ahead as showing gets underway.

I tend to show a young bird with potential only a few times in its first year, and if possible, in the company with hardened campaigners of the same kind. When fully trained and exhibited a few times a bird will respond satisfactorily even after a lengthy lapse of time, often rendering re-training unnecessary. They seem to remember what is required of them and even appear eager for an outing.

All my trained blackbirds required for showing are removed from their outside aviaries during the hours of darkness, this is to save them stress and damage. They soon get used to the procedure and settle down in their respective, prepared show cage. I use the dim light of a torch and the use of a small net for this purpose, but before transferring each exhibit to its allotted cage, I use an artists' brush and a little lukewarm water to clean beak, legs, leg-ring, feet, and toes of any dirt.

After the team has settled down, I clean away any dirt or dropped feathers from the cage, also in a dimmed light. I take the artists' brush with me to the show venue, and again tidy up the cages before handing the team over to the stewards.

Show cages for the blackbird should be well presented. They can be the desk or box type, and should have white interiors and black exteriors including the wire front. The door should be placed on the right-hand side. Points can be lost if cages are chipped or have off-white or cream interiors. The essential thing is to have everything clean; this includes the food and water vessels which should be inside the cage

No rules are laid down as to whether blackbird show cages should be decorated, it is up the individual exhibitor to decide. Two stout perches are ideal, so a judge can see a bird move to good effect. I very rarely decorate a blackbird's show cage. I place white paper on the floor, blotting paper is ideal, and sprinkle a few leaves, usually oak, over it.

Anyone interested in showing softbills or other species is advised to obtain good stock and to

IT'S NOT BLACK!

by **BERNARD HOWLETT**

I BRED this Cinnamon Pied Blackbird hen in May 1993, from a Cinnamon carrier cock and a dark-eyed White hen. I had hoped, that due to its type and size, it would make a nice show bird, but it appears a little nervous in a show cage. I hope eventually to breed a strain of Pieds to match those of my friend and fellow breeder, Alan Dawson, whose strain of lively Grizzle Blackbirds have graced our show benches for more than a decade.

Photograph by Dennis Avon

Since this short article was printed, other normal pieds were bred, but not as good as the above, and no
further cinnamon pieds were raised. (see chapter 1)
Note: White birds with black eyes are referred to as Leucism.

breed a strain of their own, this will take time but pay dividends in the end. There will be ups and downs for any newcomer, as there are for the accomplished exhibitor. There will always be someone who will decry a winning bird, by uttering words to the effect, 'I don't like it', these individuals end up sounding more like a parrot than a critic by the end of the season!

Sometimes a bird unlikely to win, will win and sometimes a bird considered to be the best on show comes nowhere. I have experienced both these scenarios, and will touch briefly on three disappointments. At a major event a normal hen blackbird bred from a visual albino cock was to be placed as best softbill in show until a steward pointed out to the judge that the bird was indeed bred from an albino, so could not be treated as normal. The bird was discarded. At another time a similar situation arose, but the steward pointed out to the judge, that the floor covering was incorrect, the paper on the floor was not entirely white, and although it was covered with leaves, again the bird was overlooked. A third occasion involved a judge when one of my entries was being put up for best British, he allegedly said. "We can't put that up, it's one of Bernard Howlett's". All these incidents were told to me by trusted friends. I take the rough with the smooth, and I advise any newcomer to do the same.

My worst memory however, is when having won most of the softbill awards on offer at a major event, a young man came up to me and said. "You didn't breed those birds, you got them from the Continent"! That was hard to take, luckily I had Ror McCluskey with me at the time, and his kind words helped me get over it. I had been lucky enough to have created several U.K. strains, and had with others, helped to promote variant softbills to the highest branch of the avicultural tree, something I can't help being proud of.

TAKING THE STRAIN

By far the best method of ensuring success on the show bench each year is, I would suggest, by way of careful selection of pairs through line-breeding from good stock. The way to achieve this is by cultivating birds of one variety or species displaying the required attributes each breeding season, many of which will contain birds whose silhouettes all share a common shape, consistent with the uniqueness of the stud.

Anyone contemplating building such a strain for prosperity, from scratch, could begin with a few specimens possibly of a chosen variety that is available. Alternatively, the acquisition of specimens of a type not kept before, may well be worth considering, depending on know-how and circumstances. Before undertaking such a venture, it is imperative to gain an in-depth knowledge of the subject bird. This must include its breeding habits, and requirements appertaining to its needs, such as food and accommodation, this will help make a difficult and challenging pursuit much easier.

About three or four pairs of the chosen variety should be considered to make up the nucleus of any programme. A buff and yellow bird should be included in any pair if at all possible, and at least five years should be allotted to the project. Careful selection of each pair, each year, and the keeping of concise records will, in time, create type in the strain. From the first sketchy plans, the project will reach its goals little by little, until such a high degree of progress has been obtained that only slight improvements are possible or expected. This standardisation process will have been achieved through line-breeding of the best inter-related birds, and a careful and controlled integration of any outside new blood.

However, the need to further improve a strain will never end, but there is no doubt that once a stud has developed sufficiently to enable a noticeable number of its exhibits to make real and sustained progress amid strong opposition on the show bench, the first of many targets has been reached. Line-breeding of a variety pursued over time will lead to its domestication. Alas, at the present time no British softbill species falls into this category, although some, such as the blackbird and song thrush are approaching this stage. Until breeders begin to specialise little progress will be made in the foreseeable future regarding the domestication of softbill species.

There are two crucial principles to grapple with when forming a strain; one is type, the other mutant genes. Both are vitally important and when present will ensure that the stud stands out like a beacon from its contemporaries. Its diversity will point towards domestication, and away from the 'wild caught' mindset of those who oppose bird keeping. Type in essence, is an improvement on nature by Fancy standards of a species through essential aspects such as size and shape. When type has been established in both normal and mutant forms, the concept of strain-building has been physically achieved.

Strain-building is a fascinating hobby in itself to pursue, because there are so many facets to consider and options to contemplate. When top birds from top studs clash on the show bench, differences between them are apparent. But their important features are similar because, while each strain has evolved separately, the same goals and ideals are sought.

Now, with the emphasis on strain-building, we must not let rare variants slip through our fingers in the future as we have done in the past. No strain will appear legitimate in this age without them, whereas any home-bred stud of type which contains variants will bring credibility to the Fancy. We have a duty to the fanciers of the future, if not to ourselves, to create strains of many kinds of softbills, in order to avert demise of our hobby, it is that important.

EXHIBITION CINNAMON SONG THRUSH

Photograph by Dennis Avon

END OF AN UNUSUAL SHOW SEASON 1995/96. PENNED APRIL 20TH 1996.

A show season in which for the first time in a decade any native bird, legally held and complying with certain regulations about ringing, was again eligible to be staged in open competition, has recently come to an end.

In many ways it was a very encouraging year as far as the staging of non-Schedule 3 British Birds was concerned. The highlight of the season came early on. In October at King's Lynn, where the East Anglian National was held, more than 30 such exhibits were on view, including cornbuntings, redstarts, wheatears and wagtails. This satisfactory tally was due to the hard work of the officials of that society, and in particular to the efforts of Alan Baldry, Andrew Moore and Dick Southgate.

I was mortified, however, to see such a poor showing of such birds at the English National itself, especially when the organisers had put on extra classes. I had envisaged seeing more than 20 such exhibits of softbills alone, but it was not to be, and of the four entered, only two were actually staged.

For many years eminent aviculturists such as Roger Caton of the British Bird Council, have worked tirelessly for the relaxation of the rules. When this came about in the form of a General Licence, the Fancy as a whole was taken somewhat by surprise. No doubt many potential show birds were short of training; also the possibility of having valuable charges blood tested may have put some fanciers off staging them.

My last show season, like my last breeding season was patchy and just satisfactory. Although I picked up the occasional special, the only bonus was when Ron McCluskey's wonderful hen song thrush escaped just prior to the National Exhibition held at the NEC. This allowed me to win with a cream blackbird, the first of its type to gain the best softbill award at this major event.

Ron and I battled for supremacy all through the season, and met head to head on several occasions, in particular at the Yorkshire BB&HC show in November, the National BB&MC centenary show at Winsford in January, and the annual show of the Eastern Federation at Swaffham in March, where he was a clear points winner every time.

The song thrush has been part of my life for longer than the last show season. Ron is a regular visitor to Norfolk. After showing at the 1994 event at Swaffham he accidently left the song thrush behind, and I had the pleasure of looking after it until mid-October of that year when I journeyed north and returned it. It had been housed in an aviary all to itself, which no doubt helped to recharge its batteries. I am now hoping that I breed a bird to rival it in the weeks ahead, or that it takes a longer holiday if it escapes again.

It is imperative that continued progress be made in establishing quality strains of as many kinds of non-Schedule 3 birds as possible, so that first-class specimens appear on the benches in greater numbers than hitherto.

The Fancy has never been better placed to take up the challenge. It has the expertise required, easier importing facilities, improved health care of birds, and quality food products at its disposal. In essence, it now possesses the tools to do the job.

SHOW SCENE APRIL 1998 WRITTEN AT THAT TIME.

During the past show season I was able to visit more venues than usual. I enjoy the camaraderie banter and meeting old and new friends. It is a pleasant way to spend weekends during the autumn and winter months – it's something that I can recommend to anyone wishing to pursue a new hobby.

The high quality of birds on display was maintained throughout the period, with greenfinches from the hardbill sections and blackbirds from the softbill classes doing well at most of the events I attended. It was also good to see big classes of goldfinches on the benches, perhaps an increase on former years. Mules and hybrids were also staged in good numbers with some beautiful birds on display. Terry McCracken's dark yellow greenfinch mule cock was perhaps the year's best exhibit. A nice redpoll x chaffinch owned by S. Shallcross was also very much admired.

PIED WAGTAIL

For me the best small softbill of the season was a pied wagtail exhibited by Gwyn Jones, a bird of good type and markings. I did not see Chris Atkinson's pied wagtail so all I can say is that it must have been impressive as it not only came out on top as best novice in show at the National Exhibition, but went one further and gained the supreme award at the Welsh event. This made it the highest achiever for many a year.

At most of the large All-British shows, the softbill judge is outnumbered by those often more interested in the seedeaters, so it is therefore very unusual for a softbill to win a supreme award at any of these events, as they tend to be at a disadvantage.

With the breeding season underway, it is hoped that more non-Schedule 3 species will be propagated in aviaries this year and exhibited in the future.

Schedule 4 species, like the black redstart and crossbill, are now well established, as are non-scheduled kinds such as the mistle thrush and hawfinch. Many others, the common redstart and pied wagtail to name but two, are being bred in numbers every year. Displays of non-Scheduled 3 varieties, if well staged in good feather, add interest to any event.

SOFTBILL SHOW SEASON 2002/03

For me, the gruelling and very competitive softbill show season for this period ended at my local event on March 2nd, 2003, when the Eastern Federation of British Bird Fanciers 28th all-British show, held at Swaffham, Norfolk, brought the curtain down for another year.

In overall terms, the quality of the exhibits was generally high, and during this period I had the privilege of judging the National Exhibition in December 2002, and was pleased to choose Ron McCluskey's magpie cock as best softbill, just beating the beautiful cinnamon hen blackbird exhibited by Gwyn Jones which gained the best colour variant award. Ron's magpie also won at the London & Home Counties. Blackbird hens were the most popular, winning three times. J. & P. Jermy's pied wagtail was the only small softbill to top a section; this bird went on to win the best in show award, the only small softbill to do so that season. There were two softbill hybrids on display, a pied wagtail x meadow pipit, bred by Norman Woodhouse, a very rare cross indeed, exhibited by the late Ken Semple and my song-thrush blackbird, both adding further interest to the British bird entries.

A number of exhibits were good enough to win at each event, with no really outstanding bird on show to dominate the season.

The main plea from many of the softbill enthusiasts was that adjudicators should judge to the standards set by the governing bodies in relation to each variety on display. A daunting and complicated task, bearing in mind just how diverse these species can be (there are about 70 of them of interest to the softbill exhibitor).

Inadequate standards

To emphasise the inadequacies of the present system, I have set out the standard of excellence applicable in 2002/03.

Points:

Size: 10

Shape - clean cut, cone shape: 15

Colour and markings - slate black and white, colour well defined: 35

Quality of feather and condition: 20

Steadiness and staging: 20

Total: 100

This description of a pied wagtail, from a judging point of view, was about as useful as a cardboard rat cage. The pied wagtail is a complex creature. Females have a greyer back than males and a smaller bib, making the drawing up of a show standard of excellence difficult. Since 2003 new standards have been set for softbill species by the British Softbill Society.

OTHER RESULTS

Yorkshire British Bird & Hybrid Club. (Pete Bailey Memorial show) I won best champion current-year bred, and best current-year bred with a normal hen blackbird, and second best champion current-year bred softbill with a normal cock song thrush.

Lancashire British Bird & Hybrid Club. I won best current-year mutation with a satinette song thrush, second best champion softbill with a normal song thrush and third best champion, also with this bird.

2003

Staffordshire British Bird & Mule Club. I won the following at this event; best colour variant softbill phaeo starling, best current-year bred normal softbill song thrush, best current-year bred colour variant softbill satinette blackbird.

National British Bird & Mule Club (All British). I won best unflighted normal softbill with hen blackbird, also second best champion softbill with phaeo starling.

London & Home Counties. Awarded best champion colour variant softbill, 2nd best champion softbill adult, best British softbill current-year bred, best champion softbill current-year bred satinette song thrush and 2nd best champion softbill current-year bred normal song thrush.

Eastern Federation of British Bird Fanciers. I won second best adult softbill with normal blackbird hen. Best colour variant in show with hen phaeo starling, and best current-year softbill with normal cock song thrush.

At the end of each show season the necessary work of planning for the next breeding season begins, with flight and aviary renovation and the selection of stock undertaken, in the hope that some home-bred winners will emerge to dominate future events.

Below is a list of the major shows I visited during this show season, together with relevant details. RESULTS WERE:

Yorkshire - There were 59 softbills, where a blackbird won for M. Milligan.

Lancashire - 81 softbills, K. Hillman's blackbird was the best exhibit.

National Exhibition - 67 exhibits on show, winner R. McCluskey with a magpie.

Staffordshire - 53 on display, winner was a waxwing shown by G. Cheesman.

National British Bird & Mule Club - 72 softbills on benches. G. Jones won with his cinnamon blackbird hen. Picture on page 244.

London & Home Counties - 59 exhibits, winner R. McCluskey with his magpie.

Eastern Federation was won with a pied wagtail benched by J.& P. Jermy; there were 26 softbills on show.

HEN PHAEO MELANIN STARLING (MANY WINS)

Photograph by Bernard Williams

**PIED WAGTAIL X MEADOW PIPIT
BRED BY NORMAN WOODHOUSE**

SOFTBILL SHOW SEASON 2003/04

The British bird show season ended on a thoughtful note during this period, when the Eastern Federation of British Bird fanciers held its 29th all-British event at Swaffham, Norfolk on March 7th.

It was dedicated to the fond memory of the late John Broadbent, a respected fancier of long standing. As a mark of respect all the club's rosettes bore his name.

Between March and the autumn, when another show season begins, minds will be focused on the breeding season.

Thoughts will turn to how the softbill section of our hobby can be improved in all its aspects, especially now that a specialist club, the British Softbill Society has been set up.

This heralds the introduction of new show standards for all the popular softbill kinds, and guidelines for exhibitors and judges alike.

From now on adjudicators will have the tools to assess each specimen in a more meaningful way than before.

It was hoped that if we worked together, aiming for the highest standards we could prosper, if we were unable to do this we might fail. We were at that time, in effect, in the last chance saloon.

The legislators and members of the anti bird keeping brigade watch our every move, so at all times we must present ourselves in the best possible light.

For some time I had pointed out the need for new show standards and made it known my willingness to assist in this regard.

In December, the Norwich aviculturist Peter Jermy asked me to give it some thought. I subsequently drew up specimen standards for 40 species of softbill and presented them to him at the Staffordshire event. Bob Partridge drew up standards for colour variant birds.

Further discussions took place there, and at the Welsh National, and the details were finalised at the All-British in Winsford in January when the British Softbill Society was formed.

The 2003/04 British softbill show season was much improved on previous years, with higher standards set, and with bigger entries at most events.

Officials at the various majors worked hard to welcome exhibitors, and staging in itself was very good.

If I had one small criticism, it was about lighting. It needs to be good so that the subtle colours of these beautiful birds can be appreciated, both by the judges and the public.

East Anglian National (October 19th) Best softbill at this commercially oriented event was a flighted garden warbler hen staged by Alan Baldry. This bird, which for me lacked a little in type, went on to win Best British overall. I liked Gwyn Jones's normal song thrush cock - a bird with strong spots and good colour.

Yorkshire British Bird & Hybrid Club (November 9th) Best softbill here was a yellow redstart cock, a good-feathered exhibit nicely staged by J. & P. Jermy. My best was a 1st of 8 with a hen cinnamon blackbird.

Lancashire British Bird & Hybrid Club (November 16th) Ron McCluskey the winner here with his cinnamon song thrush, the first in a season's hat-trick of such wins. This bird was of good colour, size and markings. I rather liked Alan Britton's lovely unflighted ring ouzel hen. It was beautifully staged and won the best current-year award. I managed 2nd best champion softbill, current-year bred with a song thrush.

Staffordshire British Bird & Mule Club (January 11th) I had the pleasure of judging this event, where I had to pick my way through some extraordinary classes. J. & P. Jermy's delightful pair of rock pipits came out worthy winners. These birds had wonderful feather quality, and were large, bold examples of their species. They were nicely marked and were clearly a matched pair. They went on to win best exhibit in show.

National British Bird & Mule Club (January 24th-25th) The largest entry for the season (118) was staged at Winsford, where a flighted yellow whinchat cock annexed the top award for Christopher Atkinson. I understand this bird had been successful at the Welsh National, winning top softbill award there.

London & Home Counties British Bird & Mule Club International (February 22nd) A second big win of the season was achieved by Ron McCluskey with his cinnamon song thrush hen, taking both the main softbill award and the overall prize for best in show at the event. A red-backed shrike was also staged - a species I had not seen represented on the show bench since the 1960s. Team England, of which I was a member, won the international team award.

Eastern Federation (March 7th) Dedicated to the late John Broadbent. Again a win for Ron McCluskey's lovely cinnamon song thrush hen. She was a bird difficult to fault, its size and shape (type) were perhaps, the best of its quality.

Of the eight events I attended, it can be seen that the winning birds were equally divided between the small and large softbills. The cinnamon song thrush was probably the best bird on view during the season. On four occasions the best bird in show came from the softbill ranks. Showing just how

good these insectivorous birds are becoming.

East Anglian National won by Alan Baldry with his garden warbler.

Yorkshire BB & HC winners J. & P. Jermy with their redstart.

Lancashire BB & HC won by Ron McCluskey with his cinnamon song thrush.

National Exhibition won by myself with my normal hen blackbird.

Staffordshire BB & MC was won by J. & P. Jermy with their pair of rock pipits.

National British Bird & Mule Club winner Chris Atkinson with a whinchat.

London & H.C. won by Ron McCluskey with his cinnamon song thrush.

Eastern Federation won by Ron McCluskey with his cinnamon song thrush.

**THE LATE
JOHN BROADBENT**

SOFTBILL SHOW SEASON 2004/05

East Anglian National October 24th 2004 and British Softbill Society Open Show, held at King's Lynn. Judge the late P. Neal. 86 birds staged. Best softbill was Alan Baldry's redstart, a lovely bird. I won two specials with a whitethroat, four with a phaeo starling and one with a colour variant song thrush, current-year bred.

The rosettes looked great in red, white and blue.

Yorkshire British Bird & Hybrid Club 2004. Softbill Judge M. Milligan. Mules and hybrids - T. Buckley. Best softbill was won by Ron McCluskey with a highly fed blackbird cock. I only won one special, second best mule or hybrid with a song thrush x blackbird. My best class win was 1st of 8 with a cinnamon blackbird hen.

Lancashire British Bird & Hybrid Club Judge T. Southcott. He placed my hen normal blackbird as best softbill and my satinette song thrush hen as best colour variant. Best current-year bred softbill was a steady ring ouzel staged by A.Britton, best current-year mutation was staged by G. Jones. The partnership of Brown and Middleton won the novice awards with a blue unflighted blackbird.

Staffordshire British Bird & Mule Club 18th open show 2005. Judge Softbills Derek Cotgrave, Mule and Hybrids Bernard Williams.

Best champion unflighted mule was my light greenfinch x canary. Best champion normal flighted softbill was my blackbird hen, second best was T. Southcott's song thrush and third best, my cinnamon hen blackbird. Best, second best and third best colour variants specials were all won by my birds, a satinette blackbird cock, a cinnamon song thrush and a pheao starling respectfully. The champion unflighted normal softbills were headed by a nice fieldfare from G. Jones, second best was a pair of dunnocks staged by R. Windle, I managed third spot with a blackbird. Middleton & Brown annexed all the novice softbill awards, the best of which was their normal coloured song thrush. 54 softbills on show.

National British Bird & Mule Club January 22nd-23rd 2005. I judged this event, an eye-catching display of softbills ranging from delicate warblers through to powerful corvids. It was a fine specimen of the former that eventually caught my eye for best in section, a delightful blackcap hen, staged to perfection by Les and Paul Neale, now both sadly missed from the exhibiting arena. Second best was a fine cinnamon song thrush benched by John Green. This bird also picked up the awards for best champion colour variant. Chris Atkinson benched a pied wagtail to near perfection to claim the award for best unflighted softbill. A. Middleton annexed the novice awards, the top bird being his cinnamon blackbird. There were 86 exhibits: Best softbill hen blackcap Les & Paul Neale.

London & Home Counties February 22nd 2005.
Best softbill cock rock pipit J. & P. Jermy.
Best current-year cock yellow nightingale A. Calvesbert.
My wins included best colour variant softbill, 2nd and 3rd best champion softbill flighted, 2nd best champion current-year bred and 2nd best hardbill hen, current-year bred with a yellow bunting.

Eastern Federation of British Bird Fanciers March 2005. Judge Chris Atkinson.
Best softbill was Ron McCluskey's normal song thrush, wonderfully staged.

LANCASHIRE 2004

SOFTBILL SHOW SEASON 2005/06

This was my 46th show season and I sent teams to five of the events mentioned. The threat of bird flu drifted ever closer to our shores, bringing in its wake human tragedy and restrictions.

I was disappointed that the World Show due to be held in Zetphen, Holland, was cancelled, for I had bred some nice song thrushes I'd hoped to exhibit there.

At home, the first main event, the Yorkshire British Bird and Hybrid Club Show, was cancelled due to the H5N1 virus. After that, and with DEFRA's approval, the big events did get underway. Here's a brief overview.

North Derbyshire Foreign, British Bird & Mule Club October 23rd 2005, Hollingwood. This event attracted a total of 53 well-staged softbills. Ron McCluskey won best softbill, and indeed best in show with his song thrush. Third best in show was C. Atkinson's pied wagtail. The second spot was taken by a hardbill.

Lancashire British Bird & Hybrid Club November 20th. Restrictions relating to the bird flu problem were thoroughly enacted (as they were at all other events during the season). Entries of softbills and the number of softbill exhibitors were down again at this show. However the birds on display were in fine fettle. Indeed, some proved to be the best of their kind as the season progressed. Coming out on top in the mule and hybrid section was my canary x buffinch; in the words of the show report, 'the largest unflighted yellow canary x bullfinch cock ever seen on the British show bench'. It took a number of prizes, including best mule or hybrid. I was also lucky enough to win the best softbill in show award with a flighted cream song thrush. The same bird took the best colour variant award. Second best adult champion was a well-marked song thrush from T. Southcott, and third best went to very nice ring ouzel staged by A. Britton. My unflighted song thrush hen won the best current-year award.

Best novice softbill and best novice colour variant went to T. Roberts with her cinnamon blackbird hen.

Cleveland British Bird & Mule Club November 27th, Trimdon. Best exhibit in show was a rock pipit staged by J.& P. Jermy. This exhibit also took the best small softbill awards. Best champion unflighted bird also went to the Jermy partnership with their cinnamon song thrush. Best large softbill was R. McCluskey's magpie, and best colour variant softbill was also staged by him, this being a cinnamon song thrush.

Bird Show U.K. November 2005. This show was staged at King's Lynn in conjunction with the all-variety event. The whole event was really well run. The quality in the softbill section was high, with many different species, and competition was keen. Best softbill was A. Baldry's redstart cock, which won best British bird overall. Best current-year bred small softbill was A. Calvesbert's nightingale. I managed to stage best flighted and best unflighted large softbills with a normal blackbird hen and a cinnamon song thrush hen respectively. My blue hen blackbird 'Two-spot' won second best colour variant current-year bred and third best large colour variant. A. Baldry took best colour variant with his silver blackbird. Best novice bird went to D. Painter's rock pipit.

Staffordshire British Bird & Mule Club January 8th 2006. Due to concern over bird flu the show was transferred from St Joseph's college to the Territorial Army Centre, Cobridge, where I believe it was held some years before. The hall chosen was excellent, well lit and roomy. The number of softbills on display and exhibitors showing them was very satisfying.

I was again in luck, staging the best exhibit, with a current-year bred normal starling, and taking best champion normal flighted with a blackbird hen, my National winner. Second best was a rock-steady waxwing from G. Cheeseman, and third best was a well-marked song thrush from G.W. Jones. A. Baldry took the second current-year normal-coloured award with his pied wagtail, and R. Windle annexed third spot with his song thrush. I also took second best adult mule or hybrid with a lightly variegated, buff greenfinch mule. Champion flighted colour variant softbills were headed by T. Southcott's good coloured cinnamon cock blackbird. My cinnamon hen blackbird and phaeo starling hen came second and third respectfully. The champion current-year bred colour variant softbills were headed by my blue blackbird hen, 'Two-spot', followed by T. Southcott's cinnamon blackbird hen and my cinnamon song thrush. Only two novice softbills were exhibited, both staged by Miss T. Roberts, a cinnamon blackbird and a normal.

The Welsh National January 15th, Port Talbot. The best champion softbill and best champion flighted small softbill was won by A. Baldry with his pied wagtail. He also took best unflighted small softbill. Best champion large softbill went to R. McCluskey with his cinnamon song thrush. This bird also took best colour variant award. J. Green won best unflighted large softbill with his song thrush.

Mrs C. Smith took the awards for best novice softbill, best novice flighted large softbill, best novice flighted, best large softbill and best colour variant softbill. Novice small softbill awards were won by Mrs S. O'Mahoney with her redstart.

National British Bird & Mule Club (All-British) January 21st-22nd 2006. Winsford Civic Hall, Cheshire, was the venue for the exhibition. Twelve softbill exhibitors entered teams. These were very well staged and contained great diversity. Coming out on top was my cinnamon song thrush hen, winning awards for best softbill, best champion unflighted softbill, best champion softbill, best champion colour variant softbill, best unflighted softbill, best large softbill, and best colour variant softbill. J. & P. Jermy took the second best softbill award with their song thrush and best small softbill award with a rock pipit.

I entered all three of my canary x bullfinches, the yellow gained awards in the northern class, winning that, a buff was also entered in this class, the second buff was entered in the sales class, and was sold.

In the novice section a well-staged pair of long-tailed tits took the top award for best softbill for Mrs S.O'Mahoney, second best was a normal blackbird from Miss T. Roberts, who also staged the best novice colour variant, a nice cinnamon blackbird hen.

London & Home Counties British Bird & Mule Club February 26th. I had the great privilege of judging this event at the Kemnel College, Sidcup, where I chose A. Baldry's yellow redstart cock as best softbill in show, a well-staged bird. Best current-year awards went to J.& P. Jermy's wheatear, a well-marked specimen. A. Calvesbert staged the best colour variant, a cinnamon starling hen, and Mrs S. O'Mahoney won both the best adult and best current-year novice softbill awards with her pair of long-tailed tits and redstart cock respectively.

Other birds of note were A. Britton's beautiful feathered ring ouzel, P. Neal's sprightly blackcap hen and A. Calvesbert's tree pipits. All these took awards. A pied flycatcher, shown by the Jermys, was also on display, an example of a species I had not seen on the show bench for many years.

Eastern Federation of British Bird Fanciers All-British Show March 5th, Swaffham. There was a good turnout of delightful entries, beautifully staged and a fitting finale to the season. Entries were staged from England, Scotland and Wales. Best softbill in show was J. & P. Jermy's flighted rock pipit; second best flighted went to R. McCluskey's cinnamon song thrush, which went on to take the best colour variant award. Third best

softbill was shown by J. Green with a cinnamon song thrush. Best unflighted softbill also went to the Jermy stable, this time with a pied wagtail. I managed one special in the softbill section. Second best young bird with a single factor blue blackbird hen, 'Two-spot'. Third place was taken by A. Baldry's redstart, he also took the best decorated cage award. There were no novices.

There was a dispute surrounding the best in show award. My young canary x bullfinch had been awarded best in show, winning the best mule and hybrid and best current-year bred bird. I understand there was an appeal of some sort, I was not there at that time, this apparently involved a goldfinch which had been chosen as best hardbill. A qualified judge who happened to be in the room, and had not been originally authorised to judge, was asked by the show manager, Terry Roberts, to give his opinion and he went for the goldfinch; overturning the original decision. Had I been present I would have appealed in writing, which was the proper thing to do, and made a strong case of which I have no doubt.

Exhibitor, winning birds and venue:
R. McCluskey song thrush. North Derbyshire.
B. Howlett satinette song thrush. Lancashire.
J. & P. Jermy rock pipit. Cleveland.
A. Baldry redstart. Bird Show U.K.
B. Howlett normal starling. Staffs.
A. Baldry pied wagtail. Welsh National.
B. Howlett Cinnamon song thrush. NBB&MC.
A. Baldry redstart. London & Home Counties.
J. & P. Jermy rock pipit. Eastern Fed.

Softbill species on show during the 2005/6 season included: tree and rock pipit, pied wagtail, waxwing, dunnock, nightingale, redstart, wheatear, blackbird, ring ouzel, song thrush, fieldfare, whitethroat, lesser whitethroat, blackcap, stonechat, whinchat, pied flycatcher, long-tailed, coal, and willow tits, jackdaw, magpie and starling. Colour variants were, cinnamon, satinette, blue and silver blackbirds, cinnamon and satinette song thrushes and cinnamon and phaeo starlings.

CANARY X BULLFINCH

Photograph by Andrew Calvesbert

A GOOD DAY OUT - 2005 LANCASHIRE.
TOP LEFT; CINNAMON HEN SONG THRUSH. BOTTOM LEFT; SATINETTE HEN SONG THRUSH.
RIGHT, YELLOW COCK CANARY X BULLFINCH.

SOFTBILL SHOW SEASON 2006/07

I sent teams to six of the main events during this period. The Suffolk bird-flu outbreak disrupted shows towards the end of the show year, but only one major event of those I usually attend was cancelled: the London & Home Counties. That was a shame because this is an international gathering of high repute.

The number of softbill exhibitors who regularly send teams to the main exhibitions is quite small but steady. There is a need for more keepers to show their birds, especially novices, to sustain the hobby for the future.

The wealth and standard of birds has not diminished, and varieties reaching a high standard are increasing. The gradual domestication of species is widening the gap between home-grown birds and those that some may presume to be akin to the wild type. Breeding techniques are streamlined nowadays, and there is a better understanding of how strains are built up. This holds the hobby in good stead.

North Derbyshire Foreign, British Bird & Mule Club, October 22nd, Hollingworth. A record for the club of 600 entries was staged altogether, 50 of which were softbills. Best British bird and best softbill was Ron McCluskey's cinnamon blackbird hen. The best novice softbill was won by Colin Preston's smart redstart cock.

Yorkshire British Bird & Hybrid Club, November 12th, Warmsworth. The 2005 event had to be cancelled due to the Scottish bird flu scare. The 2006 show was held at a new venue, the Holiday Inn at Warmsworth, in a large carpeted room, where the light was a factor (it was poor).
Best in show and best softbill was Alan Baldry's redstart cock. Second flighted was Ron McCluskey's fine cinnamon blackbird hen, which also took the best colour variant award. Third best flighted was my cinnamon blackbird hen. Best unflighted softbill went to Rob Windle's nicely staged pair of dunnocks, and second unflighted was won by Gwyn Jones's song thrush. Ron McCluskey took the third unflighted spot. Mrs O'Mahoney won the best novice award with her

well-staged pair of long-tailed tits.

Lancashire British Bird & Hybrid Club, November 19th, Lowton. I had the great privilege of judging this event and enjoyed my day. I chose Ron McCluskey's marvellous cinnamon blackbird hen as best softbill, best champion softbill, best large softbill and best colour variant softbill. It went on to take the supreme award. Best current-year bred softbill was won by a well-rounded silver blackbird owned and bred by John Green. Other birds of note were a well-spotted song thrush belonging to Gwyn Jones, and Colin Preston's lovely redstart cock, which took the best novice softbill award.

Cleveland British Bird, Mule & Hybrid Club, November 26th, Trimdon. Best bird in show, best large flighted softbill and best colour variant was Ron McCluskey's cinnamon blackbird hen. Best small softbill and best novice was won by David Painter's rock pipit.

East Anglian National Open Show, December 3rd, King's Lynn. This event was cancelled at the last minute, not because of bird flu, but owing to lack of entries, and with it the national British Softbill Society's open show - a tragedy for the fancy.

British Softbill Society's Members Show, December 10th, Talke Pits. The venue, although small was well-lit with natural light and ideal for the event. Our first members' show was held there in 2005. In the 1970s, Kidsgrove CBS had open shows at this venue.

Any new club has its ups and downs, as with the British Softbill Society, formed in 2003 but at its second members' show, the society had already come of age.

There were 35 classes and I looked first at the flighted exhibits. The titmice class included a very bright coal tit winner, owned by Bob Partridge. He also topped the warbler class with a well presented garden warbler. In the class for starts Chris Atkinson's beautiful redstart cock won easily. In the wheatear class the winner came from the stud of John Green. Chris Atkinson's whinchat headed the chats, he also took first place in the wagtail class with his famous old, pied cock bird. Rock and meadow pipits were represented in the pipit class, which was won by Ron McCluskey's fine rock pipit. Franks and Eyre came out on top in the gale/lark class with their large, well-marked skylark. In the normal song thrush class, two beautiful, well-spotted birds proved difficult to separate, but John Green's lovely type bird came out on top.

The cock blackbird class also had two similar birds, my own specimen just edging out Ron McCluskey's bird for top spot. The same scenario occurred in the hen blackbird class with my National winner beating Ron McCluskey's lovely yellow and well

shaped specimen by the narrowest of margins. A hen from my stud won the starling class. A fine ring ouzel hen won its class for John Green, and a fieldfare took the red ticket in its class for Chris Atkinson.

In the corvid class Ron McCluskey came out on top with his smart magpie. The cinnamon song thrush class was won by John Green's large, outstanding entry. The cinnamon blackbird class was headed by my hen. It went on to take the best in show awards, and won two plates. The blue/silver blackbird class attracted seven entries and was won by my 2005-bred blue hen (Two-spot). Ron McCluskey won the AOV blackbird class with a neat opal type cock bird, and the any colour variety starling class with a nice cinnamon starling.

The current-year bred section also had a high standard. In the wheatear class John Green's young bird won the red ticket. The young chat class was won by Ron McCluskey's well turned-out whinchat. The current-year wagtail class was taken by John Green's well marked pied.

The current-year pipit class had nine beautifully staged exhibits, the winner being Ron McCluskey's rock pipit. Franks and Eyre won well in the gale/lark class with their rich coloured nightingale. Eric Shallcross topped the current-year song thrush class. Ron McCluskey won the current-year hen blackbird class.

Franks and Eyre took the red ticket in the starling class, and a jackdaw won the current-year corvid class for Ron McCluskey, who also won the cinnamon song thrush class. John Green's cock silver scooped first, second and third in the blue/silver blackbird class and best current-year bird in show awards. One bird not mentioned was a huge hooded crow exhibited by Ron McCluskey, which was a talking point at the show.

Bernard Williams presented ceramic plates to the victors.

Staffordshire British Bird & Mule Club, January 14th, Cobridge. For the second year running, the show was held at the Territorial Army Centre, in a spacious room.

Best champion flighted normal softbill was a steady and well marked redstart from Chris Atkinson's stable. Second best was a superbly coloured blackbird entered by Terry Southcott. Third best was a pied wagtail from Chris Atkinson. Best champion unflighted normal softbill proved to be Ron McCluskey's steady blackbird, followed in second place by my pied wagtail hen. Coming third was Rob Windle's dunnock.

Best champion flighted colour variant was Ron McCluskey's richly coloured cinnamon blackbird hen, which was also best softbill in show. Second best was a cinnamon song thrush also from Ron McCluskey, and third best was my single-factor blue blackbird hen (Two-spot).

Best unflighted colour variant softbill was Terry Southcott's outstanding cinnamon blackbird hen. Second was Ron McCluskey's blue blackbird and third a cinnamon song thrush from Gwyn Jones. Colin Preston gained the top novice softbill award with his redstart.

Welsh National, The overall softbill winner was J. & P. Jermy's normal song thrush. I won best lizard, and best champion lizard canary awards.

National British Bird & Mule Club All British Show, (Victor Carr Memorial Show) January 27th-28th, Winsford. Winsford Civic Hall, Cheshire, was again the venue for this event. The hall was later demolished, so the 2008 show was held 12 miles further south in Nantwich Civic Hall.

Best champion softbill, best champion colour variant and best softbill was my cinnamon blackbird hen. Best champion unflighted softbill went to Gwyn Jones's cinnamon song thrush. I also annexed best champion unflighted hardbill colour variant with an Isabel mealy redpoll. In the novice section, best softbill was Mrs S. O'Mahoney's redstart, a flighted bird. Best unflighted novice went to Colin Preston's bird, also a redstart. I also won best northern exhibit with my yellow canary x bullfinch.

Victor Carr's son, Mike, presented the memorial trophies to the main winners. I was touched to receive mine as I knew Victor well, he was a great ambassador for the fancy.

Eastern Federation of British Bird Fanciers, March 4th, Mundford. This show had been caught up in the bird-flu outbreak, so was re-arranged from its original date of February 11th. Best softbill and best flighted softbill went to Craig Walker's well-coloured nightingale cock, runner up was my blue blackbird hen (Two-spot), which also took the best colour variant award. Best unflighted top award went to a fine pair of dunnocks entered and bred by Rob Windle. Again I managed second best with a buff redstart cock.

My pastel skylark hen won a red ticket and was well received, being the first of its kind ever to grace a British show bench.

Species shown during the 2006/07 season: tree, meadow and rock pipits, pied wagtail, skylark, waxwing, dunnock, nightingale, redstart, wheatear, whinchat, stonechat, blackbird, ring ouzel, song thrush, fieldfare, whitethroat, garden warbler, blackcap, long-tailed and coal tits, jackdaw, magpie, starling and hooded crow.

Colour variants included: cinnamon, satinette, silver and blue blackbirds, cinnamon and satinette song thrushes, cinnamon and pheao starlings and a pastel skylark.

National British Bird and Mule Club

Victor Carr Memorial Show 2007

Photograph by Tommy Milner

BEST SOFTBILL IN SHOW

B. HOWLETT

Photograph by Bernard Williams

**CINNAMON HEN BLACKBIRD
- BEST SOFTBILL**

Photograph by Bernard Williams

**VICTOR CARR'S MEMORIAL SHOW - WINSFORD , CHESHIRE.
NATIONAL BRITISH BIRD & MULE CLUB.
VICTOR'S SON MIKE PRESENTED THE TROPHIES**

Top British softbills at the main events

As you can see, cinnamon blackbird hens dominated the series.

Club/event	Judge	Benched	Winner	Winning Bird
North Derbyshire	D. Henderson	50	R.McCluskey	Cinnamon blackbird
Yorkshire	P. Jermy	71	A. Baldry	Redstart
Lancashire	B. Howlett	32	R.McCluskey	Cinnamon blackbird
Cleveland	C.Patterson	50	R.McCluskey	Cinnamon blackbird
British softbill members' show	B.Robinson	86	B.Howlett	Cinnamon blackbird
Staffordshire	J.Green	74	R.McCluskey	Cinnamon blackbird
Welsh National	A.Baldry	62	J.& P.Jermy	Normal song thrush
All British	A.Calvesbert	31	B.Howlett	Cinnamon blackbird
Eastern Federation	C.Mortimer	31	C.Walker	Nightingale

SOFTBILL SHOW SEASON 2007/08 (AUTUMN - MARCH)

Every cloud has a silver lining - or it does in the British bird fancy. For after negative dialogue among some factions, two new exhibitions have been added to the calendar.

Talke Pits used to stage the British Softbill Society's annual members' show, but this season the organisers broke away to stage an independent display. The BSS, somewhat depleted, continues as before, with a members' show. Secondly, the Northern Counties Native & Hybrid Club was founded and held its inaugural event. Cage numbers were down at some events, and this enabled my team to perform better than expected. Still, you've got to be in it to win it! The shows were:-

Bird Show of the Year, October 14th, Bingley Hall, Staffordshire. I mention this briefly, because I feel this could become another National where everyone could rally round. A small contingent of softbills was on display, including my own, arranged by the Yorkshire British Bird & Hybrid Club. I won the best British softbill adult and current-year awards.

North Derbyshire Foreign, British Bird & Mule Club, October 21st, Staveley. This event was held at the Speedwell Rooms, Staveley, a venue with plenty of light and excellent facilities. Alan Baldry's marvellous redstart cock came out on top in the British softbill section. Best current-year bred was a redstart hen benched by Franks and Eyre. Best novice softbill went to M. Goodale.

Yorkshire British Bird & Hybrid Club, November 11th, Dalton, Rotherham. The best softbill in show and the second best came unusually, but correctly, from the same class, both owned by Alan Baldry and both worthy of their wins. Third best softbill was my normal blackbird hen. My cinnamon song thrush annexed the best current-year award, and my cinnamon blackbird hen won the best colour variant softbill award overall. I also won 3rd best flighted colour variant with a blue blackbird (Two-spot), and best northern bird with a yellow canary x bullfinch. Best novice was P. Drury's normal blackbird cock, which was nicely displayed.

Talke Pits Open Softbill Show, December 9th 2007, Staffordshire. This event attracted an entry of more than 100 exhibits. Best in show was an immaculate cinnamon blackbird hen benched to perfection by Ron McCluskey. This exhibit also won the best colour variant prize. Best current-year bred was won by John Lennox, with a super starling. Best current colour variant was won by John Green's starling. Small softbills included large classes of warbler, whinchat and wheatear, but all were beaten by Robb Brown's well-coloured redstart, not bad for a novice! Best current-year small softbill went to Chris Atkinson's promising wheatear hen, a full-bodied bird. I was unable to attend due to bird flu in my area.

Scottish National, January 1st-2nd, Edinburgh. The British open championship was won by Ron McCluskey with his superb cinnamon blackbird hen, beating an entry of more than 1,700 birds.

Lancashire British Bird & Hybrid Club, January 6th. This event had to be postponed from November, owing to the bird flu outbreak, and was rescheduled at the usual venue, Lowton Civic Hall. There was a fine show of well-staged softbills on display, and I was lucky on the day. My cinnamon blackbird hen was judged best softbill and best colour variant softbill, and my cinnamon song thrush was awarded best current-year bred and best current-year colour variant. Best champion small softbill went to the J.& P. Jermy stable. Sadly there were no novice or junior exhibitors.

Staffordshire British Bird & Mule Club, Won best softbill, best large softbill and best champion colour variant with my cinnamon hen blackbird, and best current-year bred softbill.

Welsh National, January 20th, Port Talbot. I was pleased to judge at this event. I chose John Green's wonderful normal song thrush as best softbill. It went on to win best British bird, mule or hybrid overall. Best small softbill went to Chris Atkinson's pied wagtail. Best colour variant softbill was Terry Southcott's good coloured cinnamon blackbird. I chose Robb Brown's very nice redstart cock as best novice. Best novice colour variant softbill was also owned by Mr Brown, a cinnamon blackbird. Another novice softbill exhibitor, D. Wedder won specials with his warblers.

North East British Bird, Mule & Hybrid Club, January 20th, Trimdon, Co Durham. Another show re-arranged because of avian flu. Best exhibit, best champion exhibit, best softbill, best champion flighted large softbill was Ron McCluskey's cinnamon blackbird. Best champion flighted small softbill, was the redstart of Colin Patterson; best champion CYB large softbill, best champion CYB small softbill, John Lennox.

Northern Counties, Native British Bird & Hybrid Club, January 26-27th. This inaugural show, held at the Civic Hall, Nantwich, was well supported, especially in the hardbill and mule and hybrid sections. Coming out on top in the softbill section was my cinnamon blackbird hen, just beating Ron McCluskey's normal coloured song thrush. My cinnamon song thrush was awarded best current-year bred softbill. I scored with 2nd best current-year with a satinette blackbird and 3rd best with a pair of wrens. Best novice bird was P. Drury's normal blackbird cock. A rock pipit won the junior award for Danny Street.

National British Bird & Mule Club (All British), February 3rd. The event was held at the Territorial Army Centre, Stoke-on-Trent. My cinnamon blackbird hen was best champion softbill, best softbill, best large softbill and best colour variant softbill. Best unflighted softbill award, and second best champion softbill went to John Green with his song thrush, his Welsh winner. The novice softbill awards went to Robb Brown's cinnamon blackbird. He also won the award for best small softbill with a well-staged redstart.

British Softbill Society Members' Show, February 10th, Dalton. Held at the Silverwood Miners Welfare Resources Centre, it attracted 78 exhibits. Best in show, best large, best current-year and best colour variant, was a cinnamon song thrush from the Jermy partnership, who also won best adult colour variant, among others. Second best softbill and best small softbill was a redstart cock owned by Alan Baldry, whose pair of bearded reedlings took second best small adult softbill. I managed third best overall with a normal cock blackbird, and minor specials with a blue blackbird (Two-spot) and with a pair of wrens. S. Cowell and Franks and Eyre won specials with a cinnamon song thrush and blackcap respectively. M. Gondale won all the novice specials with a fine team of birds.

London & Home Counties British Bird & Mule Club, February 24th, Sidcup, Kent. Best softbill, best champion and best champion softbill adult were won by my normal blackbird hen. My blue blackbird hen (Two-spot) took best colour variant softbill and my cinnamon song thrush won the best current-year softbill award. The novice award was won by a pair of bearded reedling from I. Brown.

Eastern Federation of British Bird Fanciers, March 9th, Mundford, Norfolk. The Federation's 33rd all British event attracted 42 softbill exhibits. The event incorporated the open show of the British Softbill Society.

Top exhibit was the pied wagtail entered by the Jermy partnership. They also took the best current-year and best colour variant awards with their brightly coloured cinnamon song thrush. Robb Brown won with his redstart to take the novice awards.

Species on view were:
Tree, meadow and rock pipits; pied, yellow and grey wagtails; waxwings; wren, dunnock; nightingale; redstart; whinchat; stonechat; wheatear; blackbird; ring ouzel; mistle thrush and song thrush; fieldfare; garden warbler, common and lesser whitethroats; blackcap; bearded, long-tailed

and coal tits; nuthatch; jay; jackdaw; chough; magpie and starling.

Mutations included: cinnamon and satinette song thrushes; cinnamon, silver, blue, satinette, agate and opal blackbirds; phaeo and cinnamon starlings; and finally, a pastel skylark owned by me. The breeding of good quality softbills goes on at pace, with record numbers being raised each year. Novice exhibitors are increasing in number. These factors can only bring hope to the hobby.

Top British softbills at the main events.

Bird Show of the Year. Judge B. Kerr. Winner B. Howlett. Normal blackbird hen.

North Derbyshire. Judge B. Partridge. Winner A. Baldry. Redstart.

Yorkshire. Judge B. Partridge. Winner A. Baldry. Redstart.

Talke Pits. Judge D. Henderson. Winner R. McCluskey. Cinnamon blackbird hen.

Scottish National. Judge J. Lennnox. Winner R. McCluskey. Cinnamon blackbird hen.

Lancashire. Judge D. Cotgrave. Winner B. Howlett. Cinnamon blackbird hen.

Staffs. Judge C. Patterson. Winner B.Howlett. Cinnamon blackbird hen.

Welsh National. Judge B. Howlett. Winner J. Green. Normal song thrush.

North East. Judge M. Milligan. Winner R. McCluskey. Cinnamon blackbird.

Northern Counties. Judge B. Hastie. Winner B. Howlett. Cinnamon blackbird.

All British. Judge M. Milligan. Winner B. Howlett. Cinnamon blackbird hen.

BSS Members'. Judges P. Beech and B. Oliver. Winner J. and P. Jermy. Cinnamon song thrush.

London. Judge A. Rhodes. Winner B. Howlett. Normal blackbird hen.

Eastern Federation. Judge K. Bennett. Winner J. and P. Jermy. Pied wagtail.

ALL BRITISH
Photograph by Dave Cottrell

The Northern Counties, Native Bird & Hybrid Club '07
INAUGURAL SHOW
January 26/27th. 2008

BEST SOFTBILL

Photograph by Tommy Milner

Awarded to BERNARD HOWLETT

BOBBIES GET JIMMY TO THE ALLY PALLY

No doubt we all reminisce from time to time, savouring moments of glory and fond memories. Naturally the older we are, the further we are able to delve back into our history to re-live those distant events.

Like other fanciers, I have many but one which brings me particular pleasure to recall, is the time I took my first red ticket at the National Exhibition of Cage Birds some 43 years ago.

In December 1969, I was a police officer serving with the Suffolk Constabulary and stationed in the Mildenhall sub-division. I had entered the National for the first time showing as a novice. The great show that year was at the Alexandra Palace, London N22 on December 4-6th. On Wednesday December 3rd, I was due to report for duty at 10pm, so I naturally planned as carefully as I could in order to be there on time.

As darkness fell, I loaded my show team into my hitherto trustworthy Vauxhall. The team consisted of a pair of peach-faced lovebirds, a cock greenfinch, two cock yellow buntings, a pair of blackcaps, a cock blackbird, a hen song thrush, a magpie, a jackdaw and a jay - the last six housed in an assortment of rather large box-type cages. I set out in plenty of time with only the birds for company, but as I approached Alexandra Palace the red light on top of its radio aerial clearly visible in the distance, my car spluttered to a stop and refused to start again.

I sat there wondering what to do next with the roar of the capital's traffic in my ears. I considered commandeering a taxi, but concluded that any driver would not appreciate the fare. I thought about getting to the venue and securing help from fancier friends, but just then, with me still weighing up the pros and cons of the situation, out of the frosty air of that December night came a London bobby, pounding his beat.

I introduced myself to the officer and explained the circumstances. He was most helpful, using his pocket radio to summon help. After a few minutes a large van pulled up and two burly policemen emerged. For a moment I could see myself being hauled off to the Tower, but no, all was well. The officers carefully unloaded the exhibits from my car, the taller one, picking up a large cage, asked, "What have we here?" I exclaimed "O that's Jimmy, my jay, be careful with him, he swears!"

263

After all my birds had been re-loaded into the police vehicle, we set off to the show. Stopping at the rear entrance the birds were again unloaded with the help of the policemen. I admit to smiling a little on seeing them humping my cages into the hall, some eyebrows were also raised by onlookers and fellow fanciers alike, an expression on their faces of disbelief.

Once the birds had been transferred into the custody of the stewards, I was whisked away and arrangements were made for my return to Suffolk. A series of police cars was laid on and I arrived at Mildenhall in good time for my night's duty.

The Metropolitan Police took care of my car and when I returned to London on the Saturday, it had been repaired by a local garage and was ready for me.

On entering the show hall, I was delighted to discover that Jimmy, my jay had not only behaved himself impeccably, but had caught the eye of the judge G.J. Roberts of Portdinorwic, who gave him the red ticket in a full class, beating some champion birds in the process.

The jay was a large compact bird with a fair amount of blue in its wing coverts. It had won many prizes prior to this particular event, and went on to win many more, including best Large Softbill at the 1971 National Exhibition, but the winning of my first National first prize, and the way in which it was achieved, will always be most memorable for me.

"WELL DONE JIMMY"

Two 1st's, one special and two 2nd's at the National

264

Exhibition records from 1965 to 2013

I began showing birds in the 1960's, this was when I moved from Leicestershire to the Norfolk/Suffolk border. I joined a number of clubs in those early days, the most memorable of these being Bury and West Suffolk, as it was then, it is now Bury St Edmunds C.B.S., and Thetford and Breckland, of which I was secretary for some time, and which is now defunct. Listed here are most results from those times until 2013. From 2002 to March 2008 I have isolated major events and have tried to eliminate errors in the stats outlined. After which I have again recorded all results.

These wins comprised of numerous cups, medals, diplomas, rosettes, vases, plaques, cash and other awards.

My National and World show records are recorded separately.
NOVICE status:
1965: Thetford and Breckland - Cock blackbird, class win.

1969: Colchester - Magpie, best British.
Bury and West Suffolk - Members' show - Blackbird cock, best softbill.
Dereham - Pair blackcaps, best closed-ringed.
Wisbech - Magpie, second best British.
Diss - Best softbill.
Colchester - Linnet hen specials, magpie prize winner.

CHAMPION status.
1970: Stowmarket - Jay cock best softbill, song thrush second best softbill, linnet hen best current-year bred.
Thetford and Breckland Members' show - Cock jay, prize winner.
Bury and West Suffolk - Cock jay best softbill, linnet hen best current-year.
Thetford and Breckland - Cock jay, best softbill.
Diss - Cock jay, best exhibit.
Wisbech - Won prizes.
Colchester - Yellow bunting, greenfinch hen and starling cock, all won prizes.
Greenfinch cock was best current-year bred.
Breckland - Cock jay, best British, best softbill.

1971: Stowmarket - Starling cock best softbill, miniature siskin x canary cock best mule or hybrid, goldfinch cock also prize winner.
King's Lynn - Greenfinch hen and goldfinch cock, specials for both.
Thetford and Breckland - Grey wagtail cock, prize winner (members' show).
Peterborough - Grey wagtail best British bird, blackbird best current-year.
Haverhill - Cock blackbird best British bird, linnet x greenfinch cock best mule/hybrid.
Sudbury - Grey wagtail best softbill.
Cambridge - Greenfinch hen specials, blackbird cock prize.
Braintree - Blackbird second best softbill, linnet x greenfinch best mule/hybrid, greenfinch hen best current-year.
Colchester - Blackbird cock, best softbill.
Wisbech - Goldfinch cock, prize winner.
Thetford and Breckland - Jay best softbill, greenfinch hen best current-year bred.

1972: Clacton - Best current-year bird.
Cambridge - Redstart best softbill.
North Walsham - Bramblefinch cock best British bird.
Clacton - Cinnamon greenfinch hen best young hardbill, normal blackbird cock best young softbill
Stowmarket - Starling cock best British.
Thetford and Breckland - Song thrush hen, best closed-ringed British.

1973: Braintree - Rock pipit, prize winner.
Sudbury - Song thrush, prize winner.
Downham Market - Song thrush hen, best current-year exhibit.
Bury and West Suffolk (members) - Tree sparrow, best British.
North Walsham - Bramblefinch cock best British bird in show, cinnamon greenfinch best closed-ringed bird.
Clacton - Blackbird cock, best young bird.
Thetford and Breckland - Cinnamon greenfinch hen, best rare colour.
Stowmarket - Jay best closed-ringed. Bramblefinch hen, best British.

1974: Haverhill - Bramblefinch cock, best British.
Stowmarket - Blackbird hen and bramblefinch cock both prize winners.
Sudbury - Blackbird hen, best British.
Dereham - Blackbird hen, prize winner.
Diss - Greenfinch cock special, blackbird hen best British exhibit.

1975: Newmarket - Chaffinch cock, prize winner. Mistle thrush also prize winner.
Stowmarket - Chaffinch cock, mistle thrush cock and starling, all prize winners.
St. Neots - Blackbird, class win.
Bury and West Suffolk - Class wins for cock starling, cock jay and linnet x redpoll.
Haverhill - Blackbird hen, prize winner.
Sudbury - Blackbird hen, chaffinch cock and bramblefinch, all prize winners.
Diss - Bullfinch hen best hardbill, silver greenfinch rosette.
Colchester - Chaffinch cock, lutino greenfinch cock and albino blackbird all prize winners.
Bury and West Suffolk - Canary x greenfinch, prize winner.

1976: Stowmarket - Cock blackbird, best softbill.
Bury and West Suffolk - Cock blackbird, best softbill.
Haverhill - Hen bramblefinch best bird in show, cock blackbird best softbill, best mule or hybrid goldfinch x bullfinch, greenfinch hen best current-year.
Sudbury - Mistle thrush and cock blackbird both prize winners.
Cambridge - Fawn mule, best miniature mule.

1971
Peterborough

National Cage Bird Society Judge, Mr. H. Blaxhall (right) from Kesgrave, is helped by Mr. J. Walker, to judge the British bird section at the Stowmarket, Open, Cage Bird Society Show, on Saturday.

Judging my bramblefinch -1973

1976
Bury St Edmunds

Winning at Diss: photos shows lovely lines of the hen bullfinch (see national record 1975 page 274 and page 277)

1977: Stowmarket - Albino blackbird, best young bird.
Bury St Edmunds - Cinnamon blackbird, best members' bird.
Diss - Cinnamon blackbird, best softbill.
1978-1980: did not exhibit.
1981-1987: local records not available.
National records can be located for this period under National Wins.

1988: South East Ipswich - Cinnamon blackbird hen, best exhibit in show.
Stowmarket - Won best hardbill with redpoll cock and best British with cream blackbird.
Bury St. Edmunds - Best British bird cream hen blackbird, best mule or hybrid song thrush x blackbird.
Haverhill - Best bird in show, cream blackbird.
South East Ipswich - Best British bird, cinnamon cock blackbird.
Lowestoft - Best British bird cinnamon cock blackbird, best champion hybrid with song thrush x blackbird.
Diss - Blackbird hen, best British bird.

1989: Haverhill - Satinette hen blackbird best softbill, brambling cock best current-year bred and second best British.
Norwich - Won best mule or hybrid, and best British bird with song thrush x blackbird and cinnamon blackbird.
Diss - Cinnamon cock blackbird best in section, song thrush x blackbird best mule or hybrid.
Eastern Federation - Best softbill with albino blackbird.

1990: Stowmarket - Best softbill with a cinnamon cock blackbird, best mule or hybrid with song thrush x blackbird.
Eastern Federation - Best softbill.

1991: Newmarket - Won best British bird and best softbill with cinnamon blackbird cock.
Dunfermline - Best British softbill with cinnamon blackbird.
Thetford and Breckland - Won with pastel starling best British, silver greenfinch hen best current-year bred.
South East Ipswich - Cinnamon cock blackbird best champion softbill, cinnamon song thrush best current-year bred, and cock song thrush x blackbird best mule or hybrid.
Haverhill - Cinnamon cock blackbird best softbill, best pure British; best current-year softbill with a cinnamon song thrush.

1992: Stowmarket - Best in show.
South East Ipswich - Best in show.
Bury St Edmunds - Best British.
Chatteris - Best in show.
Thetford and Breckland - Best in show.
Haverhill - Best in show.

1993: St Neots 40th event - Won best British with a cinnamon song thrush.
Eastern Federation - Won best softbill with cinnamon song thrush and best Siberian with Siberian thrush.
Haverhill - Best in show with blackbird.

1994: London & Home Counties - Best adult softbill blackbird, second best adult song thrush, best current-year song thrush, second best current-year starling.
1st East Anglian National - Best softbill, cinnamon song thrush.
Yorkshire British Bird and Hybrid Club - Second best champion flighted, cinnamon song thrush.
Bury St Edmunds - Best British.
Beccles - Best in show.
Breckland - Best British.
Norwich Alliance - Best softbill, best current-year.
Haverhill - Best in show.
North Walsham - Best current-year bred, cinnamon song thrush.
South East Ipswich - Best bird in show, cinnamon song thrush, best foreign bird Siberian thrush.
Eastern Federation - Best flighted hardbill hen with chaffinch.

Photograph by Andrew Calvesbert

Ipswich 1992 My cinnamon song thrush - best bird in show and my Siberian thrush best foreign bird in show.

THIRD WIN AT HAVERHILL - 1994
Bernard Howlett with his best in show
at the Haverhill CBS open show.
Bernard will be presented with a
commemorative plaque for winning
the supreme award for three
consecutive years (C&A Birds).

RICHARD BAGLOW and my cinnamon blackbird winner - Dunfermline 1991

1995: Yorkshire British Bird & Hybrid Club - Best flighted hen hardbill with chaffinch, best softbill with hen blackbird.

1996: Stowmarket - Best in show with cinnamon blackbird hen, best hardbill current-year with cock mealy redpoll and best foreign bird with Siberian thrush.
South East Ipswich - Best softbill with blackbird normal hen.
Bury St Edmunds - Won with cinnamon current-year song thrush, best large softbill.
East Anglian National - Won with cream blackbird best current-year adult softbill and best softbill hen.
Yorkshire British Bird & Hybrid Club - Cinnamon blackbird best softbill, best colour variant in show, cream song thrush 2nd best adult softbill, cinnamon song thrush 2nd best current-year softbill.

1997: Stowmarket - Cinnamon blackbird hen best British bird.
Lincolnshire British Bird Mule & Hybrid Club - Won best champion current-year bred softbill with cream cock blackbird.
Norwich - Won best large softbill with cinnamon blackbird.
Cambridge - Won best softbill with cinnamon blackbird, best small softbill with redstart, and best current-year softbill with cream cock blackbird.
London & Home Counties - Second best champion current-year bred, cinnamon song thrush hen, third best champion softbill adult cinnamon blackbird hen.
Eastern Federation - Cream song thrush, best colour variant.

1998: Stowmarket - Cinnamon hen blackbird, best British bird.
Staffordshire British Bird & Mule Club - Blackbird hen best normal flighted, cinnamon blackbird best softbill, best colour variant, pair greater whitethroats, best current-year birds, mutation blackbird best current-year colour variant.
National British Bird & Mule club - Blackbird hen best unflighted softbill.
Eastern Federation - Second best adult champion, cinnamon hen blackbird and was best colour variant in show, third best with a redstart cock, also won best, second best and third best current-year softbill awards.

1999: Stowmarket - Cream blackbird cock, best British, redpoll cock, best hardbill.
Lincolnshire British Bird Mule & Hybrid Club - Hen blackbird, best softbill, cinnamon cock song thrush, best current-year.
Haverhill - Redpoll cock, best hardbill, cinnamon song thrush, best in show, dark linnet mule, best mule.
Colchester - Cinnamon blackbird, best British, cinnamon song thrush, best current-year.
Staffordshire British Bird & Mule Club - Cream song thrush, best colour variant, cinnamon song thrush, best current-year colour variant. Fieldfare, third unflighted bird, cinnamon blackbird hen, third flighted.
National British Bird & Mule Club - Best softbill, cinnamon blackbird hen, normal blackbird, second best softbill.
Eastern Federation - Cream song thrush, best colour variant in show, and third best adult.
London & Home Counties - Best champion colour variant, cinnamon blackbird hen, mistle thrush, third best champion adult.
Yorkshire British Bird & Hybrid Club - Best colour variant British, best current-year, second best champion flighted softbill, third best champion flighted softbill.
Lancashire British Bird & Mule Club - Best champion mutation softbill, cinnamon blackbird hen. Best unflighted softbill, cinnamon hen song thrush, second best mutation softbill, cinnamon blackbird hen, third best champion softbill phaeo starling.

2000: Stowmarket - Cream hen blackbird, best British bird, normal hen blackbird second best softbill.
Bury St Edmunds - Cream hen blackbird, best in section.
South East Ipswich - Cream hen blackbird, best softbill.
Chatteris - Best champion softbill.
Yorkshire British Bird & Hybrid Club - 60 softbills. Second best softbill and second best colour variant with phaeo starling, third best and third best colour variant cinnamon song thrush, best current-year bird with cinnamon song thrush.
Staffordshire British Bird & Mule Club - The millenium show 9th January 2000, best champion colour variant softbill current-year bred.
London & Home Counties - Best softbill with blackbird hen, third best current-year bred softbill with blackbird.
Eastern Federation - Phaeo starling best colour variant and second best softbill, blackbird hen second best current-year, second blackbird hen third best adult, and variant song thrush third best current-year softbill.
Lincolnshire British Bird Mule & Hybrid Club - Best British softbill.

2001: Stowmarket - Won best softbill, and best British with cream/cinnamon blackbird. Won second best softbill with normal hen blackbird.
South East Ipswich - Won 2nd best British bird, best softbill with normal hen blackbird, best any other variety cock with mealy redpoll.
Chatteris - Won best British bird with cream song thrush, best in show. (363 entries altogether).
Bury St Edmunds - Won best champion softbill and best British.
Yorkshire British Bird & Hybrid Club - won best softbill, and best colour variant softbill with cream song thrush, 2nd best softbill with phaeo starling, 3rd best softbill and 3rd best colour variant, cinnamon song thrush (national bird). 3rd best current-year bred with a cinnamon song thrush, entered 7 birds, won 7 firsts.
Staffordshire British Bird & Mule Club - 120 softbills, best champion flighted softbill with hen blackbird, cinnamon song thrush 2nd best colour variant. Also 3rd best champion colour variant flighted with phaeo starling, and 3rd best unflighted softbill with a redwing.
London & Home Counties - Won best British softbill in show with normal hen blackbird.
Eastern Federation - Phaeo starling best colour variant and second best softbill, blackbird hen second best

current-year, second blackbird hen - third best adult, and variant song thrush third best current-year softbill.
Lincoln British Bird Mule & Hybrid Club - Best British softbill.

2002-2008, (autumn), main events not included here. (See page 251).

2002: St Neots - Best lizard, best British-blackbird hen.
Bury St Edmunds - Cream song thrush best softbill and best current-year bred, best current-year bred hardbill phaeo house sparrow, best mule or hybrid song thrush x blackbird.
Diss - Won best British with hen blackbird adult, twite x canary won best mule or hybrid and opal canary won best self.
South East Ipswich - Won best mule or hybrid and best current-year British mule or hybrid with a cock song thrush x blackbird.

2004: St. Neots - Their 50th show, won best British softbill with a pheao starling and Best current-year with a cinnamon song thrush.
South East Ipswich and New London Fancy show - Won best champion British with a cinnamon blackbird and best champion London fancy with a jonque cock. Edward McGillian won best novice and best London fancy overall.

2005: St Neots - Best current-year bred with cinnamon song thrush.
The 2006/07 show season was cut short due to bird flu and the cancellation of the King's Lynn event.

2006 St Neots - Won best British bird and best softbill with a normal blackbird hen, (National bird),best mule or hybrid with a light greenfinch mule.
South East Ipswich - Won best British bird with hen cinnamon blackbird, best London fancy with cock bird.
Diss - Won best in section with canary x bullfinch, best current-year hardbill with yellow bunting, best hardbill with yellow bunting, and best current-year softbill.

2007: South East Ipswich Members' show - Won best in show with canary x bullfinch, best true British with blue blackbird hen (Two-spot).
Club details not available - Won with canary x bullfinch, best northern hybrid and best northern exhibit, also 2nd best current-year softbill with pied wagtail and 3rd best current-year adult with blue blackbird hen (Two-spot).

2008: St Neots, 4th October 2008 - Won second best foreign with a Java sparrow. Best British bird with a cinnamon song thrush.
Welsh National - I judged this event.
Nantwich Northern Counties - Best softbill, best champion softbill with cinnamon hen blackbird.
British Softbill Society Members' show, Yorkshire - Best large softbill with blackbird cock. 3rd best colour variant softbill, 2nd best large softbill with blue blackbird hen (Two-spot), 3rd best current-year small softbill with a pair of wrens.
South East Ipswich - Best any other variety canary with New London fancy. Best softbill, best British bird, best in show with single factor blue blackbird hen (Two-spot).
Cambridge - Best champion flighted hardbill hen with a yellow bunting. Best large softbill with a cinnamon blackbird.
Andrew Calvesbert won best softbill prize with a pair of tree pipits.
From this point, all records are out-lined.
Talke Pits, softbill show - Won best softbill with cinnamon blackbird hen and best current-year overall with yellow normal song thrush.
Diss - Best hardbill with flighted hen yellow bunting, best softbill with cinnamon song thrush flighted hen and best mule or hybrid with yellow canary x bullfinch cock

2009: South East Ipswich - Best softbill cinnamon song thrush and best mule or hybrid with canary x bullfinch.
Lancashire British Bird & Hybrid Club - Won best softbill and best colour variant in show with cinnamon blackbird hen. Presented with a watch by Jack (John) Lloyd.

This yellow chaffinch hen was bred by me in 1993, from my line-bred strain. Its sire (pictured below, top left) was best current-year bred hardbill at the Eastern Federation of British Bird Fanciers' show at Swaffham, Norfolk.

Although not large she has good feather type and colour, and performed well in front of the judges. During the 1994/95 show season, she did the double by winning best flighted hardhill hen awards at both the Yorkshire BB & HC open show and at the Eastern Federation of British Bird Fanciers' event. (see details in show reports)

Photograph by Dennis Avon

Photograph by Dave Henderson

Photograph by Dave Henderson

Talke Pits - Ecka Booton

Talke Pits - Alan Lythe

Photograph by Dave Henderson

Talke Pits - 2011

Photograph by Dave Henderson

Talke Pits - John Billing

Staffordshire British Bird & Mule Club - Won best softbill and best colour variant with cinnamon hen blackbird, best northern with canary x bullfinch.

National British Bird & Mule Club - Best softbill, host of specials, with cinnamon blackbird. Best northern mule or hybrid with canary x bullfinch.

Talke Pits - Second best large normal softbill flighted with cock blackbird, second best large normal softbill with hen blackbird (daughter of Two-spot).

London & Home Counties - Best softbill with cinnamon blackbird, best current-year softbill, third best hardbill with yellow bunting.

Eastern Federation. Best softbill with cinnamon blackbird hen. Third best current-year softbill.

2010: Northern Counties - Minor specials with softbills.

Diss - Best British bird blackbird hen, best mule or hybrid with a song thrush x blackbird.

Bury St Edmunds - Won minor specials.

2011: South East Ipswich - Second best champion hardbill cock with a yellow bunting,
Best champion lizard canary with a clear cap gold cock and best new London fancy with a jonque, this bird also gained the award for best old variety canary.

Diss - won best British with yellow bunting cock, best mule or hybrid with clear greenfinch x canary mule and seond best champion lizard with broken cap silver hen.

Talke Pits - Ron McCluskey's Memorial Show - Four firsts with cock normal blackbird, hen normal blackbird, satinette song thrush hen and current-year bred normal blackbird hen, this bird gained the current-year large softbill award.

2012: Staffordshire British Bird & Mule Club - Second best normal softbill current-year bred with hen blackbird and third best colour variant flighted with a cinnamon-ino cock blackbird.

Eastern Federation of British Bird Fanciers - Rosettes remembering Ron McCluskey. Best in show with normal hen blackbird (daughter of Two-spot). Also third best current-year bred with a normal blackbird hen. Nearly 500 birds staged, 48 of which were softbills.

South East Ipswich C.B.S cock bird table show - Best in show with a redstart (Page 273).

2013: Staffordshire British Bird & Mule Club 25th anniversary show - Won best colour variant and best large softbill with a hen satinette song thrush. Second best colour variant with a hen cinnamon starling. Judged All British for the third time.

Best Exhibit in show - Eastern Federation, 2012.

Photograph by Andrew Calvesbert

Photograph by Bernard Williams

Peter Degville and the author - 2009

Photograph by Bernard Williams

2009 Staffs

Talke Pits - 2011

Photograph by Dave Henderson

South East Ipswich Table Show - 2012

Photograph by Andrew Calvesbert

Staffs 2013 - prizes won with satinette song thrush (Page 294). I now have 42 of this type of vase and 27 plaques.

NATIONAL WINS 1969 – 2003 and 2007-2011 - lesser events

1969 - 1st with a jay.

1971 - 1st of 6 with a jay - Best large British softbill.

1972 - 1st of 2 with cinnamon hen greenfinch.

1973 - 1st of 8 with a normal cock blackbird.

1974 - 1st of 8 with a normal hen blackbird, second best closed-ringed British bird. In effect, best softbill.

1975 - 1st of 7 with albino blackbird, best large softbill. (Classes 304-324)

1st of 7 with hen bullfinch, best bullfinch hen, Jervons silver cup.

1st of 2 with cock chaffinch

1976 - 1st of 1 with albino blackbird hen, for best abnormally coloured softbill.

1st of 1 with cock mistle thrush.

1st of 3 with goldfinch x bullfinch, adult hen, special, best bird in classes 270 to 271 (Hybrid)

1977 - Silver Jubilee.

1st of 6 with blackbird.

1st of 4 with silver starling and special for best large softbill.

1st of 7 with fawn canary x redpoll (miniature).

1st of 6 with cock blackbird.

1981 - 1st of 2 with albino blackbird, best in class 360, in effect best rare coloured softbill.

1st of 3 with cinnamon cock blackbird.

1982 - 1st of 2 with albino hen blackbird, special class 369, in effect for rare colour.

1983 - 1st of 2 with albino blackbird, best in class 369, in effect special for rare colour.

1984 - 1stof 14 with flighted normal hen blackbird, and my FIRST rosette. Prior to this event, rosettes were very few and far between, special prizes usually amounted to small amounts of cash. Awarded Best British softbill with this entry.

1st of 5 with cinnamon flighted hen blackbird and special for best in class 369. Best rare colour.

1st of 15 with current-year cinnamon blackbird.

1985 - 1st of 1 with song thrush x blackbird hybrid cock.

1988 - 1st of 10 with a cinnamon cock blackbird.

1st of 3 for a dunnock.

1989 - 1st of 6 with cinnamon cock blackbird, best colour variant.

1st of 1 with current-year bramblefinch cock.

1990 - 1st of 3 with flighted silver greenfinch.

1st of 2, with current-year silver greenfinch.

1st of 7 with cinnamon blackbird cock; best British softbill, best champion softbill, best softbill and best colour variant.

1st of 3, with cock silver greenfinch.

1st of 2, with hen silver greenfinch, current-year bird.

1991 - 1st of 9 with current-year cinnamon song thrush, second best British bird, best British softbill, best champion British softbill, best champion British colour variant, best current-year hybrid or British bird.

1st of 7 with chaffinch cock.

1st of 1 with Isabel greenfinch cock

1st of 1 with silver greenfinch hen.

1992 - 1st of 11 with blackbird hen.

1st of 8 with cinnamon song thrush flighted.

1st of 5 with cinnamon cock song thrush current-year.

1993 - 1st of 12 with hen flighted normal blackbird.

1st of 9 with cinnamon flighted blackbird.

1st of 4 with cock agate greenfinch.

1st of 1 with cock chaffinch.

1st of 1 with Isabel greenfinch hen

1994 - Judged, this included judging the BEST in SHOW award.

1995 - 1st of 6 with cream blackbird hen, best champion British softbill, best softbill.

1st of 2 with a redstart.

1st of 2 with blackbird normal, best current-year softbill.

1st of 2 with redstart current-year.

1996 - 1st of 9 with colour variant blackbird, best champion adult British colour variant.

1997 - 1st of 3 with normal blackbird.

1st of 8 Best British softbill, best champion adult softbill and best champion British softbill.

1st of 3 Best champion current-year bred British softbill.

1st of 1 with colour variant blackbird.

1998 - 1st of 3 with a hedge sparrow.

1st of 10 with a blackbird.

1999 - 1st of 5 with a colour variant, and best staged British bird softbill with current-year cinnamon song thrush hen, won the K & R Books Trophy, the British Bird Breeders' Association Trophy and the Ray Fletton Memorial Trophy for best current-year bred bird of any species, second best British bird and best current-year bred hybrid or British bird.

The British Bird Breeders' Trophy - runner-up to the best British bird.

1st of 1 with colour variant hardbill.

1st of 2 with blackbird, flighted.

1st of 8 with colour variant flighted.

1st of 4 with song thrush current-year.

2000 - 3rd Best of 16, any other variety canary with new London fancy.

1st of 2 with normal blackbird adult.

1st of 4 with cinnamon song thrush current-year bred.

2001 - 1st of 8, with blackbird hen.

2002 - Judged for second and last time.

2003 - Diamond Jubilee show - 1st of 4 with blackbird flighted hen, second best British bird, best champion British bird, best British softbill, best champion British softbill and best champion adult British softbill. The British Bird Breeders' Association Trophy - runner-up to the best British bird.

1st of 1 with phaeo starling hen.

1st of 3 with cock normal song thrush current-year.

No shows staged thereafter.

2007 - Bird of the Year Show, Bingley Hall, Stafford.

The most similar event in the exhibition calendar. Java Sparrow Society Show, best any age in show, with adult hen cream.

Best softbill, best current-year bred softbill.

2008 - Best champion flighted hybrid, best mule or hybrid, Judge S. Fitzpatrick, with canary x bullfinch. Best current-year softbill with song thrush.

Best champion softbill flighted, best softbill, with cinnamon hen blackbird.

2011 - (Now called The National Exhibition) Best softbill with a cream song thrush, second best softbill with a cinnamon blackbird hen and best hybrid with a song thrush x blackbird cock.

I sent teams to 28 original English Nationals, and won at least one first at each of them, 79 in all. Won at least one special at eighteen of them and 30 rosettes overall (not many rosettes were available early on). Specials won with jay, starling, bullfinch, blackbirds and song thrushes. Best champion British once, best softbill about seven times, best colour variant many times, second best British bird four times, best current-year mule, hybrid or British bird twice and best current-year bird at the event, once. Setting a record, winning more softbill specials than any other exhibitor at the National.

National Trophies

British Bird Breeder's Association Silver Challenge Trophy for runner-up to best British bird:
Won in 1974, 1991, 1999 and 2003.
Ray Fletton Memorial Trophy for best current-year hybrid or British bird:
Won in 1991 and 1999.
A.J. Jervons Silver Cup for best bullfinch hen:
Won it in 1976.
K & R Books Silver Challenge Trophy for best current-year bred bird in the whole show (bred by the exhibitor) won 1999.

PLEASING GOLDFINCH IS BEST OF BRITISH

National Exhibition 2002 held at the Exhibition Centre

The judges, Terry Ball, Gary Cheeseman and I had a quality entry of birds before us. The best of which was a pleasing and tidy goldfinch cock exhibited by E. Stevens. Second best British bird, a greenfinch cock of good quality, was staged by novice exhibitor M. Holland. The third best British and best softbill was Ron McCluskey's magpie, which was staged in lovely condition.

Best champion current-year bred hardbill was a good coloured buff greenfinch, owned by M. Harris. The best current-year bred softbill was a tame and nicely feathered fieldfare, shown by J. and P. Jermy. These exhibitors also took the best staged award with a wonderfully decorated cage displaying a wheatear. Best champion colour variant in section was a lovely cinnamon blackbird hen, well staged by G. Jones. This bird was only narrowly beaten by R. McCluskey's magpie.

The best colour variant hardbill was an unusually dark-eyed variegated greenfinch, staged by Thundow and Lawson. The special for best bullfinch was awarded to D. Bowen's exhibit. An unusual pied wagtail x meadow pipit, staged by K. Semple and bred by Norman Woodhouse, was unable to go further than to win its class due to its ineligibility for class specials. A hen crossbill, owned by D. Footitt, took a special for current-year bred novice hardbill. Other notable exhibits were a steady lutino greenfinch cock (D. Footitt) and Chris Atkinson's cock redstart which won a good class of chats etc.

B. Howlett

Had the privilege of judging the supreme award on this occasion in 1994

Refer to above text

1974 - National Exhibition winner of the BBBA silver trophy with normal blackbird hen

Winning the Jervons Trophy, 1975 National Exhibition, with the Hen Bullfinch.
Pictured with my daughter Stella. (See Diss 1975 - Page 266)

1990 - Best Softbill National Exhibition with cinnamon cock blackbird

Photograph by Dennis Avon

Photograph by Dennis Avon

National Exhibition 1991
British Bird Breeders Association Cup (on right) and
Ray Fletton Cup both won with cinnamon song thrush.

1995 - Best Softbill National Exhibition

Photograph by Dennis Avon

1999 - National Exhibition with my current-year bred cinnamon hen song thrush
winner of British Bird Breeders Association Cup, Ray Fletton Cup and K & R Books Trophy.
(best young exhibit at the event)

Photograph by Dennis Avon

278

SCOTTISH NATIONAL CAGE BIRD SOCIETY

(only data available)

1975: Corn Market Hall, Slateford Road, Edinburgh. Sixty Second Show.
Class 355 - Won 4th place with a hybrid in class of 6.
Class 381 - Bullfinch - hen unplaced, class of 36.
Class 395 - Won 2nd place with blackbird hen.

1978: Assembly Rooms, George Street, Edinburgh. Sixty Fifth Show.
Class 368 - Won 1st with miniature canary mule.
Class 390 - Won 4th place with corn bunting.
Class 405 - Won 3rd place with blackbird.
Class 409 - Won 1st place with silver starling.
Class 410 - Won 2nd place with albino blackbird and 3rd place with cinnamon blackbird.

1981: Corn Market Hall, Slateford Road, Edinburgh. Sixty Eighth Show.
Class 432 - Entered two birds in "rare feathered class" - no data.
Class 433 - Entered one bird in "any registered bird class" - no data.

Photo (below) shows me with winning cinnamon hen blackbird at the Scottish National. I have no other details. Note: The bird is the first cinnamon I acquired. It came from the wild on Home Office Licence in 1976 and all my cinnamons can be traced back to this bird.

Fawn Canary x redpoll - 1978 class 368.
Also won at English national in 1977.

Cinnamon hen blackbird, possibly 1981.
winner of many awards in England.
(wearing licenced split ring)

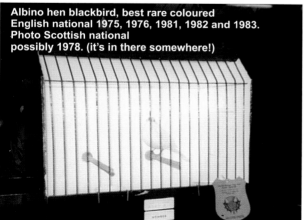

Albino hen blackbird, best rare coloured
English national 1975, 1976, 1981, 1982 and 1983.
Photo Scottish national
possibly 1978. (it's in there somewhere!)

Normal Blackbird hen possibly 1978
best softbill English National 1974

These birds won big in England - not in Scotland

WORLD SHOW TEAMS AND RECORDS

2002: Belgium - Variant song thrush gained 87 points.

2003: France - Variant song thrush gained 88 points.
Song thrush gained 90 points.
Song thrush x blackbird hybrid gained 88 points.
Lizard, team of four gained 83, 82, 77, and 81 points respectfully, total 323.

2004: Switzerland - Fieldfare gained 87 points.
"fine" New London Fancy canary hen, in class not judged for medals.
Greenfinch variant gained 89 points.
Greenfinch variant gained 91 points.
Lizard canary gained 89 points.
Lizard canary gained 89 points.
Lizard canary gained 87 points.
Song thrush gained 89 points.

2008: Belgium - Cinnamon song thrush gained 89 points.

2009: Italy - Normal yellow song thrush cock, gained 92 points and winner of the GOLD medal.
Cinnamon hen song thrush, gained 93 points and winner of the GOLD medal.
Team of four yellow buntings gained 89, 89, 89, and 89 points each, total 356, winner of the BRONZE medal.
Satinette song thrush gained 92 points, winner of the SILVER medal.
Team of four song thrushes gained 89, 87, 88, and 88 points respectfully, total 352 points.

2010: Portugal - Satinette song thrush hen gained 90 points.
Team of four normal cock song thrushes gained 89, 90, 89, and 89 points respectfully, total 357 points, winner of GOLD medal.
Satinette song thrush gained 94 points and GOLD medal.
Satinette song thrush gained 92 points, winner of BRONZE medal.
Satinette song thrush gained 91 points.
Normal song thrush cock gained 92 points, winner of GOLD medal.
Normal song thrush cock gained 91 points, winner of SILVER medal.
Normal song thrush cock gained 89 points.
Team of four yellow buntings gained 92, 90, 92 and 90 points each respectfully, total of 364 points, winner of the SILVER medal.
Yellow bunting gained 91 points, winner of BRONZE medal.

2011: France - Cock song thrush gained 89 points.
Hen Isabel greenfinch gained 90 points.
Hen satinette song thrush gained 93 points and winner of the GOLD medal.
Hen cinnamon blackbird gained 89 points.
Cock cinnamon blackbird gained 91 points and winner of the BRONZE medal.

2012: Spain - Blackbird hen gained 92 points and winner of the GOLD medal.
Song thrush cock gained 90 points.
Song thrush cock gained 92 points (no medal?).
Satinette song thrush hen gained 94 points and winner of the GOLD medal (also won gold in 2011).
Cinnamon song thrush hen gained 89 points.
Cinnamon blackbird hen gained 90 points.
Silver lizard gained 91 points.
Gold lizard gained 89 points.
Silver lizard gained 89 points.
Gold lizard gained 89 points.
Team of white Java sparrows scored 83,83,83 and 83 a total of 332 points (very young birds) they came third in their class - no medal?

2013: Belgium - Phaeo hen greenfinch (I believe a new variety) gained 93 points and winner of the GOLD medal. Among other specimens staged was a London Fancy canary in a non-competitive class. (Page 327).

A total of 16 medals; 9 gold, 3 silver and 4 bronze.
Won GOLD medals with normal song thrush (2), satinette song thrush (3), cinnamon song thrush (1), normal hen blackbird (1), team of 4 normal song thrushes (1) and a phaeo greenfinch (1). **Won SILVER medals with** normal song thrush (2), team of yellow buntings (1) and **won BRONZE medals** with satinette song thrush (1), yellow bunting (1), cock cinnamon blackbird (1) and team of yellow buntings (1) with hardbills, softbills, singles and teams. A British record.

THE PRETENDER
bred 2011 - best current-year normal large softbill Talke Pits, gold medal winner world show 2012.

Photograph by Dave Henderson

GOLDEN OAK LEAVES

Although I have exhibited birds at various World Shows with good results, it was not until the 2009 event, staged in Piacenza, Italy, in January of that year, that I managed a good win. My tally of medals amounted to two gold, one silver and one bronze. It was not a complete fluke! I had carefully scrutinised previous schedules for clues, about which classes would be most suitable for any birds I had available. So, during the breeding season of 2008, I knew what birds I needed to produce to give myself the best chance of success.

The 2008 breeding season went well for me, with a goodly number of song thrushes and yellow buntings bred. I decided to enter seven song thrushes and four yellow buntings. They were split up into five classes. There was a stam (team) of four normal song thrushes; a single normal/yellow cock that had won best current-year bird for me at the all-softbill show at Talke Pits in December 2008; a single cinnamon hen that had been narrowly beaten when I entered it in the 2008 World Show; and a single satinette hen. Together, with a stam of yellow buntings consisting of two cocks and two hens. I trained them all for the event.

On January 13th 2009, I delivered the team to the home of Cliff Griffin and his wife in Coven, Staffordshire. The thrushes were housed in show cages, giving them plenty of room, and on the floor of each I had scattered leaves from my five mature oaks. After receiving great hospitality and a cup of tea, I left the team stacked in Cliff's kitchen-diner. There was nothing left that I could do. Now it was up to the assigned members of the International Ornithological Association (IOA) to stage the birds at the World Championship Show in Italy, more than a thousand miles away, while I waited at home for the results. After the judging had taken place I was contacted by Brian Preddy, Brian Hogg and the (now, sadly) late Ron Evans. A gold medal and 92 points had been awarded to my single 2008, normal/yellow cock song thrush.

Then a second gold medal, with 93 points, to my cinnamon song thrush hen, bred in 2007.

There was a silver medal for my 2008 satinette song thrush hen, with 92 points, the same number won by my first gold exhibit. Finally a bronze for m[?] stam of yellow buntings. A gentleman who saw th[?] yellow buntings at the show said my birds were to[?] bright - I had colour-fed them. Colour-feeding is frowned on in some species by World Show judges. I duly thanked Simon Tammam for his hel[?] with the classification, Alan Robinson for his advic[?] on cage labelling, as well as Cliff Griffin, Mrs Griffin, and Brian Hogg, with special thanks to the[?] conveyors Brian Preddy and Maurice O'Connor who, with great insight, left the thrushes in my cages for their journey - this without doubt assiste[?] the results.

On collecting the birds from Cliff on their return, I noticed that the oak leaves in the thrush's cages had turned to gold. Good sign. A larger team was[?] entered in 2010 in Portugal with even better resul[?] winning 3 gold medals, 2 silver and 2 bronze, again with song thrushes and yellow buntings, making me the most successful UK World Show exhibitor in the history of the IOA, according to th[?] organisation. In 2011, in France, I won a gold medal with a satinette song thrush and a bronze medal with a blackbird. In 2012 I won two further gold medals with a blackbird and a satinette thrush, and in 2013 won gold with a phaeo hen greenfinch, new on the world stage.

2009 - MEDALS WON IN ITALY

2010 - MEDALS WON IN PORTUGAL

Photograph by Alan Hoary

Photograph by Luke Harvey

2011 - MEDALS WON IN FRANCE

Photograph by Luke Harvey

2012 - MEDALS WON IN SPAIN

2013 - MEDAL WON IN BELGIUM

GOLD

283

WINNERS IN THE EAST
All photographs by Andrew Calvesbert

Terry Roberts - Chairman, Eastern Fed.

Steve Dix - Secretary S.E. Ipswich C.B.S.

G.W. Jones - EFBBF

EFBBF - Phaeo starling 2003

Ron McCluskey - Cin. song thrush EFBBF 2004

Cin. blackbird hen S.E. Ipswich

Jim Rutter and Herbie Hatcher

Phil Shaw

Cin. blackbird hen
2006 S.E. Ipswich

F. Brankin
Best bird in show
Yellow siskin hen

Robert Windle

Les and Paul Neale

J. Harris
Best CYB
adult cock

Jason and Peter Jermy

Keith Bennett starling 2002

Single factor blue blackbird hen, 'Two-spot'

Robb Brown 2008

Eastern Fed. best softbill 2009

Roy Easter

Dave Mason

Craig Walker

P. Linder

Brian King

Luke Harvey

Nick Spencer

Andrew Calvesbert and Jay

B. Clark

Gary Cheesman

Alan Haury

A. Henry

Steve Williamson

George Carr

George Hodge

Nick Potts and son

A. Mayers

Neil Prentice and his son, Morten

M. Pybus 2012

P. Robinson 2012

JIM THEAKER AND HIS WINNING BIRDS

10 year old chaffinch - National winner

Winning Yellow Linnet mule, North Derbyshire 2000

WINNERS IN THE WEST
All photographs by Bernard Williams

Normal Starling - best softbill Staffs 2006

Jack Lloyd

John Lennox - 2006

Brian Leigh with author - 2006

2006

2007

Alan Britton - best exhibit Staffs 2008

Best softbill - cinnamon blackbird - Staffs 2008

Bernard Williams presenting

Terry McCraken

John Green

2007

Chris Atkinson - 2007

Terry Southcott

Wendy Woodward

Bernard Williams presenting 2013

Satinette song thrush winner of two gold medals World Show, best softbill 'National'. Best large softbill, best colour variant Staffs BB & MC 2013 (see prizes page 273).

Photograph by Robb Brown

Judging All British 2013.

CHAPTER TEN

British Softbill Society

Normal Yellow Hen Blackbird

Photograph by Dennis Avon

THE BRITISH SOFTBILL SOCIETY

The society was founded in 2004, its founder members being: England - A.Baldry, J. Green, B.A. Howlett, J. Jermy, P. Jermy and B. Partridge. Scotland - R. McCluskey and M. Milligan. Wales - C. Atkinson, Joint secretaries; P. & J. Jermy, Treasurer; Mrs J. Jermy.

Judges 'A' list: C. Atkinson, A. Baldry, J. Green, B.A. Howlett, J. Jermy, P. Jermy, R. McCluskey, M. Milligan, P. Neil and B. Partridge.

'B' list; A. Calvesbert, S. Dix, K. Hillman and T. Southcott.

Cage & Aviary Birds March 6th 2004 reports: The BSS is braced for possible objections to a list of recommended softbill judges to show organisers, but it argues that it is a necessary step forward.

"It's not the case of boycotting shows that refuse, it's just a case of saying let's have present day exhibitors of softbills judging softbills, not just someone who used to keep a thrush 40 years ago," said RON McCLUSKEY, who keeps around 150 softbills in his aviaries in Scotland. "When you've travelled a long way, you don't want to have birds judged by someone who's only been keeping them for a short time and doesn't know very much about them. It's a kick in the teeth. We want the softbills judged the way some of the hardbills are judged - to type and size, colour and markings, rather than giving it first because it looks a nice bird. We are saying, if you want someone to make a 500 mile round-trip to bench birds at your show, we don't want them to be judged by someone who is not on our list. We were sick of exhibiting birds and seeing them get marks for colour and markings when the important thing is breeding to type. Because of the bad standard that someone drew up 40, 50 or 60 years ago, nobody was encouraged to exhibit a blackbird cock because a blackbird hen was winning all the prizes. Hopefully now we will get people showing magpies and hedge sparrows and pied wagtail cocks and hens. We are just saying we are sick of being the poor relation for so many years and it is about time we got a fair crack of the whip."

Lessons learned from the previous softbill society. RON McCLUSKEY recalls the National British Softbill Society that existed 30 years ago, where some of the members did not even keep softbills.

"The secretary had a couple of Rhode Island reds and a robin in his hen run" he recalled. "That fizzled out around 1980 and bears no relation to today's small band of dedicated bird men united by their enjoyment of the hobby. Now we have a band of fanciers who are going to support the major shows, provided they play the game" he said, describing the new society as 'a step forward'.

"We hope we've seen the last of big softbill cages being slid about the floor and shoved in a dark corner while the hardbills are staged with so much space you could drive a bus in between the lanes. We don't want to be the main attraction, though to me and to many other fanciers they are the main attraction, but with all the work that goes into making the lovely cages and decorating them, we want equal recognition."

ALAN BALDRY also sees the new society as keeping breeding records and publishing them and picking up where the Association for the Study and Propagation of European Birds in Aviaries (ASPEBA) left off.

"The National British Softbill died when the 1981 Act came in, and everybody was on a downer, but things have steadily recovered," he said.

"Blackbirds, thrushes and colour mutation birds are being bred now. All it needs is for the standards to be pulled together to make it worth exhibiting them again."

PETER JERMY said: "We don't want to offend people which is why we have collated a recommended list of judges.

There will also be a 'B' list of judges who probably haven't exhibited softbills for quite a number of years now, but who want to come and show softbills. If they want to judge, we will recommend that they steward at three or four of the specialist shows with one of our recommended judges and we will see how they pick up on the scale of points we have drawn up. If we think they are making a very good job of it, and know what they are about, we will put them on the 'A' list."

WHAT DO I GET IF I JOIN?

So, what are the benefits of belonging to the British Softbill Society?

"We hope we can help everyone all over the country if they have got any problems with their softbills," said Peter Jermy, who has already had a big response from Cage & Aviary Birds readers to the recent news item.

"The idea is that eventually we will be able to put them in touch with someone to give them all the relevant information on that bird. If someone has lost a hen bird of one species and they are near to the breeding season, it may be that we can put them in contact with someone who can do a swap or sell them a bird. We will hold meetings now and again at one of the specialist shows, to give people a chance to attend and come up with views. We are not going to have a show just for softbills, but we will try to pick a venue for next season to have a full patronage show of the British Softbill Society perhaps at the East Anglian National in King's Lynn, which should produce one of the biggest entries for a long time."

COLOURS HOLD THE KEY

PETER JERMY believes colour variants could hold the key. "Belgians have been pioneers in colour variants, even in canaries and foreign birds, and in colours that have never been bred in this country" he said.

They've done it with thrushes and blackbirds, and because it's easy to get a vet's certificate and go over to Belgium and bring birds into the country, people have brought back colour mutations and had quite a lot of success in breeding from them.

The prices of the birds haven't been astronomical and this has enabled them to be passed on to other softbill exhibitors, and now we are seeing a lot on the benches. You can now get classes of cinnamon thrushes with 16 in, whereas several years back you were lucky to see one or two.

And protectionist societies realise that you aren't going to find white and cinnamon thrushes and blackbirds in the wild, so people do feel a bit safer, though there is no reason why they shouldn't keep any of the other softbills.

If we all stick together in the society, and someone does have the misfortune to be put upon by the protectionist society, and we feel that member hasn't done anything wrong, that member is going to be in a lot stronger position if he or she has to go to court if they have the backing of the BSS.

They will have the backing of a lot of experts, who are going to be listened to more by a court than just a Mr Smith from down the road who keeps softbills. However, if someone wanted to belong to the society and we felt they were doing something wrong, they would be told about it and if that wasn't put right, they wouldn't be allowed to be a member."

A LAST CHANCE SALOON

According to BERNARD HOWLETT, winner of the best softbill at the National with a flighted blackbird hen, the current situation is a 'last chance saloon' for a side of the fancy under threat from several sides.

The current popularity of softbills, and the trend towards breeding colour variants and mutations, which are less likely to come under the scrutiny of conservation organisations, is an opportunity to rise above speculation about origins" he believes.

We have got the legislators and conservationists breathing down our necks, and if we don't get our act together and present ourselves in a professional manner we are not going to go very far" he said.

"We have got to get together and be more professional and present the public with standards that are for colour variants or bigger birds, and breed them and move forward.

We just can't stand still bickering about what has gone. We've just got to get on with it.

We have got the foundations and can build on that now before all these birds get slapped on Schedule 4, and we are left with only a few in aviaries. We want to jump ahead of all that and get our house in order before we have people coming round and knocking on our door and saying 'where did you get your birds from?'

"We've got one or two young people coming in, but we would like to have more, and if we go about this in a professional way we will encourage new people to come in because they are going to see the birds on the show bench and know they are aviary-bred and want to join. The more people we have, the stronger we will be."

The judging standards for 41 species were all written by myself, with the exception of the colour variants, these were composed by Bob Partridge.

A members' show of the British Softbill Society was held at Talke Pits Village Hall, Staffordshire on December 11th 2005, the judge was P. Jermy and was billed as the first ever show dedicated solely to softbills. On December 3rd in 2006, The British Softbill Society held an open show in conjunction with the East Anglian National, the judge was B. Robinson, it was a great success. The second members' show took place at the same venue as the first on December 10th 2006, the judge being B. Robinson, I was able to win it with a cinnamon blackbird hen.

On February 10th 2008, the members' show was held in conjunction with the Yorkshire British Bird and Hybrid Club's annual open show at Dalton, near Rotherham, the judges being Peter Beech and Brian Oliver.

The club presented a show in conjunction with the Eastern Federation in 2008 and 2009.

From 2007 friction between the BBS and Talke Pits overflowed, this resulted in both going their separate way. While Talke Pits flourished, the British Softbill Society 'withered on the vine'. In the British Softbill Society news update February 2008, the Society informed members, 'it is in no way connected with the Open Softbill show at Talke Pits, Staffordshire'.

Breeding reports for the 2004 and 2005 British Softbill Society breeding seasons for softbill species were reported as follows:

2004 - Song thrush 21, blackbird 28, mistle thrush 5, redwing 3, fieldfare 10, ring ouzel 8, dunnock 18, wheatear 38, stonechat 34, redstart 42, whinchat 18, nightingale 11, pied wagtail 21, grey wagtail 18, rock pipit 14, meadow pipit 24, skylark 12, blackcap 22, garden warbler 14, whitethroat 21, lesser whitethroat 14, nuthatch 18, long-tailed tit 15, marsh tit 18, coal tit 19, pied flycatcher 7 and spotted flycatcher 10.

2005 - Song thrush 41, blackbird 80, fieldfare 16, ring ouzel 9, dunnock 12, wheatear 45, stonechat 17, redstart 43, blackstart, 8,whinchat 10, nightingale 10, pied wagtail 32, grey wagtail 20, yellow wagtail 6, rock pipit 18, meadow pipit 17, tree pipit 12, skylark 13, blackcap 19, garden warbler 9, whitethroat 14, lesser whitethroat 9, nuthatch 15, long-tailed tit 19, marsh tit 21, coal tit 17, pied flycatcher 8 and spotted flycatcher 15. Surprising numbers! Breeding results thereafter are not available.

Photograph by Andrew Calvesbert

The Late Ron McCluskey - founder member and judge

Steve Dix, BSS Judge

Photograph by Andrew Calvesbert

Jason and Peter Jermy - BSS judges and founder members

BRITISH SOFTBILL SOCIETY
THE FUTURE

In early December 2011 I spoke with Peter Jermy about the British Softbill Society. I started off by asking him if the club was now defunct. He assured me that it was not and affiliation fees were still being paid by the club to the British Bird Council.

Peter went on to say that, due to difficult commitments, he and Jason Jermy had not been able to give much time to club affairs, but hoped this would change in the near future.

It would appear that the club will be reassessed in early 2012, when meetings will restart, and hopefully a club show, albeit on a smaller scale than hitherto will be staged.

For my part I hope this scenario will happen. As a founder member of the original set-up, I would be happy to help in any way I could. No doubt fewer small softbills would be available to show at any future event, due to harder enforcement of the laws by the authorities; this has put fanciers off from keeping them.

The line-breeding of small species takes time and the lifespan of individuals is far too short to be of much interest to breeders in such an atmosphere. Larger softbills and their mutations would form the greater part of any future event. NOTE: Robb Brown has offered to take up the reigns and a show is envisaged for 2013.

BRITISH SOFTBILL SOCIETY - MY REPORT

September 2004

Club officials, exhibitors and judges alike approached the 2004/2005 softbill show season with some reservations, following the formation of the British Softbill Society. Among the society's mandated aims was to elevate the status of insectivorous birds within the fancy, and to ensure that, as far as possible, only BSS-recommended judges adjudicate at softbill classes in major events.

The second of these aspirations soon caused anxiety in some quarters. Clubs felt they had every right to employ a judge of their choice, while the BSS points out that only judges approved by them were acceptable to a majority of its members. Although the BSS accepted that all the judges booked by major clubs for the ensuing show season were competent, some were seen by them as more so than others. Where BSS-recommended judges are not used, softbill entry numbers would fall. Where they are installed, softbill numbers would rise as a majority of BSS members will send teams to these events.

There would be no discrimination, however, by the BSS towards any member who decided to show under a judge not listed on their panel. In a free society, it is up to the individual to decide where to exhibit.

Overall, however, I predicted softbill numbers would rise during the year and be of a better standard than hitherto, this was indeed so. I also thought that, with more than forty members signed up with the BSS, more exhibitors would participate than ever before. Even where BSS judges were not involved, this also proved to be true.

It was thought that in time the new regime would bed in. Problems would gradually evaporate. New judges would gain the experience required and, if they wished, become accepted by the new society. The concept formulated by the founder members of the British Softbill Society was for the benefit of the fancy as a whole. It was thought that over time, it would win nationwide recognition and respect, and that the life of a softbill keeper could only be made more enjoyable by the existence of a unique and strong society promoting the hobby.

JUDGE'S WORK

New standards adopted for exhibition birds by the society would give judges the tools to do the job in hand - which is a difficult one - for the first time. The judges needed to assimilate in-depth knowledge of dozens of species. This involved hard work and dedication and was the only way a judge could gain respect. Poor judging would only result in poor numbers of exhibits being shown. Exhibitors, of course, must have faith that judges scrutinise each entry, according to the new standards.

In the past, it was usual for a hen normal-coloured blackbird to beat cocks on the benches. With un-flighted birds, it was almost impossible to win a special with a normal-coloured young cock. Normal males only become jet-black in their second or third year. This is also when their bill and eye-ring look their golden-yellow best.

At long last, cock and hen birds have an equal chance of winning, providing they are in good condition, and have size and type. Surely this must be good for the fancy. It should encourage exhibitors to show more blackbird cocks, flighted and un-flighted, than in the past. Such new thinking applies across the board, whatever the sex, species or variety.

CAGES ON SHOW

In the past large, beautifully decorated cages containing various mosses, heathers, etc., have caught the judges eye and have been given more credit than the exhibit itself.

A cage like this is worth 10 points, the same as one of smaller size with less decoration. It was hoped that BSS judges consider the bird and the cage, but make sure that it is the bird within the cage that is the more important, and points should be allocated accordingly. This, it was hoped, would unify the size of cages and concentrate the mind of the exhibitor on type. It might also encourage fanciers who are not gifted in cage artistry to show their birds with more optimism than before.

A fundamental cornerstone of the new society is strain building. It will encourage breeders to create line-bred strains of our popular softbills, in particular the small ones. It is hoped that these studs will contain colour variant varieties whenever possible. BSS experts will be on hand to advise on issues appertaining to breeding or exhibiting if required.

Most top exhibitors see it as a disgrace that no visible strains of colour-variant dunnock, for instance, exist within the fancy. The domestication of this small softbill in many colours should be a priority. This species, although unusual in some sexual habits, is easy to breed. It requires an earth-floored planted aviary, with ample supplies of insects or their larvae to raise young, and will rear three or four broods in a year. Species like the redstart are more freely bred now, and large classes of this beautiful species are expected at the main shows, but over time, the winners will come from line-bred strains.

COLOUR VARIANTS

Colour variants hold the key to domestication among the fancy's softbill species, no strain is complete without them. They send the right message to the authorities that birds with these genes are bona fide bred. They are an integral part of our culture. From the wild canary we have numerous breeds. From the wild budgerigar the same applies. The modern world as we know it is awash with mutations. Agriculture is built upon them, and almost every citizen in the land has or has had a mutant pet or has grown mutation flowers.

From time to time dissenting voices are heard from individuals who object to the propagation of colour variant British birds. Their views must be respected in a free society. Others however belch out propaganda on the matter when they themselves have kept animals or growing plants, some of which were variants. These people are summarily dismissed with the contempt they deserve, for theirs is a classic example of the 'pot calling the kettle black.'

BREEDERS' CLASSES

I would like to see classes known as 'breeders' classes listed in any schedule produced by the British Softbill Society, when promoting its annual open show. Unflighted classes, which are usually included in the schedules of most main softbill events, should also be included at BSS shows. Perhaps two breeders classes could be added in the short term, one for large and one for small normal-coloured softbills. Others, to include colour variants could be included later on. These new classes would attract owner-bred birds, the winners of which could be suitably rewarded with a nice prize, such as a medal. This would further encourage fanciers to breed their own strains. The regular unflighted classes would attract bought-in birds and birds otherwise acquired. Personally, I have found it more rewarding when I have won well with a bird I have bred than with one I have brought into my team from elsewhere.

BREEDING RECORDS

It is very important for breeders of our native birds to keep concise records of all transactions concerning stock and especially records of breeding, listing ring numbers and hatching dates, and of parents' ring numbers as well.

If an aviary-bred specimen is not ringed, then a

note to this effect should be made along with any relevant detail, such as a description of the bird. Evidence of breeding is vitally important, not only can it contribute to the overall healthy state of the fancy, but can often reveal the innocence of a breeder should a complaint arise.

Strain-breeding and exhibiting will bring about new thinking now, improving this branch of the hobby for the benefit of the fancy as a whole.

JACKDAW
Large softbill

Photograph by Dennis Avon

NUTHATCH
Small softbill

Photograph by Dennis Avon

GREAT GREY SHRIKE
Medium-sized softbill

Photograph by Sergey Yeliseev

MELODIOUS WARBLER
Rare softbill

Photograph by Tony Tilford

SATINETTE BLACKBIRD
Large colour variant

Photograph by Dennis Avon

CINNAMON BLACKBIRD

Clipping from
Cage & Aviary Birds.
Photo: Dennis Avon

This cock cinnamon blackbird owned and bred by Bernard Howlett is considered by experts to be the best ever seen.

CHAPTER ELEVEN

Miscellaneous

Photograph by Dennis Avon

Cinnamon Blackbird Hen

THE SNOW BUNTING CASE

written May 5th 2003

In 1988 a licence was granted to a named member of the British Bird Council to take some wild snow buntings. The RSPB became involved, having allegedly found discrepancies in the way the licence was handled. This led to court action, where the alleged offenders were found not guilty and costs were granted against the charity.

A licence was applied for to the Department of the Environment, to take nine female and eleven male snow buntings from the coast of Cleveland. The licence was granted on March 4th 1988, and recommended that the taking of the birds should be phased over three years.

The actual licence received was to take three female and five male snow buntings in 1988. It stipulated that a report must be forwarded to the Secretary of State, and that any birds caught must be ringed and registered (as the snow bunting was a Schedule 4 species). No adult bird could be taken between March 31st and August 31st 1988, and the birds must be used for captive breeding. The licence authorised L.S. Warrillow, the then president of the BBC, or his agent.

On March 10th 1988, 18 snow buntings were trapped by the agent. The agent took the birds home and after retaining three females and five males, he released the remainder. Although the DoE requested an update, none was received from the BBC until September 26th. This delay had in no way broken any condition of the licence, which was due to expire on December 31st 1988.

Photograph by Tommy Milner

Snow Bunting

Mr Warrillow was visited by Mr Robinson and Andrew Jones of the RSPB on September 27th 1988. They said they were making enquiries about snow buntings, and at this point Mr Jones cautioned Mr Warrillow.

It turned out that the DoE had sent a copy of the licence to the RSPB in March of that year. This arrangement was, in fact in order, however disturbing it may appear. Further interjections between the parties were made, resulting in the RSPBs solicitor writing to Mr Warrillow asking him to accept a caution on each of four related charges. The RSPBs caution meant nothing in law, the RSPB being a private body, and it was rejected out of hand.

Summonses were issued by the charity on November 9th 1988, at Hartlepool. Mr Warrillow was found not guilty on all counts and the RSPB was ordered to pay costs of £2,500. Mr Warrillow's agent, Graham Barrett, was similarly charged on two counts. He too had declined a caution. His case was also thrown out and costs of £700 were awarded against the RSPB.

A request for a further licence to take snow buntings was made by the BBC in February 1989, but as legal proceedings were in progress, the DoE did not consider it. The RSPB gave notice of appeal, but later decided not to do so.

The species was bred, I understand, by Fred Astles some years later. During the past few years steady progress has been made both here and on the continent with the species. In England Alan Britton, of the West Country, has bred and exhibited some very nice examples in recent years.

L S Warrillow

Newspaper clippings courtesy Cage & Aviary Birds

RSPB pays court costs

No case to answer result

THE Royal Society for the Protection of Birds was ordered to pay costs of £3,300 following a court case in Hartlepool on April 5, brought against Leslie Warrillow, at that time hon. life president of the British Bird Council, and Graham Barratt.

The case was brought after Leslie Warrillow, on behalf of the BBC, had been granted a licence by the Department of the Environment in February of 1988 to take eight Snow Buntings which were required by BBC members for breeding purposes. Two further licences were issued with the names of BBC members who would take charge of the birds when they were caught.

The RSPB brought the case on the grounds that offences had been committed in respect on non-compliance of the DoE licence to trap the Snow Buntings. The court heard that Barratt had trapped 18 birds and taken them home to determine their age and sex prior to releasing the surplus. The court was further told that it would have been dangerous for the birds, which were not required, to be freed immediately after capture. He chose eight birds and released the other ten back into the wild a few hours later.

Leslie Warrillow was cleared of the RSPB allegation that he had control of eight Snow Buntings which were not properly ringed and registered. Graham Barratt, who caught the birds under a DoE licence, was acquitted of taking ten birds unlawfully.

The magistrate ruled that there was no case to answer.

The RSPB appealed the judgment See clipping (left)

RSPB withdraws appeal against costs order

IN the May 27 issue you published an article in which I stated that I had been awarded costs of £2,500 against the RSPB over a case involving Snow Buntings. In a later issue it was reported that the RSPB had decided to appeal. I have now been advised by my solicitors that the RSPB is not proceeding with its appeal.

Thus the unwarranted pressure which Mr Barrett and myself have had to live with for the past six months has been lifted. The unjustified proceedings will leave a bitter taste, despite the fact that we were proved innocent of the charges, and the costs awarded were some recompense for the pressures and traumas to which we were subjected.

However, we did not profit from the costs awarded, except to be reimbursed for the expenses incurred in attending the court proceedings etc.

What of the future for the co-ordinated breeding programme of the Snow Bunting? In my article of May 27, I particularly mentioned some of the conditions under which the licence was granted, and I quote "...NCC consulted who are agreeable to a licence being granted; they recommend the taking of the birds be phased over a period of three years" and that the licence shall "apply over the next two years to take remaining birds. The birds shall not be taken except in Cleveland."

I have reason to believe that it was the intention for this agreement to be honoured by the DoE/NCC, and as this prosecution case has not shaken the *status quo* I would assume the DoE would not want to renege on its position.

I was most interested to read Bernard Howlett's article (October 7 issue) about breeding Redwings and Fieldfares and that captive-bred strains should be the aim of the BBC. Mr Howlett also referred to the breeding programmes involving Crossbill and Snow Bunting and how

he would enjoy being involved.

Although I must make quite clear I have now withdrawn my services from the British Bird Council, I feel most strongly that the Council should continue the co-ordinated breeding programme for Snow Buntings, thus keeping faith with the members originally involved in the scheme, and encouraging others of the calibre of Mr Howlett to participate.

If this is not done, then the sacrifice and traumatic experiences endured by Mr Barrett and myself will count for nought. Failure to act could also give comfort and succour to the RSPB.

LESLIE WARRILLOW
Kingston-upon-Thames.

Published: December 2nd 1989

IN MEMORY OF

Ron McCluskey - 1936-2011 (June)

The fancy has lost a formidable exponent of aviculture in the passing of Ron McCluskey, and our thoughts are with his widow Anne and family at this sad time.

Ron was a dedicated breeder and exhibitor of British birds, notably softbills - a Goliath in birdkeeping terms. One who, with unparalleled expertise rose to the top of the softbill community and remained there for more than 50 years. He will be greatly missed - an irreplaceable cornerstone of our hobby.

Ron was a lovely man, quietly spoken, dedicated to the fancy and hard working. He loved travelling to England - sometimes with his dog for company - driving hundreds of miles in all conditions with his birds. He supported many clubs year-in and year-out. Their softbill stands will never be the same now he has gone. Gone with him are his wonderful blackbirds and thrushes, all perfectly trained for the shows.

He won an enormous number of top prizes including the British Open championship at the Scottish National. Most of all he won the respect from all who knew him.
Many friends mourn his passing.

I knew Ron well and visited him and Anne at their Bedford address and later at their Scottish home. We were fierce combatants, but there was never a harsh word between us in all those years. He was a mentor to many. He was my mentor and my friend.

Farewell Ron, your suffering has left you.
Rest in peace, dear friend,
where birds are sweetly singing.
Bernard Howlett.

On the morning of Ron's death I was first contacted by Mark Milligan with the news, then by Bob Hastie. Bob asked if I would write an obituary for Ron on behalf of the family. Later on Bob thanked me for my effort.

Photograph by Andrew Calvesbert

QUESTIONS AND ANSWERS
GOLDFINCHES

Caring for my goldie

BRITISH BIRDS

RECENTLY, I bought a goldfinch cock, together with a small dome-shaped cage to take the bird home from the show, which I hang on an outside wall. I need to know whether there is a proper type of cage for this type of bird.

Also, what is the proper diet and what supplements do I need to feed him to keep in peak condition?
S.C., Staffs

Bernard Howlett, leading exhibitor and show judge, replies: For a pet goldfinch, any well-made cage will suffice – ornamental or otherwise – provided it is large enough for the bird to stretch its wings fully,

with perhaps a little room to spare in all directions.

No doubt you have assessed the situation regarding predators such as cats and sparrowhawks, which will, of course, attack a bird in its outdoor cage if they locate it.

I would feed the bird a plain seed diet consisting of a canary mixture, rape and linseed, avoiding too many oil-based seeds such as hemp, niger and gold of pleasure. These can be fed, as a treat, from time to time.

Supply cuttlefish-bone, grit and fresh water, to which can be added a liquid calcium solution, bearing in mind the guidelines for doses on the container. Goldfinches relish fresh chickweed, dandelion, etc, and also apple or pear.

Goldfinch breeding basics

BRITISH BIRDS

I HAVE been given a present of a pair of goldfinches and am almost certain that I have a cock and hen. I do have some experience of breeding canaries, but feel that I need some expert advice on breeding these goldfinches. Can I breed them in a canary breeding cage, or do I need to build a flight? Also, what food would they need during the breeding season?
P.W., Dublin.

Bernard Howlett, world champion British bird exhibitor, replies:
Goldfinches can be bred in cage or aviary – I prefer small, outside flights. If you're cage-breeding, the cock bird should be removed after mating before an egg is laid, and each egg replaced by a dummy until the clutch is full. The cock can be

returned when the chicks are two or three days old.

You can use secluded wicker baskets. Incubation is 12-14 days. Young are in the nest for 12-15 days, and are dependent on adults for a further week or so afterwards. Be sure they are weaned before removing them from their parents.

A good, fairly plain seed should be available, together with soaked seed. Offer plenty of dandelion heads, sowthistle, teasel, etc, firmly placed in a container with a little water to keep fresh. Also offer a variety of livefood, which is essential to rearing in the wild.

In outside flights, house one pair in each, with no other birds. Nest-sites and livefood stations should be under cover. The beautifully constructed nest can include moss, lichens, down, hair and feathers, with cobwebs to bind the intricate structure together.

BRITISH BIRDS

HOW can I sex my goldfinches?
A.K., via email.

Bernard Howlett, leading British birds exhibitor, replies: The sexes are very similar but the slightly brighter red blaze of the male extends beyond the level of the eye, while in the hen the red reaches only to the lower eyelid. In the male, the cap and nape are black; in the female they are tinged with grey. His cheek-patches are white; hers are smoky grey. Males have black nostril bristles; females brown.

Goldfinch diet

I'M HAVING trouble keeping my goldfinches alive for any length of time. I feed them canary mix, eggfood, iodine block, grit, chickweed and cuttlefish-bone. Should I offer something else?
R.E., via email.

I ASSUME you are referring to young goldfinches, and if so I would try a varied British seed mixture, and a good-quality soaked seed mix, with added hemp, niger, chicory, teasel and safflower. Livefood is also essential, and this can be purchased from commercial supplies. Also try to add any greenfly etc that you are able to find.

As a precaution from a wasting disease known within the fancy as "going light", I would advise obtaining a sulphur drug from your avian vet. Add this to the drinking water before the birds breed, and later to the chicks for a period of time. It is effective against protozoan parasite which can cause this wasting ailment.

**British birds, mules & hybrids
Bernard Howlett**
Has kept birds for 50 years and is a qualified show judge.

BULLFINCHES

What's the truth about bullfinch pairings?

BRITISH BIRDS

WHY is it now said that a bullfinch cock cannot hybridise with other British birds? In a book from 1926 it said records exist of successful bullfinch x goldfinch and bullfinch x redpoll matings.

Also, can a British bullfinch cock be mated to a northern bullfinch hen to keep size and colour, and in what class could they be shown?
M.A., West Midlands.

 Bernard Howlett, World Show gold medallist, replies: The male bullfinch (*Pyrrhula pyrrhula*) has evolved in such a way that makes it almost impossible for it to successfully hybridise with any other species. Scientists are of the opinion that this bird has never fathered young from any other than its own kind.

The sperm of the male bullfinch has a slightly different shape to that of any other seedeater. Evolution of this species dictates that it generally mates for life, and perhaps due to this fact it has a low sperm count, and has no need to mate (copulate) often.

When using the bullfinch in hybridising or muling, writers have, on very rare occasions, mentioned the bullfinch first (which relates to the cock bird used in the mating) in error, when successful breedings were being described.

Northern bullfinches are of the same species as our bird and will successfully breed with them. (A male northern bullfinch will fertilise the eggs of our small British or Irish hens.) Northern bullfinches can be shown in the "northern" classes, and mules and hybrids can be exhibited in the regular or northern classes, depending on the rules of the promoting society.

Bullfinch pairs

Q WOULD two pairs of bullfinches breed in the same aviary? Could two bullfinch hens be paired to one bullfinch cock in one aviary? And would a pair of bullfinches breed in a breeding cage?

T.B. Cleveland

A IN A very large aviary, two pairs of bullfinches may each rear young. I advise, however, an aviary to each pair. Here again, your suggested trio might be successful, but since bullfinches pair for life in the wild, I suggest one cock to one hen. On the Continent, large numbers of these birds are bred in cages. A double breeding cage should do nicely.

**British birds, mules & hybrids
Bernard Howlett**
Has kept birds for more than 50 years and is a qualified show judge.

British winner?

Q COULD a Siberian bullfinch or its hybrid take a best British bird award?

J.D. Surrey

A SUCH a bird could win the top award. It depends on the relevant rules set out in the club's schedule. Most clubs provide northern classes for these birds and stipulate that they cannot win main awards. However, many birds with northern blood are entered in the main classes, and are subjected to the whims of the judge.

Incomplete moult

A FRIEND who breeds bullfinches once told me he bred a cock that left the nest very late, at the end of September, and didn't seem to complete its first moult. Is there anything I can do to encourage such birds to moult fully?

– R.A., Dublin.

AS A rule, bullfinches breed in late April and May, so the bird you mention was extremely late in fledging. Birds must be fit and healthy to face the moult. Slow moults are generally caused by dietary deficiencies, and products to promote a healthy moult can be found in the market place. A more natural diet can help, too. Feed the birds on tree-seeds, weeds and berries, buds of fruit frees in late winter and early spring and caterpillars when they have young, to boost their usual aviary foods.

**British birds, mules & hybrids
Bernard Howlett**
Has kept birds for 50 years and is a qualified show judge.

BULLFINCHES

Fighting bullfinches

Q I HAVE a pair of northern bullfinches, housed together in a 2.4m x 1.8m x 1.8m (8ft x 6ft x 6ft) outdoor flight since November 2005, but there has been no sign of breeding. Recently they have been fighting a lot, resulting in feathers being plucked and bald heads. One day I witnessed them feeding each and then continue fighting. She chases him all over the place. Is this normal, or should I give up on this pair ever breeding?

S.M. *Kent*

A I AM of the view that wild bullfinches mate for life, with the cock bird being very attentive to its mate at all times. Your pair is not displaying normal behaviour.

Aviary conditions restrict movement, which is part of the problem, as sometimes birds need their own space. Your flight is of good size, but needs to be furnished with plenty of plant material, constructed in such a way as to mimic a small thicket, so that a bird subjected to harassment can hide. Eventually, normality will reign.

Two separate food and water stations situated well apart should be provided together with wild buds and a varied diet to bring about breeding condition.

**British birds, mules & hybrids
Bernard Howlett**
Has kept birds for more than 50 years and is a qualified show judge.

BRITISH BIRDS

HAVING bred two young normal bullfinches the hen refused to feed them, so from six days old I hand-reared them on a commercial mix that I have used to rear other birds. All was well until the birds were just starting to peck for themselves. Then one morning one of the birds was on the cage floor on its side. It was still alive, but seemed unable to support itself on its legs. Soon after this it died, yet the other bird is fine with no problems. Have you any idea what could cause this? There was no actual injury to the bird.
D.E., Cleveland

Bernard Howlett, top exhibitor and show judge, says: Although your feeding regime may be adequate in most cases, I believe there may have been some deficiency in this instance. Birds require sodium, potassium, calcium and magnesium, vital for a healthy nervous system. You should consult a vet for a more in-depth answer.

BRITISH BIRDS

A FRIEND of mine bought in a pair of Siberian bullfinches this year to breed with and they have turned out to be both very tame and excellent parents, producing two broods. However, he has hit a major snag with both sets of nestlings when it has come to closed-ringing them. Shortly after they were ringed and put back into the nest, he went back out to find them on the aviary floor. Within minutes of returning them to the nest, he found them ejected again – it appeared that the hen didn't like the rings on the chicks' legs. Fortunately, after that she accepted them and raised three superb chicks.

Everything went perfectly with the second brood until my friend ringed the chicks, and again found the hen ejected them immediately after. The hen broke the leg of one of the chicks when trying to get the ring off its leg. Luckily my friend has been able to foster the chicks out under canaries.

Both of the parent birds are very placid and feed the chicks non-stop,

BRITISH BIRDS

WHAT would cure gape in bullfinches?
K.B., North Yorks.

Bernard Howlett, world champion British bird showman, replies: I use Mycoform-T, which has been developed by Aviform for respiratory difficulties in pigeons, but is very useful in the treatment of respiratory problems in the bullfinch when problems occur within its throat pouches. The feeding of hemp, I find, aggravates this problem.

The Bird Care Company also offers products made to ease this problem. And ivermectin will greatly help with air-sac mites in hardbills.

---

but the hen simply cannot accept the closed rings on the chicks' legs. Perhaps it's the white lettering. Is this a common problem, and is there a way around it?
Derek Faulkner, Kent.

Bernard Howlett, eminent breeder of British birds, replies: You write a sad tale. This phenomenon happens all too frequently with bullfinches. Sometimes it occurs with a single hen within a stud. Various methods are used by keepers in order to prevent these injuries.

One such method is to cover the ring with dirt, and another is to use tiny rubber bands (which are sometimes provided with puncture kits for cycles). These are placed over the ring to hide it. A third is to cover the ring with nail vanish.

Lastly, a method I sometimes use is to ring chicks a day earlier than usual. I place a tiny piece of twig (the length of the width of the ring) between the ring and the leg. If a parent pulls at the ring soon after ringing, the ring will come off and the chick will not be harmed. After a couple of days the twig will fall out, or it can be taken away when the parents are no longer interested in the ring. All are said to help discourage the hen from noticing or nibbling at the ring, or hurting the chick.

The problem appears to be the hen's sighting of the ring on the leg, and it would seem that lettering or colour makes no difference. After ringing it is advisable to tuck the legs under each chick when returning them to the nest so rings are not visible, at least for a short while after ringing.

GREENFINCHES

BRITISH BIRDS

WHEN you're breeding with pied greenfinches, do the young show pied straight away or, like pied diamond doves, does it take several months to show? S.P., Devon.

Bernard Howlett, experienced breeder of British birds replies: The genetic make-up of variegated (pied) greenfinches is not fully understood. However, both recessive and dominant modes of inheritance are present in the general population and this allows for specimens born with the visual mutation to express their variegation as soon as the feathers appear – that is, straight away.

Greenfinch pairings

WHAT offspring could I expect from a silver cock x cinnamon hen greenfinch, from which I have bred nine? Five appear to be silver, four possibly normal. Are they sex-linked for colour?
D.K., via email

FROM this pairing you can expect to breed cocks split for silver and cinnamon, and silver hens. Silver and cinnamon are both sex-linked mutations.

British birds, mules and hybrids
Bernard Howlett
Has kept birds for 50 years and is a qualified show judge.

Greenfinch pairings

CAN you tell me the expected offspring of some greenfinch pairings – and inform me whether these pairings are correct, or if I could pair them better another way?

1. Pastel cock x normal hen
2. Agate/isabel/lutino cock x isabel hen
3. Silver/lutino cock x lutino hen
4. Opal cock x normal hen
5. Normal cock x cinnamon hen.
P.H. Warwickshire

1. FROM this pairing you will breed normal/pastel cocks and pastel hens.
2. In this coupling the cocks will be agate/isabel, isabel, agate/lutino, isabel/satinette and agate/isabel/lutino, the hens will be agate, isabel, lutino and satinette (sex-linked).
3. Cocks here will be silver/lutino and lutino, hens will be silver and lutino (sex-linked).
4. Opal is unknown to me in the greenfinch. If you have one, it will be recessive, progeny will all be normal/opals.
5. This pairing will produce normal/cinnamon cocks and normal hens (sex-linked).

Agate and silver are one and the same. This and isabel are dilutes. As a rule, parents that are themselves dilute are unable to produce normals.
– B.H.

Grand old bird

Q WE HAVE a greenfinch cock that is 13 years old. Is this a record, or is it usual for this type of finch? He is in lovely condition and has paired to a hen, but I am curious as to whether he is too old to breed.
P.G. Via e-mail

A THIRTEEN years is a great age for your greenfinch; seven or eight is not uncommon in confinement. In the wild, greenfinches live for one or two years on average.
    Fertility declines with age, but with a fit bird it is likely that some eggs will be filled.

British birds, mules & hybrids
Bernard Howlett
Has kept birds for more than 50 years and is a qualified show judge.

GREENFINCHES

Which native hardbill species should I breed?

BRITISH BIRDS

I'M NEW to birdkeeping, but I am a long-term birdwatcher/naturalist.

I'm particularly interested in breeding native species – hardbills especially. Is there a species that you'd recommend for a novice?
M.M., via email.

Bernard Howlett, eminent breeder of British birds, replies: I would recommend the greenfinch as a suitable species to begin with. The bird is domesticated and is kept widely with numerous colour varieties,

making it easy to keep and breed.

The greenfinch can be raised in a roomy birdroom cage, an outside flight or aviary. A pair of these birds can be bought for as little as £40.

They are long-lived and will produce two or more rounds of chicks each year. The main setback from a health point of view is a tendency of specimens losing weight and becoming ill. This problem is known as "going light" within the fancy. It can be treated with sulpha drugs, which can usually be obtained from your local vet. I recommend you consider joining a club where you will find that the greenfinch is a common bird among its members.

BRITISH BIRDS

EVERY year for the past three years, I have lost 10-15 young greenfinches through "going light". Two vets wanted the dead birds for post mortems before they would issue medicine. Can anything be bought without all the red tape?

Also, can I breed mealy redpolls in a group of four pairs in a flight? I had my first pair this year, and there was no sign of nesting after three weeks in a double breeder. I put them in the flight and the hen built a nest and reared four chicks.

The cock was very aggressive to the pair of greenfinches in there, and nearly killed a red dimorphic cock canary. I put them back in a cage, and they have done nothing for the rest of the season. Is he a rogue bird, or are all redpolls that aggressive?
A.M., via email.

Bernard Howlett, experienced British bird breeder, replies: After the post mortems have been carried out, your vet will no doubt prescribe sulpha drugs for your birds, such as a sulphadimidine sodium, and you will need to follow instructions. When further supplies are required, these are usually made available without the need for more examinations.

"Going light" syndrome is caused in most cases by the protozoan parasites *Lankesterella* and *Coccoidian isospora*. Adults should be treated before the eggs hatch. If not, parent birds will feed the parasite(s) to their chicks.

It's a pied puzzle

Q I PAIRED a normal greenfinch cock, which is a carrier for pied, to a normal hen I bred, which as far as I know does not carry pied. They had 11 young, of which two were pied, one with pied tail and the other with pied flight feathers.

Does this mean the hen is a carrier and the rest of the young are carriers?
R.S. Shropshire

A I AM not aware of any sex-linked strains of pied greenfinches. Those I know are recessive, dominant, or a combination of the two. Dominant birds are always visual. Your strain is most likely to be recessive.

In either case – sex-linked or recessive – the nine youngsters that are not visually one of these, will be completely normal or a carrier. Only test-mating can tell.

If, however, one or both of your pied young are cocks, then your old hen is a carrier for the recessive gene. The other nine chicks will still have to be test-mated to find out whether they are also carriers of this gene.

If both pied chicks are hens, then the strain could be either sex-linked or recessive in its mode of inheritance. Further breedings would be needed to determine the issue.

Carrier, sex-linked cocks cannot produce visual young males when mated to a completely normal bird.

British birds, mules & hybrids
Bernard Howlett
Has kept birds for more than 50 years and is a qualified show judge.

Greenfinch pairing

I HAVE paired a visual normal/satinette greenfinch cock to a normal hen. Could you please tell me what colour young to expect?

R.S., Shropshire

YOUR description "visual normal/satinette" conjures some confusion in my mind. From a visual satinette cock you will breed split cocks and satinette hens. From a split cock you will breed split cocks, normal cocks, normal hens and visual satinette hens.

In greenfinches, satinette is a sex-linked mutation.

British birds, mules and hybrids
Bernard Howlett
Has kept birds for 50 years and is a qualified show judge.

LINNETS AND REDPOLLS

Redpoll deaths

MY LESSER redpoll cock, bred last year, has killed his young when they were on the sticks. Is it normal for young cocks to do this, and could he do it again?
R.S., Shropshire

INFANTICIDE is not normal, but nevertheless it happens. The reasons for such behaviour are complex and not easily understood. It may be your redpoll found his chicks a threat, or without them being around he would be able to mate again.

If you decide to breed with him again, I would advise that he is removed from the breeding-pen when the chicks hatch, to prevent such a tragedy occurring again.

**British birds, mules & hybrids
Bernard Howlett**
Has kept birds for 50 years and is a qualified show judge.

BRITISH BIRDS

I HAVE three pairs of redpolls in separate aviaries that measure 0.9m x 0.9m x 1.8m high (3ft x 3ft x 6ft). I feed them on British finch mix, eggfood, and soak seed, and I also give them dandelion heads. However, they haven't bred yet, so could you tell me what I'm doing wrong?
T.F., via email.

Bernard Howlett, leading British bird breeder, replies: Redpolls often breed through July into August, so you may yet have a brood. It is possible, however, that your pairs are of the same sex. To sex them, you need to blow the feathers around the vent of each bird to reveal the gender. If there is a tubular protrusion, the bird is a male, whereas if the ventral area is flat, the bird is a female.

Add small mealworms and waxmoth larvae to the diet just before the eggs are due to hatch. Good luck!

Can I improve my linnets' red plumage?

BRITISH BIRDS

I HAVE recently purchased two hand-reared linnets, but they are not that red in plumage. I have been given a couple of tips on how to improve the red in my birds, but none are certain to work. Is there anything I could feed my birds to ensure they get a full red plumage?
N.B., Kent.

Bernard Howlett, top British bird exhibitor, says: Linnets obtain their colour from the seeds and insects they consume. Their colour is dull during the non-breeding season, but as soon as the hot sun reveals itself, its ultraviolet radiation unmasks the redness in their feathers.

Aviary linnets remain dull during the breeding season because they are not subjected to the sun's rays in the same way as their wild counterparts.

If, for instance you had an incredibly large aviary out in the open, then the linnets within it would become as red as the wild ones.

Feeding within normal aviary conditions will not bring about this desired effect. The red pigment is already there, only the hot sun will bring it out.

Subsequently, linnets living in "sun-traps" are redder than those accustomed to the shade.

Mealy redpolls

Q I HAVE recently purchased a pair of mealy redpolls. The hen has white flight feathers – is she pied? Could you give me some advice on their diet and whether it is best to breed them in a cage or in my flight, which contains a pair of greenies and a pair of siskins?
P.B. Via e-mail

A PIED redpolls are being developed. They have white spots on their heads and shoulders. Your bird is not pied; its 'white' wings are probably due to a metabolic imbalance.

Their basic diet is British finch mixture, to which niger and condition seed can be added. Soaked seed is important and should include hemp, rape and Red Band pigeon mixture.

Softfood is also essential and to this can be added glucose, hard-boiled egg, vitamins and minerals. Perilla seed supplied in a separate dish will add medicinal properties to the diet. Supply clean dandelion, chickweed and so on when available, especially when breeding. Some pairs may take small mealworms and cleaned maggots.

It is best, in your circumstances, to breed your mealy redpolls in a suitable cage.

**British birds, mules & hybrids
Bernard Howlett**
Has kept birds for more than 50 years and is a qualified show judge.

SISKINS AND SERINS

FINCHES

I WOULD like to house some European serins and siskins in my planted aviary, which measures 3m x 2m x 3m (10ft x 6ft 6in x 10ft). It already holds two canaries.

I've been told that my new finches are rather difficult to breed, so can you give me some tips about them? For example, the best type of nest and the plants or trees they favour?

Should I breed them as pairs, or – for example – run a male with four females? And is there any behaviour in particular I should keep an eye on?
G.T., Northants.

Bernard Howlett, leading British birds breeder, replies: European serins and siskins are lively and eager breeders in captivity if suitably housed in cage or aviary. Outside, I recommend they are kept in small flights, one pair only in each. That deals with most potential behavioural problems.

The species will frequent all manner of trees, but serins tend to prefer broad-leaved trees while siskins favour conifers. However trees or bushes are not too important in a flight.

In the spring, when your birds are established, nest sites in the form of wicker baskets, placed in protected locations, can be screened by bunches of foliage.

Nesting materials can include those that are available on the market, together with moss, lichen, cobwebs, hair and feathers.

In the wild, a large amount of livefood is consumed when chicks are in the nest, so bear this in mind and add it to their diet of seed, soaked seed and eggfood. Also supply greenfood such as chickweed at this time.

BRITISH BIRDS

I HAVE recently obtained a pair of mutation siskins. The cock bird is a cinnamon brown and the hen a green agate, both I believe single factor. What description would the offspring be? Also I have a very successful pair consisting of a yellow cock (double factor) with a normal hen, which produced pastels. Would it pay me to pair the yellow cock to the new green agate hen and the brown cock to the normal hen? What would each pair produce?
A.K., Hereford.

Bernard Howlett, eminent breeder of British birds, replies: Progeny from the cinnamon brown x green agate (sex-linked mutations) will be cinnamon brown hens and cocks split for cinnamon brown and for green agate.

Pairing the yellow (double factor dominant cock) to the agate hen would produce single factor young of both sexes, the cocks of which would be split for agate. Pairing the brown cock to the normal hen would give you brown hens and cocks split for brown.

I advise you to breed good-quality cinnamon browns (cinnamons), yellow and pastel siskins (double and single factors) and agates. In other words, continue breeding with your present pairs.

Sisterly siskins

Q I HAVE been breeding siskins for the past five years and now have very good stock. This year, one of my pairs of blue siskins hatched five chicks, but sadly the cock died, so the hen had to feed all five herself. One of the other hens, which did not breed this year, also started to feed the chicks. At first the mother hen chased her off but after a while accepted her help.
Is this unusual?

R.E. Bath

A YOU tell an interesting tale. It is unusual in my view for an unrelated siskin hen to feed in this way, but not unheard of. I expect this phenomenon occurs elsewhere from time to time within the fancy, brought about, no doubt, by an overwhelming desire to breed.

Other similar scenarios exist where first-round young have been known to feed their smaller siblings, and in some birds, only a few pairs of a group will breed, with all members of that group helping to raise the chicks and therefore perpetuate the species.

**British birds, mules & hybrids
Bernard Howlett**
Has kept birds for more than 50 years and is a qualified show judge.

BRITISH BIRDS

WILL visual pastel siskins be sex-linked, i.e. through colour?
A.K., via email.

Bernard Howlett, leading British bird exhibitor, replies: Not sex-linked but dominant, therefore only a visual bird can breed a visual bird, and no normal coloured bird will carry.

MULES AND HYBRIDS

Muling a greenfinch

Q I HAVE been breeding finches and canaries for four years now and have just got myself a greenfinch cock, which I want to cross with a canary. With which canary breed would it be best to cross him, and should he be removed when she is sitting? They will be in a large breeding cage.

P.W. Via email

A GREENFINCH cocks are not prolific mulers; they can, however, be paired to any variety of canary. They can be left in the breeding cage throughout the nesting season.

Norwich canary hens are the best at producing high-class exhibition mules. Smaller kinds can be used to produce miniature mules, also for shows, or as pets for their song and pleasing ways.

British birds, mules & hybrids
Bernard Howlett
Has kept birds for more than 50 years and is a qualified show judge.

Breeding mules

Q I HAVE been told that when breeding mules you have to use a canary hen with a wild bird? Can you also use canary cocks with hens? What will then be the ideal crossing?

R.H. Via e-mail

A AS FAR as European finches are concerned many wonderful mules are bred each year using cock canaries. I have in mind canary x bullfinch, canary x crossbill and canary x greenfinch; all these are ideal. Other crossings using canary cocks, with limited success, include the canary x goldfinch.

Niger seed

Q IS IT safe to feed niger seed to my mules?

P.A. Notts

A NIGER seed (*Guizotia abyssinica*) is a native of Ethiopia, and is cultivated in warm climes as an oil seed for feeding to cage birds. The oil from it is used for cooking and paint.

Known to fanciers as 'black death', it was once used as a bait to catch wild birds. After caging, the seed was replaced by plainer varieties, because if fed extensively to cage birds it will kill them, through damage to vital organs such as the kidneys.

Niger seed is often fed to wild birds, which will gorge on it to their detriment. Feeders are manufactured for its use, but health warnings should accompany them.

When fed to cage birds, seeds should be mixed and contain 3½ parts of niger only; others in the mix can be black rape, red rape, white millet and so on. It is said to tighten the feathers and to assist in sleekness in a bird. It should never be overfed.

British birds, mules & hybrids
Bernard Howlett
Has kept birds for more than 50 years and is a qualified show judge.

Breeding the mules you want

Q COULD you please give some advice on breeding goldfinch and bullfinch mules.

R.R. Via email

A A GOLDFINCH cock two or three years old is ideal. Place it in a double breeder, in the winter, with a canary hen – Norwich for size, a coloured canary for colour, or a small yellow canary, such as a roller, for song.

When the canary hen attains breeding condition, replace the goldfinch with a canary cock (goldfinches breed later than canaries) and rear a brood of canaries with the cock bird. Remove the chicks when they are viable.

When the canary hen is ready to breed again, reintroduce the goldfinch. After mating, remove the goldfinch and replace the egg with a dummy one, then return the goldfinch. Repeat this procedure until the clutch is complete, then replace the dummy eggs with the live ones. After the chicks have hatched, allow the goldfinch to assist in their rearing. A canary cock x goldfinch hen is seldom used.

The sperm of the bullfinch is incompatible with any hen other than of its own kind, therefore the canary must be the male. Proceed as with goldfinch mules.

Fertile eggs can be fostered out. Often, supplementary hand-feeding is advisable.

A good seed mixture with added vitamins and minerals, including calcium and grit, should be given, together with livefood, soaked seed, eggfood and plant material such as dandelion heads, chickweed and sowthistle when in season.

British birds, mules & hybrids
Bernard Howlett
Has kept birds for more than 50 years and is a qualified show judge.

White mules

Q HAVING kept and bred birds for many years now, I decided four or five years ago to try breeding a few goldfinch x canary mules. I always used white Fife hens, hoping that some of the young would carry some white from the hen. It seemed I was correct in this assumption since most of the mules had either white collars or white other bits and pieces.

But I was talking to a bird breeder recently, who told me that the hen plays no part in the influence of the colour of its young. Is this correct and, if so, where has the white in my birds come from? I bred 21 mules in 2005 with a very good percentage having white markings somewhere or other.

K.B. North Yorks

A YOU pose an interesting question! In aviculture we refer to three modes of inheritance; we loosely call these sex-linked, recessive and dominant. Your friend was probably referring to the first two, since even visual variant hens cannot reproduce their visual colour in their offspring, when mated to completely normal birds. They can of course, produce splits: cocks in the first mentioned and cocks and hens in the second.

Dominant birds can, however, reproduce their visual colour in their offspring. But your stock has its limitations in this regard, and is only partially or co-dominant, allowing you to produce 'pied' birds only.

British birds, mules & hybrids
Bernard Howlett
Has kept birds for more than 50 years and is a qualified show judge.

MULES AND HYBRIDS

MULES

I HAVE a question that nobody seems to know the answer to. After a late start to the breeding season, I paired up my natives and my canaries. I had some spare birds left, which were put together in a flight cage. These were greenfinch cocks, bullfinch cocks and mules – four of which were redpoll mules and they were all nest mates.

One day I noticed one of the mule hens was carrying some nest material. After observing her for a while, I decided to put her with a cock canary so I could use her as a foster mother for some hybrids. I was hoping to breed, but when I put the cock canary in with her, he started to beat her, as did four other cock canaries I tried her with.

I decided to put another mule in with her, who was her brother. When I put them together the cock started to sing the roller canary song at his sister. Then he proceeded to feed her. They built a nest and shortly after the hen mule laid five eggs. The eggs were redpoll eggs, but slightly bigger. Because the parents were both mules, which I have been told from the age of five are not fertile, I put one of my roller canary's eggs under the mule hen along with her own five eggs to see if she would be a good foster mother.

After 10 days I had a look at the eggs and to my surprise they appeared to be full. Three days later, all six eggs hatched, but as soon as I saw them I could see the difference between the five baby mules and the roller canaries (who were pink-skinned compared to the black-skinned mules). I then removed the canary chick back to its real mother to give the young mules a better chance.

To my delight, both cock and hen mules were great parents and they reared all five chicks. At this point the chicks are 20 days old. The grandparents of these chicks are a cinnamon variegated roller canary hen and a normal redpoll cock.

Everybody I have asked says they have never heard of a mule being fertile and that it may well be a first. Have two mules every paired up before and had young, or is this a first? Will these chicks be fertile? Also, should I colour-feed them?
R. O Connor, Ireland.

Bernard Howlett, eminent breeder of British birds, replies: I will answer your three questions first, before attempting to analyse your letter and the events described therein.

Q. Have two mules paired up before and had young?
A. Yes.
Q. Will these chicks be fertile?
A. Maybe.
Q. Should I colour-feed them?
A. It's up to you!

Coloured canaries are basically mules, their ancestors propagated from a siskin and a canary. I also have personal knowledge of a fertile "mule" between a siskin and a siskin mule. If your birds are mules bred from mules some maybe fertile – especially the males.

Colour-feeding would enhance such birds, but they would be of no value on the show bench. Show mules must have 50 per cent of each of their unrelated pure "species" parents – yours do not.

If these birds are truly mules bred from mules, then your achievement is remarkable. No doubt the colour of the chicks has come down from their cinnamon variegated grandmother. If you wish, you could breed a new "fancy" bird by pairing son to mother and father to daughter next spring, thereafter gradually developing a strain using distant relatives paired together. Any strain built up could be named as a new something, perhaps canary.

BRITISH & HYBRIDS

I KNOW that a lot of fanciers cross British finches with canaries (the result being mules) or with other finches (hybrids). My question is could this be done with wagtails, or has it already been? Could a young pied and grey

Bernard Howlett replies: The best way to breed hybrids is to pair closely related species together. The pied and grey wagtails fall into this category, since they are in the same genus, *Motacilla*. They have indeed been bred in the past – J. Craig showed an example of a grey x pied hybrid at the Scottish National in 1964. The yellow x pied wagtail hybrid has also been bred.

Might my mule be fertile?

BRITISH BIRDS

I HAVE a goldfinch mule that does not sing. I've tested it and found it to be a hen bird. I thought goldfinch mules were cocks and have been told they are sterile. If it is a hen, would it be sterile?
G.D., Hemel Hempstead.

Bernard Howlett, eminent breeder of British birds, replies: Both male and female goldfinch mules are almost always infertile. On very rare occasions a fertile mule is bred, perhaps once in a lifetime – they can be used as fosters. Paired together they will often build a nest and lay a clutch of eggs. If you exchange these eggs for fertile ones, perhaps canaries', the mules would incubate them. They would probably also rear any chicks that hatch.

Keeping corvids

Q I AM thinking about keeping British jays and magpies and was wondering if you could recommend a book or some other source of information on their care and management, such as housing, feeding and breeding. I would like to find out as much information about the care of these birds as I can before I acquire them.

M.P. Via e-mail

A ALTHOUGH a lot can be learned from bird books, those dealing with aviculture leave much to be desired.

Jays and magpies require spacious flights with some protection from the weather. Although foods are available on the market, I fed mine on poultry pellets as a staple diet, together with dead rabbit, rat, day-old chicks and mice. I added fruit and berries (especially acorns for the jays) and clean water.

Some imagination is required so far as the construction of nest sites is concerned. Open boxes can be included for jays, fixed behind or within Scots pine brush to give privacy. For the magpies, bushes growing naturally within the aviary, or part of a dead one, such as thorn, positioned near the roof will entice the birds to build.

The jays will require small sticks, grasses, mud and animal hair; the magpies, sticks about 60cm (2ft) long (old pigeon nests are handy), mud and grasses.

The chicks can be fed on invertebrates, indigenous or otherwise, and carrion as I mentioned.

British birds, mules & hybrids
Bernard Howlett
Has kept birds for more than 50 years and is a qualified show judge.

BRITISH BIRDS

I HAVE purchased a pair of redstarts that I'm keeping indoors during the winter. I'm feeding them on a mixture of CeDe and Orlux softfood pate, along with a pinch of Birdcare Daily Essential3, with hardboiled egg yolk, grated cheese and either cress or broccoli, although it's only the hen that will take the latter. I also add Aviform gold plus to the drinking water. Is there anything else that you would advice me to do?
W.O., Scotland.

Bernard Howlett, top exhibitor and show judge, replies: You seem to be giving your redstarts pretty well all that they need. The only suggestion I have is to provide them with a few mealworms or similar invertebrate about twice a week, which I'm confident will improve their diet to some extent.

It seems you intend to put them outside during the warm weather. If this is so, the redstarts must be compatible if housed outside together. If they are not, they will probably injure each other.

Breeding starlings

Q I WOULD like to breed starlings, and would appreciate any information you could provide.
J.O. Via e-mail

A STARLINGS can be bred in a colony system or in a flight containing just one pair. Nest-boxes should be erected in the winter, and will be used by the birds from February onwards. High-protein foods, such as eggfood, should be provided from January onwards.

By April the birds will be in breeding condition. Straw makes the best nesting material. Starlings have a short breeding period; the first eggs usually appear by the middle of April. A second round is sometimes undertaken.

Brown crickets and mealworms, dusted with vitamin and mineral powder, will give good results. Cleaned, sterilised maggots can be added from the fifth day.

Starlings should be closed-ringed (4.4mm internal diameter ring, size 'M') on the fourth day. They fledge at the three-week stage, or can be hand-reared from the age of ten days.

More than one pair, each within sight and sound of the others is ideal, as these are colony breeders.

British birds, mules & hybrids
Bernard Howlett
Has kept birds for more than 50 years and is a qualified show judge.

SOFTBILLS AND PLANTS

Me, my young starlings and the law

Q I HAVE been hand-raising two starling chicks which I found on the farm where I live. Their nest had been destroyed by crows and I could tell that they were only a few days old because they were just starting to show their first few quills.

They are now about four or five weeks old and really thriving. I would love to be able to keep them as they are very tame and follow me around the house everywhere, constantly perched somewhere on me. I do not know the legal status of keeping them in captivity and I am worried that if I keep them I will be breaking the law. However, if I release them I do not know if they would be able to survive. Please can you tell me where I stand on this?

J.P. Via e-mail

A YOU find yourself between 'a rock and a hard place'. The starling is a protected species. Your initial actions in raising the abandoned chicks were perfectly legitimate. But now they have matured they should, if at all possible, be returned to the wild. Keeping them in an aviary for a while and giving them the minimum amount of fuss, will encourage their wild side to emerge, perhaps to such an extent that they can be safely released. If you feel this is unwise, then all you can do is retain them. Keep a written record of their history as a safeguard.

**British birds, mules & hybrids
Bernard Howlett**
Has kept birds for more than 50 years and is a qualified show judge.

BRITISH BIRDS

AFTER a period of about 30 years I have decided to return to keeping birds. As a youngster I used to breed and show Gloster canaries, but this time I would like to keep British finches. I was wondering what plants or shrubs I could plant inside a flight, as I believe that finches look better against a natural background.

N.W., via email

Top exhibitor and show judge Bernard Howlett replies: The size of your flight and the number of birds you intend to house within it will determine the size of shrubs or other plants.

In a large aviary many are suitable, including bamboo, currant, dogwood, crab-apple, buddleia, snowberry, cotoneaster, honeysuckle, small conifer, box, elder, nettles and grasses. I agree that finches look very nice against a green background - it's only trial and error that will bring about the required result.

Unseasonal behaviour

Q WE HAVE a bird box in the garden where blue tits often nest. But for the first time this autumn we have one that appears regularly, pecks away at the wood and pops in and out of the box. This is normal in the spring, but we haven't been aware of it happening at this time of year. Could you tell me what it all means?

D.B. Via email

A BLUE tits live complex lives, and they prefer oak trees in which to breed. In the autumn and winter they form flocks with other small birds to forage among reed beds and woodlands. Those that remain in gardens use their nest-boxes pretty well all year, often roosting within them during cold spells.

Now global warming is apparently upon us, birds are remaining in breeding condition longer. Some are even seen picking up nesting materials and tinkering with nest-boxes after their annual moult, and this may account for your bird's behaviour.

It is also possible that the box has been usurped by another pair, who, like anybody settling into a new home, wish to put their stamp on it.

BH

Keeping grey wagtails

MY UNCLE kept and bred grey wagtails, but died before he could teach me how to do it. Can you give me some advice on the care of these lovely birds?

S.L., Norfolk

IT IS indeed a challenge for anyone who tries to breed the beautiful grey wagtail, so it is essential to pay attention to their breeding requirements. They prefer fast-running water. They must have a planted enclosure, within which there should be a pond with a waterfall set-up. This should consist of a pump to push water up from a reservoir to a header pool, where the water can overflow off a shelf and back into the reservoir. This feature need not be elaborate.

Plants placed around the pond will bring in insect life, and the addition of a few rocks with crevices, which offer a choice of nest-building sites, should produce good results.

Grey wagtails are early breeders. They often have young in the nest before the end of April, and will require insects to bring up their chicks. Mini-mealworms and wax-moth larvae should be offered in liberal quantities, with as many other insect types as can be mustered.

**British birds, mules & hybrids
Bernard Howlett**
Has kept birds for 50 years and is a qualified show judge.

USEFUL GENETICS AND MUTATIONS

Probably the first obvious changes which came about during the early stages of domestication of wild creatures were the many different colour varieties which evolved.

Mutations have always occurred in nature with albinism being an example, but with selective breeding an array of new colour varieties have emerged. Cage birds such as the budgerigar have also undergone changes in both shape and colour. This popular bird is very different in these respects nowadays compared to its small, greenish ancestor.

In recent years many bird species have been line-bred in a host of unusual hues. These modern developments came about due to many reasons, two of which are worth mentioning here in regard to the British Bird Fancy. The first was the determination of enthusiasts to bring about a respectability of the hobby. The second was the grasping of the basic laws of genetics by fanciers to line-bred strains of colour-variants.

Heredity and genetics are vast and complex subjects, but understanding the basic modes of inheritance is comparatively straightforward and if these rules are followed they will bring about many colour variant breedings.

The first of these I loosely refer to as the recessive mode of inheritance. In this mutation a cock or hen can be a carrier or a visual variant.

The expectations from the various breeding combinations are:

Carrier to normal give 50 per cent normals and 50 per cent carriers.

Visual to carrier gives 50 per cent visual and 50 per cent carriers, cocks and hens.

Visual to normal gives 100 per cent carriers, cocks and hens.

Visual to visual gives 100 per cent visuals, cocks and hens.

Carrier to carrier gives 25 per cent visual, 25 per cent normal and 50 per cent carriers, cocks and hens (these matings in reverse give the same expectations).

The second of these modes of inheritance is that which I loosely call the sex-linked mode. Here the sex of the carrier or visual is critical.

The expectations from suggested pairs are:

Carrier cock to visual hen gives 25 per cent visual cocks, 25 per cent carrier cocks, 25 per cent visual hens and 25 per cent normal hens.

Visual cock to normal hen gives 50 per cent carrier cocks, 50 per cent visual hens.

Normal cock to visual hen gives 50 per cent carrier cocks and 50 per cent normal hens.

Carrier cock to normal hen gives 25 per cent carrier cocks, 25 per cent normal cocks, 25 per cent visual hens and 25 per cent normal hens.

Visual cock to visual hen gives 50 per cent visual cocks and 50 per cent visual hens.

It is important to note that it is impossible to breed a carrier hen from a genuine sex-linked mode of inheritance. These percentages are only average and some extremes may occur.

The third mode of inheritance under discussion here is the dominant, where the colour of the variant bird is passed on to progeny immaterial of its sex, these birds can be single (SF) or double factor (DF).The colour in the single factor seems to be darker or more intense in most cases. Pairings in reverse give the same expectations.

Dominant (SF) cock to normal hen, gives normal cocks and hens and dominant (SF) cocks and hens.

Dominant (SF) cock to dominant (SF) hen, gives normal cocks and hens, dominant (SF) cocks and hens and dominant (DF) cocks and hens.

Dominant (SF) cock to dominant (DF) hen gives dominant (SF) cocks and hens and dominant (DF) cocks and hens.

Dominant (DF) cock to normal hen, gives dominant (SF) cocks and hens.

Dominant (DF) cock to dominant (DF) hen gives dominant (DF) cocks and hens.
(Normal offspring do not carry the dominant gene)

In recent years continental breeders have added to our British achievements with a significant number of different colour varieties.
Today a great many of these commonly seen on the show bench are represented by colour mutations of one sort or another.

Those of the greenfinch, house sparrow, siskin, redpoll, goldfinch, bullfinch, song thrush, blackbird and starling are well known and long established. Others, including chaffinch, bramblefinch, jay, magpie and dunnock are bred from time to time. Although the modes of inheritance which govern such mutations are now more understood, there is much more to learn, making the breeding of colour variant British and European birds a pastime well worth pursuing.

THE CHOICE IS YOURS - 5 CATEGORIES

Anyone wishing to take up breeding and exhibiting British birds has an enormous diversity of species and varieties to choose from. From the outset, however, it is essential to have an adequate birdroom or a draught and vermin-proof shed, along with flights before any stock is obtained.
It is wise to gain knowledge about any bird of interest before buying stock, and one of the best ways to do this is to join a local or national club, where members will be glad to give advice.
It is best, I feel, to specialise in one or two kinds and to spend a little time building up numbers to form strains of the desired type. In this way, progress can be scrutinised and assessed, and beneficial changes, such as the introduction of new blood to improve a strain can be made.
The categories or groups can be loosely divided into five main sections: hardbills, softbills, mules, hybrids and colour variants.
The **hardbills** are finches, buntings and sparrows. The greenfinch is the most popular hardbill bred today. The goldfinch, a beautiful little seedeater, is also much admired and the yellowhammer is the most sought after of the buntings.
Softbills include thrushes and wagtails, which, in the main, live on invertebrates. Others like the magpie and jay are omnivores and will eat almost anything that is edible.
Mules are bred from finch and canary. Larger specimens are raised when a Norwich canary is used, and miniatures are propagated when one of the smaller breeds of canary, such as a Fife or new colour, is chosen.
Hybrids are bred from two different, non-canary species. A popular cross is one between the goldfinch and the bullfinch.

COLOUR VARIANTS

The last of these groups, and one that I have relentlessly pursued, is the breeding of **Colour variants**. Mutations occur in all varieties and kinds, from time to time, and with a basic knowledge of genetics, beautiful specimens can be bred, almost to order.
Lutino in greenfinches and cinnamon in song thrushes are two of the most popular colours and species used in this branch of the hobby.
Crossbill breeders have chicks early on; for most species, April is the month when proceedings get underway, which can go on until July, depending on the variety kept.
Most British birds will breed in outdoor flights, one pair to each is recommended. Those for softbills can be planted out with shrubs. They should be vermin proof and have sheltered areas for roosting and nests.
Some breeders prefer indoor quarters for their birds. This will include those who specialise in northern or European goldfinches and Siberian bullfinches, as they do well inside and dislike our damp conditions outdoors. Mule breeders also usually have their stock inside, where they may 'run' a goldfinch cock with a couple of canary hens. For breeders of hybrids, often success will come if an aviary can be provided for a combination of species. These could include goldfinch, linnet and greenfinch cocks and bullfinch, siskin and redpoll hens. Usually some 'pairs' will bond and a few chicks will be bred.

DIVERSE DIET

Supplementary foods should be available when the birds start breeding. Eggfood can be added to the diet of seedeaters, and various invertebrates to softbill rations. This will ensure that chicks are satisfactorily reared. Everything that is required can be purchased from commercial suppliers. Knowing the needs of the kinds of birds kept is very important.
For hardbills, foods collected around the garden and local areas could include dandelion, sow thistle, shepherd's purse, and chickweed. Worms and snails would benefit breeding softbills, the latter being especially relished by song thrushes. These wild foods will, of course, be in addition to mealworms etc. purchased from commercial outlets.
Mealworms should be offered to all breeding pairs, including hardbills, especially buntings, chaffinches and bramblefinches – species that feed their young on an insect diet in the wild.

see photographs overleaf.

COCK BRAMBLEFINCH
Hardbill

Photograph by Dennis Avon

CANARY X BULLFINCH
Mules and hybrids

SONG THRUSH AND BLACKBIRD
Softbills - colour variants

Photograph by Dennis Avon

KEEPING RECORDS

The keeping of good records offers an invaluable source of information on so many aspects of bird ownership, and if these are maintained in a simple and orderly fashion, any required information can be found within minutes.

Some fanciers use a computer to store pages of relevant data which can be retrieved at the click of a mouse; others jot down salient points, just a few items such as expectant hatching dates.

There is no golden rule, although I believe all bird keepers should at least keep records for legal and insurance purposes, whether these are hand written, computerised or in photographic form is a matter for the individual.

I maintain records on a daily basis on pretty well every aspect of my hobby. The bulk of these are kept on A4 lined sheets within a spring binder, one volume for each twelve month period from March to February. This covers my bird keeping year; breeding and exhibition.

Every bird in my collection is ringed and listed, and information relating to it is recorded throughout my ownership of it, from its birth or acquisition to its disposal.

For the serious breeder, records concerning line-breeding are very important, so that the general make-up and ancestry of any one specimen is known and understood. With this knowledge a stud can progress satisfactorily and new blood can be introduced to maintain fertility and vigour when the data suggests.

I have some 60 aviaries or flights, mostly small. Each one is numbered and the details of the birds within each, at any one time, are listed. In this way I know the whereabouts of every bird in the collection.

SEPARATE SECTION

A stud section is created for every species kept and where more than one mutation is bred within a species, it is allocated a separate record. For instance, at the present time I have several distinct colour varieties of the blackbird. The cinnamon strain goes back to 1973 and the cream to 1982. With concise records I can trace every bird back to the date it was hatched and ringed. I have details of its parents and grandparents, and the offspring it has bred, together with its exhibition record, if any. With this knowledge I can evaluate faults and improvements and much else besides, and act accordingly. I can also pass on a pedigree with a bird to any new owner and thereby advertise its strain to the best of my ability.

I obtain a new folder and pages at the beginning of my year; mid March, after the last show of the season. At the front I place all correspondence received and copies of replies and letters sent out. Next, there is a record for each aviary or flight and details of any stock housed therein, especially breeding pairs. If a bird is again moved, a note is made. A record of all rings purchased comes next, and this is followed by details of all telephone calls, incoming and outgoing, with a brief note of the substance of the call. In this way any points of interest, such as who has birds to part with, can be referred to, if required, later.

This is followed by the stud data of all birds kept at the time within each stud. These studs include British bird species, Java sparrows, Lizard and new London fancy canaries. These new lists will differ in certain respects from those kept the previous year, as some birds will have been disposed of, and on occasions, new specimens brought in. The final section deals with the exhibition scene, show, team, results, etc.

LESSONS LEARNT

A brief note is made each year as to how it has gone, highlighting any pitfalls and lessons learnt. Records kept elsewhere include all receipts for items such as seed, wire netting, live food and any legal documents.

After feeding the stock each day, I glance through the records and add any relevant notes. The time this takes is well worthwhile, not least the accumulation of first-hand knowledge. To some, no doubt, my method of record keeping may seem primitive, but for the record, I wouldn't keep birds without them.

1st of a strain which I can trace back to the 1970's through my records to this day.

Phaeo hen greenfinch at the World show, winner of Gold Medal 2013. It's in the records! (see page 167)

Young blackbirds. My records show winners here.

ALIENS IN OUR MIDST
written in 2005

Comments are often made regarding non-native animals and plants swilling around in the British countryside.

Most non-natives provide considerable benefits to society, for example, in horticulture or as pets. But those that do become invasive can damage economic interests.

In March 2005 government minister Ben Bradshaw announced the setting up of a new programme board, to ensure the threat of non-natives is tackled by the Government and its agencies. The board met in September 2005, and decided to set up a number of working groups. One of these will prepare a national strategy on non-native species. Section 14(1) of the Wildlife and Countryside Act (WCA) 1981 states that "it is an offence for any person to release or allow to escape into the wild any animal which; (a) is a kind which is not an ordinary resident in or a regular visitor to Great Britain in the wild state; or (b) is included in Part 1 of Schedule 9 of the Act".

However, no offence would be committed if the person can prove that he took all reasonable steps and exercised due diligence to avoid committing the offence or if a licence has been issued under Section 16 of the WCA and all the conditions have been complied with.

If you scan the list of species mentioned in the Act you'll recognise the names of many popular cage and aviary birds. Some are incontestably 'exotic', some are native and others are a matter of fierce debate! What they all have in common is that the Government doesn't want any more escaping into our countryside.

Listed on the 1981 Act are:

BUDGERIGAR: An Australian grass parakeet, widely kept. A very adaptable little bird. Homing budgerigars are trained to leave and return to their specially adapted quarters. I believe the Duke of Bedford had such a colony in the 1920s and 1930s.

CAPERCAILLIE: The largest British grouse, the male is turkey sized, resides in coniferous and mixed woodland in the north-east of Scotland, where there are thought to be about 1,500 individuals. The species became extinct in the 18th century. In 1837 it was re-introduced from Sweden into Perthshire.

CAROLINA DUCK: An American species, native to North America, where there are two separate populations, one western, the other eastern. An introduced bird, breeding wild in the South-East of England, mainly in Berkshire and Surrey. There are a number of collections in Britain, some of which are free-flying.

MANDARIN DUCK: Originally from Japan, China, and eastern Russia. The British wild population has bred from individuals released in the Home Counties in the 1920s and 1930s. They have since spread to the Isle of Wight, Cheshire, Norfolk and elsewhere. I enjoy watching them in an Ipswich park, where they fly freely and breed. About 2,000 pairs breed wild in Britain.

RUDDY DUCK: Introduced into Britain from North America and closely related to the European white-headed duck. At one time the ruddy duck reached an estimated 600 pairs in the UK.

On October 12th 2005 ministers announced an eradication programme for the ruddy duck, to run for five years. The programme carried out by staff of the Central Science Laboratory will cost £3.34 million, jointly funded by DEFRA and the European Commission. It will take place in conjunction with other control programmes in France and Spain. The work is being carried out by experienced staff who are under strict instructions to minimise the distress of target birds and ensure any wounded ones are despatched quickly. Where control takes place on sites designated for their nature conservation value English Nature (or its equivalent in Scotland, Wales or Northern Ireland) will be consulted before any work takes place. DEFRA is also looking at laws that will prevent the keeping of ruddy ducks, and other problem non-natives, in captivity.

WHITE-TAILED EAGLE: The huge white-tailed sea eagle became extinct in Britain in the early part of the last century. The last pair nested in Skye in 1916.

In 1968, four young birds were brought in from Norway, but the attempt to re-establish them failed. In 1976, The Nature Conservancy Council carried out a large-scale reintroduction programme in Western Scotland, bringing over a total of 84 birds, again from Norwegian eyries. This time the project was successful and they now breed in Britain every year. I have watched these on Isle of Mull.

CANADA GOOSE: Introduced into Britain from North America in the 17th century during the reign of Charles II, it soon became established, frequenting lakes and pools on many estates. By the late 1960s numbers had risen to more than 10,000 birds.

Protected in the closed season; may be shot from September 1st to January 31st (indeed until

February 20th in some areas below the high-water mark). A General Licence permits sale of captive-bred birds and their eggs.

EGYPTIAN GOOSE: Common and widespread in tropical Africa. Feral populations in Britain based in East Anglia, although scattered elsewhere. The species is very well known to me and I see pairs or small groups when I am out and about. The most I have seen feeding at the same time was on stubble in Norfolk, when I counted 42. About 500 pairs now breed in Britain.

NIGHT HERON: A mainly nocturnal bird as its name suggests. It is a vagrant here from southern Europe. I understand a feral colony exists near Edinburgh Zoo.

RING-NECKED PARAKEET: It is believed that a few of these birds were set free in the London area some 40 years ago, since then others have been freed from captivity. They probably originate from India. The population in Britain today numbers thousands. Flocks can be seen around the Home Counties, at Virginia Water, Windsor Great Park, in Thanet and elsewhere. They can survive without human handouts, living in the wild on the fruits of the forest.

CHUKAR PARTRIDGE: A bird of southern Europe, where it inhabits grassy slopes. Introduced into shooting fields of East Anglia. Licences are no longer issued and specimens are rarely seen.

ROCK PARTRIDGE: A bird confined to southern Europe and used for sport.

GOLDEN PHEASANT: The golden pheasant is a native of China, introduced into this country for its beauty and ornamental value rather than for sport in the shooting field. It is well established in Norfolk and I have often seen specimens foraging in the woodland glades. A magnificent bird of red and gold with a very long tail.
Other areas where it is established include the South Downs, Anglesey and Galloway. It is thought that about 1,500 exist in Britain.

LADY AMHERST'S PHEASANT: Native of China, south-eastern Tibet and Burma. Introduced into Britain at various times since 1900; a small population has been established in the south of England but has decreased dramatically in recent years. A recent report suggests species is probably extinct as a British breeding bird.

REEVES'S PHEASANT: Native of the highlands of north and central China. One of the longest pheasants at 1.5m (60in); very long tail. Its brown, black and off-white appearance is patterned with black-edged feathers.

SILVER PHEASANT: A Chinese species, also found in Burma. A mountain bird living in the high forests. The cock bird is easily recognised by the almost white upperparts, crimson facial skin, black crown, crest and underparts. The hen is olive-brown with the crest darker.

BOBWHITE QUAIL: An inhabitant of the United States and Mexico, where it is abundant in open fields and pine woods. Many similar species also inhabit the New World. The male is identified by a white throat and eye-line. The bird's call is a whistled 'bob-bob-white' hence its name.

EAGLE OWL: Quite a lot of fuss arose in November 2005 following a BBC2 Natural World documentary on eagle owls that have become established in North Yorkshire. A representative of the British Ornithologists Union (BOU) made a statement to the effect that these birds were not considered native to Great Britain and so are not protected by legislation. Furthermore it was suggested that there was nothing to stop people killing them, or taking their eggs from the wild.
A Government representative contacted the producer to disagree with this line of thought, and a correction was issued when the programme was repeated later in the week.
The reason for the disagreement was that the definition of a wild bird under the 1981 Act was extended so that not just birds native to Great Britain are protected. The definition of wild bird is worth committing to memory: "any bird of a species which is ordinarily resident in or a visitor to the European territory of any Member State in the wild state" and so on.
If the birds can be shown to have been captive-bred, they are not afforded protection under the WCA 1981, since any bird bred in captivity is excluded from the protection of Section 1. If the birds are present due to range-spread they would come within the scope of the protection afforded all wild birds under Section 1, as they are 'ordinarily resident in a wild state in the European territory of a Member State'.
All the chicks would be protected even if their parents were captive-bred, because their parents were not in captivity when the eggs they hatched from were laid.

BUSTARD: In 2003 DEFRA granted a ten-
ence to the Great Bustard Consortium,
ng the release of up to 50 birds a year onto
sbury Plain. The licence is subject to monitoring
and annual reviews. If there are any negative
impacts the trial will be terminated.

The project is at an early stage for anyone to guess
whether a self-sustaining breeding population will
ever be established in the wild.

Until the year 1526, the great bustard used to
breed in the UK as far north as the Scottish border
country, and in the south it was common on the
moors, downs and plains of England. Its demise
was brought about by the growth in human
population, the planting of trees and the gradual
intensification of agriculture in the wake of the
Enclosure Acts. The early 19th century saw its
extinction from Salisbury Plain - the area which
most closely resembles the open steppes the
bustard favours in Asia. In East Anglia the last
fertile egg was taken in about 1838.

Since then the great bustard has only been an
occasional, but welcome visitor to our shores. I
hope its reintroduction will prove to be successful.
NOTE: The great bustard is now breeding on
Salisbury Plain.

*4,400 ruddy ducks have been shot in the last few
years, leaving an estimated 120 in the wild.*

Photograph by Sergey Yeliseev

RING-NECKED PARAKEET

MANDARIN DUCK (female)

Photograph by Sergey Yeliseev

GREAT BUSTARD

Photograph by Sergey Yeliseev

HEART STOPPING MOMENTS

The 1997 breeding season was satisfactory for me in a number of ways. I was able to breed the common redstart and the magpie for the first time in my avicultural career, together with an albino blackbird, the like of which I hadn't bred for quite a while.

Three other blackbirds, a normal hen, a cinnamon hen and a satinette cock, which all went on to win major awards at the big events, were also produced. Other species bred included greenfinches, house sparrows, dunnocks, song and mistle thrushes.

The magpies consisted of a normal cock and a cinnamon hen. They were housed in an aviary 6ft sq x 7ft high which proved to be ideal. Nest building began in earnest in early March and was completed by the end of the month. I had collected more than 300 suitable sticks and twigs, mainly oak, each about 18in long for their use and also provided a large dish of mud and ample supplies of hair and grasses. The hen appeared to do all the work and a somewhat untidy nest complete with an entrance hole was constructed. Six eggs were laid and these were incubated by the hen alone.

They began to hatch on May 7th and four chicks emerged. Problems then arose when the parent birds declined to use most of the rearing food, road kills, dead day old chicks, etc. relying only on mealworms and maggots. Although all four chicks developed into juvenile plumage, only one survived.

In mid March I placed a redstart cock into a flight 6ft sq x 3ft and a hen in an adjoining aviary. Nest boxes were provided at each end one, a budgie-type, the other of half-open design.

I opened the connecting door, so the pair could fly together. By the end of May the hen had built a cosy nest inside the budgie-type box, and very little was seen of her during the next weeks.

At this time many of my other pairs of birds were nesting, including a pair of blackbirds, both birds being split for albino. On May 9th four eggs hatched from their first nest of the season, and one chick was a visual albino. By May 22nd, all had flown, the albino being the larger bird.

I went away on "holiday" in early June, to a room I had booked overlooking a site of scientific interest in the Cambridgeshire countryside, and left friends in charge of my birds.

I had been told on many occasions by so-called friends that one day men in white coats would take me away. This is exactly what happened on the morning of June 9th. I was watching the wildlife from my bed-sit window when men in white coats came into my room and whisked me away. All the lights went out, but came on again a quadruple heart bypass operation later at 2am the next day. A few days later I was home again, back to the science of bird breeding. My friends had done a good job and the albino blackbird was looking great. By the middle of August the bird was warbling, indicating its sex the best way it could. The young magpie was also growing.

Of all the three eggs laid by the redstart, only one hatched. The chick was successfully reared. By August 12th its sex was confirmed when male tell-tale orange breast feathers appeared. By August 19th the white forehead was also visible. The bird was 84 days old at that stage.

As the sexes of normal coloured magpies are similar I was anxious to know the gender of the youngster early on. I therefore sent some of its feathers away for sexing. When the results came back they were disappointing. The bird was a hen, therefore not able to further the cinnamon strain.

CINNAMON MAGPIE

Photograph by Dennis Avon

ᴐN FANCY CANARIES

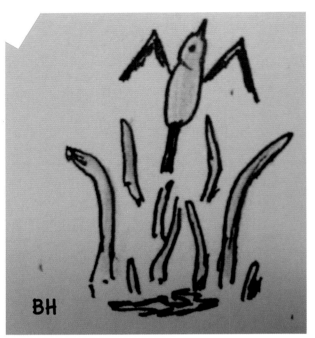

London Fancy canary....
.... rising from the ashes.

On February 15th 1997, Lizard canary expert John Record reproduced in Cage & Aviary Birds a photograph taken by Dennis Avon, of a preserved example of a London Fancy canary, bred and exhibited by A.G. Filby. In the accompanying article, he emphasized that the specimen had won a red ticket in the 1927 Crystal Palace show, and had come 2nd at the same venue in 1929. John Record had relocated the bird at the behest of well-known canary fancier Russell Liddiatt, who had seen it some years earlier, at Tring Museum. At that time I had been looking for a challenge. These revelations gave me the impetus to form the New London Fancy Canary Club during that year. I considered the term 'new' as appropriate, as the reinvention of the true London fancy seemed unlikely. I crossed Lizard canaries with opals and began to form a strain which appeared similar to the old bird.

At the 2000 National Exhibition, I entered two new London Fancy canaries, a Jonque hen and a Mealy hen, in the class for 'Any Other Variety Canaries'. These birds were bred from a Silver broken cap Lizard cock and a Opal/Lizard hen. Sixteen birds were entered in the class, which included Blue Lizards, Japanese Hoso, Raza etc; the New London Fancy Mealy hen came 3rd, a good result.

In 2002 I entered a Mealy (fine) New London Fancy in the ' Non-classified Variety Section' at the World show held, that year, in Switzerland. Further entries to this event are being considered.

In 2004, the NLFCC obtained great assistance from the committee of the South East Ipswich Cage Bird Society, of which I am a member. They allocated classes for champion and novice New London Fancies in their 2004 schedule. The birds on display were much admired by the public and fancies alike. Classes have been provided by this club for these birds ever since and long may it continue. Birds are also exhibited at local cage bird society shows.

In 2010, the New London Fancy Canary Club requested the Canary Council to accept the new London Fancy as a new variety. It was rejected 'ou of hand'. This entity had missed a great opportunity; shame on them! Had the breed been accepted, acceptance at the World Show would have probably followed with a trial period of some years, before any medals would have been allocated. As it is, work on the project will continue. During the same year, and by consensus, the New London Fancy Canary Club was re-named the London Fancy Canary Club, the only one of its kind in the U.K.

Membership is adequate. It is by association, as members are scattered over the U.K. and abroad. Officers are: President S. Savage, Chairman E. McGillian, Secretary and Publicity Officer B. Howlett, Treasurer, B. Cooper; assisted by the good officers of South East Ipswich Cage Bird Society. Some other members are Mr. D. Andrews Scientific Advisor, A. Early, S. Howlett and Sergio Palma of Italy.

Unflighted mealy new London fancy canary.

A 'fine' new London fancy canary.

'Strong' (top) and jonque (right) new London fancies.

'My new London fancy mealy hen appeared on the front cover of *Cage & Aviary Birds* in the July 7, 2005 issue, with the Houses of Parliament as a backdrop'

Bernard Howlett: saw London fancy photo in *Cage & Aviary Birds*.

Clipping from Cage & Aviary Birds.

Defining the ideal

THE scale of points for the new London fancy, laid down by the NLFCC, is as follows. Note that these criteria define the ideal bird:

Maximum colour – for richness and depth – 15
Clearness – clearness throughout the body – 20
Cap – clean and broad – 10
Wings and tail – for neatness and darkness – 20
Wing coverts – for darkness – 15
Legs, toes, nails and beak – for darkness – 10
Condition and staging – 10
Total: 100

Length 135mm; **stance** 45° (same as lizard); lizard-type show cage.

Full classification for champion and novice new London fancy exhibitors:

1. Clear or nearly clear-bodied jonque cock
2. Clear or nearly clear-bodied jonque hen
3. Clear or nearly clear-bodied mealy cock
4. Clear or nearly clear-bodied mealy hen
5. Spangled-backed jonque cock
6. Spangled-backed jonque hen
7. Spangled-backed mealy cock
8. Spangled-backed mealy hen
9. Over-year clear or nearly clear-bodied jonque cock or hen
10. Over-year clear or nearly clear-bodied mealy cock or hen
11. Over-year spangled-backed jonque cock or hen
12. Over-year spangled-backed mealy cock or hen

● Judges are requested to judge the birds as new London fancies and not as London fancies.

Photograph by Andrew Calvesbert

Class of new London fancies at South-east Ipswich show in 2004.

The London Fancy Canary at the Natural History Museum, Tring.
Photo: Dennis Avon

Breckland Beauty

Photograph by Andrew Calvesbert

When the London Fancy Canary was in its heyday some of the best birds were given stud names by their breeders, for instance John Robinson named one of his birds "Old Gold", Mrs Stokes's bird was named "London Pride" and Mr Needham named his best bird "Comy's Memorial". My 2012 mealy example is called "Breckland Beauty" reflecting my place of birth. I exhibited this bird at the 2013 World Show in a non-competitive class.

THE BLACK SENTINEL

Wizard of velvet in feather and voice,

Bird of my passion and bird of my choice;

You are a prophet and so can foretell

The longings of nature, black sentinel.

You sing, sweetly sing, your golden refrain,

And sanctify souls in sunshine and rain:

Your home's a meadow, your castle a tree,

I envy you blackbird! What you of me?

Nobly you strive with your dusky brown maid,

Tending your charges in apple green shade;

You whisper wisdom till light leaves the sky,

And teach them music and how they should fly.

O let me dwell in your magical dell

And there find contentment, black sentinel.

From the author's book - Seasons 2008.